Laval
PARC PÈRE-MARQUETTE
boul. Rosemont
page 126
Rosemont
rue des Carrières
rue Dandurand
rue St-Grégoire
PARC SIR-WILFRID-LAURIER
av. Papineau
DE LORIMIER
rue Mascon
PARC LE PÉLICAN
av. Laurier E.
PARC LAFOND
18e av.
PARC MAISON-NEUVE
boul. Pie-IX
Laurier
ST-DENIS
boul. St-Joseph Est
rue St-Hubert
av. Christophe Colomb
de la Roche
rue Fabor
av. de Lorimer
av. des Érables
rue d'Iberville
av. Bourbonnière
Serres
Trois-Rivières, Québec
boul. St-Laurent
rue St-Urbain
rue St-Denis
Mt-Royal
av. du Mont-Royal
ST-JEAN-BAPTISTE
MONT-ROYAL
rue Marie-Anne Est
rue Rachel Est
Pie-IX
Château Dufresne
Musée des Arts Décoratifs
page 168
PRÉFONTAINE
rue Hochelaga
rue Duluth
rue St-Dominique
Laval
rue Berri
rue St-Herbert
av. du Parc Lafontaine
PARC LAFONTAINE
BOURGET
rue Sherbrooke Est
Prefontaine
Joliette
page 104
LAFONTAINE
Papineau
rue Frontenac
ST-EUSÈBE
rue de Rouen
HOCHELAGA
rue Dézery
rue Davidson
des Pins Est
ST-LOUIS
Sherbrooke
avenue
rue Parthenais
rue Ontario
ST-JACQUES
rue Montcalm
rue Amherst
Frontenac
rue Moreau
av. Valois
rue Adam
rue Ste-Catherine
TERRASSE ONTARIO
STE-MARIE
Berri-UQAM
Beaudry
Papineau
boul. de Maisonneuve
rue Notre-Dame
St-Laurent
rue Ste-Catherine
UQAM
Musée d'Art Contemporain de Montréal
boul. René-Lévesque
Champ-de-Mars
av. Viger
page 78
Quai Laurier
St-Laurent (St Lawrence)
Hôtel de Ville
Marché Bonsecours
rue St-Paul
Pont Jacques-Cartier
Pont Ste-Hélène
Lac aux Dauphins
Tour de la Ronde
La Ronde
Musée David M. Stewart
Tour de l'Horloge
Quai King-Edward
Quai Jacques-Cartier
VIEUX-PORT
Quai Alexandra
PARC DE LA CITÉ-DU-HAVRE
Vieux Fort
Ile Ste-Hélène
Tour de Lévis
PARC DES ILES
Biosphère
page 170
Québec
rue St-Charles Ouest
Quai Mark Drouin
Pont de la Concorde
Lac des Cygnes
Ile-Ste-Hélène
Chenal le Moyne
Longueuil
Habitat '67
Place des Nations
Pont des Iles
20
Canal de la Rive Sud
rue Labonte
De Chateauguay
rue St-Laurent
Circuit Gilles-Villeneuve
Jardins des Floralies
Casino de Montréal
PARC DE LA VOIE MARITIME
rue Lemoyne Ouest
Ile Notre-Dame
Lac des Regates
Bassin Olympique
rue Riverside
LONGUEUIL
rue Dollard
rue Joliette
rue Gardenville
boul. Lafayette
boul. Desaulniers
rue Marquette
rue Ste-Hélène
ST-LAMBERT
Plage des Iles
PARC LOGAN
Musée Marcil
rue Logan
av. Putney
ch. Tiffin
boul. Taschereau
Plattsburg

W9-AVM-692

Other Insight Guides available:

Alaska
Amazon Wildlife
American Southwest
Amsterdam
Argentina
Arizona & Grand Canyon
Asia, East
Asia, Southeast
Asia's Best Hotels and Resorts
Australia
Austria
Bahamas
Bali & Lombok
Baltic States
Bangkok
Barbados
Belgium
Belize
Berlin
Bermuda
Brazil
Brittany
Buenos Aires
Burgundy
Burma (Myanmar)
Cairo
California
California, Southern
Canada
Caribbean
Caribbean Cruises
Channel Islands
Chicago
Chile
China
Colorado
Continental Europe
Corsica
Costa Rica
Crete
Cuba
Cyprus
Czech & Slovak Republic
Delhi, Jaipur & Agra
Denmark
Dominican Rep. & Haiti
Dublin
East African Wildlife
Eastern Europe
Ecuador
Edinburgh
Egypt
England
Finland
Florida
France
France, Southwest
French Riviera
Gambia & Senegal
Germany
Glasgow
Gran Canaria
Great Britain
Great Railway Journeys of Europe
Great River Cruises of Europe
Greece
Greek Islands
Guatemala, Belize & Yucatán
Hawaii
Hungary
Iceland
India
India, South
Indonesia
Ireland
Israel
Istanbul
Italy
Italy, Northern
Italy, Southern
Jamaica
Japan
Jerusalem
Jordan
Kenya
Korea
Laos & Cambodia
Lisbon
Madeira
Malaysia
Mallorca & Ibiza
Malta
Mauritius Réunion & Seychelles
Melbourne
Mexico
Miami
Montreal
Morocco
Namibia
Nepal
Netherlands
New England
New Mexico
New Orleans
New York State
New Zealand
Nile
Normandy
North American and Alaskan Cruises
Norway
Oman & The UAE
Oxford
Pacific Northwest
Pakistan
Peru
Philadelphia
Philippines
Poland
Portugal
Provence
Puerto Rico
Rajasthan
Rio de Janeiro
Russia
Sardinia
Scandinavia
Scotland
Seattle
Sicily
South Africa
South America
Spain
Spain, Northern
Spain, Southern
Sri Lanka
Sweden
Switzerland
Syria & Lebanon
Taiwan
Tenerife
Texas
Thailand
Trinidad & Tobago
Tunisia
Turkey
Tuscany
Umbria
USA: On The Road
USA: Western States
US National Parks: West
Venezuela
Vienna
Vietnam
Wales

INSIGHT CITY GUIDES
(with free restaurant map)

Barcelona
Beijing
Boston
Bruges, Ghent & Antwerp
Brussels
Cape Town
Florence
Hong Kong
Las Vegas
London
Los Angeles
Madrid
Moscow
New York
Paris
Prague
Rome
St Petersburg
San Francisco
Singapore
Sydney
Taipei
Tokyo
Toronto
Utah
Venice
Walt Disney World/Orlando
Washington, DC

INSIGHT CITY GUIDE

Montreal

Discovery CHANNEL

APA PUBLICATIONS
Part of the Langenscheidt Publishing Group

INSIGHT GUIDE
MONTREAL

Editor
Lesley Gordon
Art Director
Ian Spick
Picture Editor
Hilary Genin
Cartography Editor
Zoë Goodwin
Production
Kenneth Chan
Editorial Director
Brian Bell

Distribution

United States
Langenscheidt Publishers, Inc.
36–36 33rd Street 4th Floor
Long Island City, NY 11106
Fax: (1) 718 784-0640

UK & Ireland
GeoCenter International Ltd
Meridian House, Churchill Way West
Basingstoke, Hampshire RG21 6YR
Fax: (44) 1256-817988

Australia
Universal Publishers
1 Waterloo Road
Macquarie Park, NSW 2113
Fax: (61) 2 9888 9074

New Zealand
Hema Maps New Zealand Ltd (HNZ)
Unit D, 24 Ra ORA Drive
East Tamaki, Auckland
Fax: (64) 9 273 6479

Worldwide
Apa Publications GmbH & Co. Verlag KG (Singapore branch)
38 Joo Koon Road, Singapore 628990
Tel: (65) 6865-1600. Fax: (65) 6861-6438

Printing

Insight Print Services (Pte) Ltd
38 Joo Koon Road, Singapore 628990
Tel: (65) 6865-1600. Fax: (65) 6861-6438

©2007 Apa Publications GmbH & Co. Verlag KG (Singapore branch)
All Rights Reserved

First Edition 1991
Fourth Edition (Reprint) 2007

ABOUT THIS BOOK

The first Insight Guide pioneered the use of creative full-colour photography in guidebooks in 1970. Since then, we have expanded our range to cater for our readers' need not only for reliable information about their chosen destination but also for a real understanding of that destination. Now, when the internet can supply inexhaustible (but not always reliable) facts, our books marry text and pictures to provide that much more elusive quality: knowledge. To achieve this, they rely heavily on the authority of locally based writers and photographers.

How to use this book

The book is carefully structured to convey an understanding of Montréal:

◆ To understand the city today, you need to know something of its past. The first section covers its people, history and culture in lively essays written by specialists.

◆ The main Places section provides a full run-down of all the attractions worth seeing. The main places of interest are coordinated by number with full-colour maps. Margin notes provide background information and tips on special places and events.

◆ A special section of photographic features highlights lively festivals, regional architecture, the arts and the city's link with the circus.

◆ Photographs are chosen not only to illustrate the landscape and buildings but also to convey the moods of the region and the life of its people.

◆ The Travel Tips listings section provides information on getting around, hotels, shops and activities. Information may be located quickly by

using the index printed on the back cover flap – and the flaps are designed to serve as bookmarks.

The contributors

This edition of *Insight City Guide: Montreal & Quebec City* was revised by **Lesley Gordon**, who also edited *Insight City Guide: Toronto*. This new edition builds on the excellent foundations laid down by editors of previous editions, **Julia Roles** and **Donna Dailey**.

The lion's share of the guide has been comprehensively updated on the spot by **Paul Waters**, a travel writer and journalist for *The Gazette*, Montréal's English language newspaper. Waters breathed new life into the history section, and features about regional cuisine, Montrealers, the performance arts and culture, language, *Ethnic Montréal, Old Montréal, Downtown, Montréal Branché, Westmount, Outremont* and *St Joseph's Oratory*.

The other main contributor, **Helga Loverseed**, is a journalist and writer who has lived in Canada for many years. Loverseed completely revised the Travel Tips section, provided new features on the emerging Tango dance scene, the Lachine Canal, and also updated the text on jazz, the city's major festivals, the St Lawrence River and the *Québec City* and *Around Montreal* chapters.

Pierre Home-Douglas updated *Famous Montrealers, Decisive Dates* and *The Needle Trade*, while **Jim Hynes** updated *Why Ice Hockey Matters* and *Stadiums, Gardens and Islands*. **Simon Lee** provided text about the African Nights festival. Their contributions have been blended with the expertise of writers who contributed to previous editions, and whose work survives in this edition. Among the principal authors are **Paul Karr**, **Matthew Parfitt**, **Lysiane Gagnon**, **Mark Kingwell**, **Emil Sher**, **Charles Foran**, **Mary Ladky**, **Louise Legault**, **Nancy Lyon** and **Katherine Snyder**.

The photography is largely the work of **Richard Nowitz** and his daughter **Daniella Nowitz**, who lives in Montréal, and **Jackie Garrow**. Editorial assistance was provided by **Sylvia Suddes**, **Carine Tracanelli** and **Penny Phenix**, who also compiled the index. This edition was proofread by **Sarah Turner**.

CONTACTING THE EDITORS

We would appreciate it if readers would alert us to errors or outdated information by writing to:

Insight Guides, P.O. Box 7910, London SE1 1WE, England.
Fax: (44) 20 7403-0290.
insight@apaguide.co.uk

NO part of this book may be reproduced, stored in a retrieval system or transmitted in any form or means electronic, mechanical, photocopying, recording or otherwise, without prior written permission of *Apa Publications*. Brief text quotations with use of photographs are exempted for book review purposes only. Information has been obtained from sources believed to be reliable, but its accuracy and completeness, and the opinions based thereon, are not guaranteed.

www.insightguides.com
In North America:
www.insighttravelguides.com

Contents

Introduction

History

Features

Places

Photo Features

Information Panels

Travel Tips

Maps

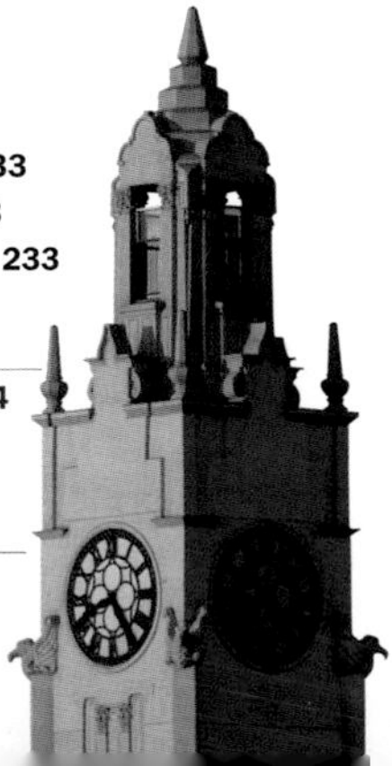

THE BEST OF MONTRÉAL

Art, culture, nature, food and festivals... Here, at a glance, are our recommendations for your visit

BEST VIEWS

- **Montréal Panorama** Views from Mont-Royal reveal the mighty St Lawrence River at the city's feet. *See page 144.*
- **The Tour de l'Horloge** (Clock Tower) At the Vieux Port provides an overview of the river, the Lachine Canal and the islands. *See pages 87, 176.*
- **McGill College** Founded by James McGill in 1821 the campus downtown climbs the slopes of Mont-Royal, known as "the mountain" by locals. *See page 113.*
- **Tour Montréal/ Parc Olympique** The sports stadium, designed by French architect Roger Tallibert for the 1976 Summer Olympic Games, is topped by the tallest inclining tower in the world. A funicular raises visitors to an observation deck at the top.

MONTRÉAL FOR FAMILIES

- **Biodôme** A combined zoo and botanical garden, this natural world reflects the four ecosystems of the Americas. *See page 168.*
- **Biosphère** Designed by Buckminster Fuller, the geodesic dome is an environmental interpretation centre on Ile Ste-Hélène. The building served as the American Pavilion during Expo '67. *See page 173.*
- **La Ronde** An amusement park on Ile Ste-Hélène, it has the highest and fastest roller coaster in Canada. *See page 174.*
- **Stewart Museum at the Vieux Fort** Costumed re-enactments at the museum during the summer. *See page 174.*
- **IMAX** At the Vieux Port, films about Outer Space, wild animals and endangered environments and Hollywood movies, adapted for large format. *See page 87.*

ABOVE: the city skyline from Mont-Royal.
LEFT: the Biosphère.
BELOW: a penguin in the Biodôme.

BEST PARKS AND GARDENS

- **Parc Mont-Royal** This landscaped park with trees and walking trails was designed by Frederick Law Olmsted who also laid out New York's Central Park. *See page 144.*
- **Mont-Royal Cemetery** One of the oldest cemeteries in North America. Guided tours of the graves of famous figures who are buried here. *See page 144.*
- **Parc La Fontaine** The city's third biggest park with a pond where you can rent pedal boats in summer or skate in winter. An outdoor theatre offers live entertainment. *See page 134.*
- **Botanical Garden** One of the world's leading botanical gardens. More than 30 themed gardens are planted with 22,000 species from around the world. A First Nations Garden showcases traditional medicinal plants and herbs. *See page 171.*

ABOVE RIGHT: mannequins in the underground city. **BELOW:** the Botanical Garden. **BELOW RIGHT:** a sculpture at the Musée des Beaux Arts.

BEST SHOPPING

- **Holt Renfrew** One of Canada's premier upscale stores with high-end designer clothing and cosmetics. *See page 227.*
- **La Maison Ogilvy** Upscale department store with a daily recital by a kilted bagpiper at 1pm, a tradition which goes back decades. *See page 110, 227.*
- **Galerie Le Chariot** This gallery has the largest selection of Inuit and First Nations art in Canada. *See page 228.*
- **Nicholas Hoare** One of a few independent bookstores that still do very good business. Difficult-to-find titles and a range of English-language topics. *See page 229.*

BEST MUSEUMS AND GALLERIES

- **Musée Château Ramezay** Exhibits trace the history of Montréal and Québec City from the time of the First Nations. The garden is planted with herbs and flowers common in the 18th century. *See page 81.*
- **Centre d'histoire de Montréal** In a former fire station the museum traces the everyday lives of Montrealers over five centuries. *See page 88.*
- **Pointe-à Callière** The Museum of Archaeology and History, across from the Vieux Port was built above excavated old city foundations. Holograms and stone remains interpret the past. *See page 88.*
- **Musée des Beaux Arts** Housed in classical and modern buildings, this is one of Canada's most important art institutions. *See page 119.*
- **Le Centre Canadien d'Architecture** A huge number of books, drawings and photographs, as well as temporary exhibits. *See page 100.*

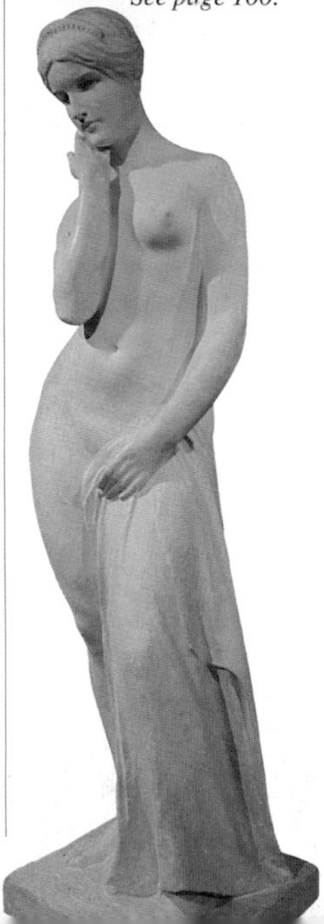

BEST FESTIVALS

- **International Jazz Festival** Probably the best known celebration in a city that hosts over 90 festivals a year. Headline acts from around the world and free events. *See page 130.*
- **Juste pour Rire (Just for Laughs)** Up and coming local acts and internationally known comedians perform in comedy clubs and theatres in the Quartier Latin. *See page 132.*
- **Festival International Nuits d'Afrique** A celebration of music from over 30 countries. *See page 139.*
- **Montréal Highlights Festival** An 11-day celebration of winter. A bacchanal of eating, and drinking, with a concert and a torchlight parade. *See page 138.*
- **World Film Festival** The city's biggest film event has a sprinkling of international stars and directors. *See page 139.*
- **Montréal Grand Prix** World class Formula 1 drivers race around the circuit on Ile Notre-Dame. *See page 174.*

BEST RESTAURANTS

- **Aux 4 Saisons d'Orford** Out of town bistro that deserves its rave reviews. Mont-Orford. *See page 196.*
- **Chalet Barbecue** Some believe it has the best barbecue chicken in the province. *See page 149.*
- **Chez Clo** Traditional restaurant that serves great Québec food. *See page 175.*
- **L'Anecdote** One of the best burger joints. *See page 136.*
- **Le Caveau** Traditional French food with rich, buttery dishes. *See page 122.*
- **Le Commensal** Tasty, inexpensive vegetarian fare. *See page 122.*
- **Moishe's** The best steaks in Montréal. *See page 136.*
- **Panache** One of the best restaurants in Canada. Serves sophisticated regional dishes. Québec City. *See page 209.*
- **Rôtisserie au Petit-Poucet** A Québec institution with a hearty buffet. Val-David. *See page 197.*
- **Verses** Hotel restaurant known for its romantic ambience and good food. *See page 99.*

BEST MARKETS

- **Atwater Market** Combine a visit to the market with a walk along the Lachine Canal. Farmers arrive at dawn with their fresh produce, which is often picked off by city chefs. Arrive early if you want to get the best of the fruit, vegetables and freshly-baked bread and pastries. *See page 59.*
- **Marché Jean-Talon** The market and surrounding stores sell some of the best produce in the city. A good selection of plants and flowers, regional products and speciality shops selling spices, oils and cheeses. *See page 51.*
- **Marché Maisonneuve** A modern building east of the city where vendors and market gardeners sell fruit, vegetables, fish and meat. *See page 227*
- **Marché du Vieux-Port** A busy farmers' market in Québec City with fresh regional produce and every kind of maple item. *See page 204.*

ABOVE: children love Montréal's street parades. **LEFT:** French-Canadian cuisine. **RIGHT:** fresh fruit at Atwater Market.

BEST GAY FRIENDLY

- **The Village** East of the Quartier Latin, within a few blocks of mainly row houses built for molasses factory workers, is the vibrant heart of Montréal's gay community. *See page 134.*
- **Gay festivals** Divers Cité (Diverse City) held in July and the Black and Blue Festival in October sees the gay, lesbian and transgendered communities strut their stuff with costume balls and over-the-top-dance extravanganzas. *See page 139.*
- **Le Parking** The city's largest gay night club. An amazing sound and light system and music, on three floors at 1296 rue Amherst. *See page 135.*
- **Taverne Normandie** Across the street from Le Parking nightclub is Montréal's first gay bar. It is very busy during happy hour. *See page 135.*

BEST CHURCHES

- **Notre-Dame Basilica** This lavish Gothic Revival cathedral has stunning stained glass windows and a gilded interior. *See page 91.*
- **Notre-Dame-de-Bon-Secours Chapel** The oldest chapel in Montréal. A small museum traces the history of the church. *See page 83.*
- **St. Patrick's Basilica** Simply called "The Irish Church" by locals. Mid-19th century building with an intricately carved oak interior. *See page 114.*
- **Cathédrale Marie-Reine-du-Monde** A tribute to St Peter's in Rome. *See page 107.*
- **Oratoire St-Joseph** A pilgrimage site on Mont-Royal founded by Brother André, a humble, pious man. *See page 159.*

ABOVE: Notre-Dame Basilica. **RIGHT:** mural art in The Gay Village.

OUT OF TOWN

La Citadelle An impressive and active military installation in Québec City. Watch the changing of the guard. *See page 206.*

Centre de la Nature du Mont-St-Hilaire Learn more about Mont-St-Hilaire, the first UNESCO Biosphère Reserve in Canada. *See page 191.*

Fort Chambly Military might and the history of the regiments that once manned this important stone building. *See page 188.*

Lac Memphrémagog A mountain-fringed lake stretching from Magog, a resort town, to Newport, Vermont, in the US. Sporting activities, art galleries and the Benedictine abbey of St-Benoît-du-Lac. *See page 194.*

Place d'Armes An historical square in the Lower Town of Québec City, where local artists display their work. *See page 202.*

Route des vins Country roads link picturesque villages in the heart of Québec's fertile wine region. *See page 192.*

St-Sauveur-des-Monts Just a few miles north of Montréal, visitors can ski and shop till they drop in a variety of factory outlets, which sell designer clothing. *See page 181.*

Tremblant Resort Busy year-round. Family fun, great places to eat out, plenty of outdoor activities (whatever the weather), festivals and, of course, skiing. *See page 184.*

THE FRENCH CONNECTION

The largest francophone city after Paris, Montréal combines Old World style with North American modernity

To understand Montréal, you should really visit the city in January, when the sidewalks are slick with icy slush and the winds that howl down rue Ste-Catherine can be cold enough to freeze a polar bear's heart. That's the real test of a city's spirit, and Montréal passes with flying colours.

Even on the iciest nights, the bars are full, the cafés are buzzing and streets like Crescent and St-Denis hum with people of all ages bouncing from one night spot to the next. It's a Canadian cliché that *joie de vivre* is Montréal's defining characteristic, but there is some truth to the old truism.

And while the city's golden age as the economic powerhouse of Canada is long gone, its movie, music and fashion industries are booming; and its four universities give it both intellectual weight and youthful flair. Throw in the river, the mountain and the city's incomparable blend of 20th-century glass towers and 18th- and 19th-century colonial buildings and there's simply no better place in Canada for shopping, dining and sightseeing.

It's not that the city's without tension. With 3 million people, it's by far the biggest city in Québec, a province that has been threatening to secede from Canada since the mid-1970s. In fact, in 1995, it was only Montréal's big bloc of non-francophone voters who kept separatists from winning the referendum. So along with the usual urban problems of crime, poverty and traffic congestion, Montréal has to contend with endless political uncertainty.

But while this squabble over language and independence can sometimes be a bit of an obsession, it doesn't really interfere with day-to-day life. If anything, it only spices up late-night bar chats and gives the local standup comics something to joke about. Political uncertainty, after all, is nothing new in a city founded by the French, conquered by the British and occupied by the Americans – all before the end of the 18th century. And Montréal has always been a haven for the politically incorrect – Loyalists fleeing the American War of Independence, priests fleeing the French Revolution, slaves fleeing the ante-bellum South and draft-dodgers fleeing the Vietnam conflict.

The result is a tolerant live-and-let-live attitude. On just about any question of personal morality, from same-sex marriage to abortion, Montréalers always poll higher than other Canadians on the "liberal" side of the ledger. ❑

PRECEDING PAGES: glass and steel towers downtown; a view of Tremblant resort across Lac Tremblant. **LEFT:** a downtown skyline with the port and Old Montreal.

THE MAKING OF MONTRÉAL

From Native Canadians to French and British settlers, the city's story has always been closely tied to its landscape, which is dominated by the river and the mountain

There are no more potent symbols of Montréal's past glories and future dreams than the St Lawrence River and Mont-Royal, the stubby little peak that gave the city its name. Montréalers call them simply "the river" and "the mountain" and the two run like contrasting threads through the whole woof and warp of the city's history. The St Lawrence, one of the great rivers of the world, is the gateway to the Great Lakes and the heart of the North American continent. It was the key to the city's economic success. Mont-Royal is more modest: at 230 metres (755 ft), it's hardly in the class of the Rockies, but it soars above the flat and fertile lands of the St Lawrence River Valley, making it a proud symbol of Montréal's aspirations. An enduring symbol, its hardened cone of volcanic basalt withstood the glacial ice that scoured the region more than 10,000 years ago, creating the complex of waterways and islands that mark the region.

West of the island on which Montréal lies, the Ottawa River, another great North American waterway, flows into the St Lawrence creating two placid lakes – Lac St-Louis and Lac des Deux-Montagnes – as well as the Lachine Rapids, a stretch of treacherous water that has contributed much to Montréal's development.

Early inhabitants

The earliest settlers of the island now known as Montréal were Indians, or more correctly, members of Canada's First Nations. The rich soil and fine fishing of the St Lawrence River Valley created ideal conditions for the members of the Iroquoian linguistic group – semi-sedentary tribes or nations who grew corn, squash and beans and built weirs to catch trout and salmon. It was members of this group – possibly Huron – whom Jacques Cartier encountered when he set foot on the island on 2 October 1525. His account speaks of an island crisscrossed with Indian trails and possessing one apparently permanent settlement, Hochelaga ("at the place of the beaver dam"). This was a circular, palisaded village whose residents lived in communal long houses. The site is probably close to where McGill University now stands.

LEFT: a family from the Iroquois First Nations tribe.
RIGHT: boats on the St Lawrence River c.1848.

The Iroquoian-speaking people included the Mohawk, Oneida, Onondaga, Cayuga, and Seneca – who formed the Five Nations Confederacy – as well as the Huron, Wenro, Erie, Tobacco, Cherokee, Susquehanna and Tuscarora. Together they dominated the Great Lakes, the St Lawrence River Valley, much of what became New England and large portions of Appalachia and the American southeast.

Cartier's mission

Jacques Cartier was a professional sailor from the French town of St-Malo. His king, Francis I, sent him west "to discover islands and countries where they say there is a lot of gold". In these early days of the Age of Discovery, France's influence in North America was unparalleled, driven by the cupidity and religious aspirations of French monarchs, and realized by the versatility and capabilities of their subjects. Cartier, for example, was a great navigator and deft diplomat. As a geographer though, he was limited by the ignorance of his times. Like everyone else, Cartier thought that North America was Asia, and that the rumoured mountains of gold and unlimited supplies of spice and silk were within his grasp. He sailed his convoy of three ships, led by the flagship *Grande Hermine*, as far as he could up the St Lawrence until impassable rapids impeded his progress.

It was here that the fateful encounter between European and First Nations that marked the beginnings of Montréal took place. Cartier dressed himself "gorgeously" for his first formal call on Hochelaga, and upon entering the village saw the horseshoe-shaped stockade typical of a Huron village. He was shown their settlement and taken to meet Agouhanna, the chief of Hochelaga.

Agouhanna decided to show him the local sights. Cartier was conveyed to the summit of the island's small mountain, and from this vantage he could see the river winding its way east for hundreds of kilometres. Here, thought Cartier, was the route to the Orient. He planted a cross, claimed the site for King Francis as the Hurons looked on baffled, and pronounced the site "Mont Royal". The derivative of this – Montréal, did not come into general usage until a century later.

Fool's gold and beaver pelts

Cartier also asked Agouhanna if he knew where to find the "shining rocks" he had heard were to be found here. The chief supplied him with some rock samples, but back in France his "gold" and "diamonds" were found to be iron pyrite (fool's gold) and quartz crystal.

However, he also brought back something far more important – the pelt of the Canadian beaver, an intelligent herbivore whose dense and furry undercoat was ideal for manufacturing the felt used to make the men's hats that were all the rage in Europe. Over the next two centuries, European demand for the pelts changed the lives of the Indians, who traded pelts for such European marvels as iron pots, firearms and, unfortunately, alcohol.

Cartier revisited Montréal in 1541, but did not linger long, and the general settlement of New France was now centred on what were to become the Canadian provinces of Nova Scotia and New Brunswick. Samuel de Champlain, whose tireless efforts to spread French influence in North America earned him the title of "father of new France", visited the island in 1611 and bought a smaller neighbouring island, now known as Île Ste-Hélène, in honour of Champlain's bride. But Champlain was more interested in developing Québec City and so Cartier's island languished until 1627 when Armand Jean du Plessis (better known as Cardinal Richelieu) entered the picture.

At Richelieu's urging, Louis XIII granted title to all land in New France to a group of shrewd French businessmen known as the Company of One Hundred Associates. It, in turn, granted subleases to likely settlers, and gave title to the island of Montréal to two fervent Catholics, Jean-Jacques Olier, later founder of the Society of Priests of St-Sulpice, and Jérôme de la Royer de la Dauversière, a tax collector from Anjou. Olier and Dauversière had met by chance in Paris, discovered a common missionary passion for converting "heathen" Indians, and determined to start a permanent mission at Montréal.

Pooling their resources, they set off in 1641 with a group of 50 missionary members of their newly created "Société de Notre-Dame-de-Montréal" under the leadership of Paul de Chomedey, Sieur de Maisonneuve. The new mission was to be established for the sole purpose of converting Indian souls to Catholicism, and Olier specified that the settlers "should have nothing to do with the fur trade". There would be difficulty enough, they cautioned Maisonneuve, in "planting the banner of Christ in an abode of desolation and a haunt of demons".

LEFT: Jacques Cartier visits Hochelaga.
RIGHT: an 18th-century engraving of a beaver hunt.

Religious fervour

Maisonneuve, a tough ex-soldier and Knight of Malta now driven by religious fervour, founded his colony, "Ville Marie", with the help of an indomitable French woman named Jeanne Mance, who built New France's first hospital. She also recruited another courageous French woman, Marguerite Bourgeoys, who established the colony's first school and founded the Congrégation Notre-Dame, an order of teaching sisters that still runs schools and colleges in Montréal, across Canada and in other parts of the world.

Life was extremely hazardous and arduous for the newly arrived settlers, who were

THE FIRST MASS

When Samuel de Champlain visited the north shore of the island of Montréal in 1615, he happened to meet two priests of the Récollet (Franciscan Minor) Order, Denis Janet and Joseph le Caron, both of whom were newly arrived from France. Together with Champlain's men, these two celebrated the first Catholic Mass in North America on 24 June 1615. The setting for this momentous event was nothing more than a humble clearing in the forest with no furnishings other than some rough wooden tables, but Champlain knelt with the two priests. Many, many more masses would be said in New France.

Religious Roots

If you walk down rue St-Denis on a Saturday night, past the bustling bars, bistros and nightclubs, it's difficult to remember just how Catholic Montréal and Québec were until a few decades ago. As recently as the 1960s, large families were the norm, weekly Mass attendance was virtually universal and the Church pretty much ran whatever social and educational systems there were, from hospitals to universities. Its army of priests, nuns and brothers – working for a pittance and the promise of future glory – educated the young, trained the professionals, nursed the sick, cared for the elderly and buried the dead. In no other North American jurisdiction, with the possible exception of Utah, did one church play such a pervasive role.

It was a system whose roots went back to pioneer days. The little band of men and women who founded Montréal in 1642 didn't brave the Canadian wilderness to get rich or make a name for themselves, but for the glory of God and the Church. Caught up in the religious enthusiasm that swept much of Catholic Europe in response to the Protestant Reformation, they wanted to create a perfect Christian commonwealth in the heart of North America. And they wanted to convert the "heathens".

Their leaders were typical of the spirit of the age. Paul de Chomedey was a fearless minor aristocrat who considered his Christian mission a "matter of honour". His chief lieutenant, Jeanne Mance, was a young woman of good family who abandoned wealth and privilege to minister to often resentful natives.

Montréal's location at the gateway to the North American interior made it inevitable that eventually commerce would trump faith. However, the ideal endured, and powerful, persuasive churchmen like François de Montmorency Laval, the first bishop of Québec, made sure that the Church played a major role in governing the colony and jealously guarded its prerogatives, especially in education.

If anything, the British conquest of 1759 strengthened the Church's role in the day-to-day lives of French Canadians. It became the sole bulwark against Anglicization, preserving language and culture as well as faith. Without the Church, it's quite possible that French Canada would be just a memory, but it was a system wide open to abuse. Many authoritarian bishops distrusted urban life and modernity. They had little time for business or engineering schools, and preferred to train the bright to be priests and lawyers and everyone else to be peasants and tradesmen.

In the 1940s and '50s, Church leaders became far too closely identified with the corrupt regime of Premier Maurice Duplessis, who used cheap Church labour to run his schools and hospitals while he spent money building roads and buying votes. Any bishops who dared defy him – like Joseph Charbonneau of Montréal, who sided with asbestos workers during a bitter strike in 1949 – were ruthlessly crushed. It was an alliance that many never forgave. After Duplessis died in 1959, Québecers turned their backs on both his party and the Church. ❑

LEFT: Jean de Brébeuf, a Jesuit priest who worked among the Hurons, is tortured by the Iroquois.

fortified by their belief that they were doing God's work. Attacks by indigenous people were a constant danger, their crops failed to thrive, and the melting snow caused disastrous annual floods. In December 1642, the confluence of the St Lawrence and St Peter rivers rose violently, lapping at the edges of the fledgling settlement. Maisonneuve, in great fear, planted a cross on the threatened bank and vowed that he would erect another on Mont-Royal if the waters receded – which they did on Christmas Day. On the feast of Epiphany (on 6 January) a procession, with a grateful Maisonneuve himself at the rear bearing a heavy wooden cross, scaled the hill and planted this token of thanks for God's mercy.

First baptism

The first baptism of an Algonquin child occurred at Ville Marie in 1642, a great victory for the embattled missionaries. After all, conversion of the pagans was their reason for enduring the hardships in New France. But as they gathered around the rough baptismal font, their thoughts may have turned to the great cost of salvation. How many more would die so that a few souls of the First Nations could be saved?

In 1644, fed up with the continual harassment of the settlement, Maisonneuve walked out like a Western gunslinger to meet the leader of the Iroquois in single combat. It wasn't by any means a fair fight, Maisonneuve having armed himself with two pistols. He succeeded in killing the chief at what is now known as Place d'Armes, where the statue of Maisonneuve and his dog stands today.

Despite the religious fervour of some at Ville Marie, the settlement flourished more as a French outpost than a centre of conversion. The quick wealth of the fur trade brought more people, including the so-called *filles du roi* – young Frenchwomen transported to Montréal to marry the male settlers.

Mountain of churches

Montréal was now North America's premier Roman Catholic city and remained so for almost two centuries. Dominated in the early days by Franciscans and Jesuits, the city later welcomed Jean-Jacques Olier's St-Sulpice fathers, and the so-called Grey Nuns (more formally known as Les Soeurs de la Charité de l'Hôpital Général de Montréal), who tended to the poor and destitute. The Oblates, Christian Brothers and Sacred Heart Sisters also found their way to the city.

The Catholic Church and its many religious orders and congregations built many of the city's most impressive buildings, including schools, hospitals, seminaries and colleges, as well as churches and chapels. When the Église Notre-Dame-de-Montréal – today a basilica doubling up as a major tourist attraction – was erected in 1829, it drew visitors from across Canada and the United States; it was at the time the largest church in North America and remained so until St Patrick's Cathedral was built in New York in 1879.

RIGHT: Montréal's Notre-Dame Basilica was built in 1829, the towers were not completed until the 1840s.

In 1874 there were 74 churches of all denominations in Montréal – one for every 2,000 inhabitants. Even at this date they were still largely Catholic, but with several tasteful additions from the Church of Scotland and the Anglican Church. Harriet Beecher Stowe, author of *Uncle Tom's Cabin*, wrote in 1860 that "Montréal is a mountain of churches", while Mark Twain took a more jaundiced view: "This is the first time I was ever in a city", he wrote in 1881, "where you could not throw a brick without breaking a church window".

Land rights and Iroquois raids

During the 1660s, the governing spirit of Ville Marie was the energetic Superior of the Sulpicians and keen amateur historian, François Dollier de Cassons (1632–1702). He was a strapping, 2.2 metre (6 ft 6 inches) ex-soldier who, with his cassock tucked up for greater freedom of movement, surveyed the town's first street plan, planned a canal to bypass the rapids, and built the first parish church and a seminary for the Sulpicians, the society of priests that was still the official owner of the island.

In 1663, however, Louis XIV took formal possession of all the land and trade of New France, and henceforth only the Crown and its representatives in Québec could grant parcels of land and trading licences. The island of Montréal was divided into land packets known as *seigneuries*; the owners, or *seigneurs*, subdividing their land into long and narrow tenant parcels known as *rangs*, which were farmed by *habitants* *(see page 24)*. For a nominal rent the habitant was given the land to work, on which he built a dwelling for himself and maintained a road. He also had to pay to grind his grain at the *seigneur's* mill. *Seigneuries* were typically divided up into long strips rather than chunks in order that every habitant could have some river access. This division is still evident in Québec estates.

But while Ville Marie seemed to be gaining a foothold on the island, the threat from First Nations did not lessen. On 4 August 1689, the worst Iroquois raid yet left 200 residents of the nearby town of Lachine dead. Another 100 were captured and never returned.

There followed 10 years of sustained fighting with the Iroquois, which effectively halted the fur trade on which Montréal's prosperity depended. The city entered the 18th century on a pensive note, but the diplomatic Governor-General of Montréal, Hector de Callières, managed to negotiate a peace treaty with the First Nations. In 1701 more than 1,300 indigenous people, representatives of 40 different nations, were persuaded to come to Montréal and camp outside the city's walls for peace talks. De Callières, skilled in smoothing over old grievances, circulated among the assembled chiefs and hammered out a deal all could accept. Surveying the hundreds of tents, campfires and milling First Nations and Frenchmen, de Callières cried: *"Voici la paix. Oublions le passé"* ("Peace is here, let us forget the past"). Peace had come, yes, but it was not destined to last for long.

The fur trade

After the peace of 1701 between the French and the First Nations, Montréal rebuilt itself, dropped the name of Ville Marie, and concentrated on becoming the trading centre its location seemed always to promise. Because the Lachine Rapids made it almost impossible for transatlantic trading ships to go any further upriver, all furs from the interior (and all trading goods going west) had to be shipped through Montréal. The pursuit of the beaver pelts was furious, sometimes unscrupulous.

The lure of quick wealth was too much for most early Montréalers to resist, and "everyone turns trader", a contemporary traveller noted. The aging Dollier de Cassons wrote of the fur trade gloomily, describing "the diabolical attractions" of quick wealth and the resulting "*perdition générale*" of Montréal.

The First Nations, however, were not the only ones to pursue the beavers into their habitat. Toughened *coureurs de bois* – French woodsmen skilled in paddling and trapping – steered fur-heavy canoes into Montréal harbour and looked for a good price. Some of them had "gone native" and barely appeared French to the civilized denizens of Montréal. Their supplies sold off, they and the First Nations would proceed to get roaring drunk on cheap liquor, collapsing in dirty heaps or copulating, fighting and drinking until dawn.

Increasing wealth

In 1721, the town fortifications were improved with 5.5-metre (18-ft) walls of stone, bastions, a citadel and more cannon. The wooden buildings inside the walls, always at risk of fire, were replaced in accordance with building regulations that called for stone walls and roofs of slate, tile or tin.

For almost five decades the little town boomed, its *seigneurs* and traders becoming wealthier as the demand for beaver furs grew in Europe. In the long winter months, leisure time was unlimited and the prosperous families of Montréal enjoyed amateur theatricals, dancing and sugaring-off picnics in which a festive party sledded out to the maple forests to collect sap for maple syrup. The more prosaic *habitants*, at least as portrayed by sentimental artists such as Cornelius Krieghoff (1812–72), loved to dance, play cards (a pursuit banned by the Church) and drink heavily.

LEFT: the *Habitants*, portrayed by Cornelius Krieghoff.
RIGHT: the death of Wolfe at the battle for Québec City.

The arrival of the British

In 1756, the Seven Years' War between the British and the French ended the prosperous peace. The conflict didn't start well for the British. In 1758, Louis-Joseph, Marquis de Montcalm, scored an impressive victory over a much larger British army at Ticonderoga. But luck and political intrigue back home did Montcalm in. In 1759 he lost a decisive battle on the Plains of Abraham outside Québec City. The fight lasted less than an hour, but left Montcalm and his British rival, Major-General James Wolfe, dead, and Québec City in British hands.

A year later the British general Lord Jeffrey Amherst entered Montréal and was met by

Vaudreuil, the governor of New France, who formally surrendered. The British flag flew over Montréal for the first time on 9 September 1760. In 1763, under the Treaty of Paris, France ceded its territories to Britain, ending the era of French control in Montréal.

However, daily life did not alter much for the average Montréaler. The British governors were sensitive to the fact that several generations of Frenchmen were responsible for whatever civilization, trade and development the colony enjoyed. No land was stripped from the *seigneurs*, and the Québec Act of 1774 accepted the French language and Roman Catholic religion as essential parts of Québec culture.

Habitants

New France's first permanent homesteads (evidence of which can still be seen today) were uniquely linked to the available water sources. The original plots were long, narrow strips of land with one end facing the St Lawrence River. In the original settlements, this water frontage was usually 200–250 metres (655–820 ft) wide, with the plot stretching away from the river to a depth of several kilometres. This division gave all settlers an equal share of good and bad land and equal access to the river.

Land tenure followed the French feudal model. The crown granted large tracts to *seigneurs* who recruited tenant farmers, or *habitants*, to clear and farm the land. Tenants paid an annual rent and were required to participate in the *corvée*, a feudal service that most often involved construction and road work. In return, the *seigneur* erected a mill and oven and handled disputes.

The linear settlement pattern established a compelling solidarity among the *habitants*. Few other colonies in Canada developed this kind of built-in interdependency. One institution reflecting the importance of neighbours was the *premier voisin* (first neighbour), usually the head of the next-door family. Invited to most family functions and included in all important decisions, the *premier voisin* helped out with any major project and was called upon for help when any emergency arose. In return, his family always received a loaf of bread on baking day or a slab of meat during the slaughtering season.

Because both France and the St Lawrence region were good dairy countries and possessed soils suitable for growing legumes, root crops, hay and fruits rather than cereals, the core diet of the *habitants* strongly echoed the typical fare of a French peasant. Along with carrots, onions, cabbage, turnips and eventually potatoes, peas and pork became central ingredients in many dishes, particularly in the form of a daily staple – pea soup. They could supplement their diet with wild berries and game, particularly wild hare and venison, as well as fish from the St Lawrence River. Folklorist Edith Fowke notes that the *habitants* would simmer eels in cream along with cider, salted pork and onions. British colonists to the south adapted this recipe, using molluscs, and it became the now famed New England clam chowder.

The *habitants*' daily menu consisted of a breakfast of pancakes, bread, salted pork and cider (until replaced by coffee and tea), followed at noon by a lunch of pea soup with fried potatoes and a garden vegetable. At around 4pm, leftovers from lunch would be consumed, accompanied by a cucumber salad and bread smeared with either pork fat or butter. The final meal of the day was eaten at 8 or 9pm, when a bowl of bread cooked in milk and maple sugar would be served along with cider.

Although today's French Canadian diet has changed drastically from that of the *habitants*, many of the old foods associated with holidays are still remarkably popular: tortières, meatball stew, sausages, onion sauce, maple sugar candies and doughnuts are among them. ❑

LEFT: the French Canadian *habitants* and *habitantes* settled along the St Lawrence in a unique fashion, founding a truly distinct society.

A cosmopolitan mix

But by this time one could hear a broad Scottish burr on the streets of Montréal, and the haughty bleat of English nobility. The demographics of the city changed radically during the next generation as the population exploded with an exuberant commercial eagerness. Montréal was still a boomtown, on whose streets leather-clad *coureurs de bois* (woodsmen), fresh from the river portages and indigenous camps, rubbed shoulders with Scottish merchants, English soldiers and aristocratic French *seigneurs*.

New civil regulations also marked the influence of English bureaucrats on Montréal. In 1765, the price of a 2-kg (4-lb) loaf of white bread (a "brick") was fixed at eight coppers; bakers were not permitted to charge more than 10 coppers for the heavier brown loaf.

Slavery was also a prevailing concern, and the governors thought it best to distance themselves officially from the buying and selling of humans so widely practised in the 13 British colonies to the south. It was decreed that "no tavern, alehouse or innkeeper do receive, harbour, or entertain any bond or servant slave or slaves, drinking, gaming or loitering in their houses, under a penalty of £5".

Americans come and go

The strategic position of Montréal made it a desirable military target, and during the American Revolution (1775–83) the city once again came under attack. The first American overture was a failure. In 1775 the garrison at Montréal heard that Ethan Allen and his famous "Green Mountain Boys" were marching along the Longue Pointe road, just east of the city.

A small force of English and French soldiers advanced to challenge the invaders and Allen was easily defeated and captured. The garrison commandant, an old soldier called Prescott, threatened to cane the arrogant Allen, and he had to be dragged off by his men. Allen was imprisoned on board the ship *Gaspé*, and Montréalers rejoiced at having "caged the great New Hampshire incendiary". The jubilation was short-lived, however, for in the autumn of 1775 General Richard Montgomery advanced towards the city with a much larger force, and the governor, Sir Guy Carleton (later Lord Dorchester), was compelled to surrender without resistance.

The attitude of the Americans was that Montréalers should be overjoyed to be freed from colonial rule. They were invited to "seize the opportunity presented to you by Providence itself" and join the not-quite-Continental Congress. But the Americans failed to reckon with other ideas of freedom – Montréalers were happy and prosperous under the British, and mocked the American deliverance. The Americans, on the other hand, found Canadian notions of liberty "monstrously ill-digested" and soon labelled the Montréalers "rascals and enemies".

Benjamin Franklin arrived in 1776 to smooth over these rough spots and court possible annexation. He tried to persuade French Canadians to join the American revolutionary cause against England, but he was rejected and withdrew.

RIGHT: General Amherst enters Montréal.

The Americans finally left in 1783, when Britain massed a large army near Montréal, and a peace treaty was signed with the new United States republic the same year.

Perhaps the only palpable benefit of the American occupation was that one of Franklin's associates, Fleury de Mesplet, decided to stay on and ply his printing trade in Montréal. In a shop on rue de la Capitale, off rue St-François-Xavier, he began producing Canada's first newspaper, *La Gazette du commerce et littéraire*. In 1788 the paper was printed in both French and English, a concrete indication that English had arrived in the city. Its lineal descendant, *The Gazette*, is now the city's only English-language daily newspaper.

Scottish Nor-Westers

Other commercial enterprises began around this time to serve the needs of the wealthy fur traders and their employees, and at the same time the influx of United Empire Loyalists fleeing the anti-monarchist revolution to the south swelled Montréal's population. The focus of the town shifted away from the harbour and towards what is now downtown Montréal.

The city's new aristocracy was largely Scottish in origin, and included several enterprising rogues who had taken advantage of the wide-open colonial life to make their vast fortunes in fur trading. Simon McTavish, Joseph Frobisher, William McGillivray, James McGill and Simon Fraser were the stars in Montréal's social and commercial firmament in this era. Their names also dot the rivers and regions of western Canada, which they were the first to explore. In 1783 a group of them founded the North-West Company, a fur-trading cooperative begun in order to challenge the hegemony of England's Hudson's Bay Company. The Hudson's Bay Company absorbed the "Nor-Westers" in 1821, but for decades it raced them to the fur trade in the west and north of Canada.

The Beaver Club

Beaver Hall Hill, site of Canada's first men's club, owes its name to the Nor-Westers. Membership in the Beaver Club was restricted to those who had wintered in Canada's wilderness, *le pays d'en haut*, and during the long Montréal winters the adventurers would gather here to tell tall stories, drink whisky and sing the canoeing songs of the old voyageurs, paddling away for all they were worth with their walking sticks, fire tongs or dress swords.

The new fur lords built their grand homes, dwarfing the châteaux of the early *seigneurs*, well away from the city centre on the southern slopes of Mont-Royal in area then known simply as "the Square Mile", which later became known as "the Golden Square Mile".

The Making of McGill

Just as their names would go down in history on the maps of the region, the Nor-Westers left their mark on their home base of Montréal. The city's main English-speaking university is built on land bequeathed by Edinburgh University graduate James McGill, who wanted the colony to have "an English college on a liberal scale".

With $10,000 and the 18 hectares (45 acres) of land known as Burnside, nestled at the foot of Mont-Royal, the oldest of Montréal's four universities was founded in 1821. The original building on the campus still stands at the end of the drive.

Now the Arts Building, this austere neoclassical structure designed by architect John Ostell, was McGill University's only building for three decades. When classes commenced the college site was still countryside, and its 20 hardy students tramped across fields full of crops and grazing cattle to reach the fount of wisdom.

They had to dress "in plain, decent and comely clothes, without superfluous ornament" and wear gowns to their lectures on medicine, classics and mathematics. The institution became one of the brightest jewels of Montréal's Scottish bourgeoisie.

By 1900 McGill University had grown to accommodate almost 30,000 students, taught by 6,200 staff.

While these Scottish "lords of lake and forest", the "hyperborean nabobs" of the fur trade (as Washington Irving had enthusiastically called them), spoke English among themselves, most were bilingual, the result of necessary traffic with their voyageur paddlers and, in some cases, of Scotland's Auld Alliance with France against the English.

Many of these Scots, including McTavish, McGill and Frobisher, also married French Canadians. They were models of biculturalism in action, happy in a city still essentially French. It was not until the spring of 1786 that an English play, Goldsmith's *She Stoops to Conquer*, was performed in Montréal by a professional troupe from Albany, New York. No other play is mentioned in the history of Montréal for almost 13 years, so presumably English-style drama did not appeal to the tastes of these northern hearties.

Molson in Montréal

In the same year, 1786, the Englishman John Molson opened his brewery on the banks of the St Lawrence. He also established a bank and a small shipping line that was to expand quickly during the next 50 years. Molson, who was a great favourite among the French *habitants* along the river, is an appropriate emblem for this golden age of commercial Montréal. Starting out with almost nothing in the new colony, he made his vast fortune by working hard to meet the simple needs of its inhabitants. He is reputed to have said that "An honest brew makes its own friends" – a slogan found on his family's beer bottles to this day. When the brewery opened, a bottle of strong beer cost five cents while mild ale went for seven cents.

Molson also built Montréal's first hotel and its first commercial theatre, the Théâtre Royal.

Molson's brewery was the first to be built in North America and, while the steamship line that used to run his two ships – the *Accommodation* and the *Swiftsure* – between Québec and Montréal is long gone, you can still enjoy Molson's lager or ale in any Canadian tavern. The Molson family continues to play a prominent, if less visible, role in Montréal.

LEFT: the men's snowshoe club turned essential winter footwear into an excuse for social activity. **RIGHT:** on the river in Montréal c.1846.

Effects of the War of 1812

With the ambitious Americans to the south, peace was unlikely to endure. War came once more in October 1813, when 5,000 troops under Major-General Hampton advanced on Montréal from the west. A decisive battle was fought at Châteauguay, where fewer than 1,000 Canadians, commanded by Lieutenant-Colonel Charles de Salaberry, defeated the Americans.

A salutary effect of the War of 1812 was that its threat to Canada's economy hastened the founding of the colony's first bank, the Bank of Montréal, which was chartered in 1817.

The war had also indicated the very real danger of moving men and supplies past the

dangerous Lachine Rapids when time was of the essence; nobody had successfully navigated the rapids that had stopped Cartier, and they remained extremely arduous. In 1821, with money "panhandled" from the provincial and British governments, the Lachine Canal was completed – almost 200 years after the far-sighted Dollier de Cassons had first suggested its construction.

Improvements were also evident on the city streets, lit from 1815 onward with gas lamps. The purpose of this innovation appeared to be mostly social – a decree said the lamps were installed so "that ladies might be induced to visit their friends much more frequently".

Also in this period (1832), the City of Montréal was incorporated, and its first mayor, Jacques Viger, was elected the following year. Viger completed a grand term in office, performing Montréal's first census and donating the land for Viger Square, Montréal's most popular park between the 1860s and 1890s.

Montréal's first mayor also coined the city motto, *Concordia Salus* ("Health lies in Concord"), giving it the distinctive coat of arms that conjoins the national symbols of France, England, Scotland and Ireland. The Societies of St Jean-Baptiste, St Andrew, St Patrick and St George were all founded at this time. *Concordia Salus*, certainly, but old ties still die hard.

Democratic demands

The prosperity and optimism of the 1820s and early 1830s were shattered by events that shook Montréal a few years later. The 1837 rebellions in Toronto and Montréal indicated that not everyone was satisfied with the colonial government and its encouragement for the rich to get richer. In Montréal, a group of reformers known as Les Patriotes, led by, among others, Louis Joseph Papineau, demanded the reform of a system that was to a large extent controlled by a clique of family interests. Representative government was a radical notion in these times, and the majority of people found the demands of the Patriotes unpalatable.

FENIAN RAIDS

Although Montréal was the first city of Canada, both commercially and strategically, the main battles of the War of 1812–14 were fought in Ontario. But Montréal did feel the effects of the unrest in the threat of "Fenian raids". The Fenians were Irish Americans whose name comes from the Irish motto Sinn Fein, which translates as "Ourselves Alone" and is today the name of the Irish Republican Army's political wing. They harassed settlers all along Canada's southern border during the War of 1812–14 and following America's bloody Civil War (1861–65).

One of their marching songs gives a better idea of their motives and mien:

We are the Fenian brotherhood, skilled in the arts of war
And we're going to fight for Ireland, the land that we adore,
Many battles we have won, along with the boys in blue
And now we're going to conquer Canada – because we ain't got nothing else to do.

The Fenians did have some bite. On 7 April 1868, men who claimed to be connected with the Fenian cause shot and killed Thomas d'Arcy McGee, one of the Fathers of Confederation, outside his Ottawa home. This had the dubious distinction of being the first political assassination in Canadian history.

Britain refused to acknowledge the 92 resolutions drawn up by Papineau and his associates, which demanded the dissolution of the appointed governing Council of Lower Canada, the Château Clique (the reference is to Château St-Louis, Québec's Government House). Papineau called for a council of elected representatives to replace the self-serving clique, which, like the Family Compacts controlling Upper Canada, doled out privilege and contracts with the arrogant disdain of absolute monarchs.

Violence and tough justice

The atmosphere in Montréal was ripe for violence. Cholera epidemics in 1832 and 1834 had ravaged the population, and political clubs and duelling societies fomented the unrest by meeting publicly to argue and fight. On 6 November 1837, a fierce riot broke out on peaceful rue St-Jacques and spilled into Place d'Armes. After dark, the house of Papineau and the offices of the *Vindicator*, a newspaper supporting him, were wrecked. Two weeks of uneasy silence were broken by the imposition of martial law when Sir John Colborne, the commander-in-chief, set up his headquarters in the Château Ramezay and dispatched troops to hunt down the Patriotes. Many, including Papineau, fled to the United States.

Others were not so resourceful. Twelve captured Patriotes, most of them young men who had worn, with a jaunty tilt, the white "O'Connell" top hat, a recognized badge of the radical, were publicly hanged by the authorities. Sixty or 70 more were banished, and Montréal's last sight of the rebellion was a chain gang of forlorn prisoners being marched down to the Bonsecours landing stage, there to embark on their journey to New South Wales or Tasmania.

The sentences may seem harsh, but despite its new metropolitan status, Montréal was still a frontier town and magistrates felt obliged to judge stiffly. In 1817, the crimes of sacrilege and shoplifting were punishable by execution, as was the more serious crime of horse-stealing.

Petty crimes were typically punished with humiliation in the stocks or the pillory, but judges were also in the habit of having small-time criminals branded on the palm of the hand with a heated iron. The brand, in the shape of a crown, was held to the flesh for as long as it took the convicted criminal to repeat *"Vive le roi!"* three times. It was more likely to be "God save the King!" however, since the session lists from these times show that the vast majority of tried criminals in Montréal were British or itinerant Loyalist Americans, and not francophone Québécois.

Political progress and setback

Britain's reaction to the trouble in the colonies was to dispatch the Earl of Durham in order to survey the state of public affairs there. Lord

Durham's famous Report on the Affairs of British North America was the first document to isolate French-English tensions as a source of political worry in Canada.

In 1841, partly as a result of Durham's suggestions, the provinces of Upper and Lower Canada (today Ontario and Québec) were joined in an Act of Union that was the beginning of modern Canada. In 1843 Montréal was made capital of the new united Province of Canada, but it enjoyed that honour for all too short a time – just five years.

In 1848, while revolution was sweeping Europe, the reactionary element of Montréal sacked the Parliament Building and burned

LEFT AND RIGHT: Montréal boomed after the Treaty of Paris, trade was brisk in such commodities as timber and ice blocks.

it to the ground after the legislators approved a bill to compensate Patriotes punished in 1837. The members of the house fled, leaving the building to be destroyed. The vandals, carrying the Speaker's ceremonial mace, ran through the streets and attacked the residences of the parliamentarians, including that of the governor-general, Lord Elgin.

After this debacle, the Canadian Parliament was moved to Toronto and alternated between that city and Québec until a permanent site was chosen in Ottawa, along the Ottawa River.

A Boston newspaper gave a gloomy picture of the city in the 1840s: "Montréal wears a dismal aspect ... the removal of the seat of government caused some 4,000 inhabitants to leave ... every third store seems to want an occupant and empty houses groan for tenants." If that weren't enough, typhus, brought to the harbour in 1847, killed more than 6,000 people; the Great Fire of 1852 – the worst in a long series – lasted for 26 days, destroying 1,200 buildings and leaving 9,000 people homeless.

Commercial advances

Despite these setbacks, Montréal was well on its way to becoming what one contemporary called "the first city in magnitude and commercial importance in British America". Although the fur trade was waning, the enterprising rich of Montréal had diversified their investments and Molson's steamship line was doing a good trade between Montréal and Québec City.

The old harbour had been renovated by some energetic young builders, including Englishman John Ostwell, who at 19 was given the job of designing the new Customs House. The Bank of Montréal building, by Scotsman David Rhind and based on the grand Bank of Scotland in Edinburgh, was erected on Place d'Armes.

The railways came to Montréal in 1853 when the Grand Trunk Railway Company began running a service to Portland, Maine, following it with a line to the still provincial city of Toronto in 1856.

A final event symbolizes this era of expansion and commercial vigour, when Montréal was the New York of Canada, its rue St-Jacques as important as Wall Street. In 1860 the 19-year-old Prince of Wales (later King Edward VII) opened the magnificent Victoria Bridge.

Confederation

The stage was now set for Montréal to assume primacy of place in the newly confederated Canada. In 1867, representatives of the colonies on the Atlantic coast decided to meet in Charlottetown, capital of Prince Edward Island, to discuss the prospects for a united Atlantic Colony. The leaders of Upper and Lower

Canada, hearing of the conference to which they had not been invited, decided to crash the party and plead their own case. At the head of this group was John A. Macdonald, the wily, alcoholic Scotsman destined to be Canada's first prime minister. His slightly irresolute portrait now adorns Canada's $10 bill.

Macdonald and his cohorts chartered the *Queen Victoria* in Québec City, loaded her with $13,000-worth of champagne, and steamed down the St Lawrence to Prince Edward Island. Despite a very modest reception – a single oyster boat – Macdonald was able, with the aid of his precious cargo, to persuade the Atlantic colonists that Upper and Lower Canada should be part of any union. The rough terms for confederation were agreed upon at what one disgusted New Brunswick editorialist described as "the great inter-colonial drunk". They were later ratified at a conference in Québec, and on 1 July 1867, the British North America Act created modern Canada by joining Nova Scotia, New Brunswick, Prince Edward Island, Ontario and Québec.

Scandalous deals

The new country was embroiled in scandal almost from the beginning. Macdonald quickly became involved in the Métis Rebellion affair, an uprising that occurred when the government purchased Rupert's Land out west but neglected to take into account the indigenous population. The Métis were of mixed French and Indian ancestry, and their leader, Louis Riel, won the sympathy of many Montréalers. When Macdonald decided to have Riel hanged, he was quoted as saying: "He shall hang though every dog in Québec should bark in his favour." Riel's death only served to entrench French-English distrust, and he is still a hero to legions of Québec schoolchildren.

In addition, to hasten a railway link to western Canada and the Pacific, Macdonald and his colleague from Lower Canada, George-Etienne Cartier, had accepted party contributions from a group of Montréal businessmen who wanted the contract to build it. The Canadian Pacific Railway (CPR) Bill was passed by Parliament in 1870, but the backroom dealing reached public attention soon afterwards. The focus of the scandal was Sir Hugh Allan, a prosperous Montréal shipper and owner of a massive estate called Ravenscrag. The estate's mansion now houses the Neurological Institute of the Royal Victoria Hospital.

With the CPR deal cut if not dried, Macdonald's ailing campaign was bolstered by "anonymous" gifts of money, first $60,000 and then $35,000. With his campaign in its final days, Macdonald foolishly wired Sir Hugh for more: "I must have another ten thousand. Will be the last time of calling. Do not fail me."

Sir Hugh considered the political financing simple tactics in good business, but the public

did not see it that way. The office of Sir Hugh's solicitor in Montréal was ransacked late one night by a confidential clerk and, as a result, the incriminating telegram appeared on the front page of Montréal's newspapers. Macdonald and Cartier had to resign and a despairing Cartier died the following year. Macdonald, a more accomplished political survivor, outlasted the public's short memory for wrongdoing and was back in office by 1878.

The railway was delayed, but not stopped. On 28 June 1886, with bands playing, the first passenger train steamed out of Montréal's old Dalhousie Station, bound for Port Moody, British Columbia. ❑

LEFT: Montréal Harbour in the late 19th century.
RIGHT: John Macdonald, Canada's first prime minister.

1566
DRY

MODERN MONTRÉAL

As Canada's focus shifts increasingly towards Toronto, Montréalers continue to squabble over language and separatism – and try to forge a new economy

Montréal approached the 20th century aglow with much optimism. Its merchants and financiers controlled the majority of the wealth of the newly unified nation and as the eastern terminus of the transcontinental railway and the westernmost port on the St Lawrence River, it was also Canada's transportation hub.

The city was spreading fast. Wealthy merchants from the old town moved their premises to larger lots on rue Ste-Catherine, rue Sherbrooke as well as on the southern slopes of Mont Royal. In 1891 Henry Morgan decisively shifted the commercial heart of the city by opening Canada's first department store – now The Bay – on rue Ste-Catherine. Even the Roman Catholic bishop, Ignace Bourget, joined the movement out of the old city by building his cathedral – a mini version of St Peter's Basilica in Rome – in what is now downtown.

Mixed blessings

The glow of these golden years was dimmed by social inequity and industrial hardship. Montréal had several desperate, disease-ridden slums. Immigration was, from the late 19th century on, both a blessing and a curse. The cheap source of labour the immigrants provided for booming industry was welcome; however, the population explosion posed serious difficulties for Montréal's housing and sanitation resources. In 1825, the city's population was 26,000. Immigration and annexation quadrupled that by 1865, when French-speakers outnumbered English-speakers for the first time since the 1820s. By 1910, the population was 500,000 and growing rapidly. The lot of many people was unremittingly hard factory work, tiny shacks to live in, and the constant threat of epidemics and fires.

The new Montréalers came from Ireland, eastern Europe, China, Greece, Portugal and especially Italy. And they followed the pattern being established in cities across North America. While the older inhabitants moved farther from the harbour and train station – in the case

LEFT: Montréal street scene c.1880.

RIGHT: registering immigrants; they provided cheap labour but put a strain on Montréal's resources.

The Quiet Revolution

The rebellious spirit of the 1960s swept through Québec with the force of a hurricane, transforming the conservative, devoutly Catholic province into one of the most militantly secular societies in North America. The popular, comic-book narrative of this *"Révolution Tranquille"*, or "Quiet Revolution", is that a handful of brave iconoclasts smashed a priest-ridden, medieval regime that had held Québecers in thrall for generations. It is an appropriate label in a country with little history of civil violence.

There is some truth in the caricature. Until the early 1960s, the Roman Catholic Church's influence was pervasive. It ran the schools, universities, hospitals and many of the social services. Many church leaders distrusted the corrupting influence of modern urban life and encouraged their flock to stay on the land as farmers rather than pursue business or professional careers in the big city. Such men tacitly allied themselves to the corrupt regime of Premier Maurice Duplessis, who ran the province for nearly 20 years with a mix of patronage, strong-arm intimidation and populist politics. He shamelessly used the provincial police force to persecute labour unions, socialists and anyone else who might threaten his power.

But this *"grande noirceur"* ("great darkness") was not entirely black. Duplessis, for all his sins, started the process of modernizing Québec. He used the Church's army of priests, brothers and nuns as free labour to staff schools and hospitals, freeing him to spend liberally on modern highways and opening up the mineral wealth of the north.

The Church had also helped establish credit unions and cooperatives, which gave francophones some clout in the economy. And the leaders of the first phase of the Quiet Revolution were not secularists but devout Catholics, like newspaper publisher Claude Ryan, leader of the Action Catholique movement and relentless critic of the Duplessis regime, and Georges-Henri Lévesque, a Dominican priest who organized the Université Laval's École des Sciences Sociales, one of the hotbeds of intellectual dissent. Such men laid the groundwork for the defeat of the Duplessis regime after the premier died in 1959 and helped reform Québec's education and social-service networks.

It was not so much the collapse of the old regime as the changes wrought in the Church itself by the Second Vatican Council that caused the old authoritarian bishops to lose their confidence, not to mention hundreds of their priests, brothers and nuns.

By the early 1970s, Québec was well on its way to becoming the most secular province in Canada. Today it has the lowest church-attendance and fertility rates in the country, as well as the highest abortion rate. The only reason its divorce rate isn't the highest is that so many Québec couples don't bother to get married – civilly or religiously.

Today francophone Québecers have more opportunity and freedom than ever. But the picture is not entirely rosy. The collapse of the birth rate means that "pure-laine" Québecers form a shrinking proportion of the population. They are not on the endangered list yet, but the future looks uncertain. The fate of nations, after all, is decided not in courtrooms or legislatures, but in bedrooms. ❑

LEFT: religion was once all-powerful in Québec.

of Montréal, farther up the hill – the new Montréalers put down their battered suitcases wherever, and as soon as, they could.

With this new diversification in Montréal, the old moneyed families began to shut their doors. No longer did the aristocrats of Montréal walk the streets like James McGill. Instead, they stayed in their estates in Westmount or the "Square Mile", or found others like themselves in exclusive gentlemen's clubs like the Canadian and the Mount Royal. Few bothered to learn French and the gap between rich and poor, English and French, widened.

Wartime loyalties

The animosity between French and English Montréal was then further exacerbated by the conscription controversy of World War I. Québecers had no particular quarrel with Britain's enemies, and many objected to being forced into the war effort. Their reluctance resulted in their vilification in the English-language press. This issue arose again during World War II, when Maurice Duplessis, premier at the time, argued that the federal government did not speak for French Canadians.

The federal government's failure to deal effectively with this crisis became a symbol of its ongoing problem with Québec, and the easy mix of French and English that had marked Montréal's early history disappeared. Economic disparity, the sense that control rested with a few privileged anglophone families, and the reality of Canada's growing anglophone population all contributed to a feeling among French-speaking Canadians that they were second-class citizens who were in danger of being assimilated.

By the 1950s, Montréal was no longer riding the strong wave of industrial and commercial success that had marked its entry into the new century. Indeed, Canada's focus was shifting away from the river ports and towards the Great Lakes, especially Toronto – a shift encouraged by the opening of the St Lawrence Seaway, which permitted large freighters to bypass the Port of Montréal. Economic power shifted to Toronto and the brokerages of Bay Street.

Revolution and separatism

In the wake of the Second Vatican Council, the Québec Church lost its confidence. With the defeat of the authoritarian Union Nationale government, led by Premier Maurice Duplessis, and the rise of the more secular Liberal Party, it also lost much of its influence over Québec's schools, hospitals and social services. The Université de Montréal and the Université Laval in Québec City, both originally church foundations, became hotbeds of dissent and debate as Québec's "chattering classes" grappled with the problems of modernity. The result was the Quiet Revolution *(see page 34)*, which rapidly transformed Québec from a deeply Catholic society into a 20th-century secular one.

RIGHT: demobbed Canadians returning home after serving in World War II.

Separatism, once a fringe movement of romantic right-wingers and fiery leftists, became respectable. Just how respectable could be judged by the delirious crowd reaction in the summer of 1967 when French President Charles de Gaulle – in Canada to celebrate the country's centenary – stood on a balcony of Montréal's City Hall and cried "*Vive le Québec libre!*" ("Long live free Québec!"). A year later, René Lévesque, one of the most popular leaders of the Quiet Revolution, bolted from the provincial Liberal Party to form the pro-independence Parti Québécois (PQ). Lévesque's new party won nearly 30 percent of the popular vote in its first electoral outing in the spring of 1970. But all those votes produced only six seats in the Assemblée Nationale, the 96-member provincial parliament. It was a situation that some saw as proof that democracy would never achieve what Québec needed.

In October 1970, the Front de Libération du Québec (FLQ) was involved in two kidnappings *(see below)*, one of which ended in tragedy. Although the FLQ's gambit failed, the group's rambling manifesto, condemning conditions in Québec and proposing an independent revolutionary state as the only viable option, struck a chord with Québec's intellectuals, labour organizations and even some clergy. Support for the PQ grew in the next election and its platform shifted noticeably leftward.

The tongue troopers

Finally, on 15 November 1976, the party gained power. One of the first laws it enacted was the Charter of the French Language, known as Bill 101, which declared French the province's only official language and pretty much forbade the public display of other languages. Inspectors – contemptuously called "tongue troopers" by the anglophone minority – ensured compliance.

In 1980, the PQ at last held its promised referendum on "sovereignty-association", or

THE OCTOBER CRISIS

On 5 October 1970, the Front de Libération du Québec (FLQ), a shadowy group that had previously limited itself to bombing mailboxes in the Westmount district of Montréal, kidnapped the British trade commissioner, James Cross, from his home on Redpath Crescent.

The action shocked the nation and sparked the so-called "October crisis". Just five days later the FLQ kidnapped the Québec labour minister, Pierre Laporte, from in front of his suburban home. The Prime Minister, Pierre Trudeau *(see page 46)* – himself a Québécois, but also an ardent federalist – responded by invoking the War Measures Act.

Armed soldiers appeared on the streets of Montréal, and police used the act's authority to round up hundreds of writers, intellectuals, labour leaders and other "troublemakers", most of whom were never charged with anything. Police eventually cornered James Cross's kidnappers, but granted them safe passage to Cuba in return for Cross's release. Pierre Laporte was not so fortunate. His kidnappers, another cell of the FLQ, were not captured until after they had killed their captive and stuffed his body into the trunk of a car. Laporte is interred in the Cimetière Notre-Dame-des-Neiges.

independence with a kind of common-market relationship with the rest of Canada. But despite the convoluted hedging of the secessionist option, the motion failed decisively.

Still, the divisiveness of the campaign and bitterness over the language laws drove many anglophones from Montréal, along with their companies. Between 1976 and 1981, an estimated 100 head offices left Montréal, taking about 14,000 jobs with them and demoting Montréal to Canada's No. 2 city.

Expo and Olympics

Despite all the political turmoil and economic uncertainty of the 1960s and 1970s, however, Montréal never really lost its exuberance – thanks in large part to its visionary and free-spending mayor, Jean Drapeau. His efforts brought the city a sparkling subway system – the métro – in 1966, and a year later the successful world's fair, Expo 67. He also won the 1976 summer Olympics for the city, an accomplishment tainted only by huge cost overruns on the facilities *(see page 170)*.

In the 1980s, the PQ was defeated and Québec and Ottawa tried to resolve their constitutional differences. Their first attempt – the 1987 Meech Lake constitutional accord, which declared Québec a "distinct society" – looked promising, but in the end the provinces of Newfoundland and Manitoba couldn't assent to its proposals and the accord failed. In 1992, the so-called Charlottetown accord was submitted to separate referendums in Québec and the rest of Canada and failed in both.

Prime Minister Brian Mulroney resigned and the Liberals, under Jean Chrétien, took power. Second place went to the brand new Bloc Québécois, a separatist party founded by Lucien Bouchard, a former Progressive Conservative environment minister who had quit the cabinet and the party over the failure of Meech Lake. The son of a truck driver from Lac St-Jean, he was the most charismatic Canadian politician since Pierre Trudeau. The amputation of his left leg after he was attacked by a bacterium only served to enhance his charisma.

But Montréal's most traumatic event of the 1980s had nothing to do with politics or constitutions. On 6 December 1989, 25-year-old misfit Marc Lépine walked into a classroom of the École Polytechnique, the University of Montréal's engineering school, with a semiautomatic rifle, and ordered the professor and male students out of the room. Lépine, who blamed his failures on "feminists", then opened fire. By the time he turned his gun on himself,

LEFT: Ile Ste-Hélène was enlarged for Expo 67.
ABOVE: the Biosphère on inauguration day in 1967.

he had killed 14 young women, the worst mass murder in Canada's history. The school slaughter deeply shocked the country, and shattered Montréal's image as a peaceable, tolerant city.

The Megacity

Meanwhile in Québec City, the PQ regained power under the hardline Jacques Parizeau. In 1995, the government organized a second referendum on independence and with Bouchard's help it came within a whisper of winning. Only a few thousand votes separated those in favour and those against. A disappointed Parizeau conceded defeat in a bitter speech that blamed "money and the ethnic vote" for frustrating Québec's nationalist aspirations. In the outcry that followed, Parizeau resigned and was replaced by Bouchard, who led the PQ to victory in a snap election in 1998.

But, despite his almost rock-star status, Bouchard failed to win the popular vote. Finally, fed up with his party's internecine squabbling, Bouchard quit politics altogether, leaving the field open for Liberal leader Jean Charest – an ardent federalist – to win the premiership in 2003.

The future

A row over amalgamating the island of Montréal's suburbs with the city *(see box below)*

The Battle of the Suburbs

In one of its last acts in power, the Parti Québécois government forced the 23 suburbs on the island of Montréal to amalgamate with the city. It was an idea that did not go down well with many proud suburbanites, especially those living in the predominately anglophone western half of the island. Most opponents of the "megacity" resented their loss of local autonomy and control, but francophones, who liked the idea of "one island, one city" saw their reluctance as echoing the bad old days of anglo hegemony.

In 2004, Premier Charest fulfilled an election promise by allowing the suburbs to vote on the mergers imposed on them, but he and his municipal affairs minister tried to rig the vote in favour of the megacity. They set tough voting criteria and promised only partial autonomy to those towns that voted to break away. Nonetheless, 13 suburbs – all but one of them predominantly anglophone – voted to regain a few shreds of their former independence.

The result offended many francophones, who concluded that the anglophones were simply trying to hang on to their privileged enclaves. It was an unfair characterization. Suburbanites' distrust of the central city's bloated bureaucracy and thuggish labour unions and their attachment to their local communities played the major part in their decision.

demonstrated that any issue in Montréal, from property taxes to policing policies, can quickly degenerate into an unseemly squabble over language. Even tragedy is not immune.

On 13 September 2006, Kimveer Gill (the son of Sikh immigrants) stormed into the city's largest English-language junior college, armed to the teeth. He killed one student and wounded 20 others before killing himself. At first the horror drew Montréalers closer together. The fluent, articulate French of the anglophone students interviewed on television helped. Then Toronto journalist Jan Wong, a former Montréaler, speculated that the province's language laws had helped spark the incident by alienating and emasculating the immigrant population.

The assertion outraged Québecers of all linguistic groups, but still it undermined some of that solidarity, fed francophone insecurity and drew a few of the so-called "angryphones" out of the woodwork to cheer Wong on.

It also demonstrated that the nationalist wars were still far from over. In mid-2006 the Parti Québécois, led by André Boisclair, was surging in the polls. It was also gaining acceptance among the growing immigrant population – a constituency that had always been dependably federalist. Newer immigrant groups – Haitian, African, Middle Eastern and Latin American – seemed particularly attracted by the party's mix of nationalism and soft socialism. Québec's generally more pacifist attitude in world affairs also appealed. Québecers, for example, were more passionately opposed to the war in Iraq than the rest of Canada, and were uneasy about Canada's combat role in Afghanistan. During the Israeli invasion of southern Lebanon, nationalist politicians like PQ leader Boisclair and Bloc Québécois leader Gilles Duceppe marched in mass demonstrations to demand that Israel halt its bombardment. Their appearance in parades that included Hezbollah flags won them no friends among Montréal Jews, but it scored well with the city's increasingly vocal Arab community, especially the French-speaking Lebanese.

LEFT: a sleigh ride past the Biosphere.
ABOVE: Habitat 67, a modernist legacy of Expo 67.

Shifting ethnicities

The question of who wins the battle for the hearts and minds of those immigrant groups is vital to the future of the city and the province. The plunging fertility rate of francophone Québecers and the continued exodus of bright young anglo professionals mean that the influence of the city's two founding races is waning. The future lies in other hands. ❑

Decisive Dates

1535 French navigator Jacques Cartier visits a Huron village, Hochelaga, later to become the site of Montréal.
1608 Samuel de Champlain, the French explorer, establishes Québec City, the first permanent settlement in Canada.
1615 First Catholic Mass in North America is celebrated on the island of Montréal.
1642 The first colonists arrive, establish a tiny colony and name it Ville Marie. The name will later be changed to Montréal after the mountain Mont Royal.

1658 Marguerite Bourgeoys, Ville Marie's first schoolteacher, begins teaching.
1716 The French decide to build a wall around Montréal to fortify it.
1754–63 While the Seven Years' War rages in Europe, tensions between the French and English escalate in North America.
1759 General James Wolfe attacks French forces near Québec City, defeating them on the Plains of Abraham. Montréal is captured by General Jeffery Amherst in 1760. The surrender of New France is signed in Montréal and British troops take over the town.
1763 Under the Treaty of Paris, the French give most of their land in Canada to the British.
1774 The Québec Act is enacted, extending Québec's borders and guaranteeing the use of the French language and freedom of religion.
1775 As the American Revolution begins, British subjects loyal to King George III of England – the United Empire Loyalists – come north. American General Richard Montgomery and his troops capture Montréal in November.
1776 Benjamin Franklin leads a group to Montréal, hoping to convince French Canadians to join the American Revolution. English troops arrive in June and the Americans withdraw from the city.
1778 The first issue of *Gazette du commerce et littéraire pour la ville et le district de Montréal* is printed. It later becomes *The Montréal Gazette*.
1792 Montréal is divided into east and west, with boulevard St-Laurent as the dividing line.
1801–20 The stone walls surrounding Montréal are demolished.
1809 Canada's first steamboat sails the St Lawrence River from Montréal to Québec City.
1812–14 The Americans attempt to invade Canada in the War of 1812, but are repelled.
1821 McGill University is founded in Montréal.
1832 Montréal is incorporated as a city.
1833 Jacques Viger is elected the first mayor of Montréal.
1837–8 French Canadians lead a rebellion against British rule; one leader, Louis Joseph Papineau, flees to the United States.
1852 After the Great Fire in Montréal, 9,000 people are left homeless.
1859 A largely Irish work force completes the 5-km (3-mile) long Victoria Bridge, the first direct link between the city of Montréal and the mainland. Built as a rail bridge, road decks were added later for cars.
1867 Québec and Ontario (Canada East and Canada West) and the Atlantic Provinces of Nova Scotia, New Brunswick and Prince Edward Island join to become the Dominion of Canada.
1885 The Canadian Pacific Railway, in Montréal, completes Canada's first continental railway.
1914 World War I army conscription divides French and English Canadians.
1929 Stock market crashes and the Great Depression ravage the city's finances. The bridge across the St Lawrence River is completed. It is named after Jacques Cartier in 1934.
1940 Montréal mayor Camillien Houde urges French Canadians to defy a government plan for conscription during World War II. Most

oppose the military draft and federal authorities put Houde in a prison camp until 1944.
1954 Jean Drapeau is elected mayor.
1959 Britain's Queen Elizabeth II and US President Dwight Eisenhower open the St Lawrence Seaway.
1963 The terrorist Front de Libération de Québec (FLQ) joins the Québec separatist movement. Between 1963 and 1968, the FLQ claims responsibility for hundreds of bombings and armed robberies in the Montréal area.
1967 Opening of the World's Fair, Expo 67, in Montréal. More than 50 million people attend.
1970 In October the FLQ kidnaps British trade commissioner James R. Cross and Québec Labour minister Pierre Laporte. Prime Minister Pierre Trudeau sends federal troops to Montréal. Laporte is murdered. Cross is released after the government guarantees his kidnappers safe passage to Cuba.
1976 The Parti Québécois wins the provincial election; the Olympic Games are held in Montréal.
1977 Bill 101 is passed, promoting the use of French on signs and in business. Access to English school is limited.
1980 Voters defeat a proposal to give provincial leaders the right to negotiate Québec's political independence from Canada.
1982 Marguerite Bourgeoys is canonised.
1987 Meech Lake Accord acknowledges Québec's "separate and distinct culture".
1990 Amid threats of Québec's separation from Canada, the Meech Lake Accord is not ratified.
1992 The 350th anniversary of Montréal's founding is celebrated.
1993 The separatist Bloc Québécois, led by Lucien Bouchard, becomes the official Opposition party in Canada's federal Parliament.
1995 Federally minded voters in Québec narrowly defeat a referendum proposal in favour of Québec's independence.
1996 Lucien Bouchard quits federal politics and becomes leader of the Parti Québécois and premier of Québec.
1998 Québecer Jean Charest takes over as leader of Québec's demoralised Liberal party. In November Bouchard calls a sudden provincial election. Although the PQ wins, the Liberals retain 43.7 percent of the popular vote. A devastating ice storm hits Montréal and Québec.
1999 An American businessman, Jeffrey Loria, purchases the Montréal Expos baseball club.
2000 Pierre Trudeau and hockey star Maurice Richard die. Trudeau's state funeral, in Basilique Notre-Dame, is the largest in Canada's history.
2001 Lucien Bouchard resigns as premier of Québec and head of Parti Québécois. Bernard Landry assumes the posts.
2002 Montréal Expos baseball club is taken over by Major League Baseball in the US. The island of Montréal becomes one municipality after an island-wide referendum. The provincial government in Québec City forces all 28 municipalities on the island of Montréal to amalgamate into a single city divided into 27 boroughs.

2003 The federalist Liberals under Jean Charest win the provincial general election, partly by promising disgruntled suburbanites a vote on the forced mergers.
2004 Fifteen of Montréal's former suburbs vote to "demerge" and reclaim their autonomy.
2005 Canada becomes the fourth country in the world to legalize same-sex marriage.
2006 André Boisclair becomes the leader of the Parti Québécois.
2007 The federalist Liberals win a close provincial election race; Jean Charest leads Québec's first minority government in 130 years. ❑

LEFT: the chief of a Mohawk Iroquois tribe.
RIGHT: Buckminster Fuller, architect of the geodesic dome at the World's Fair 1967.

Politics, Language and Identity

Québecers wrestle with the same social problems that everyone else in North America does – an aging population, a shrinking birth rate, soaring health costs, a crumbling infrastructure, high taxes, anaemic economic growth and pollution. But behind all those issues – and, in fact, colouring all of them – hangs the eternal "*question nationale*": Whither Québec? Is it in or is it out? Will it be proudly Canadian or defiantly independent? Or

something else altogether? What Québecers really want, one local comic says, is "an independent Québec in a strong Canada". Given politicians' efforts to find a formula that will give Québec autonomy without frightening the natives, that observation isn't as silly as it sounds.

In 1867, Québec, along with Ontario, New Brunswick and Nova Scotia, was one of the founding members of the Canadian Confederation. Economically, the arrangement made sense, and leaders like Sir George-Étienne Cartier believed that a federal state would give French Canada the tools it needed to protect its language, culture and religion. There's not much of that religion left, but Québec certainly has preserved its culture and language, and is, psychologically, at least, a nation in a way that Nova Scotia and New Brunswick could never be. To describe it as a province like any other might be true in law but is manifestly absurd in any other way that counts. The trick for federalists is to find a formula that will keep that nation within Canada; for sovereignists, the goal is to pry that nation out of Canada.

Winning elections

It's not that Québec lacks political power and the will to use it. Two-thirds of Canada's voters live in Ontario and Québec, and winning an election without the support of at least one of them is nearly impossible. And because until recently Québecers voted as a block for the Liberal Party, they've managed to put one of their own into the prime minister's office in Ottawa for about 60 of the country's 130 or so years. In fact, since Pierre Trudeau was first elected PM in 1968, Québecers have held the top job for all but a few months.

Despite all that federal muscle, however, Québec elected René Lévesque's separatist Parti Québécois to power in Québec City in 1976. Lévesque promised good government first, and a vote on the future later. His own particular brand of autonomy was "sovereignty-association", a hazy notion that coupled Québec independence with economic partnership with the rest of Canada. Freedom without pain, the cynics called it. But it was too painful for Québecers. When Lévesque asked them to decide the matter in a referendum in 1968, 60 percent voted to remain in Canada.

Bureaucratic irritants

That first PQ government left one enduring legacy: the Charte de la Langue Française. The charter declared French Québec's only official language and effectively banned the public display of any other languages in commercial signs and advertising. It also limited access to English-language schools to children whose parents were educated in English in Québec. Among the law's many bureaucratic irritants were the "tongue troopers" (agents of the Commission de Surveillance de la Langue Française) who prosecuted merchants who dared to put up signs in English (or Welsh). Québec's anglophones and other minority language groups were outraged, but francophones loved the law, and still do, despite its sometimes embarrassing excesses.

And there's no doubt the law has done much to protect French. Immigrants now have to send their children to French-language schools and so French rather than English has become the lingua franca of a whole cross-section of cultures, from Koreans and Vietnamese to Arabs and Latin Americans. And the anglophones who stayed rather than pull up stakes and move west to Ontario or Alberta, tended to be the adaptable ones who were quite happy to speak French, if not so happy at having their freedom to use their native tongue curtailed.

The crucial difference

The issue is all to do with language. There's really not much else to distinguish Québecers from other North Americans. They tend to be a bit more permissive on social issues like abortion and same-sex marriage and a little more addicted to state intervention in the economy, but otherwise they pursue the same personal and economic goals as the rest of the continent. But they live in a society that thinks, reads and writes in French.

Eighty percent of its citizens subscribe to magazines and watch television programmes that are foreign to the rest of Canada. Québec films regularly outsell Hollywood blockbusters in local cinemas – and sometimes even win Oscars – but are virtually unwatched in the R.O.C. (the rest of Canada). Group identity is bound up inherently with language. Says writer André Belleau: "We do not need to speak French: we need French in order to speak."

How does all this affect Montréal? The city is the heart of Québec, the metropolis, the powerhouse that drives the provincial economy. As such it has attracted an ethnically and linguistically diverse population. Its streets and neighbourhoods teem with Italians, Greeks, Jews, Asians, Africans, Arabs, Caribbeans and Latin Americans. Whole districts like the West Island and Notre-Dame-de-Grâce are anglophone. Some towns like Hampstead and Côte St-Luc are entirely Jewish, while others are virtually all Italian. All this makes Montréal a rich, exciting and interesting place to live.

But all this diversity is viewed with some suspicion in places like Lac St-Jean, the Gaspé and even Québec City, where people almost seem to think of Montréal as some kind of foreign body polluting the purity of French Québec. And so it's where most linguistic skirmishes are fought, whether it's over commercial signs or access to an English-language education.

Montréalers get along on a day-to-day basis. Friendships, families and marriages often cross linguistic lines. But everyone is careful, even diffident, about retaining a balance that won't upset the status quo or attract the ire of the more fervent nationalists. When, for example, the province agreed to build a new teaching hospital for McGill University, a similar one had to be built for the Université de Montréal. ❑

LEFT: Canadians gather in Montréal's Place du Canada in 1995 to vote against separation.
RIGHT: caricature of Britain's Queen Elizabeth II.

MONTREALERS

Montréal's French and English counterparts lead surprisingly similar – if often separate – lives of work and leisure

There was a time when it would have been reasonably accurate to describe Montréal as an open book. Viewed from the south, the text on the left-hand-page, spreading to the west, was in English, while the words on the right-hand page, opening to the east, were all French. And down the centre, like the spine of an old leather-bound volume, ran the multiethnic and multicoloured boulevard St-Laurent, the street known to Montréalers of all languages more simply and affectionately as the Main.

Life is no longer that simple. It remains true that the west still tends to be English and the east tends to be French, but the twain meet all the time. Their shared passion for good food, good times and hockey blurs the line that separates them. So does intermarriage. Rare is the anglophone family that doesn't have at least one francophone branch, and many francophone families can claim at least one anglophone in-law. Children who dream in both languages, play in both languages and grow up switching effortlessly between two languages and two cultures are increasingly common. So complete is this fusion in some people that they have difficulty identifying their mother tongue, which is defined by Québec's Byzantine language laws as the first language you learned and still speak.

Blurring boundaries

Even the geographical line is fading. Francophone executives have moved their families into the mock Tudor homes high up the hill in Westmount, and francophone professionals have moved into once solidly anglophone bastions like Notre-Dame-de-Grâce in the west end of the city and the lakeside suburbs of the West Island. However, movement the other way is less pronounced, mostly because the anglophone community has shrunk dramatically over the last few decades, but there are plenty of hip young anglophone writers, artists and media professionals living in the duplexes and triplexes of Plateau Mont-Royal and Mile End.

That's not to say the old tensions and animosities have completely disappeared. Each community perceives itself as a vulnerable

LEFT: living history at Musée Marguerite-Bourgeoys.
RIGHT: Scottish Highland Games at Douglas Hospital.

Pierre Trudeau

René Lévesque, champion of an independent Québec, found his match in fellow Québecer Pierre Elliot Trudeau, the great francophone hope of all those who believed in a strong and united Canada. Their clash was neither friendly nor civil. Lévesque, who always denied he was an ethnic nationalist, had a nasty way of emphasizing the "Elliot" whenever he mentioned his rival's name, to remind the audience that Trudeau has a Scottish mother. For his part, Trudeau contemptuously dismissed Lévesque and his separatist followers as people who sought to limit French Canada's possibilities and capitalize on its insecurities.

Trudeau was easily the most colourful and charismatic figure in federal politics. He was as eloquent in English as he was in French, and his good looks and his sense of style made him the darling of many female voters. His dating such stars as Barbra Streisand added to the glamour of his image.

But there was more to Trudeau than pirouettes and fancy clothes. As prime minister from 1968 to 1984 (excluding a brief interruption in 1979), he set about recasting the Canadian confederation in his own image. His vision was of a nationally bilingual nation where francophones and anglophones would be equally at home wherever they went.

He introduced mandatory bilingualism at all levels of government. Francophones and anglophones would get equal service from the government their taxes supported. The Official Languages Act made French and English official languages everywhere. He was determined for Canadians to see the value and necessity of bilingualism, thus undermining the Parti Québécois freedom cry.

Trudeau's proudest accomplishment was the patriation of the Canadian constitution. Canada was created in 1867 by the British North America Act, a law passed by the British Parliament in Westminster. That meant that whenever Canada wanted to change its constitution, it had to petition the British government to amend the act.

It took an endless round of negotiations with the Canadian premiers to pound out a document that everyone, or at least, almost everyone, could agree to. Finally, in 1981, Trudeau managed to find a formula that was good enough to pass muster with nine of the 10 premiers. Unfortunately, the one dissenting voice was that of René Lévesque, who accused his fellow premiers of stabbing him in the back.

Trudeau, however, pushed ahead with his plan and in April, 1982, Queen Elizabeth II, still Canada's head of state, flew to Ottawa to sign the Constitution Act. But Lévesque and his successors refused to sign.

Still, Trudeau's constitutional ploy was not a total failure in Québec. Although it steadfastly ignored any conciliatory gestures toward Québec's "two nation" ideal, its Charter of Rights and Freedoms was very popular with Québecers. The Liberals continued to dominate federal politics in Québec, and Trudeau continued to be admired by the many as much as he was despised by the few.

And his constitutional victory did bring something of a truce – a truce that lasted until Trudeau retired from politics, Lévesque died and a new generation of combatants were ready to reignite the fuse. ❑

LEFT: Pierre Trudeau was a visionary leader.

minority. The anglophones, a majority in Canada but a minority in Québec, see their numbers dwindling and fear for the survival of their institutions. The francophones, a majority in Québec but a minority in Canada, feel their whole language and culture is threatened and need to be protected by thickets of sometimes petty regulations.

But don't be misled. Montréal is not a war zone. In daily living, Montréalers have developed the art of good-humoured coexistence. On St Patrick's Day, for example, thousands of francophones and anglophones don the green and buttons reading "Kiss me, I'm Irish", or "*embrasse moi, je suis irlandais*" and descend on rue Ste-Catherine to drink green beer and cheer a parade of floats and pipe bands celebrating the Irish community that has been a fixture here since the mid-19th century.

The French spoken in Montréal is shot through with English expressions and Québec English is in turn laced with Gallicisms. An anglophone Montréaler will speak of a manifestation or even a "manif" instead of a demonstration, a cocktail for a cocktail party, a convention for a contract, a syndicat for a union, and a dépanneur (or, even more briefly, a "dep") for a convenience store. And a francophone will speak of earning "un peu d'overtime" to pay for fixing "les brakes" on his "char", a variation on car.

Religion and relationships

The relationship between francophones and anglophones is similar to that of many old married couples – marred by irritants, old hurts and misunderstandings, but deeply rooted in shared memories, mutual interest and yes, believe it or not, affection. Even the epithets they hurl at each other when they're frustrated or angry actually sound more marital than martial.

Francophones use physiognomy to insult anglophones, calling them *têtes-carrées* (square heads), while anglophones resort to consumer habits when they call their francophone neighbours "Pepsis" (indeed for decades Québec was, for some reason, the only province in Canada where Pepsi-Cola outsold Coke).

RIGHT: a merchant on Place Jacques Cartier.

Both communities have undergone enormous changes since the late 1960s. Francophone Montréal – and, indeed, francophone Québec – has all but abandoned its once fervent adherence to the Roman Catholic Church to emerge as the most secular society in North America. Church attendance percentages hover in the low teens and support for every social innovation, from abortion on demand to swingers' clubs, is enthusiastic. Francophone Québecers, for example, applauded louder than anyone else when Canada legalized same-sex marriage in 2004 – this despite the fact that only half of its heterosexual couples bother with any kind of ceremony, civil or religious.

Changing influences

Anglophone Montréalers have seen their numbers and influence dwindle. The unilingual Westmount elite, who once ran the province's business over gin and tonics in the St James Club are long gone, replaced by bright young graduates from the École des Hautes Études Commerciales and francophone entrepreneurs financed by money from Québec's government-run pension fund.

Montréal anglophones have also seen the institutions they've built so painstakingly over the generations change beyond recognition. A large number of the students at McGill and Concordia Universities, for example, are francophones who write their book reports and exams in their own language, often for francophone professors. Hospitals like the Hewish General and Royal Victoria offer fully bilingual and, indeed, multilingual services, and are often staffed by francophone doctors, nurses and cafeteria workers. The enforcers of Québec's language law, the dreaded "tongue troopers" *(see page 36)*, keep a close watch on anglophone health-care centres to make sure their staff can speak acceptable French, a Big Brother exercise that many anglophones consider humiliating.

But in spite of all their fears and uncertainties, the majority of anglophones would live nowhere else. While they fail to see the independence movement that so enraptures their French-speaking compatriots as anything more than a threat to their property values, they know they occupy a privileged position in Canada's cultural centre, open to the influences of both great cultures.

English-speaking Montréalers, for example, can laugh at the antics of both *Les Bougon* on the Radio-Canada television network and *Trailer Park Boys* on the Showcase network. The former are a lovable family of Montréal ne'er do wells who scam the welfare system and anyone else who has the misfortune to come in contact with them; the latter a tribe of hilariously hapless petty criminals who try to make a living stealing supermarket carts and growing marijuana in a Nova Scotia trailer park. They're the mirror image of each other, but Montréal anglophones are among the few Canadians who know and love them both.

In fact, modern anglo-Montréalers tend to be a breed apart. Most of those who are left speak French quite well and send their children to French or French-immersion schools. And while they often find the language laws irritating and can be highly critical of the municipal and provincial governments when they're at home, outside the province they are often passionate defenders of Québec. And many of those who left for Toronto or Calgary dream of returning and beg their family back home for care packages of bagels, smoked meats, maple syrup and DVDs of the latest Québec movies. On visits home they haunt the clubs and restaurants of the Quartier Latin and Plateau Mont-Royal with the enthusiasm of released convicts.

Joie de vivre

For their part, Montréal's francophones like to think of themselves as passionate Latins lost in a sea of cold-blooded Saxons. But, in fact, their ancestors were mostly hard-headed Normans who were quite at home with British reticence and stringent work ethics. Many of the things that seem so definitively Montréalais today, like sidewalk cafés, croissant breakfasts and two-cheek kisses, are actually of quite recent vintage. Most are imports that made their way into the province when the backpacking generation of the 1960s returned from reacquainting themselves with their French roots.

But there's no denying that Québec francophones have always had a certain *joie de vivre* sometimes lacking in their more Calvinist conquerors. They share Catholic Europe's more humane attitude toward the pleasures of the flesh – eating, drinking and, whatever.

Thanks to relatively permissive drinking laws and a kind of laissez-faire police force, Montréal was something of a wide-open city in the 1930s and 1940s, with strippers like the incomparable Lili St-Cyr and big-name jazz musicians fleeing discrimination south of the border playing its clubs and nightspots. This, at a time when Toronto closed its bars at midnight and wouldn't let women enter without an escort.

Toronto and the rest of the country have more or less caught up, but Montréal still sets the pace. The city drinks until 3am and allows diners to bring their own bottles of wine into many of its restaurants. Francophones – men and women – spend more on clothes, as well as on home furnishings, than any other community on the continent. And Montréal probably possesses as many importers of Milanese furniture as New York.

Haute culture

In Montréal you can see French and other European films while they're playing in Paris, and American films while they're playing in New York. This city's newsstands bend under their stacks of dailies in French and English – from Montréal, Paris, New York and London. TV offers several public and commercial channels in French and English, plus the big US networks and re-broadcasts of the best programmes from France, Belgium and Switzerland. The Montréal elite have always been unusually cosmopolitan. They read *Le Nouvel Observateur* and *The New Yorker*, Marguerite Yourcenar and Milan Kundera or Tom Wolfe. The city has four universities (two French and two English), one English and three French daily newspapers, a dozen French-language theatres, and a rich literary scene that serves up both the biting English prose of the late lamented Mordecai Richler and the French lyricism of Réjean Ducharme.

LEFT: Montréalers *joie de vivre* starts early.
ABOVE: friends out for a drink on Crescent Street.

Montréal is also the centre of a booming pop-culture industry, complete with its own *vedettes* (stars) like Mitsou, Stéphanie Lapointe, Natasha St-Pier, Corneille, Garou, Andrée Watters, Roch Voisine and, more recently, Eva Avila, and a whole library's worth of supporting magazines, so that fans can follow their heroes' every move. Québec movies regularly outsell Hollywood blockbusters in Montréal, and directors like Denys Arcand and actors such as Rémy Girard, Josée-Marie Croze and Roy Dupuis have the same kind of star status in Montréal as Martin Scorsese, Leonardo DiCaprio and Julia Roberts have elsewhere.

"Allophones"

But hang on. Francophones and anglophones make up only part of the story. Fifteen percent of Montréal's 3 million people – the so-called "allophones" – belong to neither group. Montréal is also an Italian, Greek, Vietnamese, Haitian and Lebanese city, a city of Ashkenazi and Sephardic Jews, of Arabs and Iranians, of Guatemalans and Colombians. Sikh temples and Muslim minarets share the religious skyline with the steeples of Catholic and Protestant churches. You never have far to walk to find lemongrass or vine leaves, falafels or smoked meat, saffron or marzipan, fresh pasta or Paris-style baguettes – not to mention the

FAMOUS MONTRÉALERS

Many internationally-known Canadians hail from the city of Montréal or its environs:

Leonard Cohen began as a controversial poet and novelist of the 1960s but really found his calling when he began making music. Cohen's smoky delivery and sultry songwriting defy categorisation. He has a home on the Plateau.

William Shatner (Captain Kirk in Star Trek) was educated at McGill but left the city to seek his fortune in Hollywood.

Maurice "The Rocket" Richard was a visible presence in the hockey arena for decades until his death in 2000; his former Montréal Canadiens team-mates **Jean Béliveau** and **Guy Lafleur** are still around.

Gilles Villeneuve had a fine career as a racing driver before his tragic death in a crash in 1982. His son, **Jacques Villeneuve**, also a racing driver, won the Formula I championship in 1997.

Andy Kim, born André Youakim, penned 1960s' and 1970s' songs "Sugar, Sugar", "Rock Me Gently", and "Baby, I Love You". But Montréal-born Kim's success as a pop musician was far eclipsed a few decades later by a young Québecer.

Céline Dion, a high-school dropout from Charlemagne, Québec, has sold more than 175 million records worldwide and was named the best-selling female artist of all time by the World Music Awards show.

world's best bagels. No, not in Manhattan nor Brooklyn will you find bagels more golden on the outside and more tender on the inside than those you buy fresh out of the old wood-stoked ovens in Montréal, made from a recipe that emanates from the *stetls* of Romania.

The easiest way to follow the waves of immigration is to follow boulevard St-Laurent, or the Main, from the narrow, noisy streets of Chinatown in the south to Little Italy in the north, with its churches, restaurants, coffee shops, cultural centres and grocery stores clustered around the Marché Jean-Talon, where all ethnic groups shop. Along the way you'll pass old synagogues, Portuguese barbecues, Greek tavernas, storefront mosques, Vietnamese noodle shops, Haitian snack bars, Hungarian butchers, and Brazilian bars as well as such Jewish landmarks as Moishe's Steakhouse and Schwartz's Delicatessen. Each successive wave of immigrants, from the pogrom-fleeing Romanian Jews of the 19th century to the Arabs and the Latin Americans of the late 20th, settled first on the Main. Many of them worked long hours for low wages in the garment industry or on construction sites, slowly acquiring enough wealth to make sure their children and their children's children had it better. And they succeeded.

LEFT: famous Montréalers Léonard Cohen and Céline Dion. **ABOVE:** cultural diversity is the city's wealth.

Montréal neighbourhoods

Most of their descendants have left the Main and their original communities for more comfortable homes in the suburbs, but many of them managed to hang on to their deep sense of community in the process. The borough of St-Léonard and Rivière-des-Prairies, for example, are mostly Italian, and the suburbs of Côte-St-Luc and Hampstead are almost entirely Jewish. Arab and Caribbean neighbourhoods, along with accompanying food stores, restaurants and cultural and religious centres, have sprung up in Notre-Dame-de-Grâce in the city's west end, while clusters of Koreans and Southeast Asians have settled in parts of Laval and the West Island suburbs.

It makes for a rich and lumpy stew, one that has changed Montréal and the attitudes of its two founding groups. The old anglo-franco quarrels mean little to recent arrivals from the Middle East or the former Soviet Union, or even to Italians, who get along comfortably with three languages. As each new group has become integrated into the life of the city, it has subtly shifted the debate away from the stale squabbles of the past to new and often more practical issues. ❑

The Jews of Montréal

For more than 100 years, the neighbourhoods along Boulevard St-Laurent have been the immigrants' first stop on the way to a new life in the New World. Thousands of families from dozens of different ethnic and national backgrounds have lived, worked and played along the street Montréalers affectionately call The Main. They've all left their mark, but none more so than the Jews. Even today, you find traces of their passage tucked between the fashionable boutiques and trendy cafés of St-Laurent.

Schreter's dry goods store still sells suits and shoes, a few blocks north of Schwartz's deli, where even on frigid January days, the lineup for a lunch of smoked meat on rye snakes along the sidewalk. Just across the street from there is Berson's monuments, where pious children can buy polished granite tombstones for their deceased parents. Farther north are the Fairmount Bagel Bakery and the St-Viateur Bagel Factory, where hundreds of light, crispy rolls are baked every day.

This is the neighbourhood immortalized by Mordecai Richler in such hardscrabble, bitterly funny novels as *St Urbain's Horsemen* and *The Apprenticeship Duddy Kravitz*. It was, Richler wrote, an all but self-contained world made up of five streets; Clark, St-Urbain, Waverly, Esplanade and Jeanne-Mance, bounded by the Main on one side, and Park Avenue on the other. On each corner were a cigar store, a grocery, and a fruit man. Outside staircases were everywhere, with an endless repetition of precious peeling balconies and waste lots making the occasional gap here and there.

From docks to sweatshops

To a large extent, it was tensions in Russia that created this unique neighbourhood and changed the face of Montréal. The assassination of Tsar Alexander II in 1881 sparked a series of pogroms leading to the first wave of Yiddish-speaking immigrants. Until then, Montréal's Jewish community was tiny and composed almost exclusively of Sephardim, descendants of the Jews expelled from Spain during the Inquisition.

The thousands of new immigrants were aware that it was their very Jewishness that had cost lives in Russia, and so they clung tenaciously to their customs. For most, it was a short trip from the docks to the sweatshop. They worked under deplorable conditions in the garment industry, toiling in cramped sweatshops with little air or light. Days were long, wages were low.

The poor working conditions proved to be fertile turf for Jews in a labour movement committed to social change. Ideologies developed in eastern Europe by such groups as the Bund, a Jewish socialist party founded in Russia in 1897, were renewed in cities like Montréal with the drive to educate and unionize workers. The Workmen's Circle saw itself not simply as a mutual benefit society but also as part of the larger labour movement, which was struggling to end capitalist exploitation.

Sidewalks became stages for social change. Bookshops were transformed into debating dens. Elstein's bookshop on Ontario Street was more than a store, it was virtually a club where anyone who read books would meet to argue politics. In August 1943 the mostly Jewish voters of the federal riding of Montréal-Cartier, centred on the Main, made history by electing Canada's first and only Communist member of Parliament.

During the Depression, small cottages sprouted into prayer houses. Hebrew resounded through forgotten lofts in industrial buildings. By 1940, 40 of Montréal's 50 synagogues were located within 1.5 km (1 mile) of each other. Few remain.

The Jewish community today is centred in Côte St-Luc, a middle-class suburb on the western edge of Montréal. Its rows of neat bungalows house the largest Jewish community in Canada. Next door is Hampstead, home of much of the community's elite.

The descendants of the rag-trade workers have become an integral part of Montréal life. Jewish professors, journalists, lawyers and doctors illuminate and enrich city life. Fluently bilingual Jewish Montréalers sit as city councillors. Socialist politicians like David Lewis have changed Canada's political landscape for ever, and magnates like the members of the Steinberg and Bronfman clans have poured millions of dollars into the city's universities, orchestras and museums. And Montréal would not be the same without the novels of Mordecai Richler, the poems of Irving Layton and the music of Leonard Cohen.

Yiddish theatre

Everywhere you look in Montréal, you'll find reminders of the vibrancy and generosity of the Jewish community – from Schwartz's deli to the Saidye Bronfmann Theatre (home of North America's only Yiddish theatre), and from the Jewish General Hospital, a world leader in cancer research and neonatal care, to Summit, a school for the mentally disabled.

Its numbers have been diminished by the same political forces that have reduced the anglophone community, and it is facing the same greying demographics as the general population. Twenty percent are over 60. But at over 96,000, the community still has a lot of life in it. Montréal is still home to the archives and offices of the Canadian Jewish Congress, a national Jewish "parliament". It has Canada's oldest and best Jewish historical museum and Holocaust educational centre.

Richler's colourful characters haven't gone; you're just more likely to run into them arguing politics at the coffee shop in the Côte St-Luc Mall, or watching their grandchildren play ice hockey at the Sam Moskovitch Arena a couple of blocks north.

Meanwhile, back on the Main, another community of Jews is making its presence felt. The Hassidim, who fervently follow all the admonishments of Torah and Talmud, are one of the fastest-growing populations in Québec. Families of up to a dozen children are not uncommon. The men walk about in their *kapotes* (black silk coats) and *spodiks* (fur hats), locks of hair curled around their ears. Women dress discreetly in modest clothing, children in tow.

They haven't had an easy time of it, clashing with city officials and some of their more secular neighbours over plans to build a synagogue. But they've also found friends. When a local columnist wrote disparagingly of these "outsiders", people who had taken the time to get to know some Hassidic families, came forward to proclaim these oddly dressed Jews the best of neighbours. ❑

LEFT: some Jews cling to old customs while others modernise. **RIGHT:** Shaar Hashomayim Synagogue in Westmount.

Le Melting Pot: The Growth of Ethnic Diversity

Fully 40 percent of Montréalers are immigrants attracted by the promise of prosperity, racial tolerance and political stability

It might come as a shock to learn that in Montréal, a city so closely identified with French culture, French Canadians have now become almost a minority. The successive waves of immigration have many explanations: foreign wars, the labour required to build a railway, the country's reputation as a place with a high quality of life, racial tolerance and political stability. Today you find Arab, Chinese, Polish and Greek areas among the ethnic neighbourhoods. The multitude of summer festivals also testifies to this diversity.

The Jewish influence has been well documented, but it is far from the only flavour here. Some 90,000 people of Asian descent call the city home, and their proportion is rising. Half of the new immigrants to Québec in the past 20 years have come from Asia.

The city's African and African-American communities are spread out these days, having once ruled the roost in Montréal's bawdy, jazzed-out Little Burgundy neighbourhood. Today only the odd Baptist church in the area testifies to the size of black Montreal; most now live on the edge of the city, in Parc-Extension or Notre-Dame-de-Grâce.

One quarter of greater Montréal's population – half a million people – come from Europe: Polish and Hungarian Jews dominate the Main; Greeks flourish on outer Parc Avenue; the Plateau's parks are filled with Portuguese footballers; and Mile-End is a crossroads of Euro-culture.

Above: there are echoes of Rio de Janeiro's carnival at the annual colourful Caribbean fiesta, which takes place in the city in July. A street parade follows a route along boulevard René-Lévesque.

Above: Korean migration to North America began in earnest in the early 20th century, and accelerated during and after the Korean War.

Right: Little Italy, or la Petite Italie, is the hub of the Italian community – Montreal's largest minority, numbering almost 200,000.

Right: Peruvian Indian children at Canada Day festivities, on 1 July.

ABOVE: the Dragon Boat races on the St Lawrence River take place every summer. Other events in the Chinese calendar include the Moon Festival in October.

BELOW LEFT: the annual Carifête is a lively celebration of Caribbean music and dance. Montréal has a sizeable African-Caribbean population.

BELOW RIGHT: Mohawk perform a pow-wow dance. The Mohawk nation and other First Nations settled in the region centuries before the French arrived.

THE CHARMS OF LITTLE ITALY

Of all Montréal's ethnic neighbourhoods, Little Italy – far from the tourist throngs – may be the most delightful to the eye and palate. The first Italians to arrive, in the late 19th century, were sailors, some of whom turned entrepreneurs and built lodgings along the river. Many of the next wave were construction labourers, living near the huge Molson Brewery and new bridge construction projects which employed them.

Prosperous Italian families soon began moving into what were then quiet areas on the outskirts of the city, and this area, around Jean-Talon, St-Laurent and Dante streets, is now the hub of the Italian community.

Walking around Little Italy, you'll notice gelato shops and cafés serving square-cut, cold, thin-crust pizza the authentic Italian way. In the north of the neighbourhood, Jean-Talon Market provides a colourful glimpse of the rest of ethnic Montréal. Westmount housewives mingle with brightly turbaned African and Indian families in the alleys of fruit and vegetables.

ABOVE: Montréal's Chinese population numbers 40,000, and the Chinatown district, with its restaurants and shops, buzzes with life at weekends.

MONTRÉAL CUISINE

It is immediately evident that the city is rich beyond its size in restaurants, rivalling many world capitals for both variety and quality

Scratch a Montréaler and you'll find a gourmet – and a chauvinist gourmet at that. Montréalers of all ethnic and linguistic stripes are convinced that it's almost impossible to get a decent meal anywhere in Canada beyond the province of Québec's borders. And until the 1970s they would probably have been right. What passed for good food then in places such as Halifax and Toronto was of the roast-meat-and-soggy-vegetables variety, served in stuffy hotel dining rooms by snotty waiters.

In Québec, on the other hand, even such smallish centres as Trois-Rivières and Matane had several restaurants where you could dine well and with flair. Even today, nowhere in Canada do people of all classes and income groups take more delight in what they eat than Québecers in general and Montréalers in particular. And it's not just gourmet fare that gives them pleasure; Montréalers are also proud of their barbecued chicken, their steamed hot dogs (*stimés*, in local parlance), their bagels (the best in the world) and their smoked meat. They even sing the praises of *poutine* (pronounced pooh-teen), a mix of french fries, rubbery cheese curds and scalding hot gravy that is Québec's very own contribution to junk food culture.

A lively restaurant scene

However, Montréal foodies – and that would include taxi-drivers and shop clerks as well as lawyers and account executives – are seldom content to stick with old favourites all the time. They are always on the lookout for something new, and the result is one of the liveliest and most volatile restaurant scenes in North America. Tourist officials claim more dining rooms per-capita than any other city in the world, it's a wonder they can keep track.

The places that survive the rough and tumble of a cruelly competitive industry cater to every pocket and to just about every taste, from Middle Eastern to Mexican with a French twist, hamburgers with foie-gras to Creole-Asian fusion. Québec schools, like the well respected Institut de Tourisme et d'Hôtellerie du Québec, keep churning out young chefs (and waiters,

LEFT: culinary art at Plus Minus Café, Tremblant.
RIGHT: Montréal's bagels are the best.

sommeliers and bartenders) eager to make their impression on the city's taste buds and ensure that the province's cuisine continues to evolve.

Local ingredients

French food in all its guises – from classic duck à l'orange and lobster thermidor at Les Chenêts to humbler *bourgeois boudin* and cod brandade at Le Paris and bistro-style steak-frites at L'Express – has long been and probably always will be a central theme in this constantly shifting scene. But the old masters in their tall white toques no longer monopolise the affections of Montréal diners. The current darlings of the dining set – young men and, increasingly, women, in baseball caps and jeans – can be seen in the public markets every morning, hunting for the best and freshest ingredients for that night's menus. They all tend to share a patriotic passion for Quebec's "produits du terroir" – pork from the Eastern Townships, shrimps from Matane, salmon from the Gaspé, veal from the Charlevoix, strawberries from Île d'Orléans, lamb from the salt flats of the Lower St Lawrence, produce from the Richelieu Valley and handcrafted cheese from almost everywhere.

The pioneer of this market-based cuisine is Normand Laprise, who was something of an enfant terrible when he opened Toqué! (the name means "Whacko") in 1993 and started

TOP TEN GASTRONOMIC TREATS

1. A smoked meat sandwich with French fries, dill pickles and Coke at Schwartz's Delicatessen. And if you don't want to be sneered at, don't ask for lean cuts.
2. Barbecued chicken at Chalet Barbecue: this is where the tradition started, and it's still a favourite with everyone from stockbrokers to cabbies (especially cabbies).
3. Spicy sausage submarine sandwiches are just about the only thing on the menu at Momesso's, but frankly who needs more?
4. Chef Martin Picard's version of *poutine* at Au Pied du Cochon – French fries, gravy and foie-gras – is about as decadent as junk food gets.
5. Cod brandade at Le Paris: never has the lowly salt cod – puréed with potatoes, cream and garlic – tasted so good.
6. The grilled T-bone at Moishe's Steak House is a gloriously thick and juicy slab of Grade A beef.
7. The lobster spaghetti at Joe Beef's features lumps of shellfish – whole claws and tails – in a light cream sauce.
8. Normand Laprise's salmon tartare and guacamole at Toqué! is still one of Montréal's most daring dishes.
9. The steak-frites at L'Express are simply the best in town.
10. The perfectly spiced meatballs at Da Emma are big enough to play tennis with (rumour has it that Johnny Depp loves them).

whipping up local products in sometimes startling combinations – salmon-tartare and guacamole, crusty scallops with cumin and jalapeno. He is now an icon of the new establishment, fighting to keep up with similarly daring chefs. One of the best is Racha Bassoul, who uses the flavours of her native Lebanon – mint, pistachios, parsley – to enliven the lamb and veal of her adopted home.

Some restaurants, such as Au Pied du Cochon, take this loyalty to Québec products a step further by reinventing old comfort foods like pea soup and braised pigs' feet, which kept the settlers of New France well-fed. Au Pied's chef, Martin Picard, even does a riff with seared foie-gras on that more modern Québec classic, *poutine*. In fact, chef Picard will add foie-gras to just about anything but ice cream.

If all that sounds too heavy, try grazing on smaller dishes such as Chinese dim-sun, Spanish tapas, Basque pinxtos (a smaller version of tapas), Japanese sushi or mini plates of angus beef and mashed potatoes. Eat as much or as little as you want and wash it down with wine. If you prefer beer, Québecers have rediscovered their taste for the real thing, thanks to dozens of brew pubs that sell homemade ales and lagers.

Foreign influence

If your wallet is on the thin side (or even if it's not), try the ethnic restaurants that have opened up in areas like Mile End, Côte des Neiges and the fringes of Plateau Mont-Royal. Russian and Georgian cuisines have made an appearance along with Guatemalan, Tibetan and Filipino. Arab, Persian, Brazilian, Thai, Vietnamese and Cambodian restaurants abound, and are almost as well established as the Greek, Italian, Portuguese and Chinese.

Many ethnic restaurants, and some good French ones like Le Pégasse and La Prunelle, allow you to bring your own wine purchased elsewhere, without the usual restaurant markup.

Provincial classics

Finally, it would be a shame to visit the city of Montréal without trying such Québec classics as *tourtière* (meat pie), sugar pie, *fêves au lard* (pork and beans), *ragoût de boullottes* (meatball stew) at La Binerie Mont-Royal, Restaurant Chez Clo or Restaurant Chez Claudette. This is traditional peasant food, plain and simple, but even at its most basic, its deft use of ingredients such as fragrant cloves, nutmeg, garlic, parsley, sage and cinnamon shows that the pioneer housewives had a pretty sophisticated sense of flavouring. Montréal's claim to culinary supremacy truly has history on its side. ❑

LEFT: dining out at Le Saint-Amour, Québec City.
ABOVE: fresh fruit on display at Atwater Market.

MONTREAL CITY OF CULTURE: PERFORMING ARTS AND MUSIC

The art scene is a rich tapestry, its colourful threads woven from theatre, music, dance, film, paintings and sculpture

Culture is more than an embellishment in Montréal; it's an industry, and an important one at that. Cut off from the rest of North America by language and isolated from the mother country by politics and an ocean, francophone Québecers have looked to their own resources to create something truly distinctive – a culture that reflects the North American experience with a distinctive French accent.

The result is that Montréal, as the continent's only French-speaking metropolis, has emerged as the centre of a thriving entertainment industry that has its own network of talented singers, dancers, actors, comedians, playwrights, painters, sculptors, film directors and rock stars. But this cultural vitality is not an exclusively francophone phenomenon. English-speaking artists of all disciplines have also benefited from the city's openness to cultural experimentation. To name a few: poets such as Irving Layton, songwriters like Leonard Cohen, playwrights like David Fennario, and rock stars like Corey Hart are also a part of Montréal's heritage.

ABOVE: Montréal has a proliferation of French-language theatres like the Théâtre du Nouveau Monde, which tends to stage such classics as Alexandre Dumas's *La Dame aux Camelias* (Geoffrey Gaquere, Anne-Marie Cadieux and Monique Spaziani pictured). Contemporary works can be seen at the Théâtre de Quat'Sous and the Rideau Vert.

BELOW: Montréalers have a passion for dance, particularly modern dance, with La La La Human Steps and Ouest Vertigo Danse among the favourites. But Les Ballets Jazz de Montréal has been pleasing fans with a more populist form of modern dance since 1972. The city is also home to the Grands Ballets Canadiens.

LEFT: the Centaur Theatre is the premiere venue for English-language productions. The company stages everything from Shakespeare to Pinter, but also provides a showcase of Montréal works such as Vittorio Rossi's *Carmela's Table*, which features Anita La Selva and Richard Zeppieri (pictured).

THE CLASSICS

Every great city needs a great orchestra, and Montréal is no exception: the Orchestre Symphonique de Montréal (OSM) is one of the world's great classical ensembles. The orchestra was founded in 1934 by Wilfrid Pelletier and was lucky enough in the 1960s and 1970s to attract such brilliant young conductors as Zubin Mehta and Franz-Paul Decker.

However, it was Charles Dutoit, who took over the podium in 1977, who made the OSM a household name. During Dutoit's 25-year reign, the orchestra travelled the world, playing concert halls in Europe and Asia. It also recorded prolifically, specializing in the repertoire of Maurice Ravel. Dutoit's reign ended acrimoniously in 2002 – his brusque, imperious style irritated many of his musicians – and he was replaced by Kent Nagano (pictured above), one of the great maestros of the day.

Of course, classical music in Montréal goes well beyond the OSM. The city's second orchestra – the Orchestre Métropolitain de Montréal – has a solid reputation, and I Musici de Montréal is one of Canada's best chamber groups. I Musici performs at Place des Arts and McGill University's Pollack Hall. But its most charming venue is the wood-panelled Tudor Room in the Ogilvy Department Store.

ABOVE: there is a host of Francophone performers like Richard Desjardins, Daniel Boucher, Les Cowboys Fringants, Les Colocs and La Chicane, but the success of Arcade Fire, which took the world by storm in 2003, shows you don't have to perform in French to be a hit.

RIGHT: Rufus Wainwright first appeared on stage at the age of 13, playing the piano for the McGarrigle Sisters, his folk-singing mother and aunt. His richly textured rock albums, full of soaring operatic solos, dense orchestrations and sweetly longing lyrics make him one of Montréal's most gifted and eccentric performers.

Why Ice Hockey Matters

Hockey is tantamount to religion for many Canadians, and nowhere in the country is its gospel preached more passionately than in Montréal

To understand ice hockey is, in some sense, to understand Canada itself. Across a frozen expanse, enterprising individuals fight their way through a series of obstacles, searching for the narrow openings that will bring them glory. And yet the individual cannot succeed – only the team, working together, can consistently come out on top.

Although it is raucous, hockey, like Canadian society, is also rule-bound: when individuals break the laws of the game, they are physically removed from their fellows, placed in the penalty box – the "sin bin" – and the team must struggle on without them ... for at least two minutes, anyway. All dirty play, from tripping and slashing to elbowing and high sticking, will draw a penalty – provided the referees can see it, of course.

Played with high emotion at high speeds, and within the tight confines of a boarded rink, tempers flare frequently in hockey. Fighting, though penalized, has always been part of the game. Like the country, hockey is wide-open and honest, at once rough and graceful, team-oriented and individual. It is like nothing else on earth – and it is Canada's game. The sport belongs to Canadians, in a way that little else does, and they know this almost from birth. And nowhere is this sense of propriety stronger than in Montréal.

Our game

Canadians are notoriously self-effacing, finding little to boast about in their own achievements. But when the talk comes round to hockey, they can rightly claim top honours.

Although the game is now played around the world, Canadians still dominate its highest levels. In the National Hockey League (NHL), the highest calibre league in the world, more than half of the more than 600 players on team rosters for the 2005–6 season were born in Canada. Canadian fans, meanwhile, remain the most loyal and discerning. Come Saturday night, Canadians of all ages tune in to the Canadian Broadcasting Corporation's "Hockey Night in Canada", the oldest and longest running sports programme in the world.

While many Americans view hockey as a cross between professional wrestling and roller derby on ice, for Canadians the game is an expression of national aspiration. Our game, our league, our players. What Canadian child has not stickhandled around the rec room, dumping an imaginary puck into the corner? What youth has not spent a winter day firing tennis balls into a net in the back lane, playing until it was too dark to see, too cold to feel toes, and ignoring the call to dinner? For all of them, the hockey announcer's traditional cry, "He shoots ... he scores!" is a dreamy mantra, a call to glory.

Desperate times

Of course there have been times – desperate times – when the Russians, Swedes, Czechs and even the Americans put Canada's hockey supremacy to the test. The first Canada–Russia series in 1972 for example. For the stars on Team Canada, it was supposed to be a light workout against a bunch of poorly equipped amateurs. But the Russians came to the Forum in Montréal, in effect the Sistine Chapel of Hockey, and beat "our boys" 7–3.

Over the next few weeks, Canadians watched in stunned silence as this eight-game foregone conclusion suddenly became a matter of national importance. Teachers even wheeled clunky school TVs into classrooms so kids wouldn't miss the daytime games. Both teams fought tooth and nail and Canadians gaped collectively until Canada's Paul Henderson scored with 34 seconds left in the eighth and final game to ensure victory and thus save national pride. That goal is still replayed, decades later, on television commercials and sports programmes as though it just happened a moment ago.

Still, a watershed had been passed. The late Montréal novelist Mordecai Richler *(see page 49)* accurately expressed the feeling that swept from coast to coast after that first international series. "We already knew that our politicians lied, that our bodies would be betrayed by age", he wrote, "but we had not suspected that our hockey players were anything but the very best.... After the series, nothing was ever the same again in Canada. Beer didn't taste as good. The Rockies seemed smaller, the northern lights dimmer." And he was only mildly exaggerating.

The birth of hockey

Within Canada, there is a lively dispute about the invention of hockey. At least four cities – Kingston, Ontario; Halifax, Nova Scotia; Windsor, Nova Scotia; and Montréal – call themselves "the birthplace of hockey". And though the matter is not likely to be resolved any time soon, one thing is for sure: on 3 March 1875, two teams gathered to play what is widely recognized as the first-ever organized game in Montréal's Old Victoria Rink. The assembled hearties were mostly winter-idle McGill University rugby players, who muscled their way up and down the long rink using "a flat piece of board" as a puck.

The most common setting for a game back then was some shovelled patch of frozen lake, pond or river. One reason for the game's early failure to fire the interest of Montréalers was the sheer effort involved in getting a game going. Imagine clearing a field every time you wanted to play lacrosse or soccer.

Early hockey had no official boundaries or rules: an indeterminate number of players could range far and wide to set up their goals. They had better be fit, however, since goals were often placed as far as 1.5 km (1 mile)

LEFT: young players are the future of the sport.
RIGHT: Tomas Plekanec, Montréal Canadiens, and Chris Phillips, Ottawa Senators, race to the puck.

apart. Some of these difficulties were overcome during the 1880s, when two enterprising undergraduates from McGill University, R.F. Smith and W.F. Robertson, codified the rules of hockey. They specified the approximate size of the playing surface, limited the skating players to eight a side (later six, and now five), and generally gave shape to the game as we know and enjoy it today. Smith also invented the hockey puck by cutting down an India rubber ball that bounced too much for good play on the ice. Permanent winter skating rinks – usually uncovered – were built to make the business of finding suitable ice less hit-and-miss.

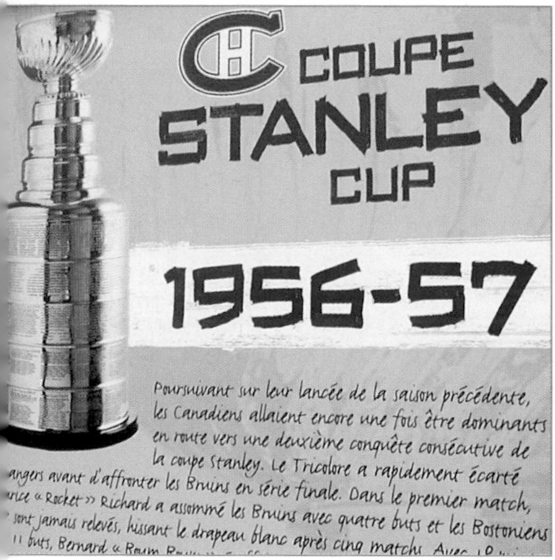

Only in 1907 was the International Ice Hockey Federation formed to govern a game that was becoming more popular by the year. The NHL did not form until 1917 – eight years after the Canadiens, the joy of Montréal, had been organized. There were five teams in that first version of the NHL: the Canadiens, the Montréal Wanderers, the Québec Bulldogs, the Ottawa Senators and the Torontos (known as the Blueshirts and later, the Arenas, St Patricks and finally Maple Leafs). The Québec team never played a game that year due to financial problems, while the Wanderers folded after their home, the Montréal Arena, burned down just six games into the season. Teams came and went, but by 1931 there were 10 NHL franchises, including a number in the United States. By 1942, because of the depression and World War II, only six remained: the Canadiens, Maple Leafs, Detroit Red Wings, Chicago Blackhawks and New York Rangers, known collectively as the Original Six. The NHL remained a six-team league until 1967.

Although Toronto won the inaugural NHL championship in 1917, Montréal teams had been a powerful force from the beginning. In 1893, the Montréal Amateur Athletic Association were the first winners of the prize for which NHL teams still vie today, the Stanley Cup. Originally called the Dominion Hockey Challenge Cup, it soon took the name of Lord Stanley of Preston, the Governor General of Canada, who purchased (for about $50) and donated it the previous year.

Les Habitants

The Stanley Cup has grown over the years, sprouting bottom layers like a tree grows rings, and the Habs (for *habitants*, an old French expression for farmers or peasants, *see page 24*), as the Canadiens are also known, have been there every step of the way. Formed in 1909, Le Club de Hockey Canadien (as it is officially known) has more NHL titles than any other team, winning Lord Stanley's Cup 24 times (once in pre-NHL 1915–16). They are without a doubt the most famous hockey team in the world, the New York Yankees or Manchester United of hockey. Montréal's former hockey temple, the Forum, was so thickly festooned with championship banners that opposing players would get distinctly woozy at the sight of its crowded rafters.

Many of the best players ever to lace up skates wore the Canadiens' sweater. First and best, perhaps, was Howie Morenz, the legendary "Stratford Streak". An Ontario boy, Morenz anchored a high-scoring 1920s line with two Québécois snipers, Billy Boucher and Aurel Joliat. In the inaugural game at the Forum, on 29 November 1924, the Morenz line scored six goals in a 7–1 defeat of the Toronto St Patricks. When he died in 1937 (due to complications from a leg broken during a game), his funeral was held at the Montréal Forum and broadcast across Canada. The stonewall in the Montréal goal on opening night was another legend, Georges Vezina (the Chicoutimi Cucumber, for keeping his "cool" under pressure), who rose to glory from a small-town family of 22 children and gave his name to the NHL trophy for goaltending excellence. Vezina collapsed in his goal during the Canadiens' home opener in the 1925–6 season and died from tuberculosis in March 1926 at the age of 39.

No player, however, has been as idolized as Maurice "The Rocket" Richard, who dominated the game in the 1940s and 1950s. Richard was so essential to Montréal's pride that his suspension for punching an official during the 1955 season sparked a city-wide riot that has been credited with kicking off the

Quiet Revolution. On ice, the hard-skating right-winger led the Habs to eight Stanley Cup victories, including five consecutive wins between 1955 and 1960. During the ceremonies marking the closing of the Forum in March 1996, Richard received a 16-minute standing ovation, thought to be the longest in Montréal history. After his death in 2000, like Morenz before him, Richard's body lay in state at the then Molson Centre. An estimated 115,000 Montréalers came to pay their respects.

LEFT: the Stanley Cup, the Holy Grail of hockey.
ABOVE: Maurice "The Rocket" Richard.
RIGHT: Henri "Pocket Rocket" Richard.

Canadien dominance

The Rocket was an aging but still considerable force when the Canadiens entered their greatest-ever period of glory, the epic five-year dominance of the Stanley Cup from 1956 to 1960, an as yet unmatched record. The team has won the Cup many times since then, including a brilliant four-year streak in 1976–79, but the team of the late 1950s was probably the best ever assembled. The roll call includes many illustrious names: Jean Béliveau; Henri "the Pocket Rocket" Richard; Bernie "Boom Boom" Geoffrion (the inventor of the slap shot); and Jacques Plant, one of the best goalies and the first to permanently don a facemask.

There will always be arguments about the merits of the dominant late-1970s team that included Hall of Famers Ken Dryden, Guy Lafleur, Larry Robinson, Jacques Lemaire, Serge Savard, Bob Gainey and Steve Shutt; but there was definitely something elemental about that 1950s dynasty. It reigned before the 1967 expansion, the birth of the rebel World Hockey Association, before the Canadiens became just another business in the NHL, and before the arrival of the first European players. For all of five years this team, composed almost entirely of Québec boys, could not be knocked off the top by the best hockey players in North America.

Canada's team?

Despite icing some strong teams in recent years, the other great team of hockey's early years, the Toronto Maple Leafs, have not won the Stanley Cup since 1967. Nevertheless, the Canadiens-Leafs rivalry remains one of the most intense in hockey. Writer Roch Carrier considered the longlasting rivalry in his short story *The Hockey Sweater*.

A Québec kid, a desperate Maurice Richard fan, needs a new hockey sweater and his mother writes away to Eaton's (the long gone Canadian department store). The resulting parcel holds a Maple Leafs sweater. *Quel désastre*! His mother will not send it back because it fits him. He is shunned by his fellow players, each wearing Rocket Richard's famous number 9, and denounced as a traitor to Mother Québec, Les Habitants, and the Rocket himself.

The Canadiens, not the Leafs, are Canada's team – well according to Montréalers anyway. Without their own teams to cheer for during the long Original Six era, and with the Habs dominating the NHL for long stretches in the 1950s, '60s and '70s, the Canadiens earned fans' from coast to coast.

In Calgary, Edmonton, Vancouver and now Ottawa, Canadiens' goals are still loudly cheered by throngs of fans decked out in the red, white and blue Habs regalia. Fans

THE LOST SEASON 2004–5

On 16 September 2004, a day after its Collective Bargaining Agreement with the NHL Player's Association expired, the NHL locked out its own players. At issue were player salaries and the league's desire to install a salary cap system to control them.

Many fans had hoped that the season could be saved as it was after a lockout in 1994, but after months of failed negotiations, the NHL had no alternative but to officially cancel what should have been its 88th season. As commissioner Gary Bettman put it, it was too little progress too late and it was no longer practical to conduct even an abbreviated season. For the first time since 1919, when a Spanish flu epidemic forced the cancellation of the finals, the Stanley Cup would not be awarded. A large number of outraged fans signed a petition at the Free Stanley website, and two Toronto hockey fans even sued the NHL to hand over the Cup, which it does not own but holds in-trust.

The impasse ended on 21 July 2005, when a Player's Association in disarray ratified a deal that included the dreaded salary cap. Although it had been feared that the year-long lockout would kill franchises in some of the league's weaker markets, attendance actually rose when play resumed in the fall of 2005.

in Winnipeg once demonstrated a better appreciation of what Les Canadiens represented, back when Winnipeg had an NHL club: the first time the Canadiens visited Winnipeg, most wore tuxedos and gowns to the arena.

Despite Winnipeg fans' loyalty, it was not enough to prevent the 1995 transfer of their Jets franchise to Phoenix, Arizona – a fate that also befell Québec City's beloved Nordiques, bitter rivals of the Canadiens who now reside in Denver, Colorado. Canada is left with just six teams, the Habs, the Leafs, the Ottawa Senators, the Edmonton Oilers, the Calgary Flames and the Vancouver Canucks.

The Habs today

In 1996, much to the dismay of many Habs fans, Le Centre Bell became the new home of the Canadiens. A vast amphitheatre built on the platforms of the old Windsor Station, it can accommodate up to 21,200 people.

The Canadiens are currently in their lengthiest championship drought, having last won the Stanley Cup in 1993, but even though the coveted Cup remains elusive, the team has led the NHL in attendance for the past three seasons, with more than 714,000 fans attending their 41 home games in 2005–6. For hockey purists, however, the NHL game has much deteriorated. Now a 30-team league, it has a diluted talent pool and too many teams favouring a boring defensive style. After a labour dispute caused the cancellation of the entire 2004–5 season *(see box, page 66)*, the NHL implemented a whole series of rule changes intended to speed up the game and therefore raise scoring. They were successful for the most part, eliminating much of the hooking and grabbing that had been bogging down play for years.

Despite the widespread support they enjoy, the Canadiens are still a family affair between city and club that is almost a century old. Indeed, the "H" on their old-fashioned sweaters is popularly taken to mean "Habitants", when it probably just means "hockey" (as in Club de Hockey).

In their hometown, the Habs are the people's team, the team that young Montréalers and youngsters from across Québec dream of playing for. A few of those wide-eyed French Canadian kids grow up to claim that birthright: donning the red, white and blue sweater, skating out onto the hallowed ice of Le Centre Bell and scoring the winner for Les Canadiens. The rest just keep dreaming. ❑

FAR LEFT: Montréal Canadiens' Sergei Samsonov. **LEFT:** "The Rocket" immortalised. **ABOVE:** old rivals – The Canadiens and the Toronto Maple Leafs.

Escapade

760

PLACES

A detailed guide to the city with the principal sites clearly cross-referenced by number to the maps

Montréal claims, with much pride and some justice, to be the second-largest French-speaking city in the Western world and the only French-speaking metropolis in North America. But in reality, it is more complex than that. Francophones (French-speakers) still predominate, but the city's anglophones (English-speakers) have had a deep and lasting impact on the city's architecture and social customs. However, it is the allophones – those whose mother tongue is neither English nor French – who represent the future. Their numbers and influence are growing at a rapid pace. Despite its linguistic tensions, this is a remarkably civil place.

Like many cities its size, Montréal is a collection of neighbourhoods, each with its own character and history and each reflecting a different facet of the city's multilayered life. For the Places section of this book we have tried to highlight the most interesting and the most representative.

Old Montréal *(pages 77–99)* explore's the city's 17th-century origins as an outpost of the French empire, while Downtown *(pages 103–23)* reveals the city's modern commercial heart and the heritage of the Scottish and English fur barons who ran Canada in the 19th century.

Westmount *(pages 141–49)* and Outremont *(pages 151–57)*, two of the wealthiest neighbourhoods, are linguistic reflections of each other, while the young and hip congregate in the bars and bistros of the Quartier Latin, Plateau Mont-Royal and Le Village, covered in Montréal Branché *(pages 125–37)*.

To understand the religiosity that played such a major role in Montréal's development, we will visit the Oratoire St-Joseph *(pages 159–63)*, a shrine that is part church and part Catholic theme park. And there are the Olympic Stadium, the Jardin Botanique and the beautiful islands of Ste-Hélène and Notre-Dame, revealed in Stadiums, Gardens and Islands *(pages 167–75)*.

Comparisons are often made between Montreal and Québec City. While the former is said to be more sophisticated, the latter is more historically intact and is considered the spiritual heart of the province. Around Montréal *(pages 179–97)* explores the city's environs, and the last chapter provides a fascinating insight into Québec City *(pages 199–209)*, the capital of French Canada. ❑

PRECEDING PAGES: the marina at Lac Tremblant; traditional architecture in the old town, Trois-Rivières. **LEFT:** remnants of the past and present Downtown.

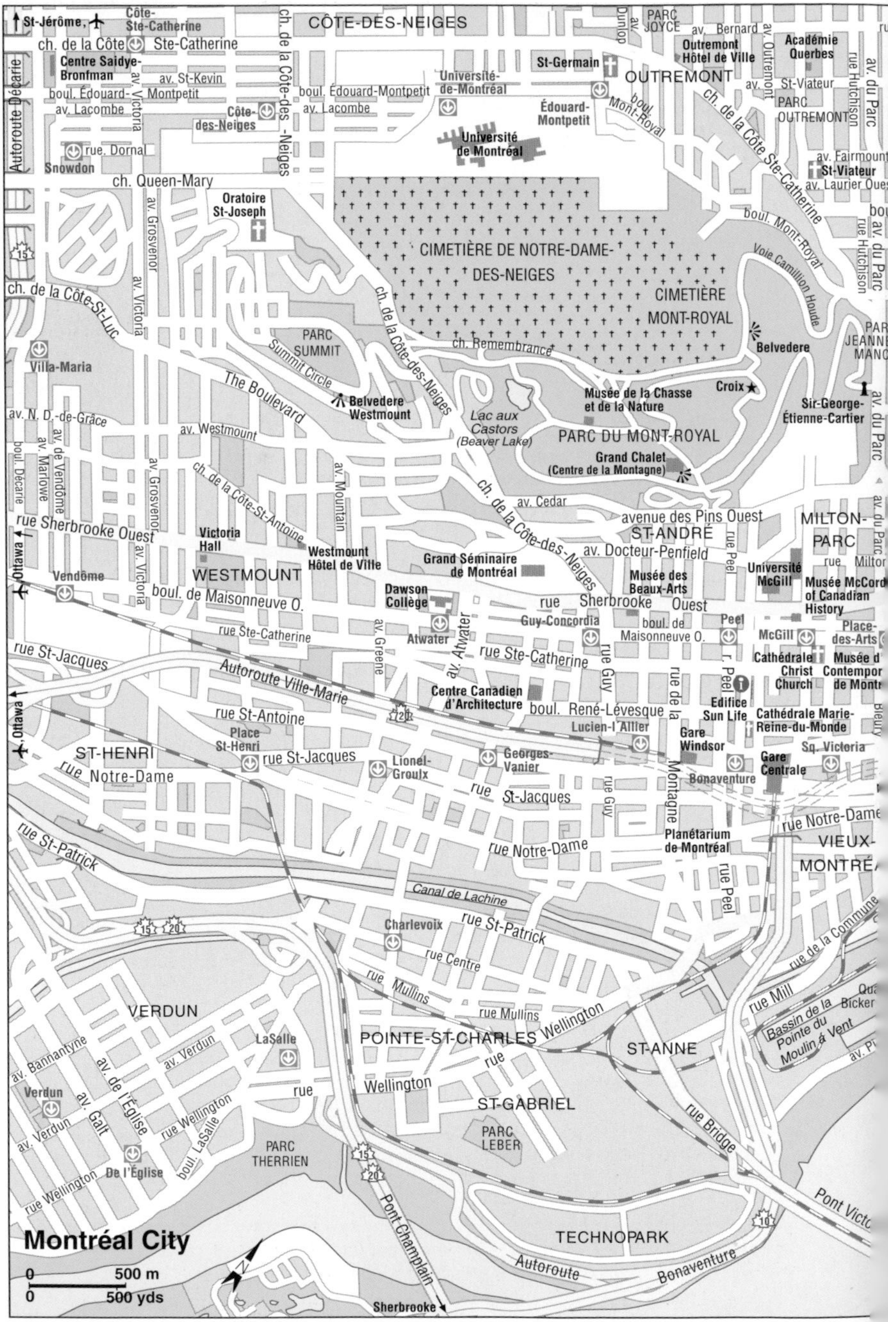
St-Jérôme
Côte-Ste-Catherine
CÔTE-DES-NEIGES
ch. de la Côte
Ste-Catherine
Centre Saidye-Bronfman
av. St-Kevin
boul. Édouard-Montpetit
av. Lacombe
Autoroute Décarie
av. Victoria
Côte-des-Neiges
ch. de la Côte-des-Neiges
Université-de-Montréal
Université de Montréal
Édouard-Montpetit
St-Germain
OUTREMONT
PARC JOYCE
Dunlop
av. Bernard
Outremont Hôtel de Ville
Académie Querbes
av. Outremont
St-Viateur
PARC OUTREMONT
rue Hutchison
av. du Parc
boul. Mont-Royal
ch. de la Côte Ste-Catherine
av. Fairmount
St-Viateur
av. Laurier Ouest
rue. Dornal
Snowdon
ch. Queen-Mary
Oratoire St-Joseph
av. Grosvenor
CIMETIÈRE DE NOTRE-DAME-DES-NEIGES
CIMETIÈRE MONT-ROYAL
Voie Camillien Houde
Belvedere
ch. de la Côte-St-Luc
Villa-Maria
PARC SUMMIT
Summit Circle
ch. Remembrance
The Boulevard
Belvedere Westmount
Lac aux Castors (Beaver Lake)
Musée de la Chasse et de la Nature
Croix
Sir-George-Étienne-Cartier
PARC DU MONT-ROYAL
Grand Chalet (Centre de la Montagne)
av. N. D.-de-Grâce
av. de Vendôme
av. Marlowe
boul. Décarie
av. Westmount
ch. de la Côte-St-Antoine
av. Mountain
av. Cedar
avenue des Pins Ouest
MILTON-PARC
ST-ANDRÉ
rue Sherbrooke Ouest
Ottawa
Victoria Hall
Westmount Hôtel de Ville
Grand Séminaire de Montréal
av. Docteur-Penfield
rue Peel
Université McGill
Musée McCord of Canadian History
Vendôme
WESTMOUNT
boul. de Maisonneuve O.
Dawson Collège
rue Sherbrooke Ouest
Musée des Beaux-Arts
Guy-Concordia
boul. de Maisonneuve O.
Peel
McGill
Place-des-Arts
rue Ste-Catherine
Atwater
av. Greene
av. Atwater
rue Ste-Catherine
rue Guy
Cathédrale Christ Church
Musée d'Art Contemporain de Montréal
rue St-Jacques
Autoroute Ville-Marie
Centre Canadien d'Architecture
boul. René-Lévesque
rue de la Montagne
r. Peel
Edifice Sun Life
Cathédrale Marie-Reine-du-Monde
rue St-Antoine
Place St-Henri
Lucien-L'Allier
Gare Windsor
Sq. Victoria
ST-HENRI
rue St-Jacques
Lionel-Groulx
Georges-Vanier
Bonaventure
Gare Centrale
rue Notre-Dame
rue St-Jacques
rue Guy
rue Notre-Dame
Planétarium de Montréal
VIEUX-MONTRÉAL
rue St-Patrick
rue Notre-Dame
rue Peel
Canal de Lachine
Charlevoix
rue St-Patrick
rue de la Commune
rue Centre
rue Mullins
rue Mullins
rue Mill
VERDUN
POINTE-ST-CHARLES
Wellington
ST-ANNE
Bassin de la Pointe du Moulin à Vent
av. Bannantyne
av. de l'Église
av. Verdun
LaSalle
rue
Wellington
ST-GABRIEL
Verdun
av. Galt
rue Wellington
av. Verdun
boul. LaSalle
PARC THERRIEN
PARC LEBER
rue Bridge
De l'Église
rue Wellington
Pont Champlain
Pont Victoria
TECHNOPARK
Autoroute Bonaventure
Montréal City
0 500 m
0 500 yds
N
Sherbrooke

Laval
boul. Rosemont
PARC PÈRE-MARQUETTE
MILE-END
Rosemont
rue des Carrières
rue Dandurand
rue St-Grégoire
PARC SIR-WILFRID-LAURIER
boul. St-Laurent
av. Papineau
av. de Lorimier
rue d'Iberville
1e av.
5e av.
10e av.
boul. St-Michel
rue Dandurand
av. Bourbonnière
rue Masson
PARC MAISON-NEUVE
boul. Pie-IX
av. Laurier E.
PARC LE PÉLICAN
PARC LAFOND
18e av.
DE LORIMIER
Laurier
ST-DENIS
boul. St-Joseph Est
St-Joseph Ouest
rue St-Denis
rue St-Hubert
av. Christophe Colomb
de la Roche
rue Fabert
av. des Érables
Serres
Trois-Rivières, Québec
av. du Mont-Royal
ST-JEAN-BAPTISTE
Mt-Royal
MONT-ROYAL
rue Marie-Anne Est
rue Rachel Est
Pie-IX
Château Dufresne
Musée des Arts Décoratifs
PRÉFONTAINE
rue St-Dominique
av. Laval
rue Duluth
rue Berri
rue St-Herbert
av. du Parc Fontaine
PARC LAFONTAINE
BOURGET
rue Sherbrooke Est
rue Frontenac
Prefontaine
Joliette
rue Hochelaga
LAFONTAINE
ST-EUSÈBE
rue de Rouen
HOCHELAGA
av. des Pins Est
avenue Papineau
rue Parthenais
rue Dézery
rue Davidson
Sherbrooke
ST-LOUIS
ST-JACQUES
rue Montcalm
rue Amherst
rue Ontario
Frontenac
rue Moreau
av. Valois
rue Adam
TERRASSE ONTARIO
STE-MARIE
rue Ste-Catherine
Berri-UQAM
Beaudry
Papineau
boul. de Maisonneuve
rue Notre-Dame
St-Laurent
UQAM
Quai Laurier
boul. René-Lévesque
Champ-de-Mars
d'Armes
av. Viger
Hôtel de Ville
Antoine
Pont Jacques-Cartier
St-Laurent (St Lawrence)
Marché Bonsecours
Lac aux Dauphins
Pont Ste-Hélène
Tour de la Ronde
Quai King-Edward
Quai Jacques-Cartier
Tour de l'Horloge
Musée David M. Stewart
La Ronde
VIEUX-PORT
Vieux Fort
Quai Alexandra
PARC DE LA CITÉ-DU-HAVRE
Ile Ste-Hélène
Tour de Lévis
Québec
Quai Mark Drouin
Pont de la Concorde
PARC DES ILES
Biosphère
rue St-Charles Ouest
Longueuil
Lac des Cygnes
Chenal le Moyne
Habitat '67
Place des Nations
Pont des Iles
rue Labonte
De Chateauguay
rue St-Laurent
20
Canal de la Rive Sud
Jardins des Floralies
Gilles-Villeneuve
Casino de Montréal
PARC DE LA VOIE MARITIME
rue Lemoyne Ouest
Ile Notre-Dame
Lac des Regates
Bassin Olympique
rue Riverside
boul. Lafayette
boul. Desaulniers
rue Dollard
LONGUEUIL
rue Joliette
rue Gardenville
Circuit
ST-LAMBERT
boul. Taschereau
rue Ste-Hélène
rue Marquette
Plage des Iles
Musée Marcil
PARC LOGAN
rue Logan
av. Putney
ch. Tiffin
Plattsburg

OLD MONTRÉAL

The original French settlement is still the most beguiling historical district in the city: a mixture of old homes, docks and churches, restaurants and squares, tiny alleys and grand public squares.

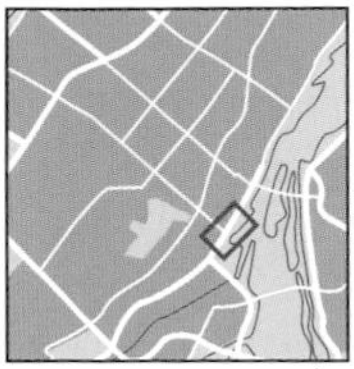

In summer, **Vieux-Montréal**, or Old Montréal, is one of the liveliest districts in the city. Its bars and restaurants are packed and throngs of partying locals and tourists crowd its narrow, cobbled streets until the early morning. Even in January, when the winds are bitter and the temperature can dip as low as minus 20 Celsius, Vieux-Montréal is still busy. Its top restaurants and boutique hotels attract visitors year round, and thanks to a booming condominium market, the area is populated with permanent residents.

Restoration

It is hard to believe that in the early 1960s Vieux-Montréal was virtually derelict. Lawyers, stockbrokers and shipping firms still had offices on rue St-Jacques, priests still celebrated Mass at the monumental Basilique Notre-Dame-de-Montréal and robed judges still meted out less-than-divine justice in the court houses near place Jacques-Cartier. But at night, as soon as the lawyers and financiers went home, the whole district shut down tight. A few artists lived in the lofts of the old warehouses near the harbour and a bar or two stayed open on place Jacques-Cartier. But the rest of the district was dark and forbidding. The narrow streets were more frightening than romantic, lined with locked and often boarded-up 18th- and 19th-century stone buildings. The Vieux-Port, or Old Port, was an industrial slum, full of empty sheds and rusting rail lines. People speculated seriously about knocking the whole mess down and building something new.

But in 1962, the Viger Commission declared the area historically invaluable. Houses were restored, buildings renovated, and restaurants, boutiques, art galleries, clubs and, some would say, far too many souvenir shops began to spring up.

Map on page 78

LEFT: the grand Basilique Notre-Dame.
BELOW: a musician performs in place Jacques-Cartier.

Old Montreal
0 200 m
0 200 yds
Québec
Tour de l'Horloge
Ottawa
FAUBOURG QUÉBEC
Bassin de l'Horloge
Quai de l'Horloge (Clock Pier)
St-Laurent
Édifice Jacques-Viger
Square Viger
rue Berri
av. Viger E.
rue St-Antoine E.
Maison Brossard-Gauvin
PARC DALHOUSIE
Champ-de-Mars
rue Notre-Dame E.
Lieu Historique National Sir-George-Etienne-Cartier
Maison du Calvet
Notre-Dame-de-Bon-Secours
Porte Bonsecours
Labyrinthe du Hangar
rue St-Denis
Place Victor-Morin
Cour municipale
Complexe Chaussegros-de-Léry
Maison Papineau
Maison de Beaujeu
Marché Bonsecours
rue de la Commune E.
Bassin Bonsecours
Quai Jacques-Cartier
le Pelican
rue Gosford
Champ-de-Mars
Hôtel de Ville
Château Ramezay
Tunnel Gosford
rue St-Claude
Pl. de Dauversière
Hôtel de Rasco
Horatio Nelson
Jean Vauquelin
Place Vauquelin
Pl. Jacques-Cartier
Maisons Denis-Viger
Poupées et Merveilles
la Minerve et le Patriote
av. de l'Hôtel de Ville
CHAMP DE MARS
Vieux Palais de Justice
Maison de la Sauvegarde
rue St-Amable
rue St-Vincent
rue de Bullion
Autoroute Ville-Marie
Cour d'Appel du Québec (Court of Appeal)
rue Ste-Thérèse
rue de Vaudreuil
VIEUX-PORT (OLD PORT)
Marché aux puces (Flea Market)
Bassin Jacques-Cartier
Quai King-Edward
Allée des Huissiers
rue St-Gabriel
rue St-Dominique
Palais de Justice
rue Notre-Dame O.
rue St-Jean-Baptiste
rue St-Paul E.
Maison de la Congrégation
Centre iSci
Bassin King-Edward
boul. St-Laurent
Porte St-Laurent
rue Clark
ruelle des Fortifications
rue St-Jacques
Aldred Building
rue de Brésoles
Cours Le Royer
Écomusée de l'encadrement
rue St-Dizier
QUARTIER CHINOIS
rue St-Urbain
Ancienne Banque du Peuple
Côte de la Place d'Armes
Basilique Notre-Dame
rue St-Sulpice
Chapelle du Sacré-Cœur
VIEUX-MONTRÉAL
rue St-Paul O.
Place de la Capitale
Pointe-à-Callière
John Young
Musée d'Archéologie et d'Histoire de la Pointe-à-Callière (Museum of Archaeology and History)
Gare Maritime d'Iberville
Quai Alexandra
Bassin Alexandra
Place d'Armes
Banque de Montréal
rue Côte
Banque Canadienne Nationale
Vieux Séminaire de St-Sulpice
Centaur Theatre Company
Ancien Édifice Merchants' Exchange
rue St-François-Xavier
Vieille Douane
Place Royale
rue de Callière
Palais des Congrès (Conference Centre)
rue Chenneville
rue Jeanne-Mance
rue de l'Hôpital
Maison de Lotbinière
rue du St-Sacrement
rue St-Éloi
rue du Port
rue St-Nicolas
rue St-Jean
rue Anderson
Molson Bank
rue St-Alexis
Cour Le Moyne
rue Evans
Centre d'Histoire de Montréal (History Centre)
Pl. d'Youville
Écuries d'Youville
Hôpital Général des Sœurs Grises
Maison de Mère d'Youville
Ancien Édifice Allan
Ancien Édifice des Commissaires du havre de Montréal
rue de Bleury
rue St-Pierre
Pl. Jean-Paul Riopelle
Centre de Commerce Mondial (World Trade Centre)
Banque Royale (Royal Bank)
Ancien Édifice du Corn Exchange
rue des Récollets
rue Ste-Hélène
Place d'Youville
rue Normand
Musée Marc-Aurèle Fortin
rue de la Gauchetière O.
rue Hermine
rue St-Alexandre
rue McGill
Édifice des Douanes
Ancien Édifice du Grand Tronc
rue des Soeurs Grises
rue de la Commune O.
Square Victoria
Place Victoria
Côte du Beaver Hall
rue de Longueuil
rue King
rue Wellington
rue William
rue Queen
rue St-Henri
rue St-Maurice
FAUBOURG DES RÉCOLLETS
Tour de la Bourse

Old commercial buildings were transformed into condos, and businesses moved into the upper floors of many old buildings, creating an intriguing contrast, with banks of high-tech electronics lined against 200-year-old fieldstone walls. The federal government razed the rotting structures along the waterfront, planted grass and trees and turned the Vieux-Port into one of the city's most popular parks.

Hotels were slower to open and until the 1990s a visitor still couldn't rent a room in the old city for love or money. But then the city built the Palais des Congrès, a huge convention centre, just north of the old city, making Vieux-Montréal a prime spot for both tourists and business travellers. Today there are more than a dozen hotels, from the luxuriously modern 300-room Inter-Continental to the charming nine-room Auberge des Passants du Sans Soucy, which is housed in an old stone fur warehouse.

The major squares

The tiny ruelle des Fortifications, which runs where the old city walls once stood, marks the northern boundary of Vieux-Montréal. From there, it's just a five-minute walk to the river, the old town's southern edge. The walk across Vieux-Montréal, from rue McGill in the west to rue Berri in the east, takes longer, but, even so, a brisk walker could cover it in 20 minutes. This small area is the Montréal that the fur merchants, tradesmen and priests of the 1790s would have known. A few of the colony's poor residents took their chances living outside the walls in huddled little "faubourgs", but for the most part, the area that is now downtown was farmland and forests.

Montréal's social and commercial life in the 18th and 19th centuries focused on four major squares – place Jacques-Cartier, place d'Armes, place Royale and place d'Youville. All four have survived to this day and all four play a vital role in the life of the old city, but none is livelier than **place Jacques-Cartier ❶**. This is the obvious place to start a visit to Vieux-Montréal.

There is a small tourist office at the north end of the square where you can get maps, advice and information on special events and concerts. The square itself, a long rectangle that runs from rue Notre-Dame to rue de la Commune on the waterfront, is paved with flagstones. Cobbled streets lined with graceful 18th- and 19th-century buildings – many of them converted into restaurants with outdoor patios in front – run down either side of the square.

In summer, the streets are closed to vehicles and the entire area becomes a crowded outdoor theatre for an ever-changing cast of jugglers, mimes, acrobats, fire-eaters, amateur comics, musicians and street artists who will paint your portrait (or draw your caricature) in minutes. More artists display their sketches, photographs and pastels

Map on page 78

An artist displays her work in the historical square, place Jacques-Cartier.

BELOW: painting the perfect portrait.

Nelson appears strangely out of place in Old Montréal.

RIGHT: a colourful re-enactment at City Hall.

on the stone walls lining tiny rues St-Amable and St-Vincent.

At the north end of the square, towering above the buildings, is a monument to Admiral Horatio Lord Nelson, an imposing if odd tribute to England's greatest naval hero. Imposing because the column on which Nelson's statue is perched stands 35 metres (115 ft) tall. Odd both because the admiral faces away from the St Lawrence, and more to the point, because he is there at all.

Given the politics of today, it's surprising that a monument to the English conqueror of a French navy has survived. Ironically, it was French-speaking Sulpician priests, not English-speaking merchants, who spearheaded the fundraising for the statue. Many of them had fled the French Revolution and were, no doubt, pleased to see the impious little Corsican Napoleon get his come-uppance.

One possible reason that Nelson is looking away from the river is so that he can keep an eye on Admiral Jean Vauquelin, one of the heroes of New France, whose statue stands in a little square just across rue Notre-Dame. **Place Vauquelin** ❷, once the site of the town jail and the public flogging ground, is not as grand as the setting for Nelson's monument, but its has a gorgeous fountain where visitors and local alike cool their feet on warm summer days.

Promenade and law courts

Just north of place Vauquelin, down a flight of stone stairs, is the **Champ de Mars**, once a military parade ground for Montréal's various militia regiments as well as a favoured place for Victorian couples and families to make their evening promenades. It was paved over and used as a parking lot until the mid 1990s, but is now a wide grassy park bisected by the excavated ruins of Montréal's old city walls.

The classical-revival building with the cupola and tall thick columns on the west side of place Vauquelin is the **Vieux Palais de Justice** ❸ (155 rue Notre-Dame Est). This old court house, dating from 1856, is currently occupied by municipal offices. Across the street,

A Living Language

Visitors from France, expecting a common language in this part of Canada, are sometimes a little bemused by what they hear. Indeed, since the French language is so dependent on pronunciation, it can actually be difficult for them to understand what their Québécois cousins are saying: *toi* and *moi* become "tway" and "mway"; a buzzing "z" transforms *petit* into "petzi" and *direct* into "dzirect"; *cheval* sounds more like "jwal"; and *ici* becomes "icitte". Aside from pronunciation, Québec French has some unique usage: *dépanneur* – "repairman" in France – here means convenience store, and "now" translates to "asteur" *(à cet heure)* as often as to *maintenant*.

As they see their language increasingly under threat, Québec Francophones tend to be more protective of it than the French. Nevertheless, some anglicisms have crept in, but always with a Gallic emphasis on the final syllable. Peanut butter thus becomes *beurre de peanut*. The French from France might not admit it, but research suggests that pronunciations and some archaic words used in Canada are closer to the original French language, so that King Louis XIV could *jaser* ("chat" here, "gossip" in France) with today's Québécois.

at 100 rue Notre-Dame Est, is a later bastion of canon and code that was used until the 1970s for criminal cases. It served briefly as a music conservatory, but now houses the **Québec Court of Appeal**. It features massive columns fronting a lovely bronze door. Above the door are bas-reliefs detailing the history of criminal law. The Latin inscription over the cornice translates as: "He who transgresses the law shall seek the help of the law in vain." Hardly comforting words for a defendant. The massive building at 1 rue Notre-Dame Est is the current **Palais de Justice**, inaugurated in 1971.

City Hall and Château Ramezay

East of Place Vauquelin stands the stately **Hôtel de Ville** ❹ or City Hall (275 rue Notre-Dame; free guided tours June–Aug Mon–Fri 9am–5pm), a Second-Empire structure with slender columns and the mansard roof so common in Québécois architecture.

The building, which dates from 1860, survived a major fire in 1922, and today it has an additional floor. At night, tiny lights outline the building's striking architectural features in a dramatic silhouette.

It was from the second-floor balcony over the main door that Charles de Gaulle addressed an adoring throng on place Jacques-Cartier in 1967 with a rousing speech that concluded with his famous – or infamous – cry of *"Vive le Québec libre!"* ("Long live free Quebec"). The crowd roared its approval, marking a new era of respectability for the notion of Québec independence.

The low lying stone manor house with the fat round tower just across the street from City Hall is the **Château Ramezay** ❺ (280 rue Notre-Dame Est; open June–Thanksgiving: daily 10am–6pm; Thanksgiving–May: Tues–Sun 10am–4.30pm; admission charge; tel: 514-861 3708), built in 1705 as the official residence of the French governor of Montréal, Claude de Ramezay. Later it served as the North American headquarters of the Compagnie des Indes, an enormously

Map on page 78

The Vieux Palais de Justice building is home to the Québec Court of Appeal.

BELOW: the striking Hôtel de Ville is lit at night.

rich French trading company with business interests in North America and the Caribbean.

American General Richard Montgomery chose the Château as his headquarters when US forces occupied the city in 1775 during the War of Independence. Statesman Benjamin Franklin stayed with the general when he came north in a vain attempt to persuade the people of Lower Canada to join the American Revolution. The Château survived these incarnations nicely, and still has the 1-metre (3-ft) thick walls and deep stone vaults ordered by its original owner. That stubby tower, however, is a later addition.

Sir George Etienne-Cartier helped to bring Québec into the Canadian Federation in 1867.

Today, the Château is a museum of life in 18th- and 19th-century Montréal. The rooms are stuffed with an eclectic collection of Aboriginal artefacts, portraits of European pioneers, coins, furniture, religious icons, rugs, and business ledgers, as well as a shiny red automobile produced by the De-Dion-Bouton company in the early 20th century for the city's first motorist. The walls of one room – the Salon de Nantes – are lined with intricately carved wooden panels imported by the Compagnie des Indes. A series of rooms recreates the interiors of diverse living quarters in New France. These include the offices of the governor, a dining room, kitchen and servants' quarters. All the rooms contain period furniture and some fine pieces, especially the cabinets. There are regular special exhibitions.

Behind the Château is the delightfully peaceful **Jardin du Gouverneur**, a re-creation of an 18th-century garden with flowers, shrubs and herbs similar to the ones that Claude de Ramezay and his wife might have planted.

BELOW: an exhibit at Musée Château Ramezay.

Etienne-Cartier's legacy

Further east on rue Notre-Dame, on the edge of Vieux-Montréal, are the two adjoining Victorian-era houses that comprise the **Lieu Historique National Sir-George-Etienne-Cartier** ❻ (Sir George Etienne Cartier Historic Site; 458 rue Notre-Dame Est; open June–Aug daily 10am–6pm; Sept–18 Dec and 8 Apr–May Wed–Sun 10am–noon, 1–5pm; admission charge; tel: 514-283 2282). They examine the life of the French Canadian statesman and financier who brought Québec into the Canadian Confederation in 1867.

The house on the east focuses on Cartier's accomplishments in commerce, railway-building and politics. The other explores the comfortable life of the Montréal bourgeoisie in the 19th century. Especially delightful is the Victorian Christmas exhibit mounted every December.

Sailors' Solace

A block south of the Cartier home is **rue St-Paul**, arguably the most charming street in the old city. Cobblestoned, the air smacking of the St Lawrence River 100 metres (109 yds) to the south, and lined with 18th- and 19th-century buildings that currently house restaurants, stores and government offices, the street is authentic without being precious, at once current and deeply historic.

Four of Montréal's most historic buildings – the Chapelle Notre-Dame-de-Bon-Secours (1772), the Maison Papineau (1785), Maison du Calvet (1770) and the Marché Bonsecours – are clustered around the intersection where rue St-Paul meets rue Bonsecours.

No symbol of the city's maritime heritage is more poignant than **Chapelle Notre-Dame-de-Bon-Secours** ❼ (400 rue St-Paul Est; open May–Oct Tues–Sun 10am–5pm; Nov–mid-Jan and Mar–Apr Tues–Sun 11am–3.30pm; free; tel: 514-282 8670). Most Montréalers call it simply the Chapelle des Matelots, or the Sailors' Church.

One must stand at the water's edge in the Vieux-Port to appreciate the church's impact. Rising above the clock tower is a statue of the Virgin Mary, her outstretched arms welcoming ships into port. For hundreds of years, seamen from Montréal and around the world have made pilgrimages to this little chapel to pray for safe passage or to give thanks for a safe arrival.

The sailors also expressed their gratitude for the Virgin Mary's protection by carving votive lamps in the shape of ships, many of which now hang from the ceiling.

Marguerite Bourgeoys

Canada's first schoolteacher and founder of the Congrègation Notre-Dame religious order, Marguerite Bourgeoys *(see page 19)*, built the first wooden chapel on this site in 1655 to give thanks for surviving her own hazardous crossing from France. Twenty years later, she supervised the construction of a grander stone chapel to house a little wooden statue of Notre-Dame-de-Bon-Secours, or Our Lady of Perpetual Help, that she had brought with her from France. It is that statue that attracted the devotion of sailors, and still does today.

The church Marguerite built is long gone – the current one dates from 1772 – but you can still see that image of Notre-Dame-de-Bon-

Map on page 78

Marguerite Bourgeoys's order of nuns was authorised by Louis XIV in 1671.

BELOW: Chapelle Notre-Dame-de-Bon-Secours.

Private function rooms are available to hire at the Musée Marguerite Bourgeoys, which also has a good museum shop.

BELOW: there are plenty of places to stop for a bite while touring Old Montréal.

Secours standing guard over Bourgeoy's tomb in the little altar on the east side of the church.

Marguerite Bourgeoys, who was canonized by Pope John Paul II in 1982, is a legend in Québec. She not only built schools and churches and founded a religious order, she also trained the *filles du roy* ("daughters of the king"), young women sent out from France to be the wives and mothers of the colony.

St Marguerite's life is examined in an attractive little **museum** (open same hours as the church; admission charge; tel: 514-282 8670) next door to the church. Museum visitors can also climb down to the archaeological excavations under the church and examine the ruins of the two original chapels as well as many other artefacts of city history. If that sounds too claustrophobic, you can climb the creaky wooden staircase to the aerial chapel and observation tower on top of the belfry.

The view of the harbour from here is impressive. Visible to the south, astride the St Lawrence, are the two most famous landmarks created for Expo '67: Buckminster Fuller's 20-storey geodesic dome and architect Moshe Safdie's cubic apartment complex, **Habitat 67**.

The dome, which served as the American pavilion at the world's fair, now houses the **Biosphère**, an interpretive centre on the ecosystems of the St Lawrence River and the Great Lakes. Habitat 67, which looks startlingly like a Navajo cliff dwelling with individual units stacked seemingly randomly at different angles, was supposed to be an experiment in low-cost modular housing, but its location on prime waterfront land has made it a prestigious address.

Papineau and Calvet

Across the street from the chapel at 401 rue Bonsecours is the **Maison du Calvet ❽**, a beautifully restored stone residence with the high chimneys and steep roof typical of 18th-century architecture. It houses a luxurious bed-and-breakfast and a couple of pricey restaurants, but it was originally the home of the notorious Pierre du Calvet, a prosperous merchant and close friend of Benjamin Franklin.

Calvet, ardently republican and anticlercial, didn't really fit in in royalist, Catholic New France. First he betrayed the French to the English in 1759 and then the English to the Americans in 1775. The second betrayal landed him in jail when the Americans withdrew from the city. Upon his release several years later Calvet sought financial compensation from the Americans for his trouble, but was refused. Next he sailed to England to protest his term in prison. Tragically, his ship sank en route, and Calvet kept his traitorous status for perpetuity.

A little further up rue Bonsecours at 440 is the **Maison Papineau ❾**, an 18th-century wooden building whose facade was painted to look like limestone. Louis-Joseph Papineau, the leader of the 1837 rebellion in Lower Canada, was born in this house, and six generations of the family, including many distinguished politicians and businessmen, have occupied it.

Maison Papineau was also the residence chosen by Eric McLean of the Viger Commission to begin the renewal of Old Montréal. When workers began to restore Maison Papineau, they eliminated two brick storeys, replaced all the windows and stripped the walls of 19 layers of wallpaper.

Stylish market

Back on rue St-Paul, the **Marché Bonsecours** ❿ (Bonsecours Market; 350 rue St-Paul Est; open late June–Aug daily 10am–9pm; Sept–May Sat–Wed 10am–6pm, Thur–Fri 10am–9pm; free; tel: 514-872 7730) was once the most photographed edifice in Montréal. It has attractive facades, especially on the river side, and a Renaissance-style dome (dating from 1864) that was the first to be erected in the city. Remember that Montréal was, and still is, a port. Ships moving down the St Lawrence from Québec would have spotted the dome and Notre-Dame church before anything else. For a sailor, riding an autumn storm and fatigued from months at sea, these markers became emblems of security and shelter.

The Marché was primarily a market and exhibition centre. The vagaries of history, however, forced it to function briefly as both house of parliament (1849) and, between 1852 and 1878, as city hall. From the mid-1960s it served as offices for civil servants, but in May 1996, it reopened as a gallery of high-quality boutiques, many of them showcasing the work of local and regional artists, craftspeople and designers. It also has a couple of ground-floor restaurants specializing in Italian and Québec cuisine.

The south doors of the Marché open on to **rue de la Commune**, a wide, sweeping arc of a street that follows the waterfront. In the days of sail and steam, when the port was alive with ships of all sorts, this was

Map on page 78

The facade of the Marché. Home to the headquarters of the Conseil des métiers d'art du Québec and the city's Institute of Design. Local designers and artists also have shops here.

BELOW: winter at Marché Bonsecours.

Busy rue de la Commune is the place to hire bicycles, skates and Segways that can be used to explore the Old Port.

a bustling thoroughfare full of carriages and transport wagons. A few of the old warehouses have been converted into hotels, and the ground floors of many of the others are now restaurants, cafés and ice-cream parlours, which in summertime set out tables on the broad sidewalk. Cars, taxis, tour buses and horse-drawn carriages move slowly along the cobbled street.

Vieux-Port

The main cause of all this modern activity along rue de la Commune is the enormous popularity of the **Vieux-Port** ⓫ (Old Port), with both Montréalers and visitors. This 2-km (1¼-mile) stretch of waterfront is the city's main outlet on the river. Visitors can sign up for harbour cruises (with or without dinner), catch a ferry to the South Shore and the islands of Notre-Dame and Ste-Hélène or take a heart-stopping (but safe) cruise on high-powered jet boats through the treacherous Lachine Rapids.

On shore, walkers, cyclists, skateboarders, in-line skaters and whole families riding contraptions that look like pedal-driven cars happily share the broad walkway that runs the length of the port. At the western end of the port, this walkway melds seamlessly into the city's most popular bike trail, a 10-km (6-mile) stretch that follows the Lachine Canal *(see page 87)* to the historic waterfront district of Lachine.

At the quays

There's not much cargo activity at the port these days, but cruise ships still tie up at the quai Alexandra, as does the occasional visiting tall ship or naval vessel. Other quais, or piers, are devoted to more recreational activities: flea markets, concerts, art exhibits, military parades, flower shows, dances and festivals during the summer; skating parties, cross-country skiing, and sleigh rides in winter.

Every two years, the **Cirque du Soleil**, the world-renowned circus of acrobats, clowns and dancers that was founded in Montréal, pitches its blue and yellow striped tents on the grounds of the Vieux-Port for a

BELOW: Vieux-Port.

summer-long run that is usually sold out before the last tent-peg is driven.

On the quai King-Edward is the **Centre iSci** ⓬ (open daily 10am–6pm; admission charge; tel: 514-496 4724, or 1-877-496 4724 toll free), Montréal's interactive science centre. Three exhibition halls cover the history of science: Life, Matter and Information. There are also two IMAX theatres and several dining areas, including one on the St Lawrence. If you're visiting chiefly to sample the **IMAX** theatre (tel: 514-496 4629, or 1-800 349 4629 toll free; www.imaxoldport.com), take note that most of the films are in French. An English-language version usually plays three times daily.

The quai de l'Horloge (Clock Pier), is home to the **Labyrinthe du Hangar** ⓭ (open mid-June–Aug daily 11am–9pm; mid-May–mid-June and Sept Sat–Sun and holidays 11.30am–5.30pm; admission charge; tel: 514-499 0099), a 2-km (1¼-mile) maze of obstacle-filled foggy corridors. At the end of quai de l'Horloge is the **Tour de l'Horloge** (Clock Tower), which was built in 1922 to commemorate the merchant mariners who died during World War I. The climb of 192 steps to the observatory is rewarded with a fine view of the city and river.

Montréal's birthplace

Toward the western end of the Vieux-Port, just off rue de la Commune are **place Royale** and **place d'Youville**, two squares that mark the origins of the city. The squares intersect each other at the site of Pointe-à-Callière, where Samuel de Champlain landed in 1611 and declared the spot a "place royale".

Thirty years later, Paul de Chomedy, Sieur de Maisonneuve chose that same site to erect the fort that became **Ville Marie**. An obelisk at the eastern end of place d'Youville commemorates the event. The inscription emphasizes that Maisonneuve ordered the simultaneous construction of a fort, a chapel and a graveyard.

It is difficult to imagine how Ville Marie looked nearly 400 years ago. Landfill has pushed the shoreline back several hundred metres and the

Map on page 78

The city is home to several circus schools including Cirque du Soleil (pictured), which has its headquarters at Vieux-Port, and L'École Nationale de Cirque and Cirque Éloize.

LEFT: there's lots to entertain children at Centre iSci.

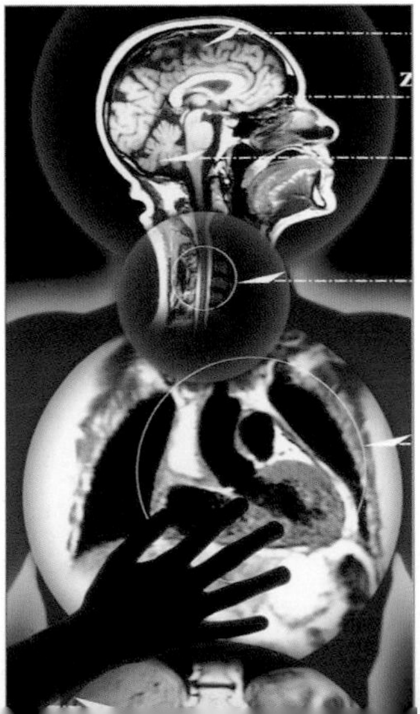

The Lachine Canal

The Lachine canal runs for 14.5 km (9 mile) from the Vieux-Port, to Lachine on Lac St-Louis. A National Historic Site operated by Parks Canada (tel : 514-283 6054; www.pc.gc.ca/canallachine), it was constructed in the 1820s and later enlarged to allow cargo vessels heading for the Great Lakes to circumvent the Lachine Rapids. By the mid-19th century the canal had helped to launch Canada's industrial revolution, but after the construction of the St Lawrence Seaway in 1959 the Lachine Canal stood unused.

It finally reopened to leisure boat traffic in 2002. Today the old factories and warehouses have been transformed into loft apartments and trendy bars and restaurants.

The towpath and the surrounding area is a city park, and the canal can be explored by boat (tours, tel: 514-846 0428), by bike (allow at least half a day to cover its entire length) or on foot. Worth a visit are a couple of small museums, a sculpture garden and the house where jazz great Oscar Peterson was born (3007 rue Delisle at the Union United Church). From the Vieux-Port head west to the Lachine Lock, or stop by the Visitor Centre at 500 chemin des Iroquois.

Rivière St-Pierre, a small stream that ran beside the fort, is now underground. The dense forest that made reaching Mont Royal an arduous journey is today a forest of skyscrapers, the walk made tricky by rush-hour traffic.

Pointe-à-Callière ⓮ remains the birthplace of Montréal, and the surrounding streets form its oldest neighbourhood. A plaque in place Royale calls the site the "first public square of Montréal", affixing the date 1657 to its creation.

As part of the city's 350th anniversary celebrations in 1992, the **Musée d'Archéologie et d'Histoire de la Pointe-à-Callière** (Museum of Archaeology and History; 350 place Royale; open July–Aug Mon–Fri 10am–6pm; Sept–June Tues–Fri 10am–5pm; admission charge; tel: 514-872 9150) was opened on the site where Montréal was founded in 1642. A multimedia display in the modern Eperon building presents the city's early history. The museum itself is built over a major archaeological excavation that reaches down to the roots of Montréal's earliest beginnings. Visitors descend in semidarkness through several layers of history, past 17th- and 18th-century stone foundations and the crumbled remains of wooden palisades to the banks of what's left of the Rivière St-Pierre and the site of the city's first cemetery.

The museum is linked by underground tunnel to the Old Customs House, a neoclassical greystone building that houses the museum's excellent book and gift shop. Outside at the southern end of place Royale is a statue of John Young (1811–79), the harbour commissioner credited with making the city a world-class port. Young's gaze still encompasses rue de la Commune and the eastern docking facilities.

Award winning jazz pianist, Oscar Peterson, was born and raised in the neighbourhood of St-Antoine, near Vieux-Port, in 1925. The son of a Canadian Pacific Railway porter, Peterson began playing the trumpet at around 5 years old and later learned to play the piano. He dominated the jazz scene for decades.

Place d'Youville

Vieux-Montréal's longest square, **place d'Youville**, is a long, narrow strip of grass that runs west for four blocks from the foot of Young's statue to rue McGill. Its main attraction is the **Centre d'Histoire de Montréal** ⓯ (Montréal History Centre; 335 place d'Youville; open

BELOW: colonial architecture near the old port.

The First Community

In a sense the "community" of Montréal dates from 1657. Before that date Ville Marie was a wildly remote fort inhabited by a singular group of people: adventurers, traders, missionaries, soldiers and their officers. These pioneers certainly had a stake in the colony, but they were not likely to produce citizens – that required settlers, ordinary people who would be devoted to establishing a life for themselves and their children. Communities are the sum of citizens, not conquistadors.

In European society the traditional symbol of a town was a public square. So, too, was this the case in Montréal.

May–Aug Tues–Sun 10am–5pm; Sept–Apr Wed–Sun 10am–5pm; admission charge; tel: 514-872 3207), formerly a stylish 1915 firehouse. The centre's exhibits focus on the city's multiculturalism and the lives of ordinary Montréalers. It also has a permanent exhibit on the role jazz has played in the city's cultural development.

Place d'Youville was once the site of the parliament for both Upper and Lower Canada. The market building here, erected after the 1837 rebellion, lasted only a dozen years before rioters, protesting against an unpopular British bill, burned it down *(see page 28)*.

Rue St-Pierre

Just south of place d'Youville on rue St-Pierre, the tall, stone, carefully preserved ruins of the **Hôpital Général des Soeurs Grises** serve as a monument to the square's namesake, Marguerite d'Youville, the founder of the Sisters of Charity and Canada's first native-born saint.

D'Youville, the widow of an unscrupulous whisky trader, took over the 17th-century hospital in 1747 and used it to shelter the sick and the homeless. She recruited a group of like-minded young women to help her, and they eventually evolved into an order officially known as the *Soeurs de la Charité* ("Sisters of Charity"). But because of the lifestyle of Marguerite's late husband and the state of many of the nuns' charges, the order was more popularly known as the *Soeurs Grises* ("Grey Nuns") – "grise" being 18th-century slang for "tipsy".

The nuns took the nickname in good spirit and adopted a uniform of grey habits. The hospital burned down in 1871, and the sisters moved to their present site on boulevard René-Lévesque, but the walls of the original hospital's west wing and the chapel still stand.

Beside the ruins is the tiny **Maison de Mère d'Youville** (138 rue St-Pierre; open by appointment only; tel: 514-842 9411), which houses an exhibit on the life of St Marguerite.

The lower part of rue St-Pierre, just south of the hospital ruins, is a heartening example of successful urban renewal. Empty for some time, the block now houses luxury apartments, law offices, architectural firms, even a fancy cheese and chocolate shop. It's also the location of the **Musée Marc-Aurèle Fortin** (118 rue St-Pierre; open Tues–Sun 11am–5pm; admission charge; tel: 514-845 6108), a small gallery dedicated entirely to the works of one of Canada's most eccentric landscape artists. Fortin (1888–1970) delighted in painting wildly colourful renditions of the Québec countryside full of higgledy-piggledy houses and unlikely trees.

Place d'Armes

A hundred metres (110 yards) north of place d'Youville and just a little to the east is **place d'Armes** ⓰, the last major historic square in the old city.

Map on page 78

From firehouse to historical archive, the Centre d'Histoire de Montréal.

BELOW: city of love.

The statue of Paul de Chomedy, Sieur de Maisonneuve, stands proud in place d'Armes.

De Maisonneuve moved the centre of the settlement to this location to escape the dangers of the capricious St Lawrence. It also marks the spot where de Maisonneuve slew an Iroquois chief in hand-to-hand combat in 1644. So it's altogether fitting that de Maisonneuve's statue should dominate the square.

In his right hand is the banner of France and at his feet are limestone representations of his fellow pioneers, including Jeanne Mance, Louis Hébert and Lambert Closse. At his back is the magnificent grey hulk and soaring bell towers of the Basilique Notre-Dame-de-Montréal, which would have pleased his devoutly Catholic heart. But de Maisonneuve would have found the rest of his surroundings disconcerting. To his left is the modern tower of the Banque Canadienne Nationale; to his left are two early 20th-century skyscrapers built by Scottish and American insurance companies, and in front of him is the neoclassical Bank of Montréal, which, with its dome and Corinthian columns, looks for all the world like a pagan temple.

Old Montréal by calèche

Parked along the southern rim of the square – come rain, shine or snow – is Montréal's venerable fleet of *calèches*, or horse-drawn carriages. They are hard to miss. If the sound of wooden wheels rattling over cobblestones doesn't prick up the ears, the bellow of the drivers certainly will. "*Un calèche, Monsieur?*" they will shout across place d'Armes. Or, sizing up a tourist, "Ride through Old Montréal for you, Sir?"

In high season the competition is fierce and drivers fan out across the square like angry bees. In winter the men sit stoically inside their vehicles, watching their breath dissipate in the frigid air. Under these circumstances, the invitation to visitors is more matter-of-fact, less convincing.

Touring Old Montréal in a carriage can be delightful. Try it during the winter, with a bear skin protecting the lower body and, ideally, a flask of something warm tucked inside the pocket. During the busy months it is often best to wait until evening to hire a carriage. Then the streets are full of moving shadows;

BELOW: a *calèche* ride around the old town.

shafts of light seep between drawn curtains, and water trapped between cobblestones glistens under the yellow street lamps. Use a ride to experience the atmosphere of Old Montréal at different times of the day and year, but don't hire one for sightseeing. Always do that on foot.

Place d'Armes is also home to the ubiquitous tour buses dropping visitors off for cursory tours of Notre-Dame and its environs. The traveller aboard one of these buses who aspires to jump ship couldn't choose a better place to do it than the square, a launching point for just about all the most interesting areas of Old Montréal. Mutinies of this kind are to be encouraged.

Notre-Dame Basilica

The **Basilique Notre-Dame** ⓱ (110 rue Notre-Dame Ouest; open daily 8am–5pm; admission charge; tel: 514-842 2925) is quite simply Montréal's most famous church, and justly so. Luciano Pavorotti has used it as a backdrop for a Christmas concert and in 2005, French actor Gérard Depardieu roamed its aisles, reciting the works of St Augustine to a silent capacity crowd. The church was also the setting for pop diva Céline Dion's wedding in 1994 and the funeral of hockey great, Maurice "Rocket" Richard, in 2000.

The first chapel, built within the fort in 1642, was covered with bark. The current structure (1829) is a little more grand. The building itself, a triumph of neo-Gothic architecture, is the work of architect James O'Donnell, a Protestant from New York who was so taken with his work and the way he was treated by the Sulpician priests who commissioned him that he converted to Catholicism and is now buried in the basilica's crypt.

What O'Donnell produced for his clerical clients was a parish church that would dwarf many of the world's cathedrals. More than 3,000 worshippers can fit comfortably under its great vaulted ceiling, and, thanks to the way O'Donnell used the natural slope of the land to incline the floor, even those at the back of the nave have a good view of the main altar. The church opened

Map on page 78

Local craftsmen produced detailed carvings of prophets that adorn the basilica.

BELOW: exterior and interior views of the landmark Basilique Notre-Dame.

TIP

Always bargain when hiring a *calèche*. The first rate quoted for a tour isn't always the best deal, especially off-season.

in 1829, but the interior was completely reworked in 1870 by Victor Bourgeau, who was inspired by the colour scheme of the 12th-century Sainte Chapelle de Paris commissioned by King Louis IX. The result is almost overwhelming.

The vast vaulted ceiling is a deep azure blue, studded with thousands of 24-carat gold stars, The reredos behind the main altar is as tall as a three-storey building and displays four larger-than-life tableaux depicting the history of sacrifice in the Old Testament. The pulpit, with its intricate curving staircase, is a monumental work of art in itself, with life-sized carvings of the prophets Jeremiah and Ezekiel at its foot. Bourgeau used local artists and woodworkers to produce his masterpiece, and the church is thus a monument to 19th-century Québec craftsmanship.

The Marriage Chapel

Behind the main altar is the **Chapelle Notre-Dame-du-Sacré-Coeur** (Our Lady of the Sacred Heart), often simply referred to as the "Marriage Chapel". In fact, so many thousands of Montréal couples celebrate their wedding in this church-sized chapel that it's often necessary to book two years ahead to get a space. It's rumoured that some would-be brides hang on to their reservations even if they're jilted or break off their engagements on the off chance they'll find someone else before their date comes up.

The chapel's interior is an interesting mix of the old and the modern. A 1978 fire seriously damaged the neo-Gothic original, and instead of trying to recreate it exactly, the Sulpicians used local cabinetmakers and sculptors to restore the nave to its ornate glory and then commissioned Québec artist Charles Daudelin to create something contemporary for the sanctuary. The result, a 70-tonne bronze depicting the stages of human life, soars 16 metres (52 ft) above a plexiglass altar. It's not to everyone's taste, but it certainly gets your attention.

The basilica's sense of the monumental is also reflected in the church's 69-metre (227-ft) twin

BELOW: a pit stop to rest after sightseeing.

A State Funeral

The grand Basilique Notre-Dame is the closest thing the city of Montréal has to a state church, and anyone of note, from former prime ministers to hockey greats, have had their final rites celebrated within its walls. During former Prime Minister Pierre Elliott Trudeau's funeral in 2000, Cuban dictator Fidel Castro shared the front east pew with fellow honourary pallbearer, former US president Jimmy Carter. Canadian Mounties in striking red uniform jackets carried Trudeau's casket into the basilica for the ceremony.

Four months earlier a state funeral was held here for Maurice "Rocket" Richard, local hero and hockey great.

towers. They were completed in the 1840s by John Ostell, who succeeded as architect after O'Donnell's death.

The west tower houses a 12-tonne bell – the Gros Bourdon – that took a dozen men to ring. Even today, powered by electricity, the bell is rung sparingly, usually when a famous Québecer has died.

For music lovers

Not surprisingly, given the size of the church, the basilica's organ is one of the biggest on the continent. Built by Canada's premier organ builders, the Cassavant brothers of St-Hyacinthe, Québec, its 7,000 pipes fill the whole back wall of the church. Music-lovers might like to try to attend the 11am solemn Mass held at the church on Sundays to hear the organ accompany the basilica's professional choir in the great classics of liturgical music; those who just want to experience the instrument's full power can show up for the end of the Mass and feel the floor shake during the organ's solo recessional.

Priestly training

Just to the west of the basilica is one of Montréal's oldest buildings – the **Vieux Séminaire de St-Sulpice** ⓲ (116 rue Notre-Dame Ouest; not open to the public). It was built in 1680 to house the Société de St Sulpice and to serve as a centre for training priests for Montréal and New France. The Société is an association of diocesan priests founded in France in the early 17th century primarily with an eye to improving priestly formation.

Its members, usually called simply Sulpicians, matched the Jesuits for intellectual rigour and religious fervour. In 1663 the Société took over missionary duties in Montréal from the Société de Notre-Dame, becoming, in effect, the landlords of all the island of Montréal. Their seigneurial reign survived the British conquest of 1760, and well into the 19th century the Sulpicians would often appeal their disputes with local authorities and even with other clerics directly to the Colonial Office in London. Today, their numbers and their influence are much decreased,

Map on page 78

The seminary clock was installed in 1701 and is considered the first public clock in Canada. Though the works were replaced by electronic movements in 1966, it still functions only periodically. Setting one's watch by it would be unwise.

BELOW: Vieux Séminaire de St-Sulpice.

The Corinthian columns of the Bank of Montréal.

but they still run the Grand Séminaire de Montréal on rue Sherbrooke Ouest, and they still train priests in many other dioceses in North and South America.

Top theatre

If Notre-Dame is the most triumphant symbol of Montréal's religious heritage, the other buildings on place d'Armes and around the basilica emphasize the city's commercial history and the values of the largely Scots and English financiers and merchants who supplanted the French priests and administrators as the movers and shakers of Montréal. In the shadow of Notre-Dame's west wall, for example, is a 1903 beaux-arts building that used to house the city's stock market, an activity that would not have pleased de Maisonneuve or those first Sulpicians. Its purpose today is hardly much better; it is home to the **Centaur Theatre Company** (453 rue St-François-Xavier; tel: 514-288 3161), Montréal's principal English-language theatre, and one of the top theatre companies in Québec.

BELOW: catch a show at the Centaur Theatre.

Bank of Montréal

Back on place d'Armes, the contrast between Notre-Dame and its commercial surroundings is even more striking. On the east side of the square is the **Aldred Building**, which looks a little like a precursor for the Empire State Building. Opened in 1931, it was Montréal's first skyscraper at 916 metres (316 ft). The nine-storey redstone building next to it was built in 1888 by a New York insurance company, but the square's most elaborate monument to Mammon is the **Banque de Montréal** ⓳ (Bank of Montréal), on the north side of place d'Armes.

The neoclassical design of this 1847 structure offers an ornate facade that has six Corinthian columns with pediment sculptures – discernible only through lenses of some sort – of a sailor, a colonialist, and two Aboriginal Canadians, one a "noble savage" and the other a recalcitrant hell-bent on rejecting civilization. The facade was designed by local architect John Wells.

The interior of the bank is stunning. The lobby is spacious, the colours gentle and the light soft at all times of day. The atrium in particular, linking the older part of the building with a 1905 addition, is lovely, lined by eight Ionic columns of Vermont granite with marble bases. The walls of the atrium are made of pink marble from Tennessee. In the majestic front hall are another 32 columns, also of granite, and counters of marble. Gold leaf covers everything and elaborate chandeliers hang from the ceiling.

The interior takes its grace from both the simplicity of the design and the continuous presence of natural light streaming down from massive windows. The bank's architects worked directly from models of Italian churches: it is hard not to remark upon the "basilica" style of the structure. A provocative gesture? Artistic inspiration? Also worth a look is a fine sculpture, *Patria*, in the atrium. The marble statue is a memorial to Canadians who died in World War I.

The Bank of Montréal has a small **museum** (119 rue St-Jacques; open Mon–Fri 10am–4pm; free; tel: 514-877 6810) off the main lobby, devoted to numismatics – money. Displays of banknotes, coins, a collection of elaborate 19th-century piggy banks and other memorabilia are to be found here. Tours are available in both official languages.

The Wall Street of Canada

In both tone and proportion the Bank of Montréal headquarters sent out a message: on **rue St-Jacques**, the street crossing the north end of the square, business would be calm, orderly and efficient. The result was the "Wall Street of Canada", an appellation applied to "St James Street" as it was called by anglophone Montréalers. Until the late 1970s, rue St-Jacques was Canada's financial centre, a street of busy Victorian buildings swathed to varying degrees in stucco, wrought-iron, columns and elaborate porticos. A trolley down the middle of the road serviced office workers.

Among the many stately edifices here are the Bank of Commerce and, across the street, the Molson Bank building at 288 St-Jacques, which was constructed in 1866 using brewery profits. The bank itself no longer exists but the building that still bears its name, like all the offices at the corner of St-Jacques and rue St-Pierre, is impressive. None, however, quite stacks up to the **Banque Royale** ⓴ (Royal Bank), constructed in 1928. Like it or not – and many Montréalers consider the building an exercise in ostentation – the former head office of the Royal Bank at 360 rue St-Jacques is an essential stop on any tour of the business district.

The exterior is grand but austere, even sober. Not so the interior. The architects who designed the building were said to have had in mind the Medici Palace in Florence, Italy – a grandiose ambition indeed. The main doors are framed in bronze replicas of coins and lead into a lobby noted

Map on page 78

The Banque Royale was for a brief period the tallest structure not only in Canada but the entire British Empire.

BELOW: the ostentatious entrance of the Banque Royale.

Map on page 78

Queen Victoria watches over place Victoria.

for its coffered ceiling and the marble steps that ascend to the main hall. Arches are covered with reddish limestone and walls are decorated with the coats of arms of Canada's provinces. Again, the ceiling is ornately coffered. There are marble walls, bronze screens, and the mosaic tiles on the floor are inlaid with Canada's royal coat of arms.

Right across from the Royal Bank is the **Centre de Commerce Mondial** (World Trade Centre; 747 place Victoria; open daily 7am–7pm; tel: 514-982 9888), a triumph of modern restoration. Developers restored the crumbling 19th- and early 20th-century buildings on rue St-Jacques and rue St-Antoine to the south and converted the shabby little lane between them into a soaring glass atrium with a fountain, trendy cafés and boutiques.

The large modern Hôtel Inter-Continental is part of the Trade Centre complex, but far more interesting is the Nordheimer Building, a 19th-century Celtic fantasy that houses an historic theatre where Sarah Bernhardt once performed.

BELOW: the Palais des Congrès convention centre.

Place Victoria

In the 1880s many commercial businesses followed the fashion and moved their offices further west to **Place Victoria** ㉑ at rue St-Jacques and rue McGill. The square was for a brief period a prestigious residential address and one of Montréal's prime shopping districts. Barely 20 years later, however, department stores, lured by the rapidly growing English community along rue Sherbrooke, moved again to rue Ste-Catherine and the whole district faded quickly.

Place Victoria itself was reduced to a tiny patch of green in a concrete sea and its bronze statue of the Queen-Empress was left to the mercies of Montréal's pigeon population. But the opening of the World Trade Centre in 1992 and the expansion of the **Palais des Congrès** convention centre a decade later brought new life to the square. The old queen now reigns over a two-block-long oasis of grass and trees ringed by some of the finest 19th century buildings in the country.

Vieux-Montréal's future as a centre of commerce, tourism, culture and entertainment is assured. Clever entrepreneurs and creative artists will continue to find new uses for old buildings and unlikely spaces. But the district's relationship to the rest of the city has changed dramatically as well. Until the 1990s it was isolated from downtown and even nearby Chinatown by a stretch of rundown buildings, and by the trench created by the Ville-Marie Expressway.

The convention centre bridges the expressway and gleaming financial buildings on rues St-Antoine and McGill have brought downtown to the old city. Although the end of that isolation gives all Montréalers and visitors easier and safer access to one of the city's most fascinating districts, it also poses challenges to those who want to preserve Vieux-Montréal's historic integrity without threatening its economic vitality. ❑

RESTAURANTS, BARS & CAFÉS

Restaurants

Aix Cuisine du Terroir
711 Côte de la place d'Armes (at rue St-Jacques). Tel: 514-904 1201. L & D daily. $$$$
Lamb from Rimouski, veal from the Charlevoix and seafood from the Iles-de-la-Madeleine make the slick and opulent dining room of the Hotel Place d'Armes a showcase for Québec products. Its comfy banquettes also make it perfect for a long and lingering meal. In summer, guests can dine on the rooftop terrace and take in the view.

Aszu
212 rue Notre-Dame Ouest (at rue St-François). Tel: 514-845 5436. L & D Mon–Fri, D only Sat–Sun. $$$.
Food and wine share equal billing in this restaurant in the financial district. The food is simple but luxurious – oysters, scallops, deer, duck, lobster and foie gras – and more than 50 wines are expertly paired with the dishes.

Bonaparte
443 rue St-François-Xavier (at rue St-Sacrament). Tel: 514-844 4368. L & D Mon–Fri, D only Sat. $$$
The service here is impeccable, the food classic French – sole *meunière*, rack of lamb in port sauce, and possibly Montréal's best crème brulée – and the ambiance is elegantly imperial.

Boris Bistro
465 rue McGill (at rue des Récollets). Tel: 514-848 9575. L & D daily. $$
The food year-round is good bistro fare – steak and salad, grilled fish, boudin sausage, and spectacular french fries cooked in duck fat – but it's in summer that Boris Bistro shines. It has created one of the city's best open-air dining spots on a large gravel terrace hidden behind the stone facade of a demolished building.

Casa da Mateo
440 rue St-François-Xavier (at rue St-Sacrament). Tel: 514-844 7448. L & D daily. $$$
Even in January, this brick-walled restaurant exudes the sunny warmth of a Mexican village. The food is authentic, the guacamole is whipped up at your table and the margaritas are made with freshly squeezed juice.

Chez l'Épicier
311 rue St-Paul Est (at rue St-Claude). Tel: 514-878 2232. L & D Mon–Fri, D only Sat–Sun. $$$
The name means "The Grocer's", and there are, in fact, shelves you can browse for gourmet foods if you want to prepare your own meal. Chef Laurent Godbout specializes in comfort food with a twist – shepherds' pie made with snails, for example – and homemade ice cream.

Chez Queux
158 rue St-Paul Est (at place Jacques-Cartier). Tel: 514-866 5194. L & D Tues–Fri, D only Sat–Sun. $$$
The location right at the foot of place Jacques-Cartier puts Chez Queux in the middle of the action, but the restaurant itself, housed in a mid-19th century building, is a peaceful haven that serves good French food at reasonable prices.

Club Chasse et Peche
423 rue St-Claude (at rue St-Paul). Tel: 514-861 1112. L & D Tues–Fri, D only Sat. $$$$
Despite the name, the dark-red leather chairs and the very masculine décor, this restaurant has nothing to do with hunting and fishing. It is, rather, the home base of Claude Pelletier, one of the city's most exciting young chefs. Try his roasted scallops with

PRICE CATEGORIES

Prices for a three-course dinner per person with a half-bottle of house wine:
$ = under $25
$$ = $25–50
$$$ = $50–70
$$$$ = more than $70

RIGHT: good bistro fare in Montréal.

puréed Jerusalem artichoke.

Da Emma
777 rue de la Commune Ouest (near rue King). Tel: 514-392 1568. L & D Mon–Fri, D only Sat. $$$
The cellar of Montréal's first women's prison hardly sounds like an enticing place to eat, but the stone walls, beams and warm atmosphere of this family restaurant make a perfect setting for hearty Roman cooking that leans toward meat and pastas. If it's on the menu, try Emma's succulent tripe a la romaine.

Les Filles du Roy
405 rue Bonsecours (at rue St-Paul). Tel: 514-282 1725. B, L & D Mon–Fri, D only Sat–Sun. $$$$
Pine tables, wicker chairs (woven by Québec First Nations tribes) and, in winter, a blazing fire in a fireplace the size of a small shed make the perfect setting for a menu that specializes in the food of New France. Try the smoked pig knuckles or the Lac St-Jean *tourtière* (meat pie flavoured with cloves).

Gandhi
230 rue St-Paul Ouest (at rue St-Nicolas). Tel: 514-845 5866. L & D Mon–Fri, D only Sat. $$
Vieux-Montréal's only South Asian restaurant is also the city's most elegant, with its buttery yellow walls and crisp linen table cloths. The food is equally refined.

La Gargotte
351 place d'Youville (at rue St-Pierre) Tel: 514-844 1428. L & D Mon–Fri, D only Sat–Sun. $$
This intimate little French restaurant with its brick walls and casement windows is one of the most romantic dining spots in the old city. In summer, the waiting staff can be seen dashing back and forth across the cobbled street to serve diners who choose to sit in the open-air terrace on place d'Youville.

Gibby's
298 place d'Youville (near rue St-Pierre). Tel: 514-282 1837. L & D daily. $$$$
The setting is authentic Vieux-Montréal – in an 18th-century fur warehouse with stone walls on place d'Youville – but the service and the food is 20th-century North American – huge portions of steak and seafood followed by gargantuan slabs of cheesecake. Gibby's barn-like size makes it a favourite with upscale tour groups.

Holder
407 rue McGill (at rue Le Moyne) Tel: 514-849 0333. L & D Mon–Fri, D only Sat–Sun. $$$
This big breezy Paris-style brasserie is full of chatter and noise, especially around noon when the local legal and business crowd pour in for a lunch of fried calamari or steak et frites. It's quieter in the evening, though, after the regulars who come for happy-hour have gone home.

La Marée
404 place Jacques-Cartier (at rue St-Paul). Tel: 514-861 9794. L & D daily. $$$$
Stiff white linens, high-backed upholstered chairs and hushed efficient service make La Marée one of Montréal's most elegant seafood restaurants. The Florentine lobster with garlic and rosemary is the kind of finicky dish its kitchen does well.

Modavie
1 rue St-Paul Ouest (at boulevard St-Laurent). Tel: 514-287 9582. L & D daily. $$$
There are few more pleasant places to eat lunch than at one of Modavie's window tables overlooking the hubbub on rue St-Paul. In fine weather, the windows are open, making the restaurant appear even more lively. There is live jazz here after 7pm and on Saturday, the cocktail lounge is open until 2am.

Le Pierre du Calvet
405 rue Bonsecours (at rue St-Paul). Tel: 514-282 1725. L & D Mon–Fri, D only Sat–Sun. $$$$
George Washington didn't eat in this dining room, but it is quite possible that Benjamin Franklin did when he visited his republican friend Pierre du Calvet. Stuffed with antique furniture, the room still has an 18th-century air, and the food is sumptuously French.

Les Remparts
93 rue de la Commune Est (at rue St-Gabriel). Tel: 514-382 1649. L & D Mon–Fri, D only Sat–Sun. $$$$
This quiet, cozy restaurant is housed in the very foundations of the old city, with stone walls that date to the early 18th century. The food, however, is up to date with such specialities as striped bass with a sweet-potato gratin or Gaspé char with wild rice.

Pub St-Paul
124 rue St-Paul (near place Jacques-Cartier). Tel: 514-874 0485. L & D Daily. $$
This brash, noisy pub has a wonderful setting in a stone-walled room near Montréal's waterfront. It specializes in honest, unpretentious grub such as juicy burgers and steak et frites and has several good local beers on tap.

Café Stash
200 rue St-Paul Ouest (at rue St-François-Xavier). Tel: 514-845 1611. L & D daily. $$
The city's oldest Polish restaurant is housed in a beautiful stone-walled dining room in the heart of the old city. Diners sit on pews rescued from a demolished church and dine on such Slavic specialities as *borscht*, *pierogi*, cabbage rolls and potato pancakes.

The crispy-skinned roast duck is a delight, try it if it's on the menu.

Titanic
445 rue St-Pierre (at rue du St-Sacrament). Tel: 514-849 0894. L Mon–Fri. $
Office workers, lawyers and stockbrokers crowd into this subterranean, rather than submarine, little dining room for salads and generously stuffed sandwiches. Try the eggplant salad or cheddar cheese and pickles on a crusty baguette.

Toqué!
900 place Jean-Paul-Riopelle (at rue St-Antoine). Tel: 514-499 2084. L & D Tues–Sat. $$$$
Chef Normand Laprise, one of the city's most revered chefs, opened the first Toqué! restaurant in a funky little storefront in Plateau Mont-Royal. The current version, in a glass and steel office tower in the financial district, has a far more corporate air, with velvet drapes and stiff napery. The food remains just as daring, however, with a constantly changing menu.

Verses
100 rue St-Paul Ouest (at rue St-Sulpice). Tel: 514-788 4000. L & D daily. $$$$
This restaurant inside Hôtel Nelligan, which is considered by many people to be Montréal's most romantic hotel. So it's no surprise that the restaurant, also has a very romantic atmosphere. The dining room is a long, stone-walled space with big plush booths and candles on the tables. The food here is no-nonsense and very good. Recommendations include the rack of venison or the lamb *osso buco*.

Vieux-Port
39 rue St-Paul Est (near boulevard St-Laurent). Tel: 514-866 3175. L & D daily. $$
Generous portions of steak and seafood accompanied by some of the city's best french fries make this restaurant very popular with the local lunch crowd. The restaurant is a little more genteel in the evening, with candlelight flickering off the old stone walls.

Le Vieux Saint-Gabriel
426 rue St-Gabriel (near rue St-Paul) Tel: 514-878 3561. L & D daily, Br Sun. $$$
The food is solid French and Italian fare, but tourists and local people come here for the 18th-century ambiance. The building dates to 1754, when it was, in fact, an inn, and its several rooms are decorated with antiques and artefacts of the period. The restaurant is a favourite wedding reception venue.

Bars & Cafés

Les Deux Pierrots
104 rue St-Paul Est (near rue St-Vincent). Tel: 514-861 1270.
Patrons are expected to join enthusiastically in the singing of Québec folk songs in this authentic *"boîte à chanson"*.

Atrium Lounge at **Hôtel Nelligan**
110 rue St-Paul Ouest (at rue St-Sulpice). Tel: 514-788 2040.
No better place for a digestive or an after-show drink than the Atrium Lounge. Grab a table by the windows overlooking lively rue St-Paul, or try the rooftop Sky Bar.

Wunderbar at **Hôtel W**
901 place Victoria (at rue St-Antoine) Tel: 514-395 3195.
The chic Hôtel W's sleek second-storey bar has one of the liveliest "cinq-à-sept" (happy-hour) scenes in the city. DJs take over and provide entertainment later in the evening.

Ben's Delicatessen
990 boulevard de Maisonneuve Ouest.
Tel: 514-844 1000.
B & L daily.
Late-night deli spot that has been a local favourite for many years; Pierre Trudeau was rumoured to be a regular customer.

PRICE CATEGORIES

Prices for a three-course dinner per person with a half-bottle of house wine:
$ = under $25
$$ = $25–50
$$$ = $50–70
$$$$ = more than $70

RIGHT: a funky little restaurant sign.

Montreal's Eclectic Architecture

ABOVE: atop the Cathedral of Mary Queen of the World on boulevard René-Lévesque, the marching tableau of saints is similar to that on St Peter's Basilica in Rome – there's no mistaking the hand of the city's considerable number of Italian immigrants.

The city's architecture is a blend of all that the French, British and other Europeans brought with them – aspirations, memories and longings

Montréal's French founders didn't come from Paris, but from Brittany and Normandy. They were seafaring men and pious women whose longing for status and recognition is sometimes sharply evident. Echoes of Parisian style can clearly be seen in such Second Empire constructions as the old Hôtel de Ville (City Hall) in the Old Port, with its slim columns and pitched roof, in the Maison du Calvet hotel's high chimneys, and on the streets of townhouses on the Plateau (around place St-Louis, for example), often incorporating fleur-de-lys woodwork.

The British influence is clearest along the Golden Mile (rue Sherbrooke), in Westmount's ivy-touched stone buildings and university, and in downtown banks (notably the Bank of Montréal in place d'Armes). It's a look characterised by ruddy sandstones and Scottish crests.

Revival periods have come and gone in Montréal, leaving stone behemoths around Square Dorchester with grand interiors. A modern hand gripped the city during the 1960s and 1970s, leaving few interesting marks – but the World Trade Centre project is one exception. The architect in charge chose to wall off an entire *ruelle* (alleyway) beneath glass, preserving an urban space.

RIGHT: the simple facade of Notre-Dame-de-Bon-Secours is reminiscent of a rural French chapel.

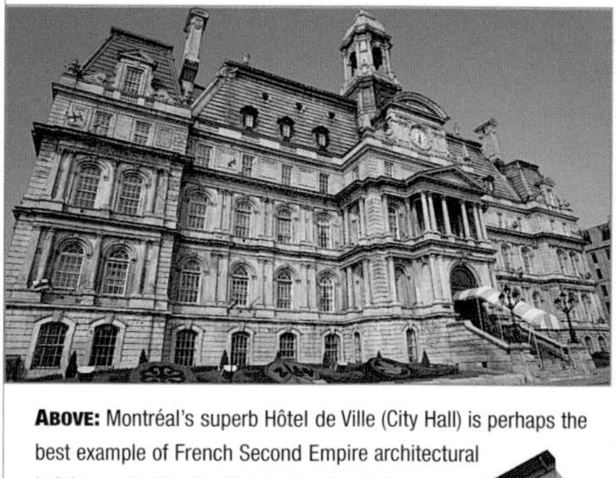

ABOVE: Montréal's superb Hôtel de Ville (City Hall) is perhaps the best example of French Second Empire architectural indulgence in the city. The city landmark is beautiful by day, and is lit up at night.

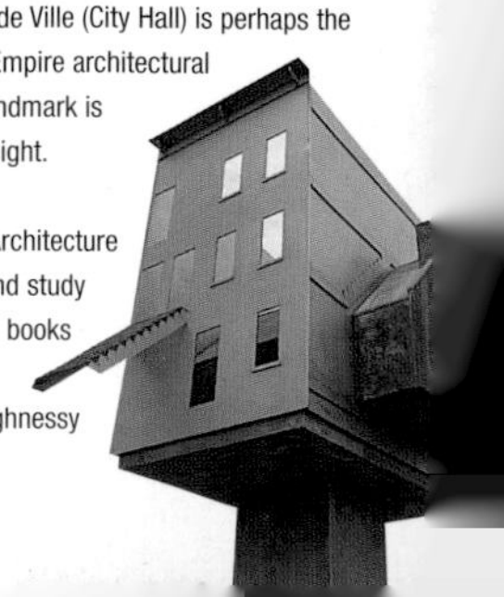

RIGHT: the Canadian Centre for Architecture on rue Baile is both a museum and study centre, with collections of plans, books and models. There are regular tours of the main building, Shaughnessy House, and the gardens.

THE NEED FOR SNOW FENCES

Some of the most notable architectural flourishes that developed in the city of Montréal were not the result of a longing for home, but simple practicality. Montréal's long, snowy winters meant that a considerable weight of snow and ice would accumulate on buildings, threatening leaks or even a disastrous collapse. Steeply pitched roofs were an obvious solution, although the long months of a frigid winter and the heavy snows it brought meant that it was still often necessary for owners to scale wooden ladders and stand precariously on high, shovelling off the snow-pack before it could cause any serious damage to the roof and the building.

Snow fences *(pictured above)* were a way of preventing mishap. A shovel-wielding home owner might easily slip, and if he did, a little iron fence was often the only thing standing between him and an icy street far below.

Even today, on modern structures where they are no longer strictly necessary, the small, delicate fences are still added as a reverent homage to days past; this is most obvious on the business district's steel and glass tower, the so-called "Batman" building.

ABOVE: founded by Champlain in 1611, Québec City is three decades older than Montréal and retains a more distinctly French look in its residential and commercial architecture.

LEFT: the *Palais des Congrès de Montréal* (Convention Centre) was designed in the late 1970s by architect Victor Prus, with the original centre opening in 1983. The distinctive modern facade of tubular steel and multicoloured glass was unveiled in 2002. It connects directly to the Metro and hotels by a series of walkways.

BELOW: the place St-Louis is lined with elegant 19th-century Second Empire style residences. Located in the Quartier Latin neighbourhood, the townhouses are much sought after and it is rumoured that some of the properties that line the square's little park are owned by celebrities.

DOWNTOWN

Montréal's heart is a spectacular architectural combination of sleek glass towers, historic churches and grand townhouses from a bygone age. Here, too, is the university campus, Chinatown and an underground shopper's paradise

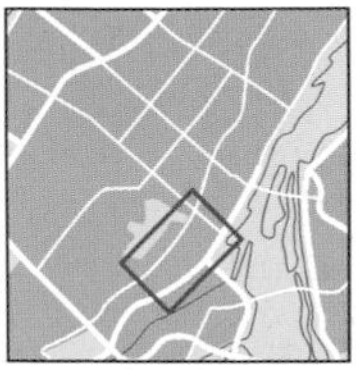

Two hundred years ago, when Montréal was beginning to feel the first stirrings of economic might, the area around what is now Dorchester Square and place du Canada would have been deep in the country and far from the walls of the thriving little metropolis on the St Lawrence River.

Today, those two little patches of green bisected by boulevard René-Lévesque are the acknowledged centre of downtown Montréal. All of the city's major department stores, malls and cinemas are within easy walking distance, as are the tallest office towers and the biggest hotels. The intersection at rues Peel and Ste-Catherine, half a block north of Dorchester Square is arguably the busiest in the city, jammed all day and late into the night with pedestrians and vehicles.

Taking the higher ground

The transformation from bucolic backwater to humming city centre was quite rapid. By the mid-19th century, it was clear that the old city by the river was just too small (and too threatened by recurrent flooding) to contain the ambitions of the fur traders and merchants guiding Montréal's destiny. The wealthiest of them started building big houses on even bigger lots on the high ground along rue Sherbrooke, where the air was cleaner, the grass greener and the views more sweeping.

Commerce followed, and the fate of the lower city was sealed in 1845 when Henry Morgan moved Canada's first department store from rue McGill on the edge of the old city up the hill to rue Ste-Catherine. Other big stores opened nearby and the rush was on. Even the churches got in on the act.

In 1859, the Anglicans built their new cathedral, Christ Church, on

Map on page 104

LEFT: Christ Church Cathedral is dwarfed by the KPMG Tower. **BELOW:** out for a drink on rue Crescent.

Downtown
0 500 m
0 500 yds
N
PARC DU MONT-ROYAL
Grand Chalet (Centre de la Montagne)
Ravenscrag (Allan Memorial Institute)
25
Stade Molson
MILTON-PARC
PARC RUTHER-FORD
ST-ANDRÉ
PARC PERCY-WALTERS
Golden Square Mile
Maison Clarence de Sola
Séminaire de Philosophie Marianopolis
Grande Séminaire (Grand Seminary)
26
Collège de Montréal
Dawson College
Place Alexis-Nihon
Forum de Montréal
Hôpital pour Enfants
Centre Canadien d'Architecture (CCA)
Musée du Centre Marguerite-d'Youville
Maison-mère des Sœurs Grises
Le Faubourg Ste-Catherine
Guy-Concordia
Musée des Beaux-Arts (Museum of Fine Arts)
21
St Andrew and St Paul
23
Erskine and American
22
Château
Holt-Renfrew
Ritz-Carlton
24
Mount Stephen Club
Maison Baxter
Résidence Forget
Ogilvy's
Pavillon des Beaux-Arts
Centre Sheraton
Second Empire Building
Dominion Square Building
2
Square Dorchester
Tour CIBC
1
Pl. du Canada
6
5
St-George
Château Champlain Hotel
Gare Windsor (Windsor Station)
Centre Bell (Bell Centre)
Le 1000 de la Gauchetière (L'Amphithéatre Bell)
Gare Lucien-l'Allier
Lucien-l'Allier
Cours Mont-Royale
7
Peel
Paramount Montréal
8
Place Montréal Trust
9
Sun Life
3
4
Cathédrale Marie-Reine-du-Monde
Bonaventure Hotel
Gare Centrale
Place Bonaventure
Bonaventure
Place Ville-Marie
10
Eaton Mall
Cathédrale Christ Church
11
McGill
Université McGill (McGill University)
18
Redpath Museum of Natural History
19
McCord Museum of Canadian History
20
Royal Victoria College
La Baie
12
Phillips Square
Maison des Coopérants
St James's United
14
Musée d'Art Contemporain
16
Place des Arts
15
Place-des-Arts
Complexe Desjardins
Spectrum de Montréal
Gesù
13
Basilique St-Patrick
Édifice Southam
Édifice Guy-Favreau
Chinese Catholic
17
Ceremonial Gate
QUARTIER CHINOIS (CHINATOWN)
Place-d'Armes
Palais des Congrès
Banque de Montréal
Centre de Commerce Mondial
Square-Victoria
Tour de la Bourse
Palais de Justice
Monument National
Musée Juste pour Rire
Cinéma Parallèle
Pl. Albert-Duquesne
Pl. Ste-Famille
Pl. du Frère-André
Sq. Chaboillez
Sq. Richmond
Georges-Vanier
rue Sherbrooke O.
rue Sherbrooke E.
boul. de Maisonneuve O.
rue Ste-Catherine O.
rue Ste-Catherine E.
boul. René-Lévesque O.
boul. René-Lévesque E.
rue St-Antoine O.
rue St-Jacques
av. Viger O.
av. Viger E.
av. des Pins O.
av. des Pins E.
av. Docteur-Penfield
Ch. de la Côte-des-Neiges
av. Cedar
Atwater
rue Guy
rue Peel
rue St-Dominique
boul. St-Laurent
rue Clark
rue St-Urbain
rue Ste-Famille
rue Jeanne-Mance
av. du Parc
rue Hutchison
rue Durocher
rue Aylmer
rue Milton
rue Prince-Arthur O.
rue Prince-Arthur E.
rue Roy E.
av. Lorne
rue Université
rue McTavish
rue Metcalfe
rue Mansfield
rue Stanley
rue Drummond
rue de la Montagne
rue Crescent
rue Bishop
rue Mackay
rue Simpson
rue Redpath
av. du Musée
Redpath Cr.
rue St-Mathieu
rue St-Marc
rue Tupper
rue Baile
rue Fort
av. Lincoln
av. Chomedey
rue Closse
av. Seymour
rue St-Martin
rue des Seigneurs
rue Coursol
rue Quesnel
rue Vinet
rue Lucien-L'Allier
av. Overdale
av. Argyle
rue Cathcart
rue Cathédrale
rue Gauchetière
rue Belmont
Côte du Beaver Hall
rue Union
rue City Councillors
rue St-Alexandre
rue Président Kennedy
rue St-François-Xavier
rue St-Jacques

rue Ste-Catherine next to Morgan's store and across from jeweller Henry Birks. Not to be outdone, the Roman Catholic bishop, Ignace Bourget, startled his flock by building his cathedral – a quarter-scale replica of Rome's St Peter's Basilica – on land in the heart of Anglo-Protestant commercial Montréal.

As the 20th century began, the old city was on its way to obscurity and neglect and rues Ste-Catherine and Sherbrooke and boulevard Dorchester (now René-Lévesque) were the undisputed centres of commerce, culture and worship. The rich built their mansions on the slopes of Mont-Royal in what became known as the Square Mile (later gilded to the Golden Square Mile, *see page 118*), while lesser merchants and tradespeople built town houses at the bottom of the hill on the sidestreets that ran north–south between Dorchester and Sherbrooke.

The Canadian Pacific Railway built Windsor Station, the eastern terminus of its transcontinental service, a block south of boulevard Dorchester on rue de la Gauchetière, and the Grand Trunk – later Canadian National – built its Central Station a few blocks to the east.

Post-war growth

The trend accelerated after World War II. The opening of the **St Lawrence Seaway** *(see pages 176–7)* in 1957 made the old port of Montréal even less relevant as oceangoing ships moved to modern harbour facilities further east.

One of the city's most dramatic growth spurts came in the 1960s and 1970s during the prolonged reign of Mayor Jean Drapeau. Visionary and autocratic, Drapeau changed the cityscape forever. A lover of all things modern, he agreed to the levelling of many old neighbourhoods, replacing them with gleaming office towers and skyscrapers. Displaced and disgruntled residents fled to the suburbs or to the characterless rows of low-rise apartment buildings in the city's north end.

Going underground

Drapeau's disrespect for the past led to the destruction of many historic buildings, but the mayor also brought the city a world's fair in 1967 and the Summer Olympics in 1976, two events that cemented Montréal's reputation as a party town. His most lasting legacy, however, is probably the Metro, the city's fast, quiet subway system, whose rubber-tyred cars changed the way Montréalers got around, especially in the cold, dark days of winter.

But the Metro is more than a transportation system. Its four lines, 65 stations, and 60 km (37 miles) of track form the backbone of Montréal's **Ville Souterrain** (Underground City), a network of subway lines and brightly lit, shop-filled pedestrian tunnels that in theory, at least, make it possible to live a full and satisfying life in Montréal without once stepping outside.

Map on page 104

The Montréal Metro rolling stock runs on rubber tires, inspired by those used in the Paris Metro in France. The decision to use rubber instead of steel wheels meant that the network had to run entirely underground because at the time of planning, in the 1960s, rubber tyre technology could not cope with the severe winter weather conditions experienced in the city.

BELOW: the Metro is Mayor Drapeau's lasting legacy.

The Corinthian columns of the Sun Life Building. Construction of the 24-storey office block began in 1913 but was not completed until 1931.

Exploring this web can be intimidating and disorienting. However, maps of the 32 km (20 miles) of tunnels that comprise the network's downtown core – the so-called RÉSO – are available at most Metro stations. And if you're staying close to the city centre, chances are your hotel is linked to the network as well.

Dorchester Square

Despite this plethora of subterranean delights, Montréalers have not evolved into a race of moles. There's still plenty to do and see on the surface. So before you get lost in that maze of tunnels, step outside and take a look around.

The downtown core is large, bordered roughly by avenues Atwater and des Pins and boulevards St-Laurent and René-Lévesque *(see page 104)*. For exploring purposes the area can be neatly split in two – the shopper's paradise that has its axis on rue Ste-Catherine, and the museums and stately homes of rue Sherbrooke and the Square Mile.

The best place to start is in the heart of that shopper's paradise, in those two neighbouring patches of green, **Dorchester Square** ❶ and place du Canada. In summer, picnic tables and benches shaded by oaks and maples make the squares a favourite gathering place for the students, office workers, shop clerks and professionals who study and work downtown.

Frequent lunchtime concerts on Dorchester Square add to the appeal, but the two mini parks are more than a green oasis in a concrete desert; they're also a kind of gallery of architecture. The buildings that surround them come in a variety of contrasting styles, from neo-Gothic to austere modern, and from Scots baronial to neoclassical, but somehow they all work together to form a pleasantly unified whole. All, that is, except the ugly little strip of bars and fast-food joints at the northern end of rue Peel that serve to remind you that this is a city, not a theme park.

The ground floor of the delightfully Italianate **Dominion Square Building** ❷ at the north end of this "city green" houses the main tourist bureau, where you can pick up brochures and maps and book-guided bus and walking tours. Incidentally, Dominion Square is what Dorchester Square was called before boulevard Dorchester's name was changed to honour Québec's first separatist premier, René Lévesque.

The most monumental presence on this "city green" is the **Sun Life Building** ❸ (1914), which fills up the whole east side of Dorchester Square and which was, until the 1950s, the largest building in the British Commonwealth. During World War II, its massive Corinthian columns and grey granite walls guarded Britain's gold reserves, which were squirrelled away in the building's vaults. It's worth taking a peek inside to see the rosy marble walls of the main hall and the ranks of brass-doored elevators.

BELOW: relaxing in the shade of oak trees in Dorchester Square.

Queen of the World

Just south of the Sun Life Building across boulevard René-Lévesque is the **Cathédrale Marie-Reine-du-Monde** ❹ (Mary Queen of the World Cathedral; 1085 rue de la Cathédrale at René-Lévesque; open daily 7am–7pm; free; guided tours available June–Sept; tel: 514-866 1661). Not everyone likes Bishop Bourget's doll-size tribute to St Peter's in Rome, and as a quarter-scale model it lacks much of the grandeur and heft of the Renaissance original. Still, it's a graceful building and its dome and rooftop row of stone saints more than hold their own amid the skyscrapers.

The cathedral, which took 20 years to build, was completed in 1884 and quickly became the centre of worship for downtown Catholic residents. Its interior is bright and airy, and the altar canopy – a reproduction of Bernini's Baldacchino in Rome – is the most notable aspect in an otherwise unexceptional design.

The tall, white, vaguely Moorish-looking building at the southern end of place du Canada is the Marriott Château Champlain Hotel. Many locals call it the "cheese grater" because that's what its rising rows of arched windows make it look like.

A forgotten history

The hulking greystone building west of the Champlain Hotel, which looks a little like a Scottish castle as imagined by Sir Walter Scott, is **Windsor Station** (1100 rue de la Gauchetière; open daily 7am–9pm), once the eastern terminus of Canadian Pacific's transcontinental railway.

Designed by New York architect Bruce Price, the building is a celebration of strength and solidity, but, sadly, it is an empty shell. Canadian Pacific left the passenger business in the 1970s, and Windsor became the terminus for the suburban commuter trains. It lost even that shred of dignity in the 1990s, when its tracks and platforms were ripped up to make way for the Bell Centre, home of the Montréal Canadiens ice hockey team.

Now even the commuter trains stop several blocks to the west at the **Gare Lucien-l'Allier**, and Windsor's

Map on page 104

On top of the Cathédrale Marie-Reine-du-Monde stand the statues of the 13 patron saints of each parish that donated them.

BELOW: the Sun Life Building with the Boer War memorial in the foreground.

The Needle Trade

The rag trade's rise to prominence here began long ago – very long ago. It began, really, when the first voyageurs returned to Montréal from the vast inland wilderness of Canada with fur-laden canoes and then shipped the pelts to France. And when the Montréal-based Hudson's Bay Company became the world's pre-eminent fur-trading post during the 17th century, the city's fate as a centre of fashion and apparel manufacture was sealed.

Ever since, it has been one of those places in the world where designers, stitchers and knitters combine their talents to shape each season's newest idea of haute couture.

While early furriers sowed the seeds for Montréal's future as a garment capital, its heyday didn't occur until the Industrial Revolution. During the late 19th century, as new factory technology from England and New England trickled northwards, Montréal's working-class quarters saw an explosion of new manufacturing plants.

The original garment district grew up downtown, along boulevard de Maisonneuve where it cuts across rue de Bleury and boulevard St-Laurent; rows of furriers and warehouses still testify to its original presence. At first, working conditions tended to be very poor – wages were low, factories were hot, and even children worked long hours – but the workers eventually struck back. There were a number of apparel-industry walkouts in the Montréal area in the early 20th century, and they succeeded in bringing public attention to the workers' continuing plight.

The garment district began moving around, first to a compact district on the Plateau centred around rue de Gaspé and then, finally, to a more northerly district closer to motorways and the city airport. A few factories can still be found tucked away on de Gaspé, but most of the city's clothing manufacturers now work out of somewhat more modern-looking facilities that line distant rue Chabanel. On Saturday mornings, many of these shops open their doors to retail customers, which results in both tremendous on-site bargains and an inside glimpse of the cutting, stitching and other handiwork that goes into the handsome garments they see in the shops and end up purchasing.

Change has come to the industry along with changing times. Working conditions, of course, have improved significantly. And while most of the clothiers had traditionally been controlled by Jewish or Italian businesses families and tailors, a growing French influence has begun to show itself, particularly in the lingerie trade, which is now one of the regional industry's most successful exports.

Most of the businesses are now small and locally owned, which has kept pricing fair and the quality of goods high. In fact, Montréal is now well-respected among the world's clothiers, and not just for its lingerie but also for the cut and quality of its menswear and children's clothing.

It won't take you long to find the home-grown, pricey lingerie or menswear shops downtown. But now, each time you find the "Made in Canada" label on an item on the rack in a clothes shop, you'll know a bit more of the story about how it got there. ❑

LEFT: Canadian-made clothing has a reputation for good quality.

great glass-covered concourse, which once buzzed with the hustle and bustle of travellers heading all over the continent, is silent. It is sometimes used for balls and exhibitions, but most of the time it's a shortcut for commuters from the train to their offices. A few photographs displayed on the old arrivals and departures board serve as a reminder of the station's past glories.

St George's

Just north of the station is **Eglise St-George ❺** (1101 rue Stanley; open Tues–Sun 8.30am–4.30pm; free; tel: 514-866 7113), which was built to accommodate Montréal's west-end Protestants. The church was completed in 1870 and is the square's oldest remaining building and arguably the prettiest Anglican church in the city. It is worth venturing inside to admire the carved woodwork covering the interior. The entire ceiling is also exquisitely carved and has managed to survive the years gracefully.

North of the church, the architecture switches to the dramatically modern with the glittering glass-fronted SNC-Lavallin Building and the Canadian Imperial Bank of Commerce Building, a tall, severe spire of black stone and glass on the northwest corner of rue Peel and boulevard René-Lévesque.

If you're a sports fan take a detour west along René-Lévesque to the Centre Sheraton. This convention hotel has no particular distinction except that it stands at the southern end of a space once occupied by the Victoria Rink, where in 1875 a group of McGill University students invented the modern game of ice-hockey, a sport that has been a city obsession ever since *(see page 64)*.

Back on Dorchester Square, the Second-Empire building just north of the Bank of Commerce is all that's left of the once majestic Windsor Hotel, whose guests have included Sarah Bernhardt, Mark Twain, Rudyard Kipling and Lilli Langtry, not to mention King George VI and Queen Mary. The **Windsor Building** is mostly offices now, but it still has a magnificent ballroom lit by enormous crystal chandeliers.

Place du Canada

Dorchester Square and **place du Canada ❻** also serve as history galleries. Place du Canada has the city's **cenotaph** and, at its north end, a statue of Sir John A. Macdonald, Canada's first prime minister, who gazes across boulevard René-Lévesque – named for a man who tried to pull the country apart – at a monument to Sir Wilfrid Laurier, the country's first French-Canadian prime minister. The most dramatic statue on Dorchester Square, however, is the monument to the veterans of the Boer War *(see page 107)*. Its rearing horse, barely under the control of a Canadian trooper, is framed by a statue of Scottish poet Robert Burns and a fountain erected to mark Queen Victoria's diamond jubilee.

Spare a few minutes to look at the

Map on page 104

A striking stained-glass window inside St George's Church, which is dwarfed by downtown tower blocks.

BELOW: St George's Anglican Church.

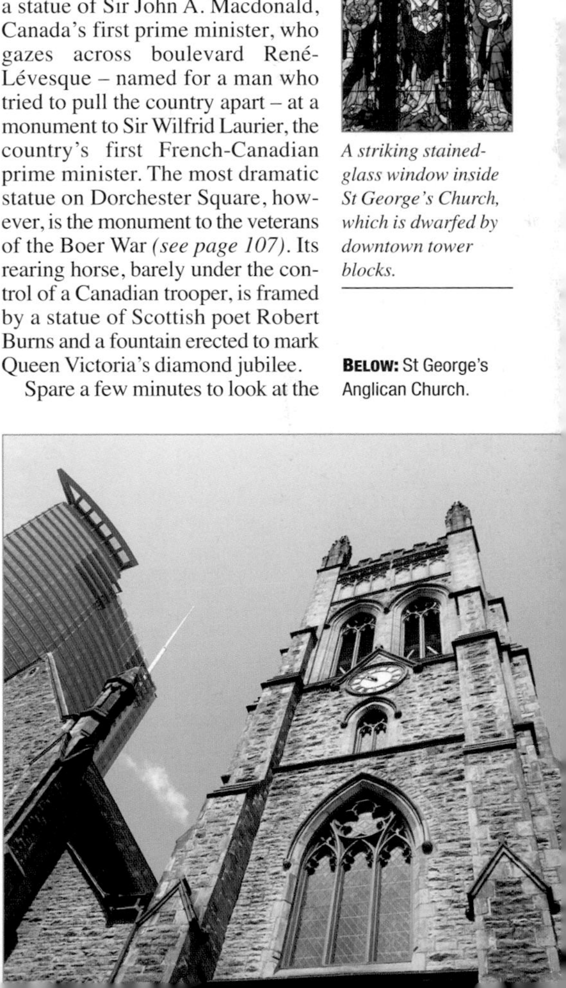

High-end goods for well-heeled city dwellers at Ogilvy's.

classic little octagonal stone building at the north end of the square. It's a lunch bar now, with a scattering of umbrella tables, but it was originally a public bathroom, one of several identical buildings erected in various city squares by Mayor Camilien Houde in the 1930s. For years, relieved Montréalers called them Camiliens in his honour.

Shopping and nightlife

To leave the square, stroll through the Dominion Square Building to see the lobby with its gilded barrel-vaulted ceiling before exiting on to the busiest shopping strip in Montréal – the stretch of **rue Ste-Catherine** between rue de la Montagne to the west and rue St-Urbain to the east.

The westernmost outpost of this stretch is **Ogilvy's**, a department store which has been selling high-end goods to the city's well-heeled since 1865. It's a store rich in tradition. Every day at noon, a kilted piper marches through the aisles, and at Christmas, children come to see Ogilvy's animated window display. Beyond Ogilvy's, the glamour factor on rue Ste-Catherine peters out quickly, although there are some interesting little second-hand bookshops further west.

However, the streets that run north–south here – especially de la Montagne, Crescent and Bishop – are another story. Together they're the heart and soul of the downtown district's night life. Between rue Sherbrooke in the north and boulevard René-Lévesque to the south, they are packed with restaurants, night clubs, bars and cocktail lounges, as well as a few boutiques and jewellers. Saturday-night traffic on Crescent – both pedestrian and vehicular – is dense.

Rue Ste-Catherine's most intense shopping, however, is to be found between rues Peel and Aylmer. From the high-end fashion shops in **Cours Mont-Royale ❼**, housed in a converted hotel, in the west to La Baie (The Bay) in the east, the shopping doesn't stop. Even the Anglican cathedral sits on a vast underground mall – one place, at least, where God tops Mammon. It is possible to walk the length of this strip, which covers

BELOW: live entertainment on rue Ste-Catherine.

Shopping Heaven

It is possible to dine, dance, work, worship, see any number of movies and plays, listen to a concert, go to a hockey game, work out, go skating, get drunk, catch a train to Nova Scotia or a bus to Ottawa, and earn a university degree without coming up for air in Montréal.

Hundreds of department stores, speciality shops, boutiques, pharmacies, discount stores and book stores all have access to the Underground City *(see page 105)*. You can buy anything from mink coats and diamonds to potato peelers and Aspirin without having to put on so much as a sweater. Maps of the network are available at Metro stations.

six city blocks, without going outside – the pedestrian tunnels of the Underground City link every mall and department store on the northern side of the street.

However, if the weather cooperates, stay outside. The passing scene is more interesting and the architecture, if you look above the modern storefronts, is worth the walk.

The street also reflects the changing face of retailing. For decades, one of the *grande dames* of rue Ste-Catherine was Simpson's, a department store that sold everything from suits to nuts and served three-course lunches, coffees and snacks to its hungry clients. It fell victim to the suburban big-box stores and closed in 1991. The art-deco buildings are currently occupied by **Paramount Montréal** ❽ (977 rue Ste-Catherine Ouest; tel: 514-842 5828), an entertainment complex with 14 cinemas and an IMAX theatre, and **Maison Simons** (tel: 514-842 1840), a Québec City-based clothing store that sells its own lines of men's and women's fashions as well as most of the big-name labels.

McGill and Ville-Marie

Off rue Ste-Catherine Ouest is **avenue McGill College**, a short but wide and beautiful boulevard lined with an interesting mix of stately 19th-century commercial buildings and shiny tower blocks. Here **Place Montréal Trust** ❾ (1500 avenue McGill College; tel: 514-843 3000) is an example of modern urban architecture in the downtown area. This shopping complex, an alternative to the labyrinthine underground city model of the 1960s, attempts to maintain a street presence – an active blend of shoppers, pedestrians, onlookers, commuters, even the proverbial "hanging out" crowd – and still allow for the ease of indoor shopping. It represents the city's continuing struggle to temper its harsh climate through experimentation in "living spaces".

At the foot of avenue McGill College is **Place Ville-Marie** ❿, the city's first real modern skyscraper and the first link in what was to become the Underground City.

The tallest of the complex's four towers – a silvery cruciform

Map on page 104

Keep track of time using the clock on rue Ste-Catherine.

LEFT: underground at Place Montréal Trust shopping mall.
BELOW: above ground on rue Ste-Catherine.

Tango

To those who love dancing, there are few sights more delightful than watching a mature couple tango dramatically across the floor, transformed into creatures of seduction and passion. In Montréal, traditional Argentinian tango is the preserve of the over-40s, many of whom don't come from South America at all.

Montréal has a sizeable Latin community made up mainly of families who fled the brutal military dictatorships of the 1970s, but the erotic dance of Buenos Aires which allows men and women to flirt and flounce and cling to one another in a seductive way, is popular with dancers of any age, especially people who consider themselves too old for clubbing or for the singles' bar scene. Recently arrived immigrants – younger folk as well as the middle aged – also find tango venues no-pressure places to socialize and meet new people. As for Montréalers, any excuse is good enough to get up and shake their booty. What all of these groups have in common is a passion for the dance.

Tango began surfacing as a dance craze in the late 1990s, after Montréal hosted a tango festival, the Festival International de Tango de Montréal, now a bi-annual event in July. As a result dance studios offering tango classes sprang up all over town with some organizing regular *milongas* – dance evenings – where novices learn the ropes or experienced dancers improve their skills.

Montréal's tango teachers, who travel to Argentina to train with the masters quickly earned a reputation for being among the best in North America. A high level of instruction is augmented by talented, locally-based tango groups such as Ensemble Romulo Larrea, Intakto and Quartango. Larrea, who specialises in the music of Ástor Piazzolla, the composer who brought tango music into the classical and jazz realms, plays the *bandoneón* (Argentine concertina) as if his heart is breaking – the essence of tango.

There are over 20 tango schools in Montréal with more springing up all the time. Some schools teach only the dance itself, usually in groups of 12–20 or on a one-to-one basis. Not having a partner is seldom a problem as instructors make sure that there is an equal number of dancers. Other tango schools, in addition to giving lessons and opening their doors for regular *practicas* (practise sessions), organise social events, Spanish-language film nights and tango workshops. A couple of tango schools even stage lavish balls (tango costume de rigeur) with live entertainment provided either by local tango ensembles or visiting musicians and dancers from South America. The oldest and most established schools include:

Tango Libre, 2485 avenue du Mont-Royal Est; tel: 514-527 5197; www.tangolibre.qc.ca

Studio Tango Montréal, 643 rue Notre-Dame Ouest; tel: 514-844 2786; www.studiotango.ca

Tangueria, 6522 boulevard Saint-Laurent; tel: 514-495-8645; www.tangueria.org

During the summer, visitors can dance tango in city parks for a nominal charge – in Verdun (Wed 7–10pm), Parc Saint-Viateur (Sun 7–10.30pm) and in Place des Vestiges in the Vieux Port (Aug and Sept Fri 8–10.30pm). Call 514-527 5197. For general information and a calendar of events visit www.milonga.ca. ❑

LEFT: tango is transforming the dance scene.

structure – dwarfed every other building in the city when it opened in 1962 and its rooftop restaurant and nightclub still have some of the best views of downtown. It was one of architect I.M. Pei's first works, completed long before he created a stir with his glass pyramid addition to the Louvre in Paris.

Place Ville-Marie's four buildings sit atop a shopping concourse that was the first to be linked to the city's new Metro in 1966. If you climb the stairs at the foot of McGill-College to the mall on top of the concourse and look north, you get a magnificent view up the boulevard to the campus of McGill University and the heights of Mont-Royal beyond.

Eaton's and The Bay

Back on rue Ste-Catherine, the next significant building on the north side of the street was another casualty of the 1990s retail wars. Eaton's department-store chain was a Canadian institution founded in 1869 by a thrifty immigrant from Northern Ireland named Timothy Eaton. He pioneered two concepts – fixed prices (no haggling) and the money-back guarantee – but his descendants were allegedly more interested in horses and collecting art than selling clothes and housewares, so the company went broke.

The Montréal store was best-known for two things: the 9th-floor café, an art-deco marvel designed to look like the first-class dining room on an ocean liner, and the mythical clerk – usually described as a "fat lady" – who couldn't speak French. The shopping concourse west of the store is still known as the **Eaton Mall**, but otherwise the family name has vanished from the Montréal retail industry. The store itself is also a mall, anchored by the upscale fashion shop, Les Ailes de la Môde.

One department store that has survived the vicissitudes of modern retailing is **La Baie** (The Bay; 585 rue Ste-Catherine Ouest; tel: 514-281 4422), so called because its parent company is the historic Hudson's Bay Company. The store is housed in a red sandstone building that used to be Morgan's,

Map on page 104

A pretty square that is ideal for a relaxing stroll after a day shopping at nearby Eaton Mall.

BELOW: Christmas in Place Ville-Marie.

Gargoyles on the Gothic facade of Christ Church Cathedral.

Canada's first department store. Its west wall on Union Street once had a plaque marking the spot where Jefferson Davis, president of the rebel Confederate States of America, lived after losing the American Civil War. It was removed in the 1990s for cleaning, but never replaced, in part because of objections from the black community.

Downtown churches

Squeezed between The Bay and Eaton's, on its own patch of green, is **Cathédrale Christ Church** ⓫ (1440 avenue Union; open daily 7am–6pm; tel: 514-288 6421), one of the prettiest churches in Montréal, seat of the city's Anglican bishop. Designed by Frank Wills of Salisbury, England, in 1857, the church is considered one of the finest examples of Gothic architecture in Canada.

The lovely narrow spire is made of treated aluminum, the original stone having been removed because of its weight. Grace and balance are also evident in the church's interior, primarily made of stone except for the ceiling. **Tour KPMG**, formerly the Maison des Coopérants, the elegant, modern glass tower behind Christ Church, incorporates the lines of the church's apses and windows in its design. During the day the spire is reflected in its tinted glass.

Just across rue Ste-Catherine is **Phillips Square** ⓬, a large open space paved with flagstones and dominated by a suitably majestic bronze of King Edward VII. With the Anglican cathedral and the linear descendant of the Hudson's Bay Company in front of him, and the venerable Birks jewellery store on his left, the king looks right at home. He doesn't even seem to mind the disrespectful attentions of the pigeons who share the square with him.

It's worth making a detour south here down Côte du Beaver Hall to boulevard René-Lévesque to visit **Basilique St-Patrick** ⓭ (460 boulevard Renée-Lévesque Ouest; open daily 8.30am–6pm; free; tel: 514-866 7379). Built in 1847, it is one of the oldest Catholic churches in the city and one of the most beautiful, but is generally neglected by tourists and tour buses.

BELOW: lunch in the shadow of Christ Church Cathedral. **RIGHT:** a bronze of King Edward VII dominates Phillips Square.

The restful interior is painted in green and gold and its high vaulted ceiling is held aloft by what appear to be impossibly slender marble pillars but which are, in fact, pine logs with a plaster facade. The wainscoting around the nave is decorated with dozens of portraits of the saints, both famous and obscure.

The church is a fitting tribute to the sturdy faith of the thousands of poor Irish immigrants who provided much of the labour for the building of the city. One of the plaques at the back of the church commemorates the priests, nuns and lay people who died tending the refugees from the Irish potato famine who arrived on fever ships suffering from typhoid.

Back on Ste-Catherine, the shops become less interesting and grand as you walk east from The Bay. Shabby storefronts of discount stores, video arcades, sex shops, fast-food places and pornographic cinemas dominate.

One welcome break in this depressing strip is **St James's United Church** ⓮ (463 rue Ste-Catherine Ouest; tel: 514-288 9245). It is hard to believe now, but from the 1930s until 2005, the stone facade of this beautiful Gothic church, with its giant rose window and unevenly sized spires, was hidden behind a grubby row of storefronts. During the Depression, the church was apparently so desperate for money that it rented out its street frontage to commercial developers with disastrous results.

St James's interior is worth a look, too. The architect, Alexandre Dunlop, seated the congregation in a large horseshoe around the sanctuary, very much like the 18th-century convocation halls at Oxford and Cambridge universities in England. The curved wooden balcony and central chandelier are striking.

Temples to arts and finance

The final stop on Ste-Catherine is **Place des Arts** ⓯. Completed in 1963, the complex's sweeping curves typify the architecture favoured during Mayor Jean Drapeau's term. The complex comprises two buildings that contain three concert halls. The larger of the two, Salle Wilfrid-Pelletier, is home to the Montréal

Map on page 104

The interior of St Patrick's includes portraits of the saints.

BELOW: St Patrick's Basilica has a high vaulted ceiling.

Contemporary art has its own museum in Montréal: Musée d'Art Contemporain.

Symphony Orchestra (MSO), but sinuous curves notwithstanding, it has never been much of a concert hall, either acoustically or aesthetically.

In 2006, the MSO and its conductor Kent Nagano announced plans to build a dedicated hall beside the Wilfrid-Pelletier. The design of the two smaller theatres in the pyramid-shaped building is interesting. Their floors and ceilings are suspended from thousands of springs, enabling the halls to be used simultaneously without fear of sound interference.

Adjacent to Place des Arts is the **Musée d'Art Contemporain** ⓰ (Museum of Contemporary Art; 185 rue Ste-Catherine Ouest; open Tues–Sun, 11am–6pm, Wed until 9pm; admission charge, free Wed 6–9pm; tel: 514-847 6226). It has had a peripatetic history, with three homes since its founding in 1964 before moving to this 4,088-sq metre (44,000-sq. ft) space above the Place des Arts parking garage.

The museum's eight rooms display post-1940s work by artists from around the world, but its permanent collection focuses on the "automatists," a group of Québec artists led by Paul-Émile Borduas and Jean Paul Riopelle. In 1948, the group published a manifesto called the *Refus Global* (Global Refusal), which challenged the political, religious and artistic orthodoxies of the day. Many consider the manifesto one of the first shots fired in the Quiet Revolution *(see page 34)*.

Directly across the street stands **Complexe Desjardins**, named for one of the distant precursors of the Quiet Revolution. Alphonse Desjardins, a devout Catholic who believed the key to securing a better future for French Canadians was to improve their economic status, started the province's credit-union movement in his living room in 1900 with total deposits of $26.40. With church help, the idea spread through the province, and Groupe Desjardins, with assets of more than $100 billion, is now one of the drivers of the Québec economy.

The group's headquarters reflects its modern prosperity. Arranged around a central atrium, Complexe Desjardins contains three office tow-

Art History

Most of Montreal's 18th- and 19th-century artists relied on church commissions to make a living, providing a glorious collection of religious art. Admittedly, much of it is derivative and dependent on European models, but artists such as Ozias Leduc (1864–1965) and Guido Nincheri (1885–1973) worked with a genuinely original verve. Not all pre-20th-century art was religious though, by capturing the daily life of the habitants on canvas, Dutch-born Cornelius Krieghoff (1815–72) popularized a more vernacular art and paved the way for painters such as Marc-Aurèle Fortin (1888–1970), whose quirky landscapes stand somewhere between folk and modern. The real break with the past came in 1948 when a group known as the "automatists", led by Paul-Emile Borduas (1905–60) and Jean-Paul Riopelle (1923–2002), signed the Réfus Global, a manifesto that challenged not only the artistic conventions of the day, but the religious and political ones as well. Their wild experiments with colour and form shattered any notion of a single Québec school. Today artists work in every style and medium, ranging from the ultra-realistic canvases of painters like Paul Fenniak to the eccentric installations of sculptors like Jean-Pierre Gauthier.

RIGHT: thousands of people gather together for the Jazz Festival at Place des Arts.

Map on page 104

ers, a hotel and the ubiquitous floors of shops and restaurants. A three-dimensional wood sculpture by the Québécois artist, Pierre Granche, serves as a centrepiece in a brown concrete interior. The atmosphere is either serene or sterile, depending on your perspective.

Chinatown

A tunnel links Complexe Desjardins to the Édifice Guy-Favreau, a federal-government building that in turn opens on to a cramped little plaza on the edge of the city's small **Chinatown**. At one end of the treeless patch of cobblestones stands the **Chinese Catholic Church**, which dates from 1835, and at the other is what is reputed to be the oldest building in Chinatown – the much battered House of Wing, a noodle and cookie factory.

Just east of the plaza on rue de la Gauchetière, an elaborate **ceremonial gate** ⓱ marks the entrance to Chinatown proper. In China, such gates were meant to ward off evil spirits; in Montréal, however, they signal the beginning of a pedestrian mall lined with many restaurants and other commercial enterprises.

Try to visit Chinatown at the weekend. On Saturday and Sunday afternoons the streets teem with families. Asians and people from other communities eat sweets and search for those hard-to-find Chinese delicacies in shops and bakeries.

The best way to explore this area is with chopsticks. Restaurants are thick on the ground, and they permit the curious epicurean to sample everything from Cantonese dim sum to spicy Szechuan beef. You can also snack on fried dough and moon cakes while you shop for Chinese herbs or cotton clothing.

Chinatown was once much bigger and home to the thousands of Chinese who began emigrating to Canada in the late 1800s. By law, the first immigrants were men only. Social and economic discrimination forced the community to band tightly together, creating a self-reliant ghetto that tended to attract some less than wholesome enterprises, including brothels and gambling dens.

The proximity of Chinatown to the

One way to explore Chinatown is with chopsticks on a culinary journey through the neighbourhood.

BELOW: gateway to Chinatown.

Statues grace the McGill campus, the oldest of Montreal's four universities.

downtown area, combined with the ramshackle condition of many of the residential buildings, made it a prime target for development. During the last two decades of the 20th century a number of the more interesting older edifices were demolished. In their place stand large government office buildings and barren parking lots. Old meets new in Chinatown, but not quite as harmoniously as in other parts of the city.

The Golden Square Mile

Downtown explorations continue in the Square Mile – also known as the **Golden Square Mile** – an area far from Chinatown in both space and spirit. In 1900, the district's 25,000 residents controlled a staggering 70 percent of Canada's wealth. But the Square Mile, too, suffered from the depredations of the modernizing wave of the 1960s. Many of its fine old homes were razed to make way for apartment towers that obscure the views of and from Mont-Royal.

Still, the area has an undeniable elegance, in spite of all the modern glitter. Even rue Sherbrooke retains some of its old dignity, despite the clusters of nondescript office towers that crowd its central stretch. Many of its greystone townhouses have been converted into boutiques, art galleries and hotels, retaining their original grace, if not their purpose.

The rich and powerful still meet for breakfast or pre-dinner drinks in the Edwardian splendour of the Ritz Carlton Hotel, where Elizabeth Taylor and Richard Burton celebrated one of their two weddings. Just down the street, Holt-Renfrew, Canada's own luxury department store, still sells furs and Armani gowns to an exclusive clientele.

The green and pleasant campus of **McGill University** ⓲ (859 rue Sherbrooke Ouest; tours available; tel: 514-398 6655), whose graduates like to refer to Harvard as the McGill of the US, dominates the eastern end of the Square Mile. Its buildings, a mix of old and new, cluster around a wide, tree-shaded lawn on the land fur-trader James McGill set aside for the school in 1828. The university held its first classes in the severe neoclassical

BELOW:
The Illuminated Crowd by Raymond Mason stands in front of the BNP Tower.

Arts Building at the northern end of the campus.

Museum tour

The fanciful temple-like building next to the university houses the **Redpath Museum of Natural History** ⓳ (open Sept–May Mon–Sat 9am–5pm, Sun 1–5pm; free; tel: 514-398 4086), whose eclectic collection runs the gamut from old coins to shrunken heads.

To get an idea of how the Square Mile's residents lived in the district's golden age, visit the **McCord Museum of Canadian History** ⓴ (690 rue Sherbrooke Ouest; open Mon–Fri 10am–6pm, closed Mon in winter; admission charge, free Sat; tel: 514-398 7100) just across Sherbrooke from the university. Its collection includes the work of a remarkable photographer named William Notman (1826–91), who made a record of the doings of the rich and powerful and their families. Other exhibits also explore the lives of humbler Montréalers with documents, clothing, fabrics and furniture.

Rue Sherbrooke's other major museum is the **Musée des Beaux-Arts** ㉑ (Museum of Fine Arts; 1380 rue Sherbrooke Ouest; open Tues–Sun 11am–6pm, Wed until 9pm; admission charge; tel: 514-285 2000). Founded in 1860, this is Canada's oldest museum, but most of its exhibits are mounted in the startlingly modern Pavilion Jean-Noël-Desmarais designed by Moishe Safdie, which opened in 1991. An underground tunnel links the pavilion to the museum's original building, the neoclassical Michal and Renata Hornstein Pavilion on the south side of Sherbrooke.

The museum's permanent collection comprises a wide range of paintings, sculptures and drawings from North America and Europe. There is a good sampling of European art from the 17th century onward, including works by El Greco, Rodin, Dalí and Picasso. Canadian art is represented by Inuit woodcarvings, soapstone sculpture and paintings by the Group of Seven – a seminal group of Ontario landscape painters – and contemporary artists such as Paul-Emile Borduas,

Map on page 104

A totem pole, an example of work produced by First Nations artists.

BELOW: exhibits at Musée des Beaux-Arts.

Grand architecture with decorative details in the Golden Mile.

BELOW: rue Sherbrooke with the Erskine and American United Church and the Château apartments.

Jean-Paul Riopelle and Betty Goodwin. The museum also houses a fine collection of decorative arts from around the world.

The religious art collection is being moved into the red-sandstone **Erskine and American United Church** ㉒ just east of the original building. Built in 1894, the church's treasures include 24 stained-glass windows signed by Louis Comfort Tiffany. The Erskine and American is one of two magnificent churches built by the Square Mile's overwhelmingly Protestant residents. The other is the **Church of St Andrew and St Paul** ㉓ (rue Sherbrooke Ouest at rue Redpath; tel: 514-842 3431), a Gothic Revival temple best known for its stunning stained-glass windows, including two designed by Pre-Raphaelite painter Sir Edward Burne-Jones.

The Château

Some reminders of how graciously the wealthy lived in rue Sherbrooke's heyday have survived the ravages of modernization. The most dramatic is the **Château** (1321 rue Sherbrooke Ouest), an imposing granite apartment building built in 1925 to resemble a castle on the Loire River in France, complete with gargoyles, coats of arms and side turrets.

Well-to-do tenants could put up visiting friends at the Ritz-Carlton across the street, whose rooms match the Château's spacious apartments in elegance and style. Several fine residences have also weathered the passing of time, notably the Maison Baxter (1201 rue Sherbrooke Ouest), the Residence Forget (1195 rue Sherbrooke Ouest) and the Corby House (1201 rue Sherbrooke Ouest), but to grasp just how flamboyantly the really rich lived in the Square Mile's exuberant age, you have to leave rue Sherbrooke.

Grand homes

One of the most grandiose homes, the George Stephen House, is actually "below" Sherbrooke on rue Drummond. Stephen, the Scottish-born founder of the Canadian Pacific Railway, spent $600,000 in 1883 – a formidable sum in those days – to line the walls of his home

with marble and oak panelling and to decorate its ceilings with Cuban mahogany. Today, this baronial building houses the exclusive **Mount Stephen Club** ㉔ (1440 rue Drummond; tel: 514-849 7338), which welcomes non-members for Saturday dinner and Sunday brunch. The brunch comes with a guided tour, which is worth it to get an idea about the life of a 19th-century magnate.

Another of Montréal's merchant princes was Sir Hugh Allan, who owned many of the ships that sailed into Montréal harbour. He built a Tuscan palace high on the slopes of Mont-Royal. **Ravenscrag** ㉕ (1025 avenue des Pins Ouest) is a steep climb from rue Sherbrooke, but worth the effort: the house is a magnificent rendition of Renaissance architecture.

There are other fine homes on avenue des Pins and the adjoining Redpath Crescent. Many have been taken over by McGill University or foreign consulates. Some reflect the origins of their owners, Clarence de Sola, for example, a Sephardic Jew from Spain, built his house at 1347 des Pins Ouest with a distinctly Moorish look. It is now the Canadian headquarters of Opus Dei, a Catholic lay organization.

Just a couple of doors west of the De Sola house at 1418 des Pins Ouest is the deceptively modest-looking house that architect Ernest Cormier, who designed the Université de Montréal and the Supreme Court of Canada building in Ottawa, built for himself. Its art deco facade is narrow and set back from the street, but the house spreads down the slope behind it in several layers. Its other famous resident was a former prime minister, Pierre Trudeau.

Catholic training ground

The final stop is back on rue Sherbrooke and has nothing to do with the Anglo-Celtic-Protestant oligarchy that ruled Montréal through much of the 19th and 20th centuries. It is the **Grande Séminaire** ㉖ (Grand Seminary; 2065 rue Sherbrooke Ouest; free guided tours in summer; tel: 514-935 1165, ext 239), built in 1860 and still used to train Catholic priests for the Montréal archdiocese.

In its front garden are two round stone towers that are the oldest buildings in Montréal, dating from the early 17th century. St Marguerite Bourgeoys used one of them as a school for young Aboriginal girls. The seminary's extensive gardens are worth seeing, as is its beautiful Romanesque chapel.

The Grande Séminaire is run by the Sulpician priests who were the *seigneurs* or landlords of Montréal through much of the French regime and well into British rule. The seminary's halls and classrooms were once packed with young men seeking ordination. There are few recruits now, and its presence is a reminder of how transitory power can be. The priests and Protestant barons who succeeded them have both been replaced by newer, brasher forces. ❑

TIP

If you're interested in architecture, head west along René-Lévesque to find the Canadian Centre for Architecture (tel: 939 7026), at 1920 rue Baile. Its collection of plans, models, books and photos is said to be the best of its kind in the world.

BELOW: study break.

RESTAURANTS & BARS

Restaurants

L'Actuel
1194 rue Peel (at Dorchester Square). Tel: 514-866 1537. L & D Mon–Sat. $$$
Moules et frites (mussels and fries) are what this restaurant is known for, but it also serves such Liege specialities as braised sweetbreads and calf's kidney. The cheerful downstairs bistro-bar is a lunchtime favourite; upstairs, is more intimate.

Alexandre et Fils
1454 rue Peel (near rue Ste-Catherine). Tel: 514-288 5105. L & D daily. $$$
The brass fittings, comfy banquettes and huge mural faithfully recreate a classic Paris brasserie. So does the food: first-rate *cassoulet* and an excellent roast beef.

Barbecue St-Hubert
1180 rue de la Gauchetière Ouest (in Gare Windsor near rue Peel). Tel: 514-866 0500. L & D daily. $$
One of the most successful restaurant chains in Québec. This is the classiest one in Montréal, with stone walls and comfortable booths. The spit-roasted chicken with gravy and fries is excellent and well-priced. For dessert, try the traditional sugar pie or *pudding au chomeur* (literally, pudding for the unemployed).

Beaver Club
900 boulevard René-Lévesque (in the Hôtel le Reine-Elizabeth at rue Mansfield). Tel: 514-861 3511. L & D Mon–Fri, D only Sat–Sun. $$$$
This sumptuous hotel dining room has discreet service, lush décor and dry-as-dust martinis that give it the feel of an elite club. The classic French menu is pricey.

La Belle Vietnamienne
1206 avenue Union (near Phillips Square). Tel: 514-866 8892. L & D Mon–Fri, D only Sat. $$
Pastel walls and cream table cloths add a splash of class to this simple dining room specializing in Thai and Vietnamese foods. On a quiet street a short walk from rue Ste-Catherine.

Bistro Gourmet
2100 rue St-Matthieu (at avenue Lincoln). Tel: 514-846 1553. L & D Mon–Fri, D only Sat–Sun. $$$
Popular, unpretentious bistro, with brick walls and paper-covered linens; good French food at reasonable prices. The table d'hote menu includes lamb shank with rosemary, and grilled tuna with sesame seeds.

Café Ferreira
1446 rue Peel (at rue Ste-Catherine). Tel: 514-848 0988. L & D Mon–Sat. $$$$
A little corner of Portugal with yellow walls, terra-cotta floors and a tile mural, but the cuisine includes nouvelle-Mediterranean choices, such as gazpacho and octopus salad, and more traditional favourites like *caldo verde* and grilled sardines.

Cavalli
2040 rue Peel (at boulevard de Maisonneuve). Tel: 514-843 5100. L & D daily. $$$$
With its pink and green velvet chairs and long illuminated bar, this brash downtown spot feels like a movie set, and stylish waiting staff add to the illusion. This may be a place to see and be seen, but it's also serious about the food. Try the seared tuna in a sunflower-seed crust.

Le Caveau
2063 rue Victoria (at avenue du Président Kennedy). Tel: 514-844 1624. L & D Mon–Sat, D only Sat–Sun. $$$
A three-storey Victorian house where the tradition of bourgeois French cooking lives on – buttery sauces, rich soups, offal and a magnificent *cassoulet Toulouse*. Flowered wallpaper and gilt-framed paintings: a perfect setting.

Les Chenêts
2075 rue Bishop (near rue Sherbrooke). Tel: 514-844 1842. L & D Mon–Fri, D only Sat–Sun. $$$$
Fussy round tables and copper pots decorating the wall. All dishes, from lobster thermidor to duck à l'orange are richly sauced and traditionally prepared. If you're on a diet, stay away.

Le Commensal
1204 avenue McGill-College (at rue Ste-Catherine). Tel: 514-871 1480. L & D daily. $$
This is the best of a homegrown vegetarian chain. Its second-floor floor-to-ceiling windows provide great views of McGill College and Mont-Royal. Salads, beans, soups and *seitan*, soy versions of shepherds' pie and *boeuf bourgignon* served buffet style and priced by weight.

Dominion Pub
1243 rue Metcalfe (near rue Ste-Catherine). Tel: 514-878 6354. L & D Mon–Sat, 11am–7pm Sun. $$
Genuine Québec-style tavern with tiled floors and wooden tables, fast, efficient, no-nonsense waiting staff. The food is traditional too. Try the pig's knuckles and sauerkraut with a pitcher of domestic draft beer.

Dunn's
1249 rue Metcalfe (at rue Ste-Catherine). Tel: 514-385 1927. B, L & D daily. $$
Long, narrow deli lined with wood and vinyl booths. Energetic service and good prices make up for the lack of ambiance, and the smoked meat, pastrami and liverwurst are the best downtown. Across

the street from the tourist office.

Entrecôte St-Jean
2022 rue Peel (near boulevard de Maisonneuve). Tel: 514-281 6492. L & D Mon–Fri, D only Sat–Sun. $$
Simple menu: sirloin steak with french fries and a walnut salad, with or without dessert. That's it. The sauce on the steak is rich and satisfying and the room is authentic Paris-style bistro.

Guy & Dodo Moralli
Cours Mont-Royal Building, 1444 rue Metcalfe. Tel: 514-842 3636. L & D Mon–Fri, D only Sat. $$$
Dodo oversees the dining room with a firm but gracious hand, while Guy rules the kitchen. Try the lobster bisque and lamb cooked in pastry, and *îles flottants* for dessert.

Hong Kong
1023 boulevard St-Laurent (near boulevard René-Lévesque). Tel: 514-861 0251. L & D daily. $$
Traditional – bright red walls, gold-tongued dragons and tables of chattering families; one of Chinatown's best. Its barbecued duck and chicken are a speciality.

Joe Beef
2491 rue Notre-Dame Ouest (at avenue Atwater). Tel: 514-935 6504. D Tues–Sat. $$$
Homey little restaurant – named for a legendary tavern owner. Chef David MacMillan makes whatever he feels like – often comfort food with a twist, like cream of chicken soup with rice, or Salisbury steak topped with foie-gras slivers – and serves it at a leisurely pace.

Julien
1181 rue Union (near boulevard René-Lévesque). Tel: 514-871 1581. L & D Mon–Sat. $$$
Bistro favourites such as baked halibut or sautéed breast of duck. In summer, guests can dine on a secluded patio. The table d'hôte lunch menu is a good deal.

Newtown
1476 rue Crescent (at boulevard de Maisonneuve). Tel: 514-284 6555. L & D daily. $$$$
Chic resto-bar owned by Jacques Villeneuve. With wraparound windows, it's a place to see and be seen. The food is good, if pricey. Try the beef Wellington à la Newton with foie gras.

Le Paris
1812 rue Ste-Catherine Ouest (at rue St-Matthieu). Tel: 514-937 4898. L & D Mon–Sat, D only Sun. $$
Comfortable but faded décor that has changed little since 1956. The menu has authentic French fare at reasonable prices. Its *branade de morue* – salt cod, cream and garlic – is famous.

Queue de Cheval
1221 boulevard René-Lévesque (at rue Drummond). Tel: 514-390 0090. L & D daily. $$$$
Chefs grill slabs of prime US beef over a charcoal pit in the middle of this brick-walled place. The steak is sold by the ounce and the fixings are separate, so it adds up.

La Rapière
Sun Life Building, 1155 rue Metcalfe (near boulevard René-Lévesque). L & D Mon–Fri, D only Sat. $$$$
Tapestries and stained-glass windows create a soothing atmosphere. The cuisine is from Gascogne in south-western France. Order anything with duck – especially the *cassoulet*.

La Rotonde
Musée d'Art Contemporain, 185 rue Ste-Catherine Ouest (at rue Jeanne-Mance). Tel: 514-847 6900. L Mon–Fri, L & D on show nights at Place des Arts. $$$
The décor is severe: white walls and red tables and chairs, huge windows offer diners a great view of Place des Arts. Good for lunch and ideal for a pre-show supper.

Le Taj
2077 rue Stanley (near boulevard de Maisonneuve). Tel: 514-845 9015. L & D Mon–Fri, D only Sat–Sun. $$
Uncharacteristically muted for a south Asian restaurant. The tandoori-roasted meats are the main draw, but the noon buffet is very good.

Trattoria Santa Lucia
1264 rue Stanley (at rue Ste-Catherine). Tel: 514-393 8623. L & D Mon–Sat, D only Sat–Sun. $$
The wood-burning oven in the back is the heart of this friendly trattoria. The thin-crust, individual-serving pizzas are among the best in the city.

Bars

Club 737
1 Place Ville-Marie. Tel: 514-397 0737.
Pricey, pretentious and loud on Thursday, but you can't beat the view from Place Ville-Marie's tallest tower.

Upstairs
1254 rue Mackay (near rue Ste-Catherine). Tel: 514-931 6808.
The perfect place for a quiet drink and a little late-night jazz.

Sir Winston Churchill (aka Winnie's)
1459 rue Crescent (near boulevard de Maisonneuve). Tel: 514-288 3414.
Open since the late 1960s, Winnie's helped transform Crescent into the liveliest night strip in the city; great for singles.

Thursdays
1449 rue Crescent (near rue Ste-Catherine). Tel: 514-288 5656.
The classic watering hole, where the action starts after work and goes on until morning.

Salsathèque
1220 rue Peel (near rue Ste-Catherine). Tel: 514-875 0016.
This popular little dance club has its own salsa instructors.

PRICE CATEGORIES

Prices for a three-course dinner per person with a half-bottle of house wine:
$ = under $25
$$ = $25–50
$$$ = $50–70
$$$$ = more than $70

MONTRÉAL BRANCHÉ

The vibrant heart of the city beats in a series of café-lined streets between St-Denis and St-Laurent. Night or day, this is where you'll find the trendy Montréal.

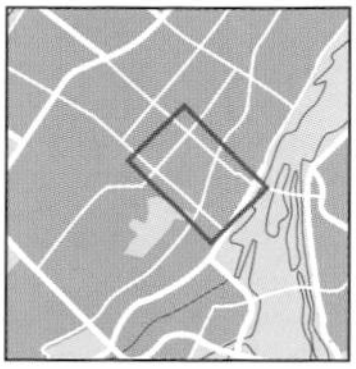

Map on page 126

Literally, the word "branché" means "plugged in" or "connected", but in Québec French, at least, it means a whole lot more. Applied to a restaurant, a bar or an entire city district, it implies a combination of trendy and cutting edge with just a dash of daring thrown in, and maybe a little lingering disrepute to give it some aroma.

Montréal's most branché neighbourhoods – the Quartier Latin, Plateau Mont-Royal and Le Village – are all roughly contiguous and all worth exploring. Their borders are blurry and not all Montréalers agree on where they begin and end, but all are distinctive with quite different histories. What they all share, however, is a checkered past.

Even the Quartier Latin, which began in the early 19th century as a comfortable haven for prosperous French Canadian businessmen and professionals, went through a long period of decay before it was resurrected as an in-place to live and play.

Gentrification

The branché neighbourhoods are also on Métro lines and close to the city centre, as well as being rich in what could be called "housing with character". All this has endeared them to young, urbane professionals, artists, writers, academics and journalists looking to live the 21st-century version of la *dolce vita*.

Some of the once rundown townhouses in the Quartier-Latin – previously the homes of the wealthy bourgeoisie – have been converted into expensive condominiums and many of the duplexes and triplexes in the Plateau – stacked housing,which was originally designed for working-class Montréalers – have been sandblasted and varnished into high-priced respectability.

But gentrification has certainly not

LEFT: hanging out in the Quartier Latin. **BELOW:** young prosperous urbanites are moving in to the neighbourhoods.

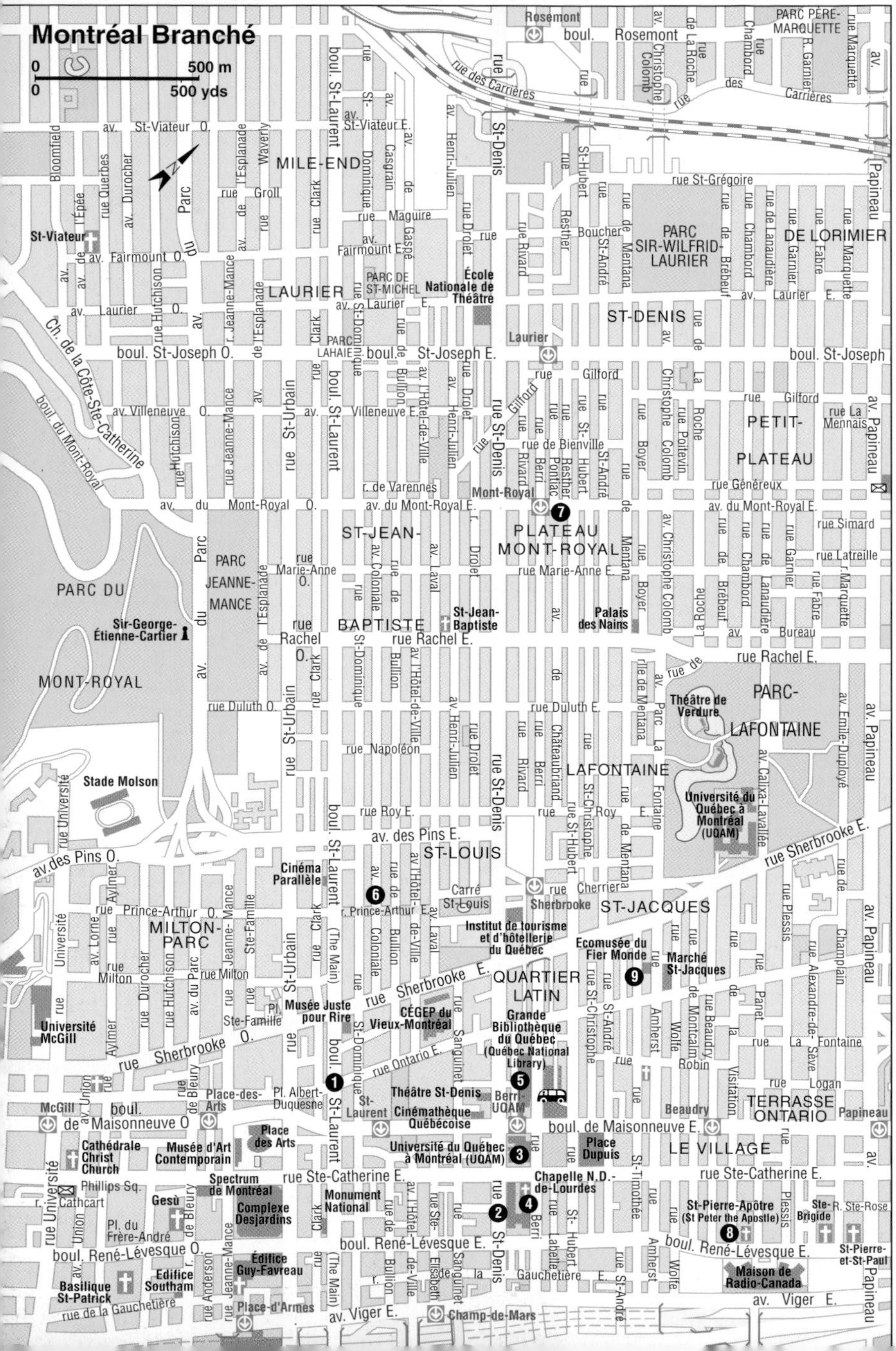
Montréal Branché
0 500 m
0 500 yds
MILE-END
LAURIER
ST-DENIS
DE LORIMIER
PETIT-PLATEAU
PLATEAU MONT-ROYAL
ST-JEAN-BAPTISTE
PARC DU MONT-ROYAL
LAFONTAINE
PARC-LAFONTAINE
ST-LOUIS
MILTON-PARC
ST-JACQUES
QUARTIER LATIN
TERRASSE ONTARIO
LE VILLAGE
PARC SIR-WILFRID-LAURIER
PARC JEANNE-MANCE
PARC DE ST-MICHEL
PARC LAHAIE
PARC PÈRE-MARQUETTE
Rosemont
Laurier
Mont-Royal
Sherbrooke
Berri-UQAM
St-Laurent
Place-des-Arts
McGill
Papineau
Beaudry
Place-d'Armes
Champ-de-Mars
St-Viateur
École Nationale de Théâtre
Sir-George-Étienne-Cartier
Stade Molson
St-Jean-Baptiste
Palais des Nains
Théâtre de Verdure
Université du Québec à Montréal (UQAM)
Cinéma Parallèle
Carré St-Louis
Institut de tourisme et d'hôtellerie du Québec
Ecomusée du Fier Monde
Marché St-Jacques
Musée Juste pour Rire
CÉGEP du Vieux-Montréal
Grande Bibliothèque du Québec (Québec National Library)
Théâtre St-Denis
Cinémathèque Québécoise
Université McGill
Place des Arts
Musée d'Art Contemporain
Cathédrale Christ Church
Place Dupuis
Spectrum de Montréal
Complexe Desjardins
Monument National
Chapelle N.D.-de-Lourdes
Gesù
St-Pierre-Apôtre (St Peter the Apostle)
Ste-Brigide
St-Pierre-et-St-Paul
Maison de Radio-Canada
Édifice Guy-Favreau
Edifice Southam
Basilique St-Patrick
Phillips Sq.
Pl. du Frère-André
Pl. Albert-Duquesne
boul. Rosemont
rue des Carrières
av. St-Viateur O.
av. Fairmount O.
av. Laurier O.
boul. St-Joseph O.
boul. St-Joseph E.
av. Villeneuve O.
av. du Mont-Royal O.
av. du Mont-Royal E.
rue Rachel E.
rue Duluth O.
rue Duluth E.
rue Napoléon
rue Roy E.
av. des Pins O.
av. des Pins E.
rue Prince-Arthur O.
rue Milton
rue Sherbrooke O.
rue Sherbrooke E.
rue Ontario E.
boul. de Maisonneuve O
boul. de Maisonneuve E.
rue Ste-Catherine E.
boul. René-Lévesque O.
boul. René-Lévesque E.
rue de la Gauchetière
av. Viger E.
Ch. de la Côte-Ste-Catherine
boul. du Mont-Royal
av. du Parc
boul. St-Laurent (The Main)
rue St-Denis
rue St-Hubert
rue Berri
rue St-Urbain
rue Clark
rue St-Dominique
av. Papineau
rue Cherrier
rue Gilford
rue de Bienville
rue Marie-Anne E.
rue Bureau
rue Logan
rue Robin
rue St-Grégoire
rue Boucher
rue Généreux
rue Simard
rue Latreille
rue La Fontaine

wiped out all traces of the districts' less prosperous past. Students can still find inexpensive walkup apartments, especially in the Quartier Latin and the McGill ghetto, and immigrants from Latin America, North Africa and the Middle East have moved into the lower stretches of rue St-Denis and boulevard St-Laurent. There's still a vibrant Portuguese community in Plateau Mont-Royal, even though many of its second- and third-generation families have moved to the suburbs.

All this means, that branché boutiques, restaurants, bars and cafés share commercial space with fish-and-chip joints, Portuguese rotisseries and secondhand clothes stores.

The Main

No talk of this part of town would be complete without a description of **The Main** (or Le Main), Montréalers' affectionate nickname for **boulevard St-Laurent** ❶ the long, colourful street that splits their city into west and east. Since the mid-19th century, waves of immigrants – Chinese, Jews, Greeks, Slavs, South-east Asians and, most recently, Latin Americans – have swept up St-Laurent, transforming it every generation or so. And every group that has come and gone has left traces of its passing.

The street's lower reaches, below rue Ste-Catherine are seedy and intimidating, lined with strip clubs, pornographic cinemas and lunch counters specializing in greasy french fries and hot-dogs, "*stimés*". In the middle of this grubby mess is the **Monument National** (1182 boulevard St-Laurent; tel: 514 842 7954). Built in 1893, it was an essential stop for such Vaudeville greats as Edith Piaf and Emma Albani. The École Nationale de Théâtre now uses its beautifully restored theatre to stage its student productions.

The Main really comes alive north of rue Sherbooke, where it skirts both the McGill Ghetto, the warren of narrow streets just east of the McGill University campus where many students and faculty members live, and the Quartier Latin before entering Plateau Mont-Royal.

For more than 10 blocks both sides are lined with restaurants, bars, delicatessens, boutiques and shops of all descriptions. There is a mix of high and low, chic and normal here that keeps the area both unpretentious and unpredictable. Discount shoe stores stand next door to hip cafés, while Greek bakeries and art galleries share old warehouse space. Come to St-Laurent to walk, browse and, most importantly, to eat.

Honest food

The Main is known for its smoked meat delis, and delis are known for lots of honest food at honest prices. Try Schwartz's Delicatessen (officially the Charcuterie Hébraïque de Montréal) at number 3895, which makes the best smoked meat in town; Rubin Schwartz brought the curing recipe with him when he

Map on page 126

Moishe's serves what some local people consider to be the best steak in town.

BELOW: rue Ste-Catherine.

Au Pain Doré bread is produced using traditional French methods and baked in stone ovens. The bakery chain has branches across Montréal.

RIGHT: view down busy rue St-Denis.

emigrated from Romania. Moishe's Steakhouse at number 3961 opened in 1938 on the site of the restaurant where Moishe himself had been a busboy, and it is still Montréal's best address for backroom power steak lunches or dinners.

A good place to admire the old buildings of St-Laurent is along the block between numbers 3640 and 3712, once called the Baxter Block. The attached buildings have impressively large arched windows and still retain the original central heating system. Also worth checking out is **Cinéma Parallèle**, at number 3684, which houses a café and arts cinema.

Quartier Latin

Six blocks east of the Main is **rue St-Denis** ❷ an elegant street of Victorian and Second Empire townhouses that form the backbone of the Quartier Latin. With its mixture of cafés, pâtisseries, boutiques, fine restaurants, bookstores, theatres and cinemas, some suggest that nowhere else has such a Parisian or European flavour, but the truth is that nowhere is more essentially Montréal.

This is the focal point of several of the festivals that now fill the summer months and where, traditionally, Québécois separatists gather whenever nationalist feeling runs high. However, most of the time francophones and anglophones, whether federalist or separatist, mingle easy in the clubs and convivial cafés of the Quartier Latin where conversation is conducted multi-lingually and at high volume.

Rue St-Denis was originally carved out of the estates of two leaders of the 1837 rebellion against British rule, Denis-Benjamin Viger and Louis-Joseph Papineau. St-Denis became the main street of a posh residential district named the Faubourg St-Laurent, one of Montréal's first suburbs when the city overflowed its old defensive walls.

Once home to the premier of the province and the elite of the business class, the majority of the original buildings were destroyed by the Great Fire that devastated Montréal in 1852. A significant number of the wealthy moved north and west, but the district remained quite fashion-

The Film Scene

It's appropriate that Canada's National Film Board offices are located in Montréal, in a rather unusual facility in the Latin Quarter, with the Cinémathèque Québécoise just down the street. The city harbours a surprisingly large film and studio community, bolstered by its bilingual labour pool and good local training programmes.

Any time of year, walking through the Plateau or downtown, you're likely to see barricades and parking notices. If you do, keep your eyes peeled: filming is probably going on, and it's often a major Hollywood motion picture in the works. That could be Denzel Washington or Bruce Willis tucking into dinner in that chic St-Laurent restaurant, glad (for once) to be just a little bit incognito.

In summer, a raft of film festivals – Asian, B-movie, art-film and Québecois are just a few of them – parade through the city, culminating in the grand Montréal International Film Festival.

In 1999 ExCentris – a huge new multi-screen art-film complex – opened its doors on the Main to mixed architectural reviews. Too drab and post-industrial, said some. Others were too busy sipping designer coffee and working on their screenplay in the café inside to complain.

able until well into the 20th century. The Victorian and Second Empire elegance of some of the townhouses can be discerned in neoclassical and Art Nouveau embellishments on some upper storeys (particularly the Mendelson Apartments at boulevard de Maisonneuve).

People first started calling the district the Quartier Latin in 1897, when Québec City's Université Laval opened a centre next to the Eglise St-Jacques, a centre that eventually morphed into the independent Université de Montréal.

In 1915, the Bibliothèque Nationale du Québec built the stately Beaux-Arts building at 1700 rue St-Denis to store the province archives, adding to the district's scholarly air. For nearly the next half century, the Quartier Latin was the academic heart of francophone Montréal. But in the 1940s, the Université de Montréal abandoned the district for its opulent new campus on the northern slopes of Mont-Royal and the Quartier Latin slid slowly into genteel squalor.

Homes that once housed prosperous professionals and merchants became rooming houses for itinerants and day labourers; families with money moved out to the suburbs.

In the 1960s, city planners made brave attempts to revitalize the area by making it a transportation crossroads. But the construction of the city's main bus terminus on rue Berri only congested the roads. In 1966, the Berri-de-Montigny Métro station (now Berri-UQAM) opened at the corner of rue Ste-Catherine. It was the central transfer station in the slick new métro system, but for the most part easy access to underground shops left commuters without any special reason to venture upstairs to the streets to patronize local business.

Prosperity returns

Money, if not respectability, returned to the district during the late 1960s and 1970s as St-Denis cafés gained notoriety as a hotbed of separatism and radicalism. Enterprising restaurateurs began to move in and renovate. Among the first was Le Faubourg St-Denis.

There was no lack of vitality, as

Map on page 126

Cookies galore from a Canadian baking institution.

BELOW: the corner of Ste-Catherine and Berri Square.

The Jazz Scene

For 10 days in early July, the Montréal International Jazz Festival books 1,000 performers from around the globe into venues all over the city. From the first event organised in 1979 by Alain Simard, then aged 29, the event has grown in popularity.

What makes this festival extraordinary is that the music venues include not only pricey clubs and concert halls but also entire streets, blocked off to allow thousands to hear free concerts at stages erected at major intersections on rue St-Denis and rue Ste-Catherine. These nightly block parties lend the city a euphoric jazz atmosphere that makes the festival the highlight of Montréal's summer – and one of the best jazz events in Canada. With an attendance exceeding two million, the festival now rivals Montreux and Monterey.

Big names from around the world attend the prestigious festival and it has helped to launch the careers of Canadian performers such as Michael Bublé, pianist and vocalist Diana Krall and the Suzie Arioli Band whose guitarist, Jordan Officer, has been compared with Django Reinhardt.

One of the most renowned performers to emerge from Montréal is pianist Oscar Peterson *(see page 87)*, who began his career at 17 playing swing in the Johnny Holmes Orchestra at Victoria Hall in Westmount. He created his own sound in a trio that performed in the Alberta Lounge opposite Windsor Station, and later found international fame. Peterson took piano lessons from his sister Daisy Sweeney who also taught Oliver Jones and Joe Sealey, well known Montréal jazz piano players.

Peterson and Jones grew up in the rough-and-tumble working class area of St-Antoine, as did Milton Sealy (no relation to Joe), who died in New York in 2000. Just before his death Sealy had released a CD of his own compositions with singer Jeri Brown, who is a staple of the Canadian jazz scene.

The smoky tones of jazz divas such as Ella Fitzgerald and Sarah Vaughan live on in the vibrant voice of Montréal-based Ranee Lee. Born in Brooklyn she moved north in 1972. The Big Band era is also alive and well in the form of the Vic Vogel Big Band, whose avuncular, genial leader has been a fixture on Montreal's jazz scene for more than four decades.

Vogel, an accomplished arranger and composer and mentor to young musicians, began playing piano as a child, later graduating to the trombone and the tuba.

Montréal doesn't limit itself to the jazz festival, the art form can be explored as part of a degree programme in jazz studies at McGill University, and the city is home to the record label Justin Time Records Inc., the recording company for singer Karen Young, bassist Michel Donato and the Montréal Jubilation Gospel Choir. There are also several good music venues around town (Grumpy's, The Upstairs Jazz Club, The House of Jazz) where jazz musicians give regular concerts or just jam together.

The dance company, Les Ballets Jazz de Montréal *(see page 60)*, adds another dimension to the portrait of jazz in the city. To music ranging from Gershwin to Pat Metheny, sometimes exploring social themes such as gender relations and nuclear holocaust, it has presented exuberant and accessible ballets to audiences worldwide. ❑

LEFT: a colourful character at the Jazz Festival.

the street would explode with celebrations and demonstrations every year on June 24, the feast day of St. Jean-Baptiste (St John the Baptist), patron saint of French Canada.

The scene looked much the same whenever the Montréal Canadiens hockey club won the Stanley Cup, a regular event during the 1970s. Among the intellectual and artistic community that gathered here, the youth of Montréal defined themselves no longer as "French Canadians" but as "Québécois", and "la St-Jean" became le Fête Nationale.

People-watching

However, it was a fresh injection of academic life that really brought the area back to life. In 1979, the **Université du Québec à Montréal** ❸ opened its main campus in the Quartier Latin. UQAM (pronounced Oo-kam by francophones and You-kwam by anglophones) is not a particularly pretty campus. Its huddled brick buildings, which fill two city blocks along St-Denis between boulevards René-Lévesque and de Maisonneuve, look more like bunkers than schools. The only things that save them from utter dreariness are the fragments of the old **Eglise St-Jacques** poking up amid the dreck. But the university has about 22,000 students, whose liveliness more than makes up for the tedium of their campus.

On the south side of rue Ste-Catherine in the heart of the campus stands one of the most flamboyant pieces of church architecture in Montréal, the **Chapelle Notre-Dame-de-Lourdes** ❹ (430 rue Ste-Catherine Est; open 7.30am–6pm Mon–Fri, 9am–6pm Sun). The lavishly decorated interior is the work of Napoléon Bourassa, who considered the chapel his finest work.

The area around UQAM is most alive during the summer festivals, of which there seem to be no end. Among these events, the most important is the **Montréal International Jazz Festival** *(see box opposite)* held every year in the first two weeks of July. For much of the festival, the street is closed to traffic and becomes a carnival arcade with tens of thousands milling along the street. It

Map on page 126

A stilt walker has a bird's eye view of the Jazz Festival fun.

LEFT: waiting for the music to begin.
BELOW: the Montréal Jazz Festival has a street parade.

Jokers descend on Montréal for the Just For Laughs event, which began in 1983. Today the festival also includes short films and more than 700 performers.

seems the whole city comes out to hear the free concerts on temporary stages set up at the intersections, and to watch unofficial street performers juggle, mime and eat fire. With no less than 1,000 musicians from five continents, and up to 50 concerts daily, the festival has helped to make avid jazz enthusiasts out of many a Montréaler.

But St-Denis is also a focus for the Just for Laughs comedy festival *(see box below)*, the Festival International de Nouvelle Danse, which is held every two years, the World Film Festival as well as the International Mime Festival. Each of these is among the largest in its medium and draws performers and fans from around the globe.

Provincial archive

Just north of the UQAM campus stands the **Grande Bibliothèque du Québec** ❺ (Québec National Library, GBQ, 475 boulevard de Maisonneuve Est; open Tues–Fri 10am–10pm; Sat–Sun 10am–5pm; tel: 514-873 1100). This five-storey glass and steel building not only houses Québec's archives, but serves as a kind of provincial lending library as well, with more than a million books and thousands of CDs and DVDs. The majority of the works are in French; about 30 per cent are in English. If you're an insomniac, it's worth remembering that the periodicals room is open until midnight every night.

One block north of rue Sherbrooke, the street opens onto Carré St-Louis, one of the prettiest squares in the city with its tall trees and large Victorian fountain. It is also surrounded on three sides by fine Second Empire homes that are occupied by some of Québec's more successful actors and artists.

The ugly modern building on the square's eastern end houses the **Institut de tourisme et d'hôtellerie du Québec** (3535 rue St-Denis; tel: 514-282 5120; 514-282 5161 for the Restaurant de l'Institut), a school that trains chefs, bartenders, and hotel managers. It also has a restaurant and a small hotel where the students can practise their skills. Unfortunately, the square itself has

RIGHT: poet's corner.

Comedy Central

This is a city that enjoys a laugh. Comedians have so pervaded everyday life here that they often star in television commercials.

Montréal is chock-full of festivals in summer, but the annual Festival Juste pour Rire (Just for Laughs) in late July is one of the most anticipated. It's the last of the great comedy festivals in North America – a 10-day romp of street pantomime, magicians, jokes, juggling and a lot more – when an appreciative city turns out in force to laugh it up along several closed-to-traffic blocks of boulevard St-Denis in the Latin Quarter. Inside the Théâtre St-Denis and venues across the city, famous and soon-to-be-famous comedians such as John Cleese, Bill Cosby, Jerry Seinfeld and a parade of young Québécois jokesters entertain audiences.

And the laughs don't end with the festival. The Musée Juste pour Rire (2111 boulevard St-Laurent; open by reservation, entrance charge, tel: 514-845 5105), said to be the only such museum in the world, uses exhibits and audiovisual presentations to convey the brightest lights of the regional comedy scene. A sign that, no matter how cold the winter gets, Montréalers will do anything for a laugh.

become a haunt of skateboarders and scruffy looking men sipping liquid refreshment from brown-paper bags. Still, it's worth a visit.

Prince Arthur restaurants

To the west the square connects to **rue Prince-Arthur** ❻ a street that represents a small triumph for the pursuit of simple pleasures in the heart of the big city.

In 1981, the city closed the five blocks of Prince-Arthur between Carré St-Louis and boulevard St-Laurent to traffic, paved them with brick, and spruced them up with trees, poster-pillars and a small fountain. At about the same time, the Greek restaurants that were opening in the area discovered a loophole in the province's Byzantine liquor laws that permitted their clients to bring their own wine.

"Apportez-votre vin" (Bring your own wine) signs appeared in windows all over the district, a money-saving measure that became an instant hit with the city's budget-conscious epicures. Now you can pop into a liquor store or *dépanneur* (corner grocery store) and pick up a bottle of something for a reasonable price to drink at dinner. The waiter will gladly uncork and serve it as lovingly as if it had come from the restaurant's own cellars.

Diners can choose from a range of menus on Prince-Arthur, but big Greek restaurants serving kebabs, stuffed vine leaves, grilled chicken, swordfish and shellfish from the Maritime provinces or the tiny Îles-de-la-Madeleine still predominate.

On weekend nights the mall fills with a meandering crowd of diners, often distracted by jugglers, musicians and sketch artists who have discovered an ideal forum to show off their skills. Diners at second-storey windows get a view of the whole parade of life below. Tables arranged out on the mall itself allow customers to eat under the sun or stars, or in the shade of a parasol.

Plateau Mont-Royal

North of rue Cherrier and Carré St-Louis, the Quartier Latin district gradually gives way to the **Plateau Mont-Royal** ❼, one the liveliest and most desirable neighbourhoods in Montréal. Originally, its rows of duplexes and triplexes were designed to house large working-class families, who in turn supported the huge parish churches that sprinkle the area. What Montréalers call duplexes and triplexes are actually two- and three-storey apartment buildings with each floor comprising a single flat.

The living spaces themselves are quite spacious but tend to be long and narrow like a railway car. Sometimes they have a corridor but often the rooms just open onto each other. To save interior space, upper storeys are often reached by curving outdoor stairways that are pretty to look at but treacherous to climb, especially in winter.

In summer, the stairways and balconies become a kind of outdoor

Map on page 126

Property at premium rates on the edge of St-Louis Square.

BELOW: Montréalers make good use of their green spaces and parks.

Staircases become a summer meeting place in Montreal.

social space where the locals meet to talk, sip wine and beer and maybe barbecue some steaks or seafood. If a Montréaler tells you he's spending his summer in "Balconville", he means he's staying in town and spending his days socialising with the neighbours that share his stairs.

The take over

Starting in the mid-1980s, young professionals and artists began to take over, pushing many of the older working-class and immigrant families further north and east. But the district is not yet an exclusive yuppie haven; families, students and urban nomads remain.

The stretch of rue St-Denis that runs through the Plateau is packed with good restaurants, bars, nightclubs, *fripperies* (selling secondhand and recycled fashions), and stores with everything from soap and furniture to ice cream and sex toys. Avenues Mont-Royal and Duluth are both good for dining, shopping and night life as well. They're also the places to go if you want to get a tattoo or have your navel pierced.

BELOW: peace in Parc Lafontaine.

Pious past

The young professionals and artists live in a neighbourhood that was once deeply religious. The most dramatic reminder of those days is the **Eglise St-Jean-Baptiste** (309 rue Rachel Est), an enormous, 3,000-seat temple sumptuously decorated with pink marble and gilded wood. It's usually locked up tight, but it opens for mass on the weekend when you can pop in for a look. Its impressive Cassavant organ and first-class acoustics make it a popular venue for concerts and choir recitals.

The huge working-class families that filled the church in more pious days could spend their leisure time in the pretty **Parc Lafontaine** (3933 avenue Parc-Lafontaine; open 9am–10pm; tel: 514-872 9800), whose 40 hectares (100 acres) of mature trees and landscaped lawns enclose a waterfall, a fountain and two linked ponds where visitors can rent a pedal boat in summer and skate on the ice in winter. The park is also home to the Théâtre de Verdure, which stages open-air plays and concerts during the summer.

The Village

The Plateau shares Parc Lafontaine with Le Village, the vibrant heart of Montreal's gay community which skirts the park's southern edge. Stretching east to west along rue Ste-Catherine Est, mainly between rue St-Hubert and avenue Papineau, it can be accessed from Berri-UQAM or Beaudry Métro stations.

This area has had a somewhat mixed history, but is now one of the largest gay neighbourhoods in the world, known for its nightlife and lively events. The Divers Cité (Diverse City) gay pride parade in August and the Black and Blue Party in October both draw huge crowds. But the best way to get a feel for the place is to stroll along the north-south side streets between rue Sherbrooke and boulevard René-Lévesque.

Lovingly restored old homes, shady back gardens and colourful window boxes characterise this revitalised area. Around rue Amherst and boulevard de Maisonneuve is an increasing range of antique and speciality shops to browse, as well as bars and nightclubs catering to the gay and lesbian community.

From the southern end of rue Amherst there is a striking view of the Clock Tower in the Old Port and further east along René-Lévesque, towards rue de la Visitation, you can see the modern Radio Canada building rising up in front of the Jacques-Cartier Bridge. The fortress-like walls of the 200-year-old Molson Brewery building are visible near the port.

The beautiful **Église St-Pierre-Apôtre** ❽ (Church of St Peter the Apostle, 1201 rue de la Visitation), is a good example of Québec Gothic Revival architecture, was built in 1853. Designed by architect Victor Bourgeau, it features flying buttresses and a 70-metre (230-ft) spire. In the finely decorated interior, the Chapel of Hope is dedicated to victims of Aids.

Two other nearby churches worth a look include **Ste-Brigide** (1153 rue Alexandre-de-Sève), not only for its Romanesque Revival style but also for its lovely 19th-century lamps; and **St-Pierre-et-St-Paul** (1151 rue de Champlain), which serves as Montréal's Russian Orthodox cathedral. Rue Ste-Rose, behind all of these churches, is an elegant street lined with beautifully restored old houses with mansard roofs and wrought-iron carriage gates.

Industrial history

In the northern part of The Village on rue Amherst between rue Ontario and rue Sherbrooke is the **Ecomusée du Fier Monde** ❾ (2050 rue Amherst; open Wed 11am–8pm, Thur–Fri 9.30am–5pm, Sat–Sun 10.30am–5pm; entrance charge; tel: 514-528 8444). The old Art Deco public bathhouse is home to a museum dedicated to the period in the social and economic history of this neighbourhood when it was one of the birthplaces of Canada's industrial revolution. ❑

Map on page 126

TIP

Even though the Art Deco building that houses the Ecomusée du Fier Monde has been carefully and skillfully restored, it is only worth paying the entrance charge for the museum if there is an interesting visiting exhibition.

BELOW: a bar in The Village.

RESTAURANTS & BARS

Restaurants

Quartier Latin

Buona Notte
3518 boulevard St-Laurent (near rue Sherbrooke). Tel: 514-848 0644. L & D Mon–Sat, D only Sun. $$$$
The waiting staff look like fashion models and at the weekend hip-hop music thumps loudly. But you can dine well if you stick to the simple pasta dishes such as veal and mushroom lasagna.

Café Méliès
3540 boulevard St-Laurent (near rue Prince-Arthur). Tel: 514-847 9218. L & D daily, B Sat–Sun only. $$$
In the ExCentris complex; a favourite of actors and writers. Classic comfort dishes: grilled tuna and seared calf's liver.

Globe
3455 boulevard St-Laurent (near rue Sherbrooke). Tel: 514-284 3823. L & D Mon–Sat, D only Sun. $$$
Popular with trendy urbanites. Comfort food with style – slow-cooked back ribs in red-wine sauce, stewed rabbit, roast chicken with mashed potatoes.

Laloux
250 avenue des Pins (at avenue Laval). Tel: 514-287 9127. L & D Mon–Fri, D only Sun. $$$
Chef André Besson's contemporary take on French cuisine works best with seafood. Try crab ravioli followed by sea bream with olive oil, herbs and diced tomatoes.

Maestro SVP
3615 boulevard St-Laurent (at rue Prince-Arthur). Tel: 514-842 6447. L & D Mon–Sat, D only Sun. $$$
Owner Ilene Polansky's wooden oyster bar has bivalves from all over the world. For something more filling try the excellent clam chowder and scallops flambéed in brandy in the dining room.

Med Grill
3500 boulevard St-Laurent (near rue Sherbrooke). Tel: 514-844 0027. L & D Mon–Sat, D only Sun. $$$
Flamboyant showcase for chic 30-somethings. The food's good too, try the pepper-crusted tuna with sweetbreads.

La Paryse
302 rue Ontario Est (near rue Sanguinet). Tel: 514-842 2040. L & D Tues–Sun. $
Some say this child-friendly institution in the heart of the Quartier Latin has the juiciest burgers in town, but it's roast-turkey sandwiches and milk-shakes are worth a try.

Santropol
3990 rue St-Urbain (at avenue Duluth). Tel: 514-842 3110. L & D daily. $
A genuine neighbourhood institution that is popular with students and artists. It specializes in big, healthy, mostly vegetarian, sandwiches and pot pies.

Plateau Mont-Royal

Ail Y'ail Y'ail
4563 boulevard St-Laurent (at avenue Mont-Royal). Tel: 514-849 8185. D only daily. $$
Iberian cuisine and garlic is king here, it is in everything from seafood to french-fries, and even in the rice and spicy chorizo sausage.

L'Anecdote
809 rue Rachel Est (at rue St-Hubert). Tel: 514-526 7697. B, L & D daily. $
One of Montreal's best burger joints. Burgers of all kinds including veal and deer. There's a small table where little ones can look at books.

Aquaterra
285 avenue Mont-Royal Est (at rue Jeanne-Mance). Tel: 514-288 3005. D only Tues–Sun. $$$
The chefs blend Italian and Japanese cuisine, which can lead to European dish with a twist. Try grilled quail with braised Asian pear.

Binerie Mont-Royal
367 avenue du Mont-Royal (near rue St-Denis). Tel: 514-285 9078. B, L & D Mon–Fri, B & L Sat–Sun. $
Eight stools and two tables in the ultimate hole-in-the wall diner, but the service is friendly and the food is authentic Québécois: *tourtière* (meat pie), *pâté chinois* (shepherd's pie), *feves au lard* (pork and beans).

Bistro Cocagne
3842 rue St-Denis (near rue Roy). Tel: 514-286 0700. $$$
The food is more daring than traditional bistro fare. Try the charcuterie plate with three kinds of sausage and home-smoked deer tongue and wild-boar bacon.

Chez Doval
150 rue Marie-Anne (at rue Hôtel-de-Ville). Tel: 514-843 3390. L & D daily. $$
Neighbourhood grill where chicken, sardines and grouper are cooked to perfection. Choose between the noisy tavern or the more subdued dining room.

L'Express
3927 rue St-Denis (near avenue Duluth Est). Tel: 514-845 5333. L & D daily. $$$
Bistro with tiny tables, zinc bar and a noisy crowd of regulars every night. Excellent steak-frites, or try the calf's liver tarragon.

Moishe's
3961 boulevard St-Laurent (near avenue Duluth Est). Tel: 514-845 3509. L & D Mon–Fri, D only Sat–Sun. $$$$
Once you get past the ugly exterior, dining at Moishe's is like a good men's club in the 1940s. The best steaks in Montreal.

Au Pied du Cochon
536 avenue Duluth (near rue Berri). Tel: 514-281 1114. D only Tues–Sun. $$$

Chef Martin Picard braises pigs' hocks in maple syrup, serves crispy pork skin and an irresistible sugar pie. He also scatters foie gras on just about everything.

Le Pégase
1831 rue Gilford (at rue Cartier). Tel: 514-522 0487. D only Tues–Sun. $$
Bring your own wine to this casual bistro. Try a thick, juicy grilled caribou steak. Great desserts.

La Prunelle
327 avenue Duluth Est (at rue Drolet). Tel: 514-849 8403. $$
Classy restaurant with a bring-your-own wine policy that make its French cuisine affordable. Try the Guinea hen stuffed with Parma ham and caramelized pears.

Pintxo
256 rue Roy Est (near avenue Laval). Tel: 514-844 0222. L & D Wed–Fri, D only Mon–Tues and Sat. $$$
The Basque version of tapas. Build a meal with morsels of duck-stuffed mushrooms, salmon tartar, seared scallops, and grilled tuna, or order a main dish like beef cheeks braised in wine.

Restaurant de l'Institut
3535 rue St-Denis (on Carré St-Louis). Tel: 514-282 5161. B, L & D Mon–Sat, B & D Sat, B only Sun. $$$
Restaurant of the Institut de Tourisme et d'Hôtellerie du Québec, where student chefs, waiters and bartenders are trained. The food is good and the service is charming.

St-Viateur Bagel and Café
1127 avenue Mont-Royal (near rue Christophe-Colombe) Tel: 514-528 6361. Open daily 6am–midnight. $
Some say Montréal bagels are the best bagels. Filled with cream cheese and smoked salmon and served with a bowl of soup, they make a perfect meal.

Schwartz's Delicatessen
1895 boulevard St-Laurent (near avenue Duluth Est). Tel: 514-842 4813. B, L & D daily. $
No one makes a smoked-meat sandwich better than this no-frills deli, where the service is brusque and the lunchtime lines long.

The Village

Area
1429 rue Amherst (at rue Ste-Catherine Est). Tel: 514-890 6691. L & D Tues–Fri, D only Sat–Sun. $$$
There are no main dishes at this little restaurant on the edge of the Gay Village. Diners assemble meals out of an assortment of soups, amuses bouches and desserts. Try a tiny dish of Angus beef with mashed potatoes, as well as a few crispy tempura shrimp.

Au Petit Extra
1690 rue Ontario Est (near avenue Papineau). Tel: 514-527 5552. L & D Mon–Fri, D only Sat–Sun. $$
Good food, impressive wine list and excellent service have made this bistro the darling of the trendy Plateau Mont-Royal set. Try the bouillabaisse or the duck confit.

Ô Chalet
1393 boulevard René-Lévesque Est (at rue Plessis). Tel: 514-527 7070. D only Tues–Sat. $$$$
Kitsch decor. Try the halibut with Riopelle cheese or the pork chops with truffle butter and chopped walnuts.

Resto du Village
1310 rue Wolfe (at rue Ste-Catherine). Tel: 514-524 5404. Open 24 hours. $
There's nothing fancy about the decor or the food: burgers, roast pork and mashed potatoes, fried chicken. But what it does it does well.

Saloon Bistro Bar
1333 rue Ste-Catherine Est (at rue Panet). Tel: 514-522 1333. B, L and D daily. $$
Laid-back atmosphere and a menu with dishes from Southeast Asia to Mexico.

Bars

Quartier Latin

Cheval Blanc
809 rue Ontario Est. Tel: 514-522 0211.
A 1940s-style tavern with a variety of beers brewed on the premises.

L'Île Noire
342 rue Ontario Est. Tel: 514-982 0866.
A wide selection of single-malt whiskies; an ideal place for a quiet after-dinner drink.

Jello Bar
151 rue Ontario Est. Tel: 514-285 2621.
Lava lamps and love seats decorate this wildly popular dance club. Music from salsa to R&B.

Plateau Mont-Royal

Le Big Cheeze
4479 rue St-Denis. Tel: 514-845 9010.
An unpretentious jazz bar with reasonably priced drinks and live music; a young crowd. Downstairs is the smaller, quieter Quai des Brumes (tel: 514-499 0467).

Le Dogue
4177 rue St-Denis. Tel: 514-845 8717.
The best place in the Plateau to dance, arrive early if you want a seat.

Sofa
451 rue Rachel Est. Tel: 514-285 1011.
Thirty-somethings lounge on big sofas, sipping cocktails.

The Village

Cabaret Mado
1115 rue Ste-Catherine Est. Tel: 514-525 7566.
Both gay and straight enjoy the show here.

Jet Club
1003 rue Ste-Catherine Est. Tel: 514-842 2582.
Clubbers of all ages and orientations, dressed to kill, pack the dance floor. The VIP lounge is a little quieter – but not much.

PRICE CATEGORIES

Prices for a three-course dinner per person with a half-bottle of house wine:
$ = under $25
$$ = $25–50
$$$ = $50–70
$$$$ = more than $70

FESTIVALS

From the Dragon Boat Race to the St Patrick's Day Parade and the Jazz Festival, there's a party most months of the year

Montréalers are known for their *joie de vivre* and in any month of the year there's a celebration. Chilly winter weather is no deterrent. While the bigger festivals run during the summer and autumn, there are also events in January and February, the most popular being the **Montréal Highlights Festival**, an 11-day bacchanal of eating and drinking, with photography exhibits, concerts and a torchlight parade. The city hosts around 90 festivals every year, from small, community happenings to celebrity-laden events that attract thousands of visitors. The gay community struts its stuff at the **Divers/Cité Festival** in July and the **Black and Blue Festival** in October with its themed costumed balls and dance extravaganzas. Montréal is home to more than 80 ethnic groups that lend their own touch to festivities by commemorating their roots in events as diverse as the **Montréal International Dragon Boat Race Festival** and the colourful, noisy **St Patrick's Day Parade** *(see opposite)*. The noise level at the Dragon Boat Race is equally ear-splitting. Dozens of drummers boom out a beat for thousands of paddlers who compete in a nail-biting competition staged at the Olympic Basin in Parc Jean-Drapeau in late July.

ABOVE: over 100 balloons dot the skies above the Richelieu Valley during the annual L'International de Montgolfières de Saint-Jean-sur-Richelieu in August. **RIGHT:** nutty acts and silly jokes are the heart of the comedy fest, Juste pour Rire. Follow the crowd and laugh along.

ABOVE: warm summer nights resound with bangs and crackles interspersed with oohs and aahs from thousands of spectators as they watch fireworks blaze across the sky above La Ronde, site of the International Fireworks Competition.

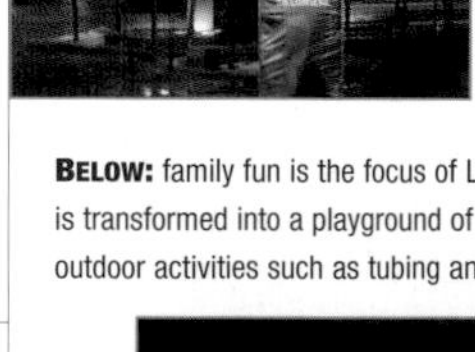

LEFT: winter chills are no deterrent to Montréalers who turn out in droves at the end of February to party and listen to live entertainment. Diehard revellers pull an all-nighter on the last evening – the grand finale of the Festival Montréal en Lumière.

BELOW: family fun is the focus of La Fête des Neiges when parc Jean-Dra is transformed into a playground of snow and ice where youngsters can e outdoor activities such as tubing and dogsledding.

RIGHT: glamorous get-ups and dazzling drag queens lend a festive air to Gay Pride week, held in July.

BELOW: little gremlins in green hats, bundled up against the brisk March temperatures, take part in the St Patrick's Day Parade. The lively event in Montréal, which has been running for over 180 years, is North America's oldest St Patrick's Day celebration.

FESTIVAL HIGHLIGHTS

The Montréal International Jazz Festival launched Montréal as Canada's prime festival destination. The jazz fest format – hundreds of concerts, many free or almost free, staged at outdoor venues as well as in theatres – has been copied elsewhere. The 10-day event attracts over two million jazz aficionados every summer.

Juste pour Rire (Just for Laughs) is a month-long comedy festival in the Quartier Latin in July. It's a giggle-a-minute in comedy clubs and at Théatre St-Denis, where events are hosted by the likes of John Cleese and Bill Cosby. Up-and-coming comedians and street performers add to the fun.

Festival International Nuits d'Afrique in mid-July is a celebration of music from over 30 countries, showcasing the best performers from Africa, the Caribbean and Latin America. Hundreds of musicians and singers perform at Place Émilie-Gamelin, downtown.

The World Film Festival is an annual celebration of cinema in September. Six weeks later the lesser-known **Festival du Nouveau Cinéma** attracts a devoted following. It screens over 180 independent films made by innovative Québecois and foreign feature and documentary film makers.

RIGHT: the maple leaf is the symbol of Canada and nowhere is this more evident than on 1 July, Canada Day, a national holiday when the country is awash in a sea of red and white flags and Montréalers enjoy lavish celebrations.

WESTMOUNT

Built on the western slope of Mont-Royal the neighbourhood is historically home to well-to-do Anglophones.

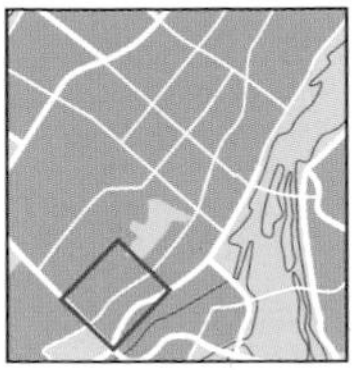

Map on page 142

The metro ride west from the rue Peel station in the heart of downtown to the Atwater station takes just five to 10 minutes. But if you then follow the signs to Westmount Square and climb back to the surface at the avenue Greene exit, you will find yourself in a different world. This is Westmount, which bears a stronger resemblance to a prosperous market town in England than a French-speaking metropolis in North America.

An anglophone stronghold

It's an impression that grows only stronger as you walk west along boulevard de Maisonneuve or rue Sherbrooke. The streets that climb steeply up the slopes of the "petite montagne" – Mont-Royal's western shoulder – are lined with elegant Victorian homes and century-old oaks and maples.

The even grander mansions near the summit tend to be mock-Tudor, faux-Norman, Scottish baronial or just plain modern ostentatious. Neo-Gothic churches, a City Hall that looks like a medieval guildhall, and large, informal parks all add to the feeling. And if it's a sunny summer day, you might just catch a glimpse of the members of the Westmount Lawn Bowling Club at 401 avenue Kensington in their crisp whites rolling balls across a perfectly manicured stretch of grass.

For a large number of younger francophones, all this Britishness makes Westmount something of a caricature of anglophone attitudes. For some older francophones, however, this green and grassy suburb covering the western edge of central Montréal is something a lot more sinister – a metaphor for the bad old days of anglophone privilege. And indeed, the prosperous 19th-century merchants and traders

LEFT: climbing the mountain.
BELOW: a statue in front of the Globe building.

Take a calèche ride through parc du Mont-Royal. Wrap up warm in the winter.

who founded the city of Westmount were deliberately trying to establish an exclusive enclave that didn't have a lot of room for French-speaking Canadians.

Those exclusionary days are long over. Although English is still the dominant language in the suburb, Westmount today is home to many francophone residents. In fact, francophones began moving into the area as early as the late 1890s, and one of the suburb's most beautiful buildings is the neo-Romanesque Église St-Léon, built in the 1920s to accommodate Westmount's French-speaking Roman Catholics.

But this suburb's diversity goes well beyond adding some francophones to the mix. Although Westmount's population remains largely white and Western European, its prime location within walking distance of the downtown skyscrapers has made it a magnet for the prosperous and successful of all races and ethnic groups. And they have brought a dash of colour to Westmount's staid image.

In the beginning

In the 1670s, the Society of Priests of St Sulpice established an outpost on what is now rue Sherbrooke Ouest, close to the dividing line between the cities of Montréal and Westmount. Two circular defence towers stand on the north side of the street in front of the Grand Séminaire de Montréal complex as reminders of this early settlement.

Eventually, the Sulpicians began to cede lands on the *petite montagne* to a community of farmers. Old Aboriginal trails and horse tracks connected these farmers to the city but, by any standard, they were isolated, and it wasn't until the mid-1800s that the community on the *petite montagne* grew in size.

As transportation gradually became more efficient, the area's

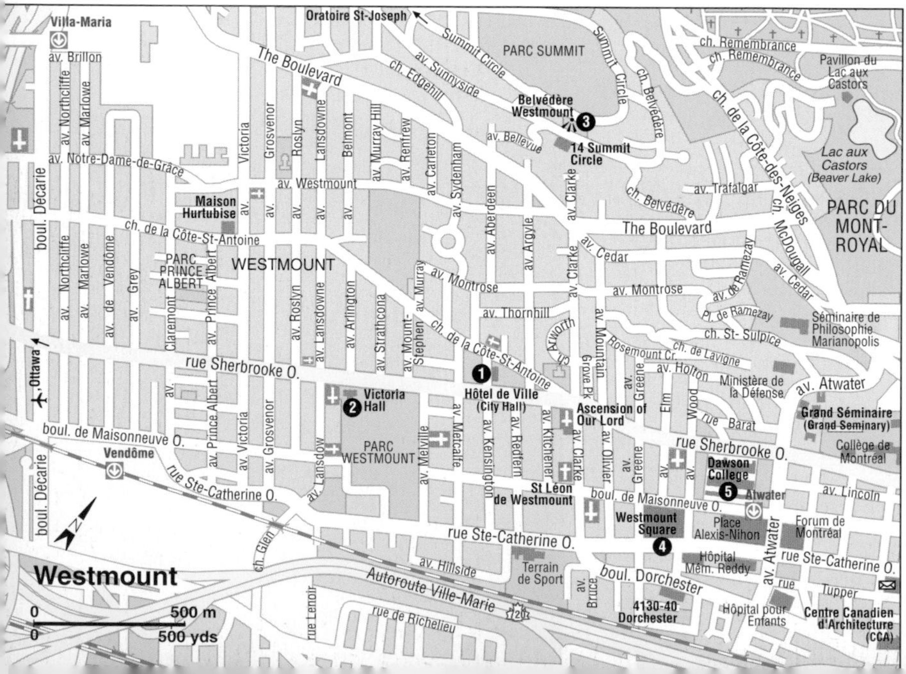

splendid views, clean air and lower property taxes made it a tempting alternative to the Golden Square Mile *(see page 118)* as a haven for Montréal's growing middle and professional classes.

Prosperous English and Scottish fur traders, merchants and financiers, as well as a great number of the city's lawyers and doctors began to settle in the area, and in 1869, the first English school was established in what was then called the village of Côte St-Antoine.

As more people settled in and around the village, a movement developed whose aim was to preserve the residential, non-industrial character of the community. In 1890, the Côte St-Antoine Improvement Committee was formed and, composed of mainly anglophone residents, created a city plan for municipal buildings and parks. The committee was very successful at regulating commercial development, and for many years it banned the "gathering of families under one roof" in apartment houses.

Its enthusiasm was fuelled by a desire for a peaceful residential community and a deep distrust of the Montréal city government.

A suburb is born

In a vote that was nearly defeated, the city council changed the name of the village to Westmount in 1895, and the city of Westmount received its charter in 1908. As the local population became more homogeneous, a distinct enclave of middle-class anglophone Montréalers became established, but that distrust of city politics persists to this day.

When Québec's provincial government forced the island of Montréal's 23 suburbs to amalgamate with the central city in 2002, Westmount led the fight to reverse the decision. At the first opportunity, the residents of the 405-hectare (995-acre) enclave voted resoundingly to regain their independent status.

Sport for all

Westmount residents appear to have been strict teetotallers and avid sportsmen at the turn of the 20th century. In fact, they seem to have

Map on page 142

A monument to Sir George-Etienne Cartier (see page 82), stands in parc Mont-Royal. Cartier is known as the father of Canadian Confederation.

BELOW: a view of the city from Mont-Royal.

Parc Mont-Royal

You can see it from just about anywhere in Montréal, whether you're buying a magazine at a newsstand, gazing idly out from a kitchen window or taking the dog for its nightly walk. Mont-Royal – or, as Montréalers call it, *la montagne* (the mountain) – looms up in the middle of the city like a natural obelisk proclaiming the city's presence.

For Montréalers, the mountain embodies a kind of grandeur, a place where nature's sublime and wild moods play freely across a landscape blissfully untouched by the heavy hand of urban development. Mont-Royal is more than a park. It is like an unmistakable family trait, a cherished reminder of the city's rich and vibrant history.

Indeed it was here in 1535 that French explorer Jacques Cartier was led by the First Nations through wooded hills and up rocky crests all the way to the summit. And today all kinds of modern Montréalers can be found sunning, sledding, strolling, folk-dancing and picnicking on this mountain.

That Mont-Royal is not covered by a network of roads, walking trails, cafés, electric cable cars and vast amphitheatres is largely owing to the aesthetic sensibilities of Frederick Law Olmsted, the man who was hired by the City of Montréal in 1874 to design the park. Olmsted, who also designed Manhattan's Riverside Drive as well as the elegant Morningside and Central parks, firmly believed that nature was a source of spiritual sustenance and that parks, properly designed, could provide urban dwellers with some relief from the oppressive routines of metropolitan life.

Olmsted urged Montréal to preserve its gracious mountain and warned off voracious developers and, so far, he has been heeded.

Most of Mont-Royal's pleasures can be enjoyed in any season: a stroll through its 200 hectares (495 acres) along winding trails, a walk to the summit for a look at the 30-metre (100-ft) cross. Now illuminated by electric lights, but the original cross was raised in 1643 by Paul de Chomedy, Sieur de Maisonneuve, when the fledgling colony of Ville Marie was saved from a flood. Visitors can also take a jaunt to one of the park's two lookouts for a spectacular view of central Montréal, the St Lawrence River, and the Montérégian mountains.

Horse-drawn carriages *(calèches)* are a relaxing and romantic way to traverse the park and, in warmer months, free nature walks, conducted in both French and English, start at Smith House, a stone cottage that also houses an exhibit on the park's history and a coffee shop. In winter, skaters take to Beaver Lake (an artificial pond) and cross-country skiers travel along tranquil tracks. Toboggan runs attract shoals of enthusiastic children.

On the park's northern boundary are two graveyards – the Catholic Notre-Dame-des-Neiges and the Protestant Mount Royal Cemetery. Together they cover more than half the mountain with elaborate monuments, lush vegetation and hundreds of kilometres of sinuous trails. The cemeteries' permanent occupants are quite an eclectic lot, ranging from Calixa Lavalée, composer of Canada's national anthem, to Anna Leonowens, whose life was dramatized in the musical *The King and I.* ❑

LEFT: a peaceful read on *la montagne.*

been absolutely wild about sport. Westmount established a golf course, a Toboggan and Snow Shoe Club, and a Cricket Club. The town hosted the 1894 Canadian Speed Skating Championships. It was also the site of what is thought to be the first lacrosse match ever played under lights and, as every Canadian nationalist knows, lacrosse, not hockey, is Canada's national sport. Today, the city is renowned for its parks; a reflection, no doubt, of this long tradition of outdoor pursuits.

The haves and have nots

Cutting a large swathe from north to south, Westmount comprises two roughly defined districts – Lower Westmount, which encompasses everything south of rue Sherbrooke, and Upper Westmount, which covers the slopes of the *petite montagne* from Sherbrooke to Summit Circle. As little demolition has taken place except at the southerly edge of Westmount around the boulevard de Maisonneuve, both parts of the city are rich in 19th-century architecture.

Despite the stereotypes, not all of Westmount is affluent. Some parts of Lower Westmount – notably the stretch of stone tenements below the Canadian Pacific Railway tracks and the Autoroute Ville-Marie – are largely occupied by relatively poor immigrant families.

Several of the businesses in the commercial district along the south side of rue Ste-Catherine near avenue Atwater have a rundown air, and Westmount High School has a reputation for being one of the roughest on the island.

But the majority of the suburb's residents are solidly middle class. Even a Lower Westmount address has plenty of cachet, and to live in Upper Westmount is a sure sign of success and prosperity. However, Westmount's real dividing line is not rue Sherbrooke, but a wide thoroughfare called simply The Boulevard *(see page 146)* that cuts across the suburb about halfway up the slope of the *petite montagne*. Hence, living "above The Boulevard" is the litmus test of true wealth and power.

Residents who share that rarified air include the executives of many of the city's major corporations, federal and provincial cabinet ministers and at least one former prime minister, Brian Mulroney.

Westmount's heart

The municipal centre of Westmount is at the foot of the mountain, and is loosely arranged on the English "green" model. The **City Hall ❶** (Hôtel de Ville) at 4333 Chemin Côte St-Antoine, is an imposing Tudor-style structure surrounded by colourful beds of flowers. One of its architects, Robert Findlay, was also responsible for the design of Westmount's other municipal buildings.

Across the street at 4574 rue Sherbrooke, right next to the beautifully landscaped Westmount Park, is the municipal library, **Victoria**

Map on page 142

City Hall was designed by Robert Findlay and his son Frank. They created a castle-like building, with a square tower and corner turrets.

BELOW: sculpture in Westmount's commercial district.

Hall ❷, which opened in 1899, when free libraries were still a new idea. It is distinguished by an unusual Romanesque style, with leaded-glass windows and delightful bas-reliefs that glorify "knowledge". The attached domed conservatory, which was also built in the course of the 19th century, still functions, and it beautifies Westmount's parks and streets with its winter-grown plants.

Colourful flowerbeds brighten up the gardens and parks in Westmount.

Victoria Jubilee Hall, although echoing the design of the city hall, is intended to resemble English medieval buildings and is used for a variety of public functions. the work of local artists' is also showcased here from time to time.

Religious difference

Just east of all these grand municipal buildings stand Westmount's two Roman Catholic churches, one built for the anglophones and the other for the francophones. The two churches stand back to back and in their own way illustrate some of the differences between Montréal's two founding cultures.

BELOW: distinctive architecture.

Anglophone Catholics worship at **Ascension of Our Lord** at 375 avenue Kitchener, a lovely little neo-Gothic church, all sharp spires and pointed arches, that looks as if it has been ripped out of some English country village and dropped into the middle of North America. Its interior is rather austere but beautifully proportioned.

Behind this church, at 4311 boulevard de Maisonneuve, is **St Léon de Westmount**, a domed neo-Romanesque beauty that looks almost Byzantine. It has gorgeously florid murals, Italian marble floors and richly-coloured windows, which are the work of Guido Nincheri, a prolific Italian-born artist who was also responsible for decorating several of Montréal's grandest churches, as well as the Château Dufresne. Both churches are very Catholic, but very different.

Going up the mountain

The oldest building in Westmount – the **Maison Hurtubise** at 563 Côte St-Antoine – predates the modern suburb's founders by a couple of centuries. It was built in 1688 by Pierre Hurtubise on land that had been granted to his father by Montréal's founder, Paul de Chomedy, Sieur de Maisonneuve. The house is the last remaining farmhouse dating back from the 17th century in Westmount.

With its steeply gabled roof, fieldstone walls and dormer windows it stands like a defiant little outpost of New France surrounded by a forest of Victorian and neo-Tudor upstarts. Because the house was built so far from Montréal (Ville Marie), the early inhabitants named it *la haute folie*.

The Boulevard is a particularly lovely street, lined with imposing houses of every shape and size. These homes mirror not only the eclectic tastes of their original owners, but also more recent technical advancements in construction.

Wreathing the top of the mountain are **avenue Sunnyside** and **Summit Circle**. Number 14 avenue Sunnyside, built in 1911 for Charles A. Smart, a member of the Québec provincial Parliament, is thought by many to be one of the most impressive residences in all of Westmount.

Across the street, some steep stairs *(see page 140)* lead to Summit Circle, where you'll find the **Belvédère Westmount** ❸, or Westmount Lookout, a small park and viewing area. It affords a breathtaking panorama to the west of the flat river valley and the scattered peaks of the Montes Regis, or "mountains of the king".

The houses that surround the lookout seem a little precarious but are in fact sturdy; the dramatic views from their living rooms wouldn't appeal to anyone afraid of heights. Above lies the wooded peak of the *petite montagne*. In 1928 McGill University sold the land, once the site of a botany laboratory, to Westmount, stipulating that it could never be developed. It is now a sanctuary for hundreds of species of birds. The park is particularly popular in the month of May, when flocks of passerines stop here for a break during migration.

Lower Westmount

Sometimes referred to as Lower Westmount, the streets below rue Sherbrooke are full of interesting row houses. While obviously less grand than the residences gracing the slope of the mountain, these houses display everything from the fortress style to mansard roofs, with numerous examples of stone and wood designs.

Of particular note are the towers at numbers 4130–40 Dorchester (Westmount's first terrace), and those at numbers 41–47 Holton (which show the classic Montréal pattern of alternating units).

The district of Westmount isn't all vintage architecture, however. Indeed, **Westmount Square** ❹, which is bounded by avenue Green, boulevard de Maisonneuve, rue Ste-Catherine and rue Wood, is one of

Map on page 142

Each Sunday evening in summer, and other evenings when the mood strikes, drummers congregate beside the Sir George-Etienne Cartier monument at the base of parc du Mont-Royal to drum in a collective "tam-tam jam". Dreadlocks are prevalent – but not required.

LEFT: a bird's-eye view.

Winter Parkland

The city of Westmount extends just 4 sq km (1½ sq miles), but within that compact area are 13 parks and green spaces that are much used by locals year-round. In winter, when you would expect people to be tucked up inside somewhere warm and cozy avoiding the freezing temperatures and heavy snow, Montréalers hit the parks.

Children and adults pull on their down coats and winter boots and head out to the outdoor skating rinks, which are usually open from mid-December to mid-March. There are many ice rinks throughout Montréal, and several within the confines of Westmount, including King George Park (Murray Park; avenue Westmount), Devon Park (between avenues Lansdowne and Belmont), Queen Elizabeth Gardens (avenue Wood and rue Sherbrooke), Westmount Park (chemin Academy), and Stayner Park (avenue Greene and rue Stayner). You can also book skating lessons at Westmount Arena (4675 rue Ste-Catherine Ouest).

Parc du Mont-Royal remains popular in the winter too, with cross-country skiing and calèche rides. There is a 2-km (1-mile) ski trail, but you must supply your own equipment.

Map on page 142

Ludwig Mies van der Rohe (1886–1969) is considered to be one of the 20th-century's most influential modern architects. Not only did he design Westmount Square in 1967, but he also created the austere steel and glass Toronto-Dominion Centre in Toronto, the Seagram Building in New York and the 860 Lake Shore Drive Apartments in Chicago.

the island of Montréal's most celebrated modern commercial and residential complexes.

One of the city's most prestigious addresses built in the 1960s, it was designed by architectural guru Ludwig Mies van der Rohe, and you either love it or hate it, but it is widely considered to be one of the eminent architect's finest projects. Its three severely cubical buildings – all black stone and glass – rise abruptly from a broad, flat plaza.

Much to the dismay of discriminating purists, the complex's owners punched several skylights through that vast plaza in the 1990s to allow some natural light to filter into the dungeon-like shopping mall that lies beneath. For this temerity, the experts roundly condemned them as Philistines, but shoppers certainly find the atmosphere a lot more inviting.

Westmount Square also offers an interesting counterpoint to the fashionable antiques shops, art galleries, boutiques, speciality stores and upscale restaurants that line the rest of the avenue.

BELOW: Westmount's café culture.

Centre of learning

Farther east, toward Montréal's downtown via rue Sherbrooke, is **The Mother House of the Congrégation Notre-Dame**, an order of teaching nuns founded by St Marguerite Bourgeoys. Now the campus of **Dawson College** ❺ (3040 rue Sherbrooke Ouest), Québec's largest anglophone CEGEP (Collège d'Enseignement Général et professionnel, or College of General and Vocational Education), it is impossible to miss. An awe-inspiring edifice designed by J. Omer Marchand in 1904, its distinctiveness is derived, in part, from the well-judged use of pale-coloured stone and a flamboyant Beaux-Arts style.

At one time the building was used simultaneously as a hospital, retirement home, school and headquarters for the religious order. The College is linked underground to the Atwater Métro station.

Commercial Westmount

Westmount has two distinctly different and widely separated commercial districts. The trendier one is the area around Westmount Square and avenue Greene. Here you'll find shops selling antiques, furs, toys, high-end fashions, and books. There are also several posh day spas in the district, which will provide a variety of beauty treatments and pampering at the end of a busy day exploring.

Avenue Greene, a pedestrian-friendly thoroughfare with wide brick sidewalks and restricted traffic, is particularly well known for its restaurants and bistros.

The other commercial district is on rue Sherbrooke on the western edge of the suburb. This is where Westmounters do their banking, pick up their prescription drugs and shop for groceries and hardware. But it, too, is beginning to sprout its own interesting selection of restaurants and boutiques. ❑

RESTAURANTS

Restaurants

Bistro on the Avenue
1362 avenue Greene (near rue Ste-Catherine). Tel: 514-939 6451. L & D Mon–Sat, Br & D Sun. $$
A gem of a bistro with a checkerboard floor, yellow walls and long wooden bar. It's a favourite with locals for brunch, but the evening menu is also satisfying. Try the roasted chicken breast with mashed Yukon potatoes.

Chalet Barbecue
5456 rue Sherbrooke Ouest (at boulevard Decairie). Tel: 514-489 7235. B, L & D daily. $
This rather shabby but beloved restaurant, with its worn booths, pioneered Montréal-style barbecued chicken, and it still serves the best in the province.

Claremont
5032 rue Sherbrooke Ouest (at rue Claremont). Tel: 514-483 5881. L & D Mon–Sun, Br Sat–Sun. $$
The decor of pale yellow walls, burgundy banquettes and vintage photos contribute to the casual, chic atmosphere that is almost standard in Westmount. Standard, too, is the burgers-to-seared-tuna menu, but the service is great and if you prefer a light nibble, try the tapas menu.

Kaizen
4120 rue Ste-Catherine Ouest (at avenue Wood). Tel: 514-932 5654. L & D Mon–Sat, D only Sun. $$$$
The poshest Japanese restaurant in Montréal, with floor-to-ceiling red drapes, light murals, high-backed sofas and a sushi bar that glows. The sushi selection is extensive and adventurous. If it's on the menu, try the oysters Tri-Afeller with spinach, shallots and béchamel sauce.

Maison de Séoul
5030 rue Sherbrooke Ouest (near rue Claremont). Tel: 514-489 3686. L & D Mon–Sat, D only Sun. $
Traditional Korean restaurant where charming waitresses grill chicken, beef and pork at your table and bring endless plates of fermented cabbage and spicy condiments. In summer you can eat on a terrace overlooking rue Sherbrooke.

Mess Hall
4858 rue Sherbrooke Ouest (near rue Victoria). Tel: 514-482 2167. L & D Mon–Sat. $$
This hot little restaurant is popular with the west-end yuppie crowd. An eclectic menu with everything from fancy burgers to seared tuna with lavender. The homemade ice-cream is excellent.

Sapori Pronto
4894 rue Sherbrooke Ouest (near rue Victoria). Tel: 514-487 9666. L & D Mon–Fri, D only Sat. $$
Perhaps the best Italian restaurant west of downtown, and a charming place too. Chef Peppino Perri specializes in "modernized" Italian cuisine. Try the duck with strawberries or the *escargot risotto.*

Tavern on the Square
1 Westmount Square (at rue Ste-Catherine). Tel: 514-989 9779. L & D Mon–Fri, D only Sat. $$
The chic, casual Tavern with its huge terrace and comfy décor draws a crowd of prosperous young Westmounters and their families. The main dishes are good – try the seared tuna with braised kidney beans – and desserts such as the almond cake with pineapple cubes can be close to spectacular.

Vago
1336 avenue Greene (near rue Ste-Catherine). Tel: 514-846 1414. L & D Mon–Fri, D only Sat. $$$
Trendy little Italian restaurant. The cuisine is standard Italian, but very well prepared. Try the veal piccata.

PRICE CATEGORIES

Prices for three-course dinner per person with a half-bottle of house wine:
$ = under $25
$$ = $25–$50
$$$ = $50–$70
$$$$ = more than $70

RIGHT: culinary inspired art.

AIME TON DIEU
LES CIEUX ET PAIX SUR LA TERRE AUX HOMMES

OUTREMONT AND MILE-END

Outremont lies on the eastern slope of Mont-Royal. It is the traditional home of the French-Canadian elite, with gracious residences, leafy public spaces and a lively commercial district

There was a time not that long ago, the 1970s, when Outremont could still have been called the bourgeois capital of Canada. Solidly francophone, solidly Catholic and solidly middle class. It felt, despite its mock-tudor homes and anglo street names like Plantagenet and Hartland, rather more like a fashionable Paris arrondissement than a North American suburb.

The haute-bourgeoisie – the financiers, industrialists and political leaders – lived in the mansions along avenue Maplewood high on the northeastern shoulder of Mont-Royal. Lesser but still wealthy neighbours – bank officers, merchants and judges – shared the lower slopes, while successful professionals, writers and academics occupied the comfortable homes on the flats north of chemin Côte-Ste-Catherine.

Outremont's humblest residents – shopkeepers and landlords – occupied the fringes along the commercial strip on avenue Van Horne and row homes of rue Hutchison.

It's still a prosperous district and with more than its fair share of commercial and political movers and shakers among its residents. In fact, Maplewood is still sometimes referred to as *"l'avenue du pouvoir"*, or "avenue of power". But Outremont is not what it was.

Expanding frontiers

The area is not even a separate municipality any more, just a district or ward of Montréal. Merger was forced on the town in the 1990s by the Parti Québécois government, but its residents couldn't be bothered to reclaim their autonomy when offered the chance in 2001. It is no longer solidly Catholic or solidly French – even on the *"avenue du pouvoir"*, you find non-francophone names.

Much of Outremont remains a francophone version of wealthy

Map on page 152

LEFT: Eglise St-Enfant-Jesus.
BELOW: time out in Mile End.

Westmount *(see page 141)*, but its northern neighbourhoods are also a source of cheap housing for immigrant families from the Philippines, south Asia and Latin America.

In the east, along rues Laurier and Bernard in particular, Outremont has become trendy rather than bourgeois respectable, with bars and cafés that attract the young and fashionable. The trendiness has spread east beyond Outremont's old borders into neighbouring Mile-End, a once rundown district of working-class homes, taverns and cheap restaurants.

Trendy bars and cafés have spread beyond the area's official borders.

In the minds of many Montréalers, eastern Outremont and Mile-End have merged into one, and indeed, it's difficult to tell where one begins and the other ends.

The changes haven't come without friction. One of Montréal's most interesting cultural battles rages intermittently along the Outremont's eastern edge, where a growing and vibrant Hasidic Jewish community has taken up residence. The Hasidim – distinctive for their large families, strict adherence to Jewish law and the 19th-century black dress of their men, began moving into the area and the adjoining Mile-End district after World War II.

For decades, they coexisted peacefully with their working-class and petit-bourgeois francophone neighbours. But in the 1980s, as avenues Bernard and Laurier became popular with young, urbane and intensely secular Québécois, relations deteriorated. Particularly silly was the so called "Battle of the Eruv" *(see page 154)*.

Rural beginnings

Located far from the river and the crowded little city on its banks, Outremont remained rural for generations. In fact, produce from the area, especially Montréal melons, were much praised and in the 19th century were to be found on the menus of

BELOW: chic stores in Outremont.

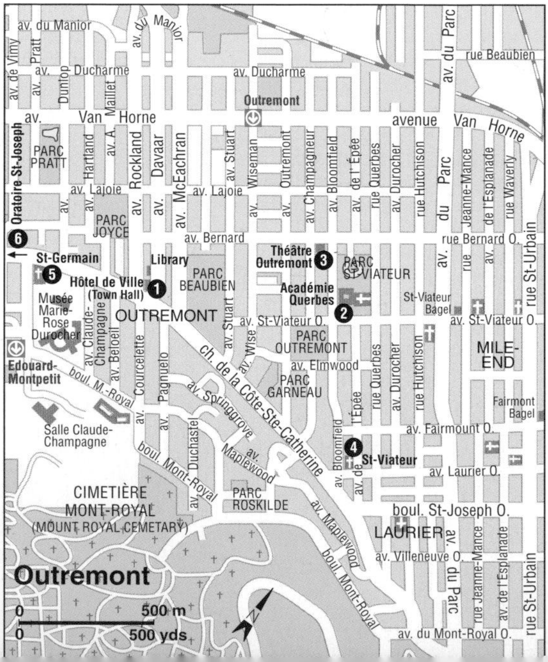

Map on page 152

some of New York city's better hotels and restaurants.

In the mid-1800s the two largest landowners, besides the St-Viateur religious order, were two farming families by the names of Bouthillier and Beaubien. The latter's power quickly translated into political influence when a son became mayor.

Outremont's population quadrupled between 1900 and 1911. While the first settlers were primarily Scottish and English, newcomers included French Canadians attracted to the less expensive homes and the proximity of Catholic churches. Jewish families also moved in and many set up shops along avenue Van Horne.

Like Westmount citizens, Outremont residents, fuelled by the fears of overdevelopment, formed a beautification committee. They were successful in obtaining more park land and regulating the size of apartment buildings. In its greatest coup, the committee persuaded the utility companies in 1914 to bury their telephone and electrical wires underground, thus eliminating unsightly poles and wires on the streets.

The boundaries

Outremont's boundaries are roughly defined by the commercial **avenue Van Horne** and **avenue Laurier** and the residential **chemin de la Côte Ste-Catherine** and **rue Hutchison**. These boundaries are not strict, however, and the neighbourhoods which stretch beyond them are deemed to be "adjacent" or "outer" Outremont.

The gentrification has reached deep into the once run-down district of **Mile-End**, which spreads east to just beyond rue St-Urbain. Today, being on the edges of this chic section of Montréal is good enough to secure a higher rent from prospective tenants or a better sale price. An address in Outremont or Mile-End suggests that you will be a francophone, a dyed-in-the-wool urbanite, and wealthy.

Outremont's attractions

The municipal centre is rather understated. Outremont's **Hôtel de Ville** ❶ (Town Hall) and public library are located off Côte Ste-Catherine. Ironically, the city hall is housed in a stately private residence

A patriotic pooch out on the town.

BELOW: out walking on a leafy street.

The Théâtre Outremont was inaugurated in 1929 and for years showcased the city's Francophone musical and theatrical talent but in the 1980s it closed and fell into disrepair. In 2001 the beautiful theatre building reopened, fully restored. Reservations, tel: 514-495 9944; closed on Sunday.

thought to have once been a trading post of the British-owned Hudson's Bay Company. It is one of the oldest buildings in Outremont, constructed around 1800. The library is also located in an old private home behind city hall.

The finest architecture in Outremont is found in its public buildings: churches, cinemas and schools. One of the most striking is **Académie Querbes** ❷, at 215 rue Bloomfield. Built in 1915 by J.A. Godin in the Beaux-Arts style, the edifice lends a distinctly European atmosphere to the otherwise typical North American residential architecture. Today, it houses a primary school.

Preserving the past

Residents had to fight hard to save the **Théâtre Outremont** ❸ at 1248 avenue Bernard Ouest. Plans to convert the playhouse into a multi-use complex were blocked by a public campaign and a determined petition drive. The bas-reliefs on the outside of the building are remarkable, despite the considerable damage they have suffered due to harsh weather. The interior is abundantly grand and reminiscent of Montréal's ornate old theatres, including the Strand, Loews and the Capitol.

At the corner of avenues Laurier and Bloomfield is the imposing **Eglise St-Viateur** ❹, completed in 1913. Its Gothic Revival style is strongly represented in the church's facade, which towers above the modest apartment buildings around it. Notably, the sides of the church aren't as elaborate as the front – a frequent feature of buildings where the architect concentrated on the facade.

At Côte Ste-Catherine and avenue d'Indy are two other interesting public buildings. **Eglise St-Germain** ❺, at the intersection of these two roads, was built in 1931 and has a magnificently large bell tower. The other building, facing out on Côte Ste-Catherine, was once the Pensionnat du St-Nom-de-Marie. Designed in 1903, its most striking feature is the classically designed portico, which incorporates a remarkable number of other architectural styles.

The residential areas of Outremont are generally organized around a

BELOW: art for sale.

Battle of the Eruv

Historically the communities who have made Outremont their home have lived in relative peace. That is, until tempers flared in the 1980s. A particularly silly squabble erupted in what was dubbed the "Battle of the Eruv" *(see page 152)*. It revolved around a length of fishing line the Hassidim string around whole city blocks to make it lawful for them to carry out certain tasks on the Sabbath. The line was barely visible, but for some reason it shocked some of the non-Jewish residents' sensibilities so much that they had Outremont city workers tear it down. The dispute ended in court, with a victory for the Hassidim.

Map on page 152

number of parks. The houses around Parc Outremont are beautiful simply because of the fine construction techniques and the regularity of their design. The unique detailing makes them noteworthy: one can see a variety of stained-glass designs, wood and iron trims and stone bas-reliefs inserted into the brick facades. These houses have the best views of the changing seasons on the mountain. Parc Joyce and Parc Pratt, which take their names from the farmers who once owned the land, also afford views of the mountain and the campus of the Université de Montréal and Oratoire St-Joseph (St Joseph's Oratory, *see page 159*).

Cimetière Mont-Royal

Also on the mountain, on the edge of Outremont, is the Protestant **Cimetière Mont-Royal** (Mount Royal Cemetery). Its sylvan landscape attracts species of birds found nowhere else in Québec.

In these idyllic settings many famous French Canadians have lived and some still do. The former premier of Québec, Lucien Bouchard, lives in Outremont, as did the late premier, Robert Bourassa, and the popular writer Maurice Tremblay. The late Prime Minister Pierre Trudeau grew up on rue McCullough.

Lively contrasts

Finally, there is a lively contrast between the quiet, tree-lined residential streets of Outremont and its commercial areas, which hum with activity day and night. Along avenues Laurier and Bernard you'll find a wealth of clothing shops, cafés and bakeries. A kind of architectural recycling goes on here. Many buildings on these two streets have been transformed from parking facilities into multi-use centres, or from garages into galleries. You can take your cat to a "postmodern" veterinary clinic or buy the latest in light fixtures. On avenue Laurier, there are also some fine French-language bookshops.

The gentrification has not been uniform, however. The farther east you walk, the spottier it becomes. Fast-food restaurants and old neighbourhood bars survive alongside chic establishments. Trendy food shops and restaurants share space along rue Bernard with kosher bakeries and butchers. And while Mile-End is full of expensive boutiques and hosts some of the city's finest restaurants, most people know it better as "the place" to go to buy bagels. It's a matter of continuing debate as to which of the area's two bakeries make the better ones – St-Viateur or Fairmont – but both bake them the old-fashioned way in wood-burning ovens.

Gentrification is least pervasive on avenue Van Horne, which until the 1960s and 1970s was just an ordinary thoroughfare lined with nondescript commercial and residential buildings. It has yet to undergo the same renaissance as Bernard and Laurier, but a few good restaurants and shops have opened amid the barbecued-chicken restaurants and hardware stores. ❑

Eglise St-Germain on avenue Vincent d'Indy hosts concerts of chamber music.

BELOW: Outremont's stores are chic.

RESTAURANTS, BARS & CAFÉS

Restaurants

L'Assommoir
112 rue Bernard Ouest (near avenue de l'Esplanade). Tel: 514-272 0777. D daily, L Thur–Sun. $$$
Part bar, part dance club and very much part restaurant, this is one of the hottest spots in the district, especially for the young, who crowd the dance floor and the brushed-chrome bar most nights. The menu focuses on the exotic, with a long list of *ceviches*, essentially raw fish steeped in citrus juice. Try the sockeye salmon with passion fruit, or if you'd like something cooked, try the pork braised in whisky.

Azuma
5263 boulevard St-Laurent (at rue Maguire). Tel: 514-271 5263. D Tues–Sun, L Thur–Fri. $$
Little booths separated by bamboo and rice paper fill this dim, quiet little restaurant. The sushi choices are always good, but for something more substantial, try the *donburi* made with chicken and lightly boiled eggs, or order the Japanese fondue and leisurely cook your own dinner.

Bistro Bienville
4650 rue de Mentana (at rue Bienville). 514-509 1269. L & D Wed–Fri, L only Tues, D only Sat. $$.
There's room for only about 20 diners in this tiny, sparsely decorated restaurant, and the place is always full and lively. And no wonder: the quality-to-dollar ratio of the food on is astonishing. The short menu features such delicacies as sily sweetbreads and monkfish served with barley and almonds. Recommended dishes include the calamari stuffed with veal and bacon.

Le Bistingo
1159 avenue Van Horne (at avenue Bloomfield). Tel: 514-270 6162. D daily, L Mon–Wed. $$
Big bay windows, sage-green walls and bright orange tablecloths give the Bistingo a warm and sunny feel even on the dreariest days. The food, inspired by the cuisine of southwestern France, matches the décor. And make sure you don't skip dessert. Dishes like the sautéed pear on gingerbread with ice cream and caramel sauce is worth saving room for.

Café Souvenir
1261 rue Bernard Ouest (near avenue Outremont). Tel: 514-948 5259. B, L & D daily. $$
The ultimate Outremont café, with a huge sidewalk terrace where you can linger for hours over an espresso and watch the stylish passing scene. If you need more sustenance than that, there is a choice of excellent sandwiches, quiches and salads.

Chao Phraya
50 avenue Laurier Ouest (at boulevard St-Laurent). Tel: 514-272 5339. D daily. $$$
Orchids decorate the tables of this fashionable Thai restaurant overlooking busy avenue Laurier. The food is spicily authentic. Try the fried halibut in red curry sauce with lime juice.

La Chronique
99 avenue Laurier Ouest (at rue St-Urbain). Tel: 514-721 3095. D Tues–Sat. $$$$
This little 36-seat restaurant with its ruby walls and black-and-white photos has been a mecca for serious foodies since 1995 when chef Marc de Canck opened the place, and it continues to produce some of the city's most adventurous food. Try the veal sweetbreads with chorizo.

Frites Alors
5235A avenue du Parc (at avenue Fairmont). Tel: 514-948 2219. B, L & D daily. $
The name, which translates roughly as "Wow, fries", pretty much sums up the place. But they're the best fries in Montréal. Long, thin, crisp and good enough to help you overlook the basic décor. For fast food Belgian style, have a heap of them with a sausage or two.

Kilo Cafe
5206 boulevard St-Laurent (near avenue Fairmont Ouest). Tel: 514-277 5039. Br, L & D Mon–Fri, L & D Sat–Sun. $
A great local cafe best known for its cakes, pies, pastries and desserts. But diners also enjoy sandwiches, salads, light meals and a variety of snacks.

Lester's
1057 rue Bernard Ouest (at avenue Durocher). Tel: 514–276 6095. B, L & D Mon–Sat. $
Most Montréalers swear that Schwartz's has the best smoked meat in town – but not all. Comic Jackie Mason declares that Lester's is the best, and the charismatic Lucien Bouchard, Québec's former premier, comes here for a regular fix of spiced brisket on rye. Both Lester's and Schwartz's share an utter lack of interest in décor.

La Moulerie
1249 rue Bernard Ouest (near avenue Champagneur) Tel: 514-273 8132. L & D daily, B Sun. $$
Two things distinguish La Moulerie – a prairie-sized terrace with a great view of one of the city's most stylish streets and a dazzling selection of mussel dishes. You can have Belgium's favourite mollusc with any of two dozen or so sauces,

including marinara, Thai, Indian, Roquefort and local.

Mythos Ouzerie
5318 avenue du Parc (near avenue Fairmont). Tel: 514-270 0325. L & D daily. $$
Zorba wannabes crowd into this brick-lined semi basement every Thursday, Friday and Saturday night to dance to live *bouziki* music and feast on such traditional Greek delicacies as stuffed vine leaves, grilled squid, braised lamb and moussaka. The rest of the week the restaurant is a little more subdued, but the food is just as good.

Paris Beurre
1226 avenue Van Horne (at avenue Champagneur). Tel: 514-271 7502. D daily, L Mon–Fri. $$
This busy bistro is winning praise from local food critics for its cuisine. It offers diners solid French comfort food and one of the best *crème brûlées* in the city.

Raza
114 avenue Laurier Ouest (near rue St-Urbain). Tel: 514-227 8712. D Tues–Sat. $$$
France meets Latin America in chef Mario Navarrete's take on Peruvian, Mexican, Cuban and Brazilian cuisine. The foie gras *empanadas* are a case in point, as are the fish croquettes with a *mojo criollo* sauce. For dessert, try the delicious *dulce de leche* ice cream.

Rumi
5198 rue Hutchison (near avenue Fairmont). Tel: 514-490 1999. L & D Tues–Sun. $$
Persian carpets and hardwood floors create a perfect backdrop for central Asian dishes infused with the flavours of saffron, mint, cilantro (coriander), lemon, nuts, raisins and olive oil.

Senzala
177 avenue Bernard Ouest (near avenue de Gaspé). Tel: 514-274 1464. L & D daily, B Wed–Sun. $$
There's live music on Thursday and Friday and samba on Saturday, so this packed little restaurant is no place to go for a quiet evening. It's hard to beat, though, for authentic Brazilian fare like shrimps with manioc and coconut milk. Breakfasts like poached eggs in avocado with grilled fruits make it a morning favourite with the local crowd.

Vasco da Gama
1257 avenue Bernard Ouest (near avenue Outremont). Tel: 514-272 2688. L & D daily. $$
This chic little Portuguese restaurant on trendy rue Bernard is the perfect spot for a light lunch or supper. It specialises in paninis, seafood salads and quiches.

Wilensky's Light Lunch
34 avenue Fairmont Ouest (at rue Clark). Tel: 514-271 0247. B & L Mon–Fri. $
Wilensky's devised its menu when it opened during the Great Depression – about the same time it bought its furniture – and hasn't changed much since. Novelist Mordecai Richler immortalised the place in *Duddy Kravitz*, and it's still the place to go for a grilled bologna sandwich on a bun with a hand-mixed cherry cola. Don't plan to linger, though; the staff is less than subtle about cleaning up once you've finished.

Bars & Cafés

BU
5245 boulevard-St-Laurent. Tel: 514-276 0249.
Oenophiles can munch on antipasto snacks until 3am while they sample the 30 or so different wines that BU serves by the glass.

Fûtenbulle
273 rue Bernard Ouest. Tel: 514-176 0473.
The best and largest selection of beers in Montréal attracts a lively mixed crowd to this trendy Outremont bar.

Whisky Café
5800 boulevard St-Laurent. Tel: 514-278 2646.
Even the bathrooms in this place are stylish enough to be a tourist attraction (check out the women's urinals – really), but it's a warm comfortable slickness that attracts a pretty sophisticated crowd.

PRICE CATEGORIES

Prices for three-course dinner per person with a half-bottle of house wine:
$ = under $25
$$ = $25–$50
$$$ = $50–$70
$$$$ = more than $70

RIGHT: Chao Phraya serves authentic, spicy Thai fare.

ST JOSEPH'S ORATORY

Celebrated as one of Christendom's outstanding monuments of faith, this is the Grand Central Station of devotional Catholicism in Montréal. Built in honour of Canada's patron saint, the shrine attracts more than 3 million visitors a year

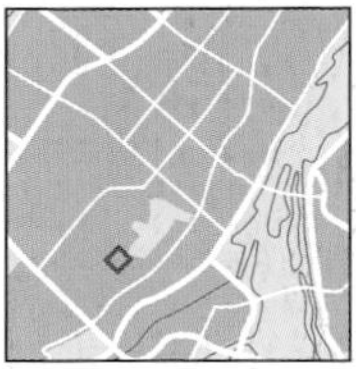

The word "oratory" literally means "house of prayer" and St Joseph's Oratory is just that, albeit a big one. The original chapel on the site was smaller than the current imposing shrine, which towers above the city's rooftops, a magnet to millions of visitors every year.

Religious theme park

A rather uncharitable critic once called the **Oratoire St-Joseph** ❻ (St Joseph's Oratory; 3800 chemin Queen-Mary; open mid May–mid Sept: daily, 7am–9pm; rest of the year: daily, 7am–5.30pm; free; tel: 514-733 8211) a kind of Catholic theme park, and indeed the place does have some of the less attractive characteristics of such places. Here you will find souvenir shops, a cafeteria, sometimes kitschy exhibits, large groups of visitors on guided tours and a parking lot full of rumbling tour buses.

The world's largest shrine to the earthly father of Jesus (and patron saint of Canada) draws more than 3 million visitors per year, and most are pilgrims on a journey of faith. A considerable number of the devout climb the 99 steps from chemin Queen-Mary to the church's front door on their knees, begging forgiveness for their sins or seeking relief from their suffering.

Their destination is an immense building of grey Canadian granite that dominates the northern slope of the western shoulder of Mont-Royal. Everything about St Joseph's is big: its main church can seat 3,000 worshippers on folding steel chairs (or squeeze in 10,000 standing); the church's transept is 65 metres (210 ft) across, the length of a good-sized urban church; and the dome, with a diameter of 39 metres (125 ft), is one of the largest in the world.

The dome is also a Montréal

Map on page 152

LEFT: the mighty cupola of Oratoire St-Joseph.
BELOW: a pilgrim pays homage.

landmark. At 263 metres (865 ft) above sea level, it is visible from all over the island and beyond. For the casual visitor, it offers an intriguing glimpse into a Catholic culture that, at one time, permeated almost every aspect of French-Canadian life.

TIP

The nearest Metro stop to St Joseph's is Côte-des-Neiges, north of the observatory.

Founding times

Work on the present building did not begin until 1914 and the basilica interior wasn't finished until 1967, long after the religious fervour that had prompted the church's construction had waned.

The person most responsible for building the oratory was a remarkable man named André Besette. The son of poor farmers, he spent much of his youth working as a factory hand in the textile mills of New England. On his return to Québec, he joined the Holy Cross religious order as a brother and spent the rest of his life as a porter at Collège Notre-Dame, a private boarding school and classical college on chemin Queen-Mary attended by well-to-do Catholic boys.

From his post at the door, Brother André gazed across at the slopes of Mont-Royal and dreamed of building a shrine to his favourite saint. In 1904 he and a few friends constructed a humble chapel on the mountain and rapidly began receiving visits from Montréal's sick and distressed. There were reports of miraculous cures, and Brother André's vision caught the imagination of church leaders and ordinary Montréalers. Over the next few decades, public subscription raised millions of dollars and construction on the present shrine was started.

BELOW: the landmark church is lit at night.

Polyglot congregation

The crypt-church, the first stop for most visitors, was completed in 1917. It is a humble, even drab little church with ponderous stone walls that create the sensation of being sealed underground. A larger than life-sized statue of Joseph holding his son carved out of a single block of white carrara marble dominates the sanctuary, but the rest of the decor is timeworn and eminently forgettable. Far more memorable are the people who worship here.

The 8pm mass on Sunday, in particular, attracts Catholics of every possible ethnic group and colour – Africans, Latin Americans, South Asians, First Nations and Filipino among them. Nurses, domestic servants, and labourers share pews with a scattering of professionals, students and university professors. This polyglot congregation represents the most vital remnant of Montréal's Catholic church.

Illuminated chapel

Adjoining the crypt-church is a room that glitters with the flames of 10,000 votive candles lit by pilgrims as a sign of devotion or to emphasize a request for a favour. More than 3,000 of them burn in front of the central statue of St Joseph and the rest flicker in front of plaques

Map on page 152

that commemorate some of the saint's titles (and hint at the favours the candle-lighters are hoping for): Guardian of Virgins, Terror of Demons, Protector of the Church, Hope of the Sick, Patron of the Dying, Comfort of the Afflicted, Mainstay of Families and Model of Workmen. The walls of the room are hung with hundreds of crutches and braces, "testimonies" left by pilgrims cured by the oil found in a basin beneath the statue of St Joseph. (The oil is also on sale in the gift shop.)

Founder of St Joseph's

Brother André, who died in 1937 at the age of 91, is entombed in a dim little room behind the central statue of St Joseph. Every day, hundreds of visitors come to pray and press their hands against the sides of his black stone coffin. Brother André was beatified by Pope John Paul II in 1982 – one step below Roman Catholic sainthood.

Visitors who want to see the main church under the dome have two choices: they can climb the outside stairs, all 179 of them, or they can ride the escalators inside. Halfway up either way is a wide, stone-flagged terrace that affords excellent views of the north end of the city and the Laurentian Mountains.

Inside, behind the terrace, is a small **museum** (open daily, 10am–5pm; donations; tel: 514-733 8211) dedicated to the life of Brother André. Exhibits include a replica of the austere cell Brother André occupied while a doorkeeper and a reproduction of the hospital room in which he died. More startling is the little shrine that displays Brother André's preserved heart, which was allegedly kidnapped and held for ransom in the 1970s.

Basilica and gardens

The basilica itself is immense – 105 metres (341 ft) long and 37 metres (120 ft) wide. Its austere concrete walls have little in the way of decoration or colour other than the stained-glass windows created by artist Marius Plamandon.

All attention is focused instead on the dramatically elongated crucifix behind the huge main altar. A door

An act of devotion – pilgrims climb the 99 steps to the church door on their knees.

LEFT: offering hope to the sick and infirm. **BELOW:** in the grounds of Oratoire St-Joseph.

Map on page 152

Many visitors find peace wandering through Louis Parent's Way of the Cross. *Work on the sculpture garden was completed in 1950.*

BELOW: foliage and statuary reflect the mood of each station.

at the western side of the sanctuary leads to the original little shrine that was built by Brother André. This small building, with its faded and chipped plaster statues and pressed tin ceiling, lacks the grandeur of its next-door neighbour but it has an endearing and simple charm. Humble and worn out, the chapel is a welcome contrast to the pomposity of its descendent.

The Oratory's expansive gardens provide pilgrims with a place to pray privately and to meditate. It is here that Québec sculptor Louis Parent (1908–82), created the now famous Way of the Cross, a 15 stone tableaux, which represent the stages of Christ's death and resurrection.

Each station of the cross includes foliage carefully chosen to reflect a mood. At the third tableau, where Christ is shown falling on the way to crucifixion, the predominant colour is red to denote the flow of blood. Where Veronica wipes the face of Christ, the colours are delicate pastels to suggest tenderness. And at the 13th station, where Christ is taken down from the cross, the colours are bland and austere, conveying grief and desolation.

Commercial aspect

Finally, a trip to St Joseph's would not be complete without a visit to the gift shop at the bottom of the hill. Almost every kind of Catholic religious paraphernalia can be found, from statues of St Joseph, whose heart (assuming the statue is plugged in) will glow an ethereal rose, to miniature versions of the saint that are specially designed to take pride of place on the refrigerator door.

There are almost 100 varieties of rosary to choose from. Those made of expensive red crystal have beads shaped like hearts, while an economy model is made of lightweight plastic.

Here, with numerous visitors pawing through bins of plastic medallions and glow-in-the-dark rosaries, St Joseph's commercial side is brazenly exposed. While celebrating the transcendent human soul, the shrine is also a monument to a culture capable of generating a commodity from even it most immaterial aspects. ❑

Restaurants & Bars

Restaurants

Le Béarn
5613 chemin Côte-des-Neiges (near chemin Côte Ste-Catherine). Tel: 514-733 4102. L & D Mon–Fri, D only Sat. $$$
In a sea of ethnic and fast-food restaurants, this little island of old-fashioned French cooking stands out. Comfort dishes like veal kidneys Dijonnais and rack of lamb with tarragon are prepared with care.

La Caverne
5184 chemin Côte-des-Neiges (near chemin Queen-Mary). Tel: 514-738 6555. L & D daily. $
The steep steps down to this basement restaurant are offputting, but the stone-walled room is a pleasant place to sample authentic and inexpensive dishes from the former Soviet Union. There are cabbage, rolls and dumplings, but for lighter fare try the Georgian egg and cheese boat or stuffed vine leaves.

Camelia des Tropiques
5024 chemin Côte-des-Neiges (near chemin Queen-Mary). Tel: 514-738 8083. L & D Tues–Fri, D only Sat–Sun. $$$
The pleasantly formal ambiance match the aristocratic version of Vietnamese food that is the speciality here. Try the sizzling platter of diced *filet mignon* on a bed of watercress with coconut rice. Bring your own wine.

Cracovie
5349 rue Gatineau (near avenue Lacombe) Tel: 514-731 3388. L & D Tues–Fri, D only Sat–Sun. $
The cacti in the window don't seem to have much to do with Poland, but the rest of this bright, restaurant is authentically Slavic: the sausages are close to a foot long, the cabbage rolls are fat and sweet and the *borscht* is rich and satiny. For a treat, try the roast duck.

Duc de Lorraine
5002 chemin Côte-des-Neiges (near chemin Queen-Mary). Tel: 514-731 4128. B & L daily. $
One of the best pâtisseries in Montréal; there's always a line at the takeout counter. The bright dining room is the ideal place to prepare for a morning visit to the Oratoire St-Joseph with some Québec cheese, a croissant and a bowl of café au lait. It's also good for an afternoon espresso and a pastry, or to stock up on sandwiches, pâté and cheese for a picnic on Mont-Royal.

East India Company
3533 chemin Queen-Mary (at chemin Côte-des-Neiges). Tel: 514-344 2217. L & D Mon–Fri, D only Sat, noon–8pm Sun. $$
The imported statues of elephants and temple dancers and the inlaid wood tables give this Indian restaurant a dash of exotic sophistication. The best bets are the vegetarian dishes, especially the *palak paneer* of spinach and homemade cheese. The fresh nan bread is excellent.

Le Georgia
5112 rue Decarie (near chemin Queen-Mary). Tel: 514-482 1881. L & D 1–11pm daily. $$
The décor – velvet drapes and hanging brass lamps – has the feel of a 19th-century Russian parlour. But the cuisine is Georgian, and the flavours of cilantro (coriander), pomegranate seeds and walnuts add an exotic dash of Persia to the more common Slavic garlic and onions. Chilled vodka is the ideal accompaniment to most meals.

Mavi
5192 avenue Gatineau (near avenue Dupuis). Tel: 514-340 9664. L & D Mon–Sat. $
The front of this Portuguese hole-in-the-wall is unprepossessing, but the excellent grilled chicken and sardines, the crunchy french fries and reasonable prices make it a favourite with students. You can order takeout or eat at the back. When you phone to reserve, tell them what you want – everything is grilled from scratch so the wait can otherwise be long.

Talay Thai
5697 chemin Côte-des-Neiges (at chemin Côte-Ste-Catherine). L & D Mon–Thur, D only Fri–Sun. $$
One of Montréal's most cheerful Thai restaurants. The food is good and inexpensive, making the place a favourite with staff from the hospital across the street. Try the Panang Kai sliced chicken in a red curry and coconut sauce with peanuts.

Bars

Pub Richard McCarold
2715 avenue Lacombe. Tel: 514-738 2971.
This noisy Irish pub has frequent live music and a great selection of Québec and Irish beers. Good spot for burgers, Irish stew and fish and chips.

Grande Gueule
5615A chemin Côte-des-Neiges. Tel: 514-733 3512.
The name – French for "big mouth" – says it all. Université de Montréal students come here to unwind, drink and argue.

Price Categories

Prices for a three-course dinner per person with a half-bottle of house wine:
$ = under $25
$$ = $25–50
$$$ = $50–70
$$$$ = more than $70

When the Circus Comes to Town

Don't expect to see lions, or dancing elephants. This city is a magnet to acrobats, clowns, tightrope walkers and jugglers

If, as a child, you dreamed about running away to join the circus then look no further than Montréal. The city is home to the famous Cirque du Soleil, Cirque Eloize and L'Ecole Nationale de Cirque (National Circus School). The circus school is the only one of its kind in Canada and one of the best in the world. Housed in a purpose-built centre in a reclaimed part of the St-Michel district, known as Tohu, the school attracts would-be circus performers from all over the world. The professional training programme accepts just 100 students, while young Canadians aged 9–17 can take part in a two-week intensive summer camp. Circus skills taught at the school include contortion, acrobatics, the trapeze, and the unicycle. Graduates have joined circuses worldwide, while others stayed close to home. The founders of Cirque Eloize, a small but internationally-renowned circus, attended the school. Established in 1993, Cirque Eloize performs in theatres rather than a traditional big top, and one of the creators of its show, *Rain*, also helped to design the acrobatic closing ceremony of the Winter Olympics in Torino in 2006.

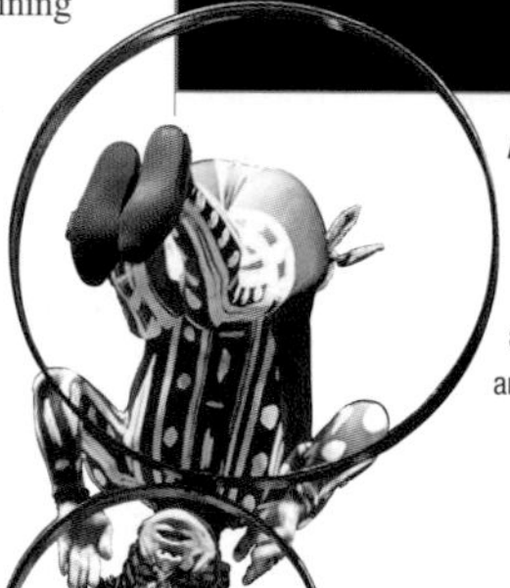

Above: the spectacular triple trapeze act appears in Cirque du Soleil's *Varekai*, which is loosely based on the Greek myth of Icarus. The show premiered in 2002 and toured in Canada, the US, Australia and New Zealand.

Left: a performer from Le Cirque Eloize proves that a bicycle has more than one use. The Québec-based touring troupe, combines circus techniques with theatre, music and dance and has appeared at prestigious events and venues worldwide including the Edinburgh Festival, the Royal Albert Hall in London and the Sydney Opera House.

Above and Right: Cirque du Soleil unveiled *Dralion* in 1999. The show combines traditional Chinese circus art with an avant garde approach. It features innovative hoop diving (above left) and a ballet on lightbulbs (right), with performers who balance on pointe on the bulbs, revealing remarkable strength and grace.

CIRQUE DU SOLEIL

The Circus of the Sun was born out of an idea by Guy Laliberté for a show that would be part of the 1984 anniversary celebration of Jacques Cartier's first landfall in Canada. Laliberté and his associates Daniel Gauthier and Gilles Ste-Croix, who had established a street theatre in Baie-St-Paul, near Québec City, had dreamed of creating a travelling circus troupe.

Although Cirque du Soleil is essentially a touring circus – it does not have a permanent home venue – its grand chapiteau (big top) is erected once every couple of years in Montréal when it unveils its latest offering. Performances combine elements of theatre, opera, ballet, live music with traditional and innovative circus skills such as clowning, acrobatics, diabolo, and daring trapeze and contortionist acts that take their audiences breath away. Over the years the company has grown in size and reputation, earning international recognition for its spectacular touring shows such as *Dralion*, *Alegría*, *Varekai*, *Quidam* , *Saltimbanco* and *Corteo*, which have toured throughout North America, Europe, Australia, New Zealand and Asia. There are also resident shows in Las Vegas, New York and Orlando. The circus employs over 700 artists within a staff of more than 3,000, of which almost 2,000 work out of the Montréal headquarters located in a redeveloping part of the St-Michel district of the city, the National Circus School is a neighbour. The building complex includes the administrative offices, a training room, dance studio and workshops.

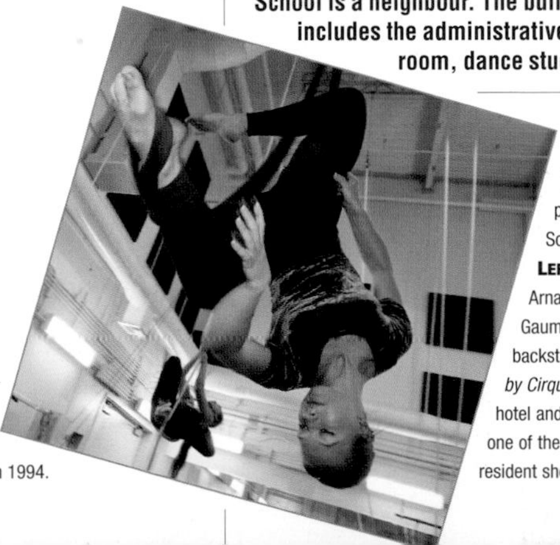

TOP RIGHT: Stiv Bello applies his make up backstage before a performance of Cirque du Soleil's *Varekai.*

LEFT: aerialists Ekaterina Arnaoutova (front) and Elizabeth Gaumond rehearse a routine backstage for *The Beatles Love by Cirque du Soleil* at the Mirage hotel and casino in Las Vegas. It is one of the company's popular resident shows in the US.

VE: manipulation is performed by a young ıe du Soleil artist in *Algería*, which ıres performers aged 11 to 64. It launched in 1994.

STADIUMS, GARDENS AND ISLANDS

Olympic Park, with its associated museums and gardens, makes a worthwhile day-trip. There's also entertainment on the city's two island playgrounds, Ile Ste-Hélène and Ile Notre-Dame

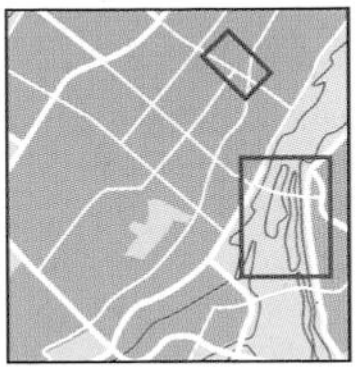

The skyline in eastern Montréal is dominated by a massive sports arena, the main venue of the Olympic Games in summer 1976. Venture out of downtown for the day and you will discover that nearby the stadium there are also pretty parks and gardens, museums, a casino and an island playground.

The "Big O"

Take the Métro to station Pie-IX or travel east along rue Sherbrooke and the **Stade Olympique** ❶ (Olympic Stadium; 4141 avenue Pierre-de-Coubertin; bilingual tours daily every hour starting at 10am; entrance charge; tel: 514-252 4737 or 1-877 997 0919) looms up suddenly amid rows of unassuming duplexes, as though a mollusc-shaped starship had landed.

Futuristic, grandiose, impractical and incredibly expensive, controversy still surrounds the "Big O", as the stadium is known, a long time after the memory of the Olympic Games has faded.

Roger Taillibert, the French architect who designed the stadium, claimed that sports arenas are the cathedrals of our age. The metaphor appealed to a city with a history of building magnificent churches but the plan for the new sports dome – designed to assert the city's modern, cosmopolitan flair rather than its Roman Catholic history – was far more ambitious, and ultimately it demanded even more financial sacrifice. And just as the slow construction of St Joseph's Oratory *(see page 159)* had depended upon the personal charisma of Brother André, so the Montréal Olympics and its centrepiece facility were only possible through the force of one man: the irrepressible Jean Drapeau, mayor from 1954 to 1986. He gets credit for sheer visionary ambition.

Maps on pages 168, 170

LEFT: the Chinese Garden and the Tour Montréal reflected in the water.
BELOW: the Biosphère, Ile Ste-Hélène.

In 1977 the final performance of Pink Floyd's In the Flesh Tour *ended in a riot. The Montréal concert erupted in violence after the rock band's singer and bass player, Roger Waters, spat at a fan whom he thought was making too much noise. The incident inspired Waters to write* The Wall, *one of the best selling albums of all time. In it he reflected on his growing awareness that stardom had alienated him from his audience.*

Unobstructed view

The Olympic Stadium's revolutionary design includes the **Tour Montréal ❷** (Olympique), a leaning tower 55 storeys high, from which a membrane roof descends along cables over the playing field. At least it was supposed to descend; it never really worked properly.

Roof problems aside, tower and stadium alike are imaginatively modelled in fluent curves that soar at beautiful and seemingly impossible angles from the rather drab working-class neighbourhood surrounding it.

You need only ride the **funicular cable car** that runs up the spine of the tower to the observatory deck to appreciate the architect's imagination. While the top overhangs the roof of the stadium, the hollow base forms the roof of the Olympic pools, with wing-like lobes that spread out on either side.

Thirteen storeys of office space fill up about two-thirds of the tower, with a three-floor observatory at the summit where the tower broadens as its three corners begin to sweep apart. The exterior double-decker cable car carries up to 76 passengers and, emerging into the open air about a third of the way along its path, offers an increasingly spectacular view.

From the top observation deck, the view extends about 80 km (50 miles) and includes an unobstructed westward view of Mont-Royal and the city skyline, with the St Lawrence River winding from the left. There is also a vertiginous view into the stadium.

The cables that suspend the roof pass down from a niche only a short distance below the deck, affording a unique perspective on the operations that once raised and lowered the 65 tonnes/tons of fabric. Forty-six winches had to operate in precise synchronicity to unfurl the retractable roof over an area covering more than 18,500 sq metres (200,000 sq ft).

BELOW: Stade Olympique.

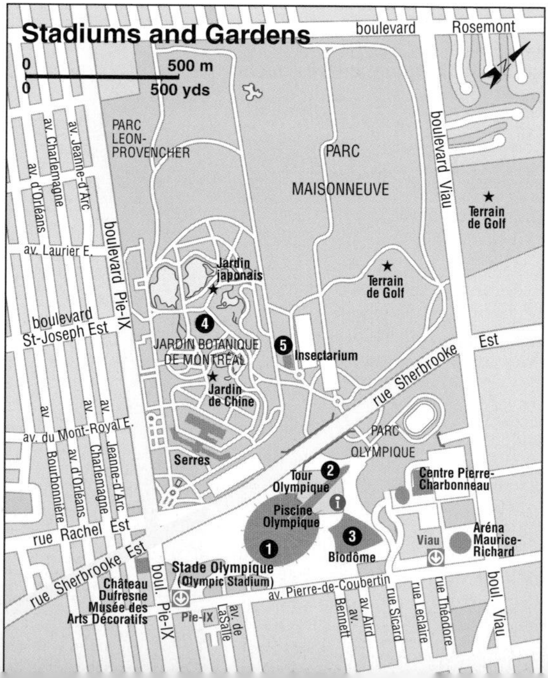

Pregnant man

For all his achievements, Mayor Drapeau must also shoulder a large part of the blame for the Big O's other unofficial nicknames: "the Big Owe" and the "the Big Uh-Oh". Montréal's stadium may be the most spectacular sports arena in the world, but there is no question that it is the most expensive. The price tag of $1.2 billion gives it the distinction of being one of the most costly buildings ever constructed, and the bill was only paid off in 2006 – 30 years later. In 1984, an accounting firm determined that the Big O had cost only slightly less than all the other domed stadiums in North America combined – and that was before it had a roof.

Drapeau had promised Montréal "modest games" that would pay for themselves through revenues from tickets and souvenirs. He remains notorious for his assurance that the Olympics could no more run a deficit than a man could have a baby. Predictably, local cartoonists enjoyed depicting the former mayor heavy with child.

The reasons for the exorbitant price tag are easy enough to find in hindsight. The concept of a retractable canopy roof suspended from a tower leaning at 45 degrees had never before been attempted on this scale. Since the top of the tower had to be centred over the stadium's roof, the circular opening in the centre of the stadium slants slightly towards the tower, so that the end of the ellipse near the tower's base is lower than the far end. The pleasing asymmetry of this design made the task of casting the huge, irregular concrete ribs of the stadium extremely tricky and delicate – and, of course, expensive.

But the real construction headaches were caused by the rigid deadline that Olympic Games always impose upon the host city. The clock ticked away as the builders waited for detailed plans from the architect. In the end, they built most of the complex in just two years, between 1974 and 1976.

At the opening ceremonies, the city had a magnificent stadium, but there was still no tower and no roof. Nevertheless, in the giddy flush (and

Map on page 168

A funicular cable car runs up the spine of the Tour Montréal to an observation deck, which affords panoramic views of the city. It is closed from early January to mid-February.

LEFT: jogging by the stadium.

The "Retractable" Roof

For all its nifty engineering, the retractable roof of the Stade Olympique did not entirely eliminate rain delays even when it worked. If an unexpected shower occurred in high winds, the game or event had to wait until the winds let up before the roof could be unfurled. The roof could not be lowered if winds were stronger than 25 kph (15 mph), while the roof of Toronto's SkyDome can operate in winds up to 65 kph (40 mph).

As it took almost 45 minutes to drop the roof into place, stadium officials normally let weather predictions determine whether the roof should be lowered for an event, rather than waiting for the rain. The original retractable roof, made of Kevlar, was permanently fixed in place in 1992. Also prone to ripping, the original roof (an ugly orange on the inside) was replaced in 1998 by one made of fibreglass and Teflon. Unfortunately that has also been problematic, with part of it collapsing under the weight of ice and snow in January 1999. The stadium was being readied for the Montreal Auto Show at the time of the collapse and so it's no surprise that that particular event has not returned.

relief) of the moment, the city gave Drapeau a standing ovation. The tower would take another decade: it was not completed until 1987.

Today the stadium hosts all sorts of events now that a fixed roof allows year-round use: trade shows, monster truck shows and rock concerts. Special events, such as the visit of Pope John Paul II or the spectacular production of Verdi's *Aïda* that came complete with a 12-metre (40-ft) sphinx, live elephants and over 1,000 singers, occasionally convert even die-hard pragmatists to the Big O.

Originally seating more than 70,000, the stadium was renovated for baseball in the 1990s and 12,000 seats were removed. The rock group Pink Floyd holds the stadium's attendance record, performing before 78,322 fans on 6 July 1977.

Locals often grumble about the archaic seating and astronomical cost. Being Montréalers and wedded to tradition, though, they would never suggest closing or demolishing the structure now.

The big exit

In 1977 the stadium became home to Les Expos, Montreal's professional baseball team, which was plagued by poor attendance in later years. Even so, sports fans were outraged when critics questioned the team's need for such an extravagant a home.

However, history has had the last laugh. The city's Canadian Football League team, the Alouettes, abandoned the Big O first for the smaller, somewhat decrepit Percival Molson Stadium downtown. Even the Expos had planned to move downtown. But in 2005 the team was moved to Washington DC, in the US, and renamed The Nationals.

Biodôme

Spreading out from the base of the Olympic Pools, the Vélodrome was built to accommodate the cycling

In the Tropical Forest area of the Biodôme daytime temperatures range from 24–28°C (75–82°F), perfect for colourful birds such as the Scarlet macaw.

BELOW: a King penguin in the Biodôme.

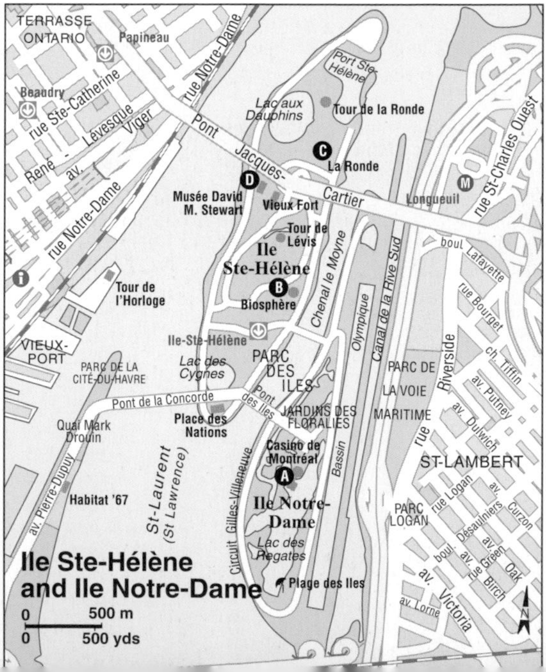

Map on page 168

events at the 1976 Olympic Games. However, another celebratory spin-off from the city's 350th anniversary resulted in the conversion of the space into an unusual life-sciences museum called the **Biodôme** ❸ (4777 avenue Pierre-de-Coubertin; open June–Aug: daily 9am–6pm; Sept–May: daily 9am–5pm; closed Mondays mid-Sept–Mar; entrance charge; tel: 514-868 3000). City botanists, biologists and zoologists have created four different ecosystems under one roof: a tropical jungle, a polar environment, a northern forest and the habitat along the St Lawrence River.

Characteristic plants, animals and birds have been installed within each miniature world. Thanks to cleverly situated underwater cameras, visitors can even observe beavers hard at work inside their elaborate lodges.

Botanical Garden

The Biodôme complements the glories of nature on display across rue Sherbrooke. More than 26,000 species of plants repose in tranquillity at the **Jardin Botanique** ❹ (Botanical Garden; 4101 rue Sherbrooke Est; open mid May–Aug: daily 9am–6pm; Sept–Oct: daily 9am–9pm; Nov–Mar: daily 9am–5pm, closed most Mondays; entrance charge; tel: 514-872 1400).

If Montréal, with its harsh winters, seems an unlikely setting for one of the world's largest botanical gardens, consider the pleasure of sitting in the warmth of the tropical greenhouse, among pineapple plants and orchids, during a December blizzard. However, most of the two million people who visit every year are more interested in houseplants and exotic gardens than they are in a chance to come in from the cold.

Located on a 73-hectare (180-acre) rectangle across the street from the Olympic Park, the garden complex has been steadily evolving since Brother Marie-Victorin founded the project in 1931. A modest statue of the monk stands to the right, just beyond the main gate.

Although nine greenhouses protect the tropical flora from the elements, spring and the autumn are still the best seasons for a visit, since

All kinds of visitors are attracted to the Botanical Garden. Spring and autumn are the best times to visit.

BELOW: the Biodôme.

the vast majority of plants are divided among the various outdoor gardens. Different plant groups bloom each month between April and October.

The Friendship Hall is the central feature of the Chinese Garden.

A garden tour

Even those visitors who can't tell a begonia from a rhododendron can enjoy a stroll among the blooms, but those who prefer a chauffeur can take a 45-minute guided tour on the mini-train (runs May–Oct: daily, every 10 mins from 9.30am). With about 30 plots in which the plants are grouped according to particular themes. Some gardens are as much educational as sensory experiences.

The **Monastery Garden** has displays of medicinal herbs that recreate the quiet enclaves of medieval monks in the age of Charlemagne. Information panels offer useful trivia about such topics as the aphrodisiac power of absinthe and the laxative properties of liquorice. The poisonous plant section is only a short distance away. These plots are located just beyond the perennials and test gardens, to the left after the entrance.

BELOW: colourful and witty plant display.

Winding paths, ponds thick with lilies, rock gardens, and a "flowery brook" make a poetic setting at the centre of the gardens. An assortment of birds live among the aquatic plants in the ponds. In the Alpinum, flora from the world's mountain ranges are gathered together beside a quaint waterfall. Beyond the ponds behind the Alpinum, the Arboretum is more like an open park, with its trim heaths, dwarf spruces, shade trees and chestnuts. In the fall the maples begin to turn a splendid colour.

The **Chinese Garden** is the largest outside Asia, with seven pavilions built in the Ming Dynasty style around a lake; the Botanical Garden staff worked closely with the City of Shanghai on this project. The **Japanese Garden** is all serenity, with bubbling streams full of carp, and a tea room. Next to the **Rose Garden**, a section collects forest specimens from a series of six villages called Montréal, located in various parts of France.

The greenhouses recreate the climates of the warmer parts of the globe: an equatorial rain forest has the musty bouquet of orchids; then a hot, dry desert with human-sized cacti; and a Mexican villa with a popular collection of carnivorous plants.

Several permanent and temporary exhibitions are housed under glass here, as well; a computer controls the climate of each of the ecosystems. There are trivia-quiz computer games for the kids to play, and audio-guides in French and English.

Bugging out

The small but intriguing **Insectarium** ❺ (4581 rue Sherbrooke Est; open: mid May–Aug: daily, 9am–6pm; Sept–Oct, daily 9am–9pm; Nov–Mar: daily, 9am–5pm; entrance charge; tel: 514-872 1400) was opened in 1990 following the initiative of an enthusiastic collector named Georges Brossard, a Québec native. Part museum and part zoo, the project was designed to educate children and adults about creatures that usually receive only negative attention from humans. Inside this pavilion, which is itself shaped like an insect, kids and grown-ups alike can peer into display cases and absorb their minds in games and puzzles that shed light on the fascinating world of bugs.

An extraordinary variety of perfectly preserved insects, from butterflies to golden scarab beetles, is mounted on the walls, while an assortment of living insects is housed behind glass. Some of these creatures seem to be a little shy of the spotlight, but they are easy enough to find with a little patience. All together, there are about 130,000 specimens here. Brave visitors may want to time their visit to coincide with the annual insect tasting event. Roasted crickets, anyone?

Expo islands

For another entertaining day-trip, visit the two islands in the St Lawrence River, opposite Old Montréal, that function as the city's fairgrounds.

Until the 1960s, there was only one island here, **Ile Ste-Hélène**, which was about half its present size. However, the earth excavated from the freshly-dug Metro tunnels was used to expand the original island and to create a new one next door: **Ile Notre-Dame**.

This park land became the site of Expo '67, the great world exposition that drew no less than 50 million visitors during the summer of Canada's centennial year, 1967. The plans called for temporary structures that would stand for the summer of the exhibition and then disappear, but several of the 83 pavilions were so sturdy and impressive that it made no sense to demolish them. So Expo survived for 14 years as Terre des Hommes (Man and His World).

Island playgrounds

Today, the former Expo site has taken on a new persona. On Ile Notre-Dame, the old French pavilion was converted in 1993 into the **Casino de Montréal** Ⓐ (tel: 1-800 665 2274 or 514-392 2746). In 1995 the casino expanded into a neighbouring building, the Pavilion du Québec, connected by a futuristic walkway. Casino authorities claim it is one of the world's largest gaming places, and both Montréalers and visitors do indeed come out in droves to enjoy a game of chance.

Still on Ile Ste-Hélène, the famous **geodesic dome** designed by Buckminster Fuller has gone through a dramatic transformation. Despite a devastating fire burning away its outer skin in 1976, the former American pavilion still stands 20 storeys high. With no internal supports, it encloses 198,240 cubic metres (7 million cubic ft) of air.

In 1995, with the opening of the **Biosphère** Ⓑ (open: mid June-mid Sept 10am–6pm, mid-Sept–mid June, 12–5pm; entrance charge; tel: 514-283 5000) the pavilion became

Maps on pages 168, 170

TIP

The Insectarium organises an insect tasting event every year. Insects have a high protein content, but they also contain vitamins and minerals. For more details tel: 514-872 1400.

BELOW: business is booming at Casino de Montréal.

Map on page 170

A re-enactment at Vieux Fort, Musée David M. Stewart.

both an interpretive centre and a hub for the vast network of eco-watchers along the St Lawrence River and the Great Lakes' water systems. Through satellites and computer technology, visitors exploring the four interactive exhibition halls receive a graphic lesson on the importance of water.

An amusement park built more than 40 years ago, **La Ronde** Ⓒ (Ile Ste-Hélène; end of May–mid-June: daily 10am–8pm; mid-June–early-Sept: daily 10am–10.30pm; Sept–Oct: Sat noon–8pm, Sun noon–7pm; closed Nov–Apr; entrance charge; tel: 397 2000 or 1-800 361 8020), is still going strong.

It is now part of the Six Flags family of parks. The original Mini-Rail and cable-car SkyRide still seem novel ways to get around the park. Montréalers with children make an annual pilgrimage to La Ronde to experience the thrills of rides such as Goliath, one of the world's biggest and fastest roller-coasters built at a cost of $18.7 million in 2006. During two weeks in the early summer, admission to La Ronde includes a ringside seat from which to view the annual **International Fireworks Competition** *(see page 138)*. Each night for two weeks a different national team attempts to put on the most spectacular pyrotechnics display over the river and the city skyline.

In mid-June the roar of Formula One racing cars from the Grand Prix of Canada can be heard on the **Circuit Gilles-Villeneuve**, the race track on Ile Notre-Dame. A refuge from all this noisy excitement is not far away: a part of Ile Ste-Hélène is still green, wooded and quiet, bar the traffic on the Jacques-Cartier Bridge.

At the **Vieux Fort** (completed in 1824) near the bridge is the **Musée David M. Stewart** Ⓓ (Stewart Museum; 20 chemin Tour-de-l'Ile; open mid-May–mid-Oct: daily 10am–6pm, Thur until 9pm; rest of the year: Wed–Mon 10am–5pm; entrance charge; tel: 514-861 6701). Naval and other military paraphernalia is on display and during the summer the Compagnie Franche de la Marine and the 78th Fraser Highlanders re-enact parades, dressed in 18th-century costumes. ❑

BELOW: a night view of the ferris wheel at La Ronde.

RESTAURANTS & BARS

Restaurants

La Bécane Rouge
4316 rue Ste-Catherine Est (at avenue Létourneux). Tel: 514-252 5420. L Mon–Fri, D Tues–Sun. $$
High ceilings, fire-engine red walls and dark wood wainscoting have made this a local favourite. The menu changes daily, but look out for the duck legs with pear chutney or the horse tartare.

Buffet la Bonne Carte
1 avenue du Casino, Ile Notre-Dame. Tel: 514-392 2708. L & D Mon–Fri, Br & D Sat–Sun. No under 18s. $$
The big windows overlooking the St Lawrence River make this casino restaurant great for a weekend brunch. The buffet has varying themes (roasts Mon–Tues, Asian Wed–Thur and surf-and-turf Fri–Sun). Live entertainment weekend evenings.

Chez Clo
3199 rue Ontario Est (near boulevard Pie-IX). Tel: 514-522 5348. B, L daily, D Mon–Fri. $
A traditional restaurant with plain tables and stools at the counter, it serves great Québec food like *tourtière* (meat pie) and meat-ball stew. This is one of the few places of its kind left, and its pork-heavy menu includes the best pea soup in town. Don't miss the *pudding au chômeur* (literally, pudding for the unemployed), a heavy upside-down cake with brown-sugar sauce.

Festin du Gouverneur
Fort Ste-Hélène, Ile Ste-Hélène. Tel: 514- 879 1141 or 800-713 0111 (toll-free). $$
One of the stone-walled powder magazines in the Old Fort on ile Ste-Hélène has been turned into a dinner theatre, where guests dine on chicken Wellington while being entertained with a raucous and slightly bawdy interpretation of life in New France. Songs and audience participation.

Hélène-de-Champlain
200 Tour de l'Isle, Ile Ste-Hélène. Tel: 514-395 2424. $$$
The food is reliably French and the service attentively formal, but it's the setting that makes this restaurant special. It sits in its own rose garden in the middle of an island park overlooking the St Lawrence River. Just a five-minute drive from downtown, it has the air of a country estate.

Nuances
1 avenue du Casino, Ile Notre-Dame. Tel: 514-392 2708. D daily. No one under 18. $$$$
The wood panelling is mahogany, the china Villeroy & Boch and the views of the city skyline are magnificent. This is the Casino de Montréal's premiere restaurant. Try the loin of lamb baked in a clay dish or the lobster and asparagus risotto.

Bars

Le Bureau
4303 rue Ste-Catherine Est. Tel: 514-253 1748.
Comfy booths and subdued lighting make this an oasis for a quiet drink.

L'Escale.
4474 rue Ste-Catherine Est. Tel: 514-254 9036.
This neighbourhood favourite features dart games and cribbage tournaments.

Casino de Montréal
1 avenue du Casino, Ile Notre-Dame. Tel: 514-392 2746.
Grab a quiet drink or waltz the night away to live music at La Rotonde bar on the casino's main floor. For something a bit edgier, climb to the third floor's zen-like Le Carré for a spectacular view of the city skyline at night (and music administered by a DJ Thursday, Friday and Saturday nights).

PRICE CATEGORIES

Prices for three-course dinner per person with a half-bottle of house wine:
$ = under $25
$$ = $25–$50
$$$ = $50–$70
$$$$ = more than $70

RIGHT: Le Festin du Gouverneur, on Ile Ste-Hélène.

THE ST LAWRENCE: RIVER OF HISTORY

The St Lawrence River has been a lifeline for Canada's hinterland, a highway between the Great Lakes and the Atlantic Ocean

The reason Montréal came to be established where it was is simple – it sits beside a large river that connects the Atlantic Ocean (and thus Europe) with Canada's vast inland lakes and forests. The St Lawrence was essentially the highway to the West, and is the true mother of Montréal, Québec City and modern Canada.

As the interior of Canada gradually opened up, a parade of steamships sailed up and down the river, carrying furs and wheat to France. Between 1830 and 1850, the line of stone piers along the waterfront was extended until it stretched for more than 6 km (4 miles), and the total freight handled in the port increased more than thirty-fold. A complex of grain elevators and silos was constructed to process the wheat coming downstream from Central Canada and by World War I, Montréal was the second most important port in North America after New York City. In 1959 the St Lawrence Seaway opened – a parallel series of channels which diverted freighters around the rapids and navigational obstacles along the river's course. Eventually the Seaway led to the port being overshadowed by those at Toronto and Chicago. However, the Seaway is too narrow to accommodate modern mega-ships and Montréal port is once again one of the busiest in North America, and Canada's top container port.

ABOVE: St Lambert lock on the St Lawrence River links the Great Lakes with the Atlantic.

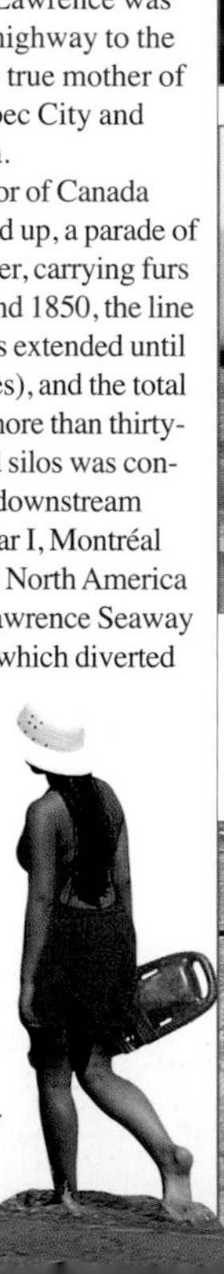

ABOVE: the Tour de l'Horloge (Clock Tower) and Jacques Cartier Bridge are landmarks of the Old Port. The tower was built in 1922 to commemorate the merchant mariners who died in World War I.

LEFT: a kite skier on the frozen St Lawrence River. Participants in the exhilarating sport can reach high speeds on the snow or ice.

BELOW: sportsmen drag and paddle 22-kg (50-lb) canoes across the frozen river in the ice-canoe races at La Fête des Neiges, which is held every January.

MONTREAL'S HIDDEN RIVIERA

Montréal's impressive Vieux Port, the less commercial end of the harbour, has been turned into a riverside playground for locals and visitors alike. Attractions include an IMAX movie theatre, state-of-the-art Centre iSci science complex (King Edward Pier), and the ubiquitous fast-food outlets. On Quai de l'Horloge is Tour de l'Horloge (Clock Tower). Climb to the top of the tower for a splendid view over the city and the river. Children of all ages will enjoy exploring Shed 16 Labyrinth (Tel: 514-499 0099), a maze of dark alleys and obstacles housed in an old hanger. The port also has a lively events calendar, summer and winter. Try the outdoor ice skating rink.

Sightseeing boats – some offering dinner and entertainment – leave from the Jacques Cartier Pier. Cruise ships dock at the Alexandra Pier, but there's no access to the Iberville passenger terminal until you are due to sail. The best time to see these stately floating hotels is in the fall, when many ships sail the St Lawrence River on leaf peeping and autumn colour cruises.

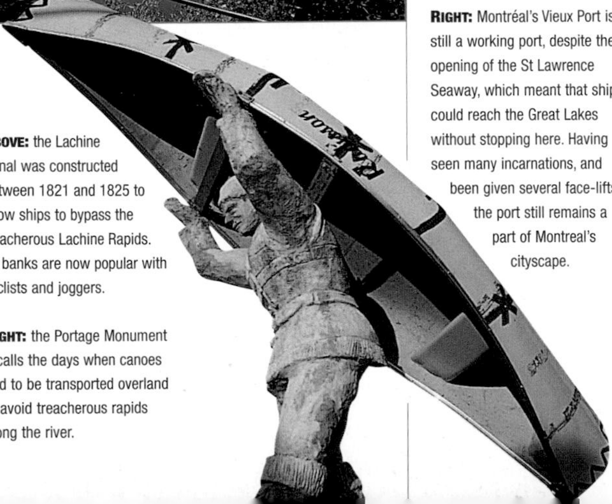

ABOVE: the Lachine Canal was constructed between 1821 and 1825 to allow ships to bypass the treacherous Lachine Rapids. Its banks are now popular with cyclists and joggers.

RIGHT: the Portage Monument recalls the days when canoes had to be transported overland to avoid treacherous rapids along the river.

RIGHT: Montréal's Vieux Port is still a working port, despite the opening of the St Lawrence Seaway, which meant that ships could reach the Great Lakes without stopping here. Having seen many incarnations, and been given several face-lifts, the port still remains a part of Montreal's cityscape.

AROUND MONTRÉAL

Excursions from Montréal include everything from fast flowing rivers to chamber music, flashy ski lodges to peaceful monasteries, French resorts to rural farm towns

Montréal is ideally situated for quick getaways to an astonishing variety of year-round adventures: whitewater rafting on the Rouge River; ice-fishing on Brome Lake; hiking, snowshoeing, mountain biking and skiing in all its forms in the mountains of the Laurentians and the Eastern Townships; pleasure boat cruises; gondola rides and water slides; historic forts and ports. All this, and a lot more beside, is available within a couple of hours' drive of Montréal.

Where to go

In the north loom the woods, glacial lakes and alpine villages of the Laurentian Mountains (les Laurentides, or "up North" in local parlance), resting on the oldest rock formation on the planet – the Canadian Shield.

To the southeast of Montréal lie the Cantons de l'Est, or Eastern Townships (simply "the Townships" to residents), a land of rolling pastures, brightly painted barns and villages crowned by elegant white-steepled churches and handsome clapboard homes with wraparound verandahs. It's like a francophone version of New England.

The Laurentians and the Townships are the two main playgrounds for Montréalers. Between Montréal and the Eastern Townships is the historic Richelieu Valley, battleground of the Iroquois, French, English and Americans, and the scene of the 1837 Patriots' Rebellion against the British regime.

Map on page 180

Seasonal activities

Summer brings another medley of pleasures to the Laurentians and the Townships – canoeing, sailing, horseback riding, camping, fishing, swimming and water skiing. Then there are the delights of autumn – hunting for antiques, going to

LEFT: a seaplane takes off on Lac Tremblant. **BELOW:** mountain bikers at Mount Tremblant.

Around Montreal
0 20 km
0 20 miles
Montréal
Laval
Longueuil
Sherbrooke
Drummondville
St-Hyacinthe
Granby
Magog
Sorel
Joliette
St-Jérôme
Victoriaville
Les Cantons-de-l'Est
Montérégie
Québec
Laurentians
Ontario
Vermont
U S A

country fairs, visiting the wineries, popping into an artist's studio, hiking in the woods or just driving the backroads, enjoying the fall colours.

If you plan to drive to either region on weekends, be warned that the traffic leaving the city is likely to be heavy. Both the Laurentians and the Townships are "cottage" country for Montréalers, many of whom spend weekends at their holiday homes in those regions.

Summer is "construction season" as well, since roads cannot be repaired in the winter, and this too can cause delays. So head out of the city early in the afternoon if travelling on a Friday.

The "saintly" villages

Heading north from Montréal, you pass a cluster of villages named after what sound like saints – St-Jérôme, St-Sauveur-des-Monts, Ste-Adèle, Ste-Agathe-des-Monts and so on. In fact, the majority of these Laurentian "saints" were local politicians or entrepreneurs who, in pioneer days, helped to build up the community, opening businesses, constructing homes and building churches.

The main road north is autoroute 15, a fast multi-lane highway, but, if time permits, try to take the more scenic route 117, the old road that was in place before the Laurentians became a major resort area.

In the beginning, skiers used to head up north on **Le Petit Train du Nord** (tel: 1-800-561 6673; www.laurentians.com; free car parking at designated points), the "little train" that opened up the Laurentian wilderness to the outside world and helped to launch the fledgling tourism industry. The construction of the highways rendered the train obsolete, but in 1996 its route was reborn as a 200-km (124-mile) linear recreational trail. Running from St-Jérôme at the southern end of the Laurentians, it terminates in Mont-Laurier. In summer and autumn it's popular with cyclists, and cross-country skiers use it in winter.

St-Sauveur-des-Monts ❶ (or simply St-Sauveur), at exit 60 of autoroute 15, heralds the start of the Laurentian tourist region. It's the archetypal French Canadian village with a huge, silver-spired Catholic church and a main street – rue Principale – lined with small, brightly painted wooden houses.

St-Sauveur is also a great shopping destination. Over 100 boutiques, art galleries, craft shops, studios and restaurants are housed in those old-fashioned buildings, selling everything from maple syrup to hiking boots. **Factorerie St-Sauveur** (100 rue Guindon; tel: 450-227 1074) is a shopping centre with factory outlets selling designer clothing at discount prices.

Travel north to **Ste-Adèle** ❷, a lively ski resort and a thriving writers' and artisans' colony by the shores of Lac Rond and the slopes of Mont Ste-Adèle. There's quite a lot to see and do here, including a train museum, the amusement park

Map on page 180

The Auberge Victorienne inn at St-Sauveur.

BELOW: autumn colours.

On the main street in Ste-Adèle.

Au Pays des Merveilles (In the Country of Wonders; 3575 de la Savane; tel: 450-229 314; www.paysmerveilles.com; June–early Sept). The park has more than 40 activities and games aimed at adults as well as children, including a spooky haunted house. Costumed characters such as Alice in Wonderland, Snow White and Little Red Riding Hood wander the grounds.

Chocoholics will relish a visit to **À la Chocolaterie Marie-Claude** (1090 rue Valiquette; tel: 450-229 3991; Thur–Sun except Nov), for an insight into the process of making confectionery the traditional way, in small batches.

On a sticky summer day, a good place to cool off is the water sports park, **Super Splash** (1791 boulevard Ste-Adèle; tel: 450-229 2909; www.supersplash.qc.ca; late June–late Aug; entrance charge). There are a number of hotels, inns and bed-and-breakfasts in the town.

Heading north, just beyond Val-Morin is 38-metre (125-ft) high **Mont-Condor** and the awesome 22-metre (72-ft) **Condor Needle**, one of the few rock pinnacles in Eastern Canada. Rock climbers flock to both to test their skills.

Continuing north, you soon reach **Val-David** ❸, well known for its abundance of traditional Québécois houses with steep roofs, its attractive inns and fine cuisine, and also for its talented painters and artisans. **1001 Pots** (2435 rue de l'Église; tel: 819-322 6868; www.1001pots.com) is an annual summer exhibition that showcases the work of local potters and ceramicists.

If you fancy a snack while sightseeing, pop into the Boulangerie Biologique La Vagabonde (1262 chemin de la Rivière; tel: 819-322 3953), a craft bakery that sells home-baked bread and pastries. The smell alone will lure you into the tearoom.

Santa Claus also lives in Val-David, at **Village du Père Noël** (987 rue Morin; tel: 819-322 2146; www.noel.qc.ca; early June–early Sept and over the Christmas holidays), where children can sit on Santa's knee and whisper their requests in his ear. This theme park has a number of attractions, including a playground and a petting zoo.

The last town on this excursion is **Ste-Agathe-des-Monts** ❹, the metropolis of the Laurentians, and a hot spot for both Québécois and international celebrities. Its beautiful sandy beach by the picturesque lake attracts sailors, sailboarders and sunbathers.

To get an idea of the Laurentians' old-guard wealth, take a quick cruise around **Lac des Sables** on the Bateau Alouette (Les Croisières Alouette; tel: 819-326 3656 or 1-866-326 3656; www.croisierealouette.com). You'll see the estate built by 20th Century-Fox tycoon William B. Fox and the 42-room "summer cottage" built by a millionaire who kept his own orchestra to play for him day and night, and a greenhouse in which he cultivated only roses.

Outdoors

Canadians are avid tourists in their own country, with many urbanites spending regular weekends at their holiday homes in the country, which are known as "cottages", regardless of their size. In fact some families spend entire holidays in their favourite national or provincial parks in pursuit of outdoor activity. Sailors head for the waters for the swimming, sailing, waterskiing and windsurfing, and tenters take to the back-roads. Autumn can be awesome in the region as the leaves turn a burnished copper, drawing hikers to the hills and valleys. Birdwatchers, fishermen and canoeists, too, find plenty of space for their gentle pursuits. If all that sounds too tame then there is also ample opportunity for whitewater rafting and parasailing. Most of the parks have supervised beaches, hiking and cycling trails.

In the winter the ice and snow are welcomed by many. The weather transforms walking trails into cross-country ski and snowshoeing trails; fishermen cut holes in the ice, dog team enthusiasts have race meets and others enjoy sleigh rides, while alpine skiiers head to the mountain slopes and ski resorts such as those found in the Laurentians and Eastern Townships.

National park

Further north, taking autoroute 117 when the autoroute 15 peters out at Ste-Agathe-des-Monts, is the magnificent Parc National du Mont-Tremblant. Nowadays when people refer to Mont-Tremblant, they inevitably mean the man-made resort *(see page 187)* that has sprung up around the mountain, but the name encompasses much more – the mountain itself, a provincial park and a nearby village.

It's worth making a stop at **St-Faustin** ❺, especially if you're interested in nature and the great outdoors (though you might want to save your energies for the park proper). The **Education and Tourism Centre of the Laurentians** (5000 Chemin Lac-du Cordon; tel: 819-326 1606; entrance charge) gives a detailed overview of the region. Two hiking trails and six interpretation trails wind around Lac du Cordon over rustic boardwalks and footbridges.

You can set off for a hike in the wilderness with an audio-guide or, opt for a guided walk with one of the bilingual naturalists. If you don't have time for a hike, pick up brochures with descriptions of Québec's forests. Naturalists will show you the inside of a jack pine cone or let you sniff some oil extract of white pine. The exhibits on display at the Interpretative Pavilion will tell you everything you wanted to know about trees, and more.

Next is St-Jovite, a typical Québecois village with a large church and a main street where attractive old houses have been turned into boutiques, galleries and restaurants. Turn off autoroute 117 here at the Mont-Tremblant signpost and continue east for 22.5 km (14 miles).

The **Parc National du Mont-Tremblant** (tel: 819-688 2281; www.sepaq.com; entrance charge) protects 1,510 sq km (583 sq miles) of wilderness. This nature enclave was Québec's first provincial park, established in 1894 as a protected "government forest reserve". Within its boundaries lie 163 km (101 miles) of hiking trails, 400 lakes, numerous waterfalls and six rivers, three of them major.

Watersports and wildlife

The **Rouge**, **Matawin** and **du Diable** rivers provide great swimming and fishing for trout or landlocked salmon, and there are riverside camping places. If you've never tried canoeing, that most Canadian of water sports, this is the place to learn, and there's kayaking along the 15-km (9-mile) **Rivière Assomption**, with rapids ranging in difficulty from level one to four.

The park is thick with maple and pine forests, and it shelters all manner of Canadian wildlife – black bears, deer, lynx, wolves, beaver and nearly 200 bird species. Bird watchers can tramp along the trails armed with a checklist, spotting such common birds (at least in these parts) as great blue herons, blue jays

Map on page 180

Pretty blooms grow in abundance in both domestic gardens and mountain habitats.

BELOW: a sunny day in Mont-Tremblant.

Twilight in Tremblant resort, where the après-ski activities can provide as much fun as the slopes.

and pileated woodpeckers. If you're near a dead tree just listen for their distinctive drumming as they hammer on a trunk looking for insects. Listen out too, for the haunting cry of the loon (the bird that features on the one-dollar coin, giving it the nickname "loony"), most commonly heard at dawn or dusk.

Tremblant Resort

North America's first alpine ski ropetows were erected in the Laurentians (at Prévost) in 1930 and at St-Sauveur-des-Monts in 1934. Montréalers soon flocked to the region to try the new-fangled sport and the glamour and fun of skiing began to catch on, enduring to this day. Today, acrobatic skiing, snowboarding, cross-country skiing by torchlight, tubing (which involves scooting down a hill on a large inner tube) and tobogganing, or sledding as Québecers call it, are all hugely popular.

The Laurentians have the largest concentration of alpine ski centres in Eastern North America. There are more than 20, many of which have lighted runs. Not surprisingly, the Laurentians have consistently been voted the leading ski destination in this part of the world.

Mont-Tremblant ❻ is the highest of the Laurentian peaks (986 metres/3,235 ft) and is the centrepiece of **Tremblant Resort** (1000 chemin des Voyageurs; tel: 1-888-736 2526 or 819-681 3000; www.tremblant.com), a year-round tourist destination. The mountain is the highest skiable peak in Eastern Canada, with a vertical drop of 650 metres (2,132 ft), and has the longest trail in Québec at 5 km (3 miles) long.

The "trembling mountain" was given its name by the First Nations, who lived here long before the Europeans. One version of the story (and there are quite a few) is that when you look into **Lac Tremblant**, a 14-km (8-mile) long lake, you can see the shimmering reflection of the mountain behind it.

The resort was the brainchild of Vancouver-based Intrawest Corporation, one of Canada's flagship companies. A global leader in the design, development and operation

BELOW: Tremblant resort in the Laurentian Mountains.

Map on page 180

of four-season resorts and clubs, Intrawest has changed the face of ski centres across North America. (In 2006 it was announced that an American company would take over some of Intrawest's operations.)

The prototype for the Tremblant Resort, which the company started developing in the early 1990s, was Whistler/Blackcomb in British Columbia, one of the best ski resorts in North America and the main site for the 2010 Winter Olympic Games. The pedestrian-only holiday village at Tremblant Resort, which curves around the base of the mountain, is actually a smaller version of its Western Canadian cousin.

The streets, named after famous Québécois skiers, are anchored by place St-Bernard, which looks remarkably like the "sainted " villages *(see page 181)* or the old parts of Québec City *(see page 199)*, albeit a more manicured version. Like the old stone structures in the provincial capital, Tremblant's buildings are small in scale, topped by cheery red and green roofs with rows of dormer windows, but their appearance is deceptive. Behind those picturesque facades are hotels, condominiums, boutiques, restaurants, pubs and a cinema, all of which spell fun for skiers seeking après-ski diversions.

West of Montréal

The Laurentian tourist region is not confined to the area "up North". Indeed, part of it lies just to the west of Montréal and is much closer to the city, so if you have only half a day to spare, this area is ideal. There are several places of interest, including a provincial park, a historic abbey, a fun ferry ride, the pretty village of Hudson – a popular weekend getaway for many Montréalers – and Oka.

Take autoroute 15 north, then off at exit 21 onto route 640 west. Route 344 west, running along the water's edge, is a scenic alternative route from downtown Montréal.

Colourful sailboards float like confetti off the silvery 7-km (4-mile) long beach of the **Parc National d'Oka**, and the lake's shallow waters are ideal for trying out the sport, with a range of rental

Take time out to relax at Le Scandinave Spa (tel: 819-425 5524), which is on the banks of the du Diable River, in the Laurentians. Open daily 10am–9pm. Over 18s only.

BELOW: picture-postcard Tremblant.

The mountain resorts are popular weekend and holiday spots.

facilities close by. The most exotic recreation here, though, is a canoe excursion through the marsh around Grand Bay. Paddle through a floating garden walled by rushes and cattails, carpeted with flowering lily pads and delicate duckweed, with marsh ducks, muskrats and Great Blue Herons in your wake. You might even arouse the curiosity of beavers at work.

The park office (2020 chemin d'Oka; tel: 450-479 8365; www.sepaq.com) can provide information about excursions led by park staff.

Oka

The village of **Oka** ❼ is at the western end of **Lac-des-Deux-Montagnes** (Lake of Two Mountains) at the point where it joins the Ottawa River. French-Canadian Sunday-school songs describe pilgrimages to Oka to buy cheese made by monks at **l'Abbaye Cistercienne d'Oka** (1600 chemin d'Oka; tel: 450-479 8361; www.abbayeoka.com). Unfortunately, the monks no longer make the famous cheese – a task now undertaken by a manufacturer – but it tastes just as good. Visitors can buy it at any number of local supermarkets or, better still, at the monastery store.

Visitors to the monastery and its grounds are greeted at the reception area by a friendly monk, who gives directions to places of interest within the complex. The Cistercian Order was founded in France in 1098 and these monks, called Trappists in North America, adhere to strict rules and observances. Visitors can sit in on some religious services.

Another fascinating site, to be found east of the village, is the **Oka Calvary**. Favoured by keen hikers as well as those who come for its religious significance, it's at its best in the autumn, when the leaves are starting to change colour and from the top – it's a steep hike – you have terrific views over the lake. The Stations of the Cross along the route were built between 1739 and 1742 to inspire the local aboriginals, and three of the seven original chapels have been preserved. Since 1870, people of the First Nations and pilgrims from all over Québec have

After the Snow

Mont-Tremblant is an important ski resort with 94 trails and three snow parks, all kept in tip-top condition by constant grooming and a battery of snow guns. Winter sports practiced here, other than skiing, include ice skating, dogsledding and ice climbing.

The area also has more to offer than snow and après-ski. Fair weather activities include golf at one of the seven championship courses such as Le Diable, Le Géant, mountain biking or cruising on Lac Tremblant (from Federal Wharf, opposite Pinteau Resort, tel: 819-425 1045). In summer and autumn, a gondola (chairlift) , which operates year round, whisks visitors to the top of Mont-Tremblant, where they are free to wander along a dozen well-maintained hiking trails ranging in length from 1 km (a half mile) to 9 km (5½ miles). Alternatively you can climb an observation tower to enjoy the panoramic views of the mountain range.

Contact Tourisme Mont-Tremblant (5080 montée Ryan, Mont-Tremblant Village, tel: 1-800-322 2932 or 819-425 2434) for more detailed information about the activities and attractions available in and around the resort.

come to Oka to celebrate the Feast of the Holy Cross on 14 September.

Montérégie

From Oka you can take the tiny car ferry across to **Hudson** ❽, which is in the tourism region of Montérégie. The seasonal ferry (tel: 450-458 4732; Apr–Nov) leaves from the dock on rue des Anges next to the Argenteuil Manor. In winter, when the water freezes over, you can drive over an "ice bridge", which is an adventure in itself. Driving on ice may sound a little nerve-wracking, but Canadians take it in their stride.

A description of Hudson nearly always includes the adjective "cute", which is particularly apt during the Christmas holidays, when the village is decorated to the hilt. The buildings represent an amazing array of architectural styles, ranging from stately Victorian mansions with wraparound verandas to modern "*chateaux*" overlooking the lake. One of the more charming old structures is **Hudson Town Hall**, a red brick building with a white-pillared entrance.

Many of these heritage buildings have been turned into speciality stores. Legg & Compagnie (422 Main Road; tel: 450-458 5222) is a former hardware store that sells sporty clothing and fancy sweaters. Across the street is the century-old Hudson Emporium (403 Main Road; tel: 450-458 1867), specialising in knick-knacks for the home.

From Hudson, you can drive on to **Rigaud** ❾, charming site of a traditional "sugar camp", the **Sucrerie de la Montagne** (300 chemin St-Georges; tel: 450-451 5204.) The sugaring off season, when the sap of the sugar maples starts to run, is late March to early April, but at other times of the year it's worth calling ahead to check if somebody is on site, because you may be able to pay a visit.

Rouge River rafting

A little further west, lying at the confluence of the Rivière Rouge and Ottawa River at the southwestern corner of the Laurentians tourist region, **Grenville-sur-la-Rouge** is one of Québec's most popular white-water rafting destinations. To get there take autoroute 15 north from Montréal, then highway 50 west (exit 35), which feeds onto route 148 west.

The rafting season runs from April to September but the run along a 25-km (15-mile) course between **Harrington** ❿ and the former village of Calumet (merged with Grenville-sur-la-Route in a 2002 provincial reorganization) is particularly exciting in spring, when melted snow turns the water into a foaming, hissing obstacle course. The names of the rapids say it all: Confusion; Turbo in the Morning; Avalanche; Washing Machine; Slice 'n' Dice; and The Monster. Steep Throat, with a drop of 3.7 metres (12 ft), has been called "the Everest of rafting in Canada". Don't be put off by the

Map on page 180

Cheese, a famous Oka speciality, which used to be made by monks from the town's abbey.

BELOW: the national park at Oka is ideal for windsurfing.

A pollution-free way to travel through the pristine waters.

scary monikers. Experienced river guides will brief you on "body surfing", "hydraulic action" and "ledge drops" and be there to pull you back into the raft in less than 30 seconds should you unintentionally bail out.

Most day packages provide 5–6 hours of rafting (approximately 18 km/11 miles) and include a lunch break, along with all the necessary equipment, one experienced river guide per raft, shuttle service from the base camp and a post-dinner video of the day's adventures. Contact Rafting Nouveau Monde (Tel:1-800 361 5033; www.newworld.ca) for more information and bookings.

The upper Richelieu River

To the east of Montréal, the tourist region of Montérégie is split into two parts – the area north of the St Lawrence River and territory to the south of the city. The spine of Montérégie – and the most interesting part for a visitor – is the 130-km (81-mile) **Richelieu River**, which flows out of Lake Champlain, then snakes north before emptying into Lac St-Pierre at Sorel.

BELOW: Lac-des-Deux-Montagnes at sunset, Parc d'Oka.

A logical starting point is **Chambly**, and there are several ways to get to the town – autoroute 20 south, autoroute 10 or highway 112 – depending on where you set off in Montréal. The main problem once you get there is finding Fort Chambly *(see below)*, the starting point of the river drive. You need to wend your way through a maze of confusing subdivisions and unless you keep your eyes peeled, you might miss the brown plaques that indicate Québec's historic sites.

The first impression of the river, named for Cardinal Richelieu, the ruthless chief minister of Louis XIII, is that of a sleepy backwater, but in Québec's early days it was part of a bustling transportation network – a vital link in New France's fur trade and, during the 19th century, a strategic route for the British military.

The imposing **Fort Chambly National Historic Site** ⓫ (2 rue de Richelieu; daily end May–early Sept; Wed–Sun spring and autumn; entrance charge; tel: 450-658 1585; www.pc.gc.ca) is perched on the edge of the **Richelieu Rapids** and the names of the heroes of New France are carved in stone at its gates. A towering stone structure, it was part of a chain of military installations that in the 17th and 18th centuries guarded the corridor from New York to Québec City. It takes its name from Captain Jacques Chambly, of le Régiment de Carignan-Salières, who built the first (wooden) fort on the site in 1665 to defend against Iroquois attack.

His soldiers were young men press-ganged from taverns in France and "persuaded" to join the colonial army. Few of these lads had a clue what harsh living conditions awaited them over the ocean – meagre rations, minimum wages and interminable winters.

The first European settlement on the Richelieu River grew up around the fort, becoming the town of Chambly. In 1709–11 the wooden building was replaced by the massive, imposing structure with five-sided corner bastions that stands today, and it was occupied by the French until 1760, by the English until 1775 and by the Americans under General Montgomery until 1776. It later held American prisoners during the War of 1812 and rebels during the Patriot Rebellion of 1837–8.

After exploring the fort, head over to **Canal Chambly National Historic Site** (1899 boulevard Périgny; tel: 450-658 6525; www.pc.gc.ca). The canal opened in 1843 and for over a century, heavily loaded barges carried lumber from the forests of Québec's interior, bound for the United States. From the closest three locks to the fort you can watch boaters "locking through" or go canoeing in the Chambly basin, which is just below the Richelieu rapids. The former towpath is now a 19-km (12-mile) recreational trail for hikers and cyclists.

A summer retreat

Head south from Chambly to **St-Jean-sur-Richelieu** ⓬ to stroll through the old section of this historic military town, along rues Jacques-Cartier, St-Charles, Longueuil and St-Georges, and also on the promenade along the Chambly Canal. St-Jean, with its graceful riverside setting, has a long history as a summer resort for Montréalers.

During the exciting 10-day festival of **l'International de Montgolfières de Saint-Jean-sur-Richelieu** (tel: 450-347 9555; www.montgolfieres.com) colourful hot-air balloons float over the rooftops and steeples of the town. Cruises on the Richelieu River (tel: 450-346 2446 or 1-800 361 6420; www.croisieresrichelieu.com) leave from the wharf at the foot of rue St-Georges.

Drive south on route 223 from St-Jean-sur-Richelieu on the west side of the Richelieu River to St-Paul-de-l'île-aux-Noix. At the visitor centre on 61st Avenue you can buy a ticket which includes admission to Fort Lennox and parking as well as a ferry ride to the island.

Fort Lennox

L'Île-aux-Noix is an idyllic spot for picnicking and hikes along the marshy riverbank to observe painted turtles, muskrats, bullfrogs and diving kingfishers. At its southern tip, only 12 km (7 miles) from the US border, is the impressive star-shaped **Fort Lennox National Historic Park** ⓭ (mid-May–late June: daily 10am–5pm, to 6 pm weekends; late June–early Sept daily 10am–6pm; early Sept–mid-Oct weekends only; tel: 450-291 5700; www.pc.gc.ca), complete with a moat 18 metres (60 ft) wide by 4.5 metres (15 ft) deep.

The French built Fort Lennox in 1759 to defend against a British advance, but they evacuated it the following year under British siege. In 1775, the Americans captured

Imposing Fort Chambly has five-sided corner bastions.

BELOW: Festival of Montgolfières.

TIP

For general information about the Montérégie tourist region contact: Tourism Montérégie, tel: 1-866 469 0069 or 450-469 0069; www.tourisme-monteregie.qc.ca

l'Ile-aux-Noix and used it as a base from which to launch attacks on Montréal and Québec City, but a year later a smallpox epidemic forced them to abandon the fort.

Lively animated tours of Fort Lennox take you through the guardhouse (dating from 1824), gunpowder magazine, officers' quarters, prison, barracks and commissary, and a museum exhibiting military equipment and documents. On special days actors perform re-enactments of 18th-century skirmishes, using replicas of period uniforms and weapons.

The Lower Richelieu River

There isn't enough time to explore both the Upper and Lower Richelieu River and take in the sights all in one day, so take another trip north along the river, taking autoroute 10 east to exit 29 (signposted Richelieu) then follow highway 133 along the eastern bank.

The highway is also known as "chemin des Patriotes" as it is named for the mostly French and Irish rebels of 1837–8 who challenged the powers of the colonial government and the merchant elite (mostly Scottish and English) while seeking greater autonomy for Lower Canada (as the province of Québec was then called).

BELOW: Fort Lennox.

Around Mont St-Hilaire

The communities along the shore have traditional *maisons canadiennes*, with steep roofs, thick walls of stone and multi-paned windows. **Mont-St-Hilaire** ⓮, an eye-catching village in front of an oddly-shaped mountain that rises out of nowhere, is well worth a stopover.

When the wind is calm and the air balmy, you can lie for hours on "Sugar Loaf", the flat rocky summit, taking in the contours of the land below. The Montérégian hill is only 410 metres (1,345 ft) above sea level, but it rises abruptly from the St Lawrence plain, affording a dreamy view of its sister peak, Mont-Royal, in the heart of downtown Montréal, the Richelieu River and the sinewy St Lawrence.

Mont St-Hilaire is a thriving ecological marvel only 35 km (22 miles) from Montréal – an environment so unspoiled that UNESCO designated it the first Biosphere Reserve in Canada. This, the highest of the eight Montérégian hills shelters the last vestige of the dense woodland that once covered the St Lawrence Valley. In a lush hardwood forest with canopies of 30-metre (100-ft) red oaks and 250-year-old white pines, there are hundreds of mosses and ferns, 600 species of flowering plants, 32 of flowering trees and 187 species of birds.

Hiking trails wind through an aquatic zone, a wildflower meadow, lush fern areas along Lac Hertel – a lake once humming with seven mills – and up to an exposed windy summit with Arctic vegetation.

The countryside around here is also ideal for birdwatching, cross-country skiing and snowshoeing.

The **Centre de la Nature du Mont Saint-Hilaire** (422 chemin des Moulins; tel: 450-467 1744; www.centrenature.qc.ca) is a good source of information about the area. This is apple-growing country and a couple of orchards sell their produce by the roadside. In the autumn you can also pick your own and taste the aromatic local cider at **Les Vergers Petit et Fils** (1020 chemin de la Montagne; tel: 450-467 9926; www.auxvergerspetit.com).

The aptly-named **Belœil** ⓯, founded in 1694, lies across the Richelieu River from Mont-St-Hilaire's apple orchards, with a bridge connecting the two sides. Belœil's yacht harbour, boutiques, art galleries, artisan shops, restaurants and cultural centre attract Montréalers in all seasons, and Vieux Belœil's magnificent old buildings include a presbytery which was built in 1772.

North of Belœil, it's fun to dot back and forth across the river, especially if you're travelling with children who will love the opportunity to get out on the water. This stretch of the Richelieu River is served by little cable ferries (crossings are well signposted) that creak back and forth all day (May–Sept, nominal charge). The journey takes less than five minutes.

Rebel country

Travelling northward again, to **Saint-Charles-sur-Richelieu** ⓰, which is crowned by a 19th century stone church with a silver roof and spire. Like the other churches along the Richelieu River, it was used as a navigational landmark in a bygone era. Other vestiges of the past are all around. Don't be surprised, in this fiercely traditional corner of Québec, to see homes flying the flag of green, white and red horizontal stripes adopted by the Patriotes.

The story of the rebels is recalled in St-Denis-sur-Richelieu at the **Maison Nationale des Patriotes** (610 chemin des Patriotes; tel: 450-787 3623; www.mndp.qc.ca). Set in a stone building dating from 1809, which once belonged to Jean-Baptiste Mâsse, a sympathizer of the Patriotes' reform movement, this museum, like Fort Chambly, has costumed guides who explain the local history, laced with interesting anecdotes from the past.

From St-Denis-sur-Richelieu, the river wends its way northwards to Tracy and Sorel, where you can explore another waterway, Lac St-Pierre. If time is short, pick up autoroute 30, a faster route back to Montréal, rather than retracing your route along the river.

To Granby

Further east from the Richelieu River, the region of **Les Cantons-de-l'Est** (Eastern Townships) has been correctly described as encapsulating Québec *joie-de-vivre* laced with New England charm. Hugging the border with Vermont (and with Maine and New Hampshire at the

Map on page 180

Shops and boutiques in the Laurentians have funky displays for Halloween.

BELOW: traditional transport.

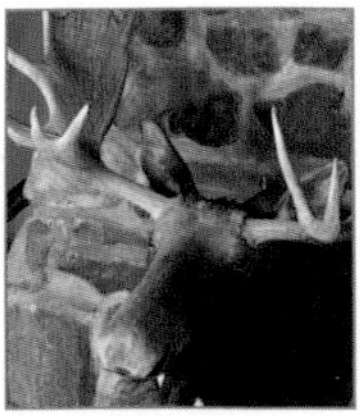

A moose head on display at Hotel du Lac.

far eastern end), the area was first settled by Loyalists – Americans who wanted to continue living under the British Crown after the American Revolution – and that makes this particular region of Québec very different from the francophone heartland.

Like the Laurentians, this is prime ski country with four major centres within an hour's drive of Montréal and of one another *(see box below)*.

If you're travelling *en famille*, stop by **Granby Zoo** ⓱ (525 rue St-Hubert; tel: 1-877-472 6299 or 450-372 9113; entrance charge; www.zoodegranby.com). This is one of the oldest and largest animal sanctuaries in Eastern Canada, sheltering more than 1,000 creatures, representing 250 species from around the globe – from Andean condors to gorillas, whose antics look a little too much like our own. Within the zoo's landscaped grounds is Amazoo, a waterpark with an Amazonian theme (end May–mid-Oct only).

Other family-oriented attractions in the Granby area include the **Lac Boivin Interpretation Centre** (700 rue Drummond; tel: 450-375 3861), which has a 10-km (6-mile) trail across a marsh, a great spot for birdwatching. There is also a 21-km (13-mile) bike trail, **l'Estriade**, which runs to Waterloo. The bike path, laid down on former railway tracks, is an easy run for youngsters because it's fairly flat. Park at place de la Gare, Granby's former railway station, where you can rent bikes at Velo Gare (71 rue Denison Est; tel: 450-777 4438).

Wine country

Heading south from Granby on route 139, across autoroute 10, you'll pass through Cowansville with its handsome Loyalist buildings, where you'll start seeing blue and white signs indicating the *route des vins* (wine route) leading to **Dunham**, Québec's wine-growing country. A picturesque hamlet with old stone houses, Dunham's farmland is rich and fertile, supporting fruit and vegetables (look out for stands selling fresh produce) as well as vines.

Skiing in Les Cantons-de-l'Est

Like the Laurentians, Les Cantons-de-l'Est is prime skiing country with four major centres within a one hour drive of the city of Montréal: Bromont, which is lit at night; Mont-Orford; Mont-Sutton and Owl's Head. However, the choice of winter sports is not limited to skiing alone. Other popular activities include cross-country skiing, snowshoeing, dogsledding, ice-fishing and winter camping. The area is also well known as the capital of snowmobile country with around 2,000 km (1,243 miles) of designated trails. It's an exhilirating experience bobbing along on the snow at high speed. The fastest way to reach the Cantons from Montréal is along autoroute 10 east (also called the Eastern Townships autoroute), plan to leave the highway as soon as you arrive at the Townships, at exit 68.

One of the joys of the region is meandering along the back roads, stopping here and there to sample a lunch of local specialities, to visit a winery or for the spectacular mountain scenery. Maps and other practical information are available from Tourisme Cantons-de-l'Est (20 rue Don-Bosco Sud, Sherbrooke, tel: 1-800-355 5755 or 819-820 2020; www.easterntownships.org).

RIGHT: horseback riding and trekking.

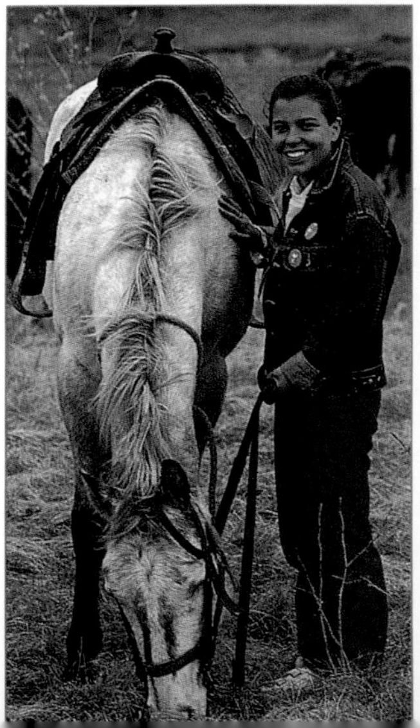

It might seem surprising that grape vines can grow in an area better known for its ski hills, but this part of the Townships has a mild micro-climate that allows the plants to survive the Québec winters.

There are 13 wineries in the region, offering tastings and tours. **Vignoble de l'Orpailleur** (1086 rue Bruce; tel: 450-295 2763; www.orpailleur.ca), also has a small museum documenting the history of wine. Pack a picnic (you can pick up ingredients at the wineries) then circle back to Montréal via picturesque Frelighsburg, Stanbridge East and tiny Mystic, north through Farnham, to autoroute 10.

Lac Brome and Sutton

Another popular destination in the Eastern Townships, to the south of Granby, is **Lac Brome** ⓲ a village and a lake, though the largely English-speaking village is commonly known by its former name, **Knowlton**. It lies south of autoroute 10, off exit 90.

A millpond cuts through the heart of the Victorian village, and colourful shops in 19th-century houses give it a festive air. Brome Lake Books (264 chemin Knowlton, Mill Pond Plaza; tel: 450-242 2242) is one of the few places in this neck of the woods that stocks English-language books and magazines.

Knowlton is a pleasant spot for lunch, brunch or coffee with wickedly rich desserts, and is known for its white ducks, raised at a factory on the edge of town. Local restaurants serve this gourmet speciality, especially during the annual Duck Festival (end Sept–early Oct).

In stagecoach days, Knowlton was a stop on the Boston to Montréal run. The old coaching inn – Auberge Knowlton, built in 1849 – still stands today, anchoring rue Lakeside and chemin Knowlton, the main crossroads.

The story of Knowlton's past is told in the **Pettes Memorial Library**, established in 1894 as the first free library in Québec, as well as in the **Musée Historique du Comté de Brome** (Brome County Historical Museum; 130 rue Lakeside; mid-May–mid-Sept Mon–Sat, 10am–4.30pm, Sun, 11am–4.30pm; entrance charge; tel: 450-243 6782).

The museum's buildings house Abenaki First Nations artefacts, pioneer bric-à-brac such as foot-warmers and pill-making machines, a local history archive (survey maps and old letters), a military collection, general store, blacksmith shop, fire tower and county courthouse. The white brick building was the original village school (1844) and contains a World War I Fokker biplane with the camouflage covering still intact: it was sent to Canada in 1919 as part of the war reparations.

Sutton ⓳ bustles with hikers and skiers bound for the winding, wooded trails of Mont-Sutton, as well as shoppers bent on finding quilts and woven rugs, ceramics and pewter in **Farfelu** (20k rue Principale

Map on page 180

Delicious preserves made from local ingredients can be found at farmers markets in the Eastern Townships.

BELOW: lakeside architecture.

The Orford Arts Centre, home of the renowned annual Orford Festival.

Nord; tel: 450-538 5959) the local artists' cooperative. The main street of this ski resort at the base of **Mont-Sutton** is flanked with graceful old houses, auberges, craft shops, art galleries and tempting restaurants and outdoor cafés.

In summer the Saturday flea market on Curley Street (open mid-May–early Oct 8am–3pm) is lively, and on Sunday it's a local tradition to have brunch followed by a hike up Mont-Sutton. Star-gazing soirées are popular, as is summer mountain biking. Local topographical and cycling maps give the best routes for excursions on 10-speed or *tout-terrain* mountain bikes. For information and maps on all the cycling routes in the area, contact Tourisme Sutton (24a rue Principale Sud; tel: 450-53 8455 or 1-800 565 8455).

After some healthy outdoor exercise, you may be tempted to pile on the calories at **Chocolaterie Belge Muriel** (8 rue Principale Sud; 450-538 0139). The chocolate shop turns out fragrant delicacies that are hard to resist and in the chocolaterie's museum there are exhibits that explain the manufacturing process, from cocoa bean to chocolate bar.

Another mouth-watering store is **Atelier Bouffe** (14 Principale Sud; tel: 450-538 2766), a kitchen shop filled with spices, teas and gadgets, you can also sample varieties of olive oil. At the back is Chez Matis (tel: 450-538 6444), a catering business specialising in French cuisine. After watching the chef roll out a length of pastry, you can nibble on a slice of his delicious apple pie.

BELOW: cycling is a popular way to see the area.

Eastern Townships

This excursion heads further east, to a pretty section of the Eastern Townships that overlooks **Lac Memphrémagog**, a 42-km (26-mile) long glacial lake, ringed by mountains, that stretches into Vermont. From Montréal, follow autoroute 10 east to exit 115.

Mont-Orford ⑳ (tel: 819-843 6548; www.orford.com), which lies within a provincial park, is a centre for outdoor activities such as downhill and cross-country skiing, skating, snowshoeing and snowboarding in winter, and hiking, swimming, golfing and camping in summer and autumn. Classical music rings in the woodland air during Festival Orford, which is organised by the **Centre d'Arts Mont-Orford** (3165 chemin du Parc, route 141 nord; concert season: July–mid-Aug; tel: 819-843 9871 or 1-888 310 3665; www.arts-orford.org), a renowned music school where young musicians hone their skills with the help of professional performers, who also give public concerts.

Magog ㉑, at the head of Lac Memphrémagog, is linked to Mont-Orford by a recreational trail (or drive along route 112 if you want to take the easy way), which runs into a linear park along the water. The gravel-covered trail snakes through forest, then passes agricultural land before paralleling chemin Roy, across a railway line, to downtown Magog. In town, you can "refuel" with a snack at any number of pubs and eateries or just flop down on one of the two sandy beaches. In winter the waterfront trail is transformed into a skating rink.

From Magog, you can take a cruise, rent a sailboat with a private skipper, fish for *ouananiche* (landlocked salmon), test your balance on a sailboard, or see Lac Memphrémagog through a snorkelling mask or while dangling from a parachute 46 metres (150 ft) in the air. Parasailing is an exhilarating and effortless way to see the lake. Don a harness attached to a parachute, which is then towed by a motor boat. Sports Nautiques Estrie (tel: 819-838 5000; www.sportaventuremagog-orford.com) organises tours of the lake.

The Benedictine abbey of **St-Benoît-du-Lac** 22 (tel: 819-843 4080; www.st-benoit-du-lac.com) looms over a peninsula on the north west shore of Lac Memphrémagog like a fairytale castle. Designed by Dom Paul Bellot (1876–1944), a French monk who settled in the area in 1937 and became one of Québec's main ecclesiastical architects. The abbey has octagonal granite towers, triangular gables and narrow pointed windows. In stark contrast to the rest of the monastery, a modern church designed by Montréal architect Dan S. Hanganu was added to the building in 1994. The 40 or so monks of the Benedictine order of Solesmes, France, are the only inhabitants of this independent municipality.

You can tour the abbey's rich mosaic interior, pick apples in the orchard in the autumn, or buy cider and the monks' award-winning cheeses (St-Benoît, Ricotta and l'Ermite). It is made on the premises and sold at the monastery store (Mon–Sat, 9–10.45am and 11.45am–4.30pm), which also stocks a selection of religious books and artefacts. Best of all, time your visit to hear the monks during Vespers (daily 5pm, except Thur 7pm). The ethereal sounds of Gregorian chant will transport you into another world. ❑

Map on page 180

Apples grown in the orchard at St-Benoît-du-Lac can be picked in autumn.

BELOW: St-Benoît-du-Lac Abbey.

RESTAURANTS, BARS & CAFÉS

Restaurants

Belœil

Hostellerie Rive Gauche
1810 boulevard Richelieu. Tel: 450-467 4477. L & D. $$–$$$$
This pretty country inn on the shores of the Richelieu River dishes up fine cuisine. The rather adventurous menu includes *merguez* (spicy sausage), salmon tartare, foie gras, ostrich and venison. There's also a good selection of Québec cheeses.

Chambly

Le Grand Meux
1717 avenue Bourgogne. Tel: 450-447 7474. L & D. $$
In the shadow of Fort Chambly, overlooking the Richelieu River, this restaurant, formerly a crêperie, still serves delicious pancakes (a favourite with the locals and visitors), but it has augmented its menu with grilled meats and chicken dishes.

Granby

Bistro le Picollo
225 rue Denison Est. Tel: 450-405 4782. L daily, D Tues–Sat. $$–$$$
This restaurant is in a charming boutique hotel and spa, which was built in 2004, alongside Lac Boivin and l'Estriade bike trail. It Specialises in authentic Mediterranean cuisine, with an emphasis on fish and seafood as well as a choice of pastas and soups.

Hudson

Auberge Willow Place
298 rue Main. Tel: 450-458 7006. L & D. $$–$$$
Faithful reproduction of an 1820 inn which burned down in 1989. Great view over Lac-des-deux-Montagnes. There's a patio restaurant, as well as an inside dining room (dover sole, rack of lamb, chicken stuffed with Oka cheese) and a pub serving favourites such as fish and chips and steak and kidney pie.

Lac Brome (Knowlton)

Le Relais Restaurant-Bistro
286 chemin Knowlton. Tel: 450-242 2232. L & D. $$–$$$
Renovated 1849 coaching inn with a menu showcasing locally-raised Lac Brome duck, served with wines from the Dunham area, wine country.

Magog

Restaurant l'Ancrage
1150 rue Principale Ouest. Tel: 819-843 6521. L & D daily. $$–$$$$
Set in the patio area and dining room of Auberge l'Etoile-sur-le-Lac on Lac Memphrémagog. Haute cuisine with regional touches – duck foie gras, medallion of caribou, roast rack of lamb. Lots of garlic. Occasional live jazz on weekends.

Mont-Orford

Aux 4 Saisons d'Orford
4940 chemin du Parc. Tel: 819-868 1110. L & D daily. $$–$$$
This bistro, with its minimalist décor and full-length bar earns rave reviews for its adventurous cuisine. Specialities include warm duck salad, roast lamb flavoured with coffee and chocolate, filet of beef in a mustard-flavoured cheese sauce.

St-Jean-sur-Richelieu

Coq Rapide
365 boulevard du Seminaire. Tel: 450-348 1191. L & D. $$
Known for its tasty roast chicken and fast, friendly service.

St-Sauveur

Restaurant des Oliviers
239 rue Principale. Tel: 450-227 2110. L & D Wed–Sun; daily July–Aug. $$
A slice of Provence in the heart of St-Sauveur. Chef Christian Robitaille dishes up Provençal specialities in a décor that takes you to the South of France on a summer's day. Good wine selection from all five continents.

Restaurant Papa Luigi
155 rue Principale. Tel: 450-227 5311. D daily. $$–$$$
Italian specialities, seafood platters and sizzling steaks served in

a spectacular way in a cosy setting. The restaurant has two fireplaces and a sommelier poised to recommend one of the 80 varieties of Italian wine.

Ste-Adèle

L'Eau à la Bouche
3003 boulevard St-Adèle.
Tel: 450-229 2991.
B & D daily. $$$–$$$$
The dining room more than lives up to its name, which means "mouthwatering". Back in the 1980s, chef/owner Anne Desjardins was one of the first female chefs in Québec to promote fresh, regional cuisine – still a staple of her exquisite food.

Sutton

Mocador Restaurant
17 rue Principale N. Tel: 450-538 2426. L & D Tues–Sun. $$–$$$
A lively bar with fireplace that's a fixture on the après-ski scene. Tex Mex, salads, sandwiches and pasta.

Tremblant Resort

Bullseye Bar & Steak House
Place St-Bernard. Tel: 819-681 2855. L & D. $$
Steak, seafood and grilled meats in a Wild West setting.

Le Chalet du Smoked Meat
Place des Voyageurs.
Tel: 819-681 4664. L. $
Fast food with a Montréal theme. Expect *Poutine* (fries covered in cheese curds), smoked meat, roast chicken.

Le Shack
Le St-Bernard. Tel: 819-681 4700. L &D. $–$$$
Burgers, fish, steaks and a family menu at lunch time in this busy (and noisy) sports bar with a giant screen. The terrace overlooks the main square from which you get a great view of the live acts during the summer.

Windigo
Fairmont Tremblant, 3045 chemin de la Chapelle. Tel: 819-681 7000. L & D daily, Br Sun. $$–$$$
A modern version of the traditional chateau railway hotels so typical of the former Canadian Pacific Hotels & Resorts, now Fairmont, who built this property in 1996. This establishment serves up international cuisine; themed buffets as well as à la carte.

Val-David

Rôtisserie au Petit-Poucet
1030 route 117. Tel: 819-322 2246. B (all day) & D. $–$$
A Québec institution, this giant log cabin serves hearty, country-style buffets with a traditional twist – meat pies, maple-flavoured ham and other calorie-laden dishes.

Bars & Cafés

Lac Brome (Knowlton)

Café Inn
264 rue Knowlton. Tel: 450-243 0069.
Run by a couple who moved here from Toronto via California and Great Britain. This is a popular hangout known for tasty thin-crust pizzas. Live entertainment Friday.

Magog

Café St-Michel
503 rue Principale Ouest.
Tel: 819-868 1062.
Noisy bar with *chansonniers* (nightclub singers) and great place for people watching. Pub menu and beers from around the world.

St-Jovite

Microbrasserie La Diable
100 chemin des Voyageurs.
Tel: 819-681 4546.
Six types of beer brewed on the premises to wash down salads, open sandwiches, sausages and sauerkraut.

Ste-Adèle

Café de la Gare
1000 rue St-Georges.
Tel: 450-229 5886
Located at the 25 km (15 mile) point on Le Petit Train du Nord, the café is the perfect place to rest your weary legs after cycling or skiing all day. Healthy snacks, fondues in winter and speciality coffees. Live entertainment.

PRICE CATEGORIES

Prices for a three-course dinner per person with a half-bottle of house wine:
$ = under $25
$$ = $25–50
$$$ = $50–70
$$$$ = more than $70

LEFT: Dunham is in Québec's wine country.
RIGHT: a slice of Provence in St-Sauveur.

QUÉBEC CITY

This is the political and spiritual heart of the province. It is rich in history, culture and beauty and the Old Town is a living museum

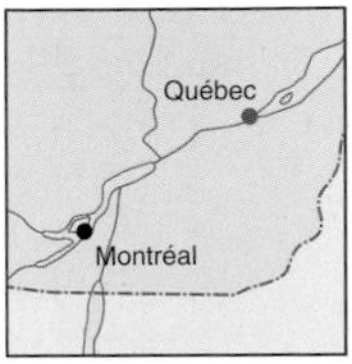

Map on page 200

The spectacular geographical position – on a clifftop, at the neck of the mighty St Lawrence River – that made Québec so appealing to the French colonists had actually been noted thousands of years earlier by First Nations Canadians. They had settled a small community here, Stadacona, from which they ruled a small riverside territory known as "the village" ("Canada" in their language).

Jacques Cartier sailed up the river to the village in 1535 and returned home with a cargo of "fool's gold" (pyrite) and beaver pelts. Though the "gold" was worthless the pelts led to Québec becoming an important trading post. However it was Samuel de Champlain who established the city in 1608, the settlement would later become New France and eventually Canada. But it wasn't all plain sailing for the French, other colonial powers had their eye on Québec too.

Arrival of the British

The British coveted the river city for its strategic position and for its port. From here they could both explore Canada's vastness and control their restless American colonies to the south. Finally conflict over the land led to a full-blown battle.

It was a terrible fight. The British had used a surprise strategy to reach the Plains, somehow climbing the undefended cliff walls that the Québécois believed could never be breached. Both generals, the French Montcalm and Wolfe, were killed, but the Québécois forces were routed. Soon the British would move upriver to Montréal; the Union Jack was raised above that city on 9 September 1760. For a time the French lost control of the city. The French agitated continually, however, and the British were

LEFT: Château Frontenac.
BELOW: a violinist plays in front of a trompe l'oeil place Royale.

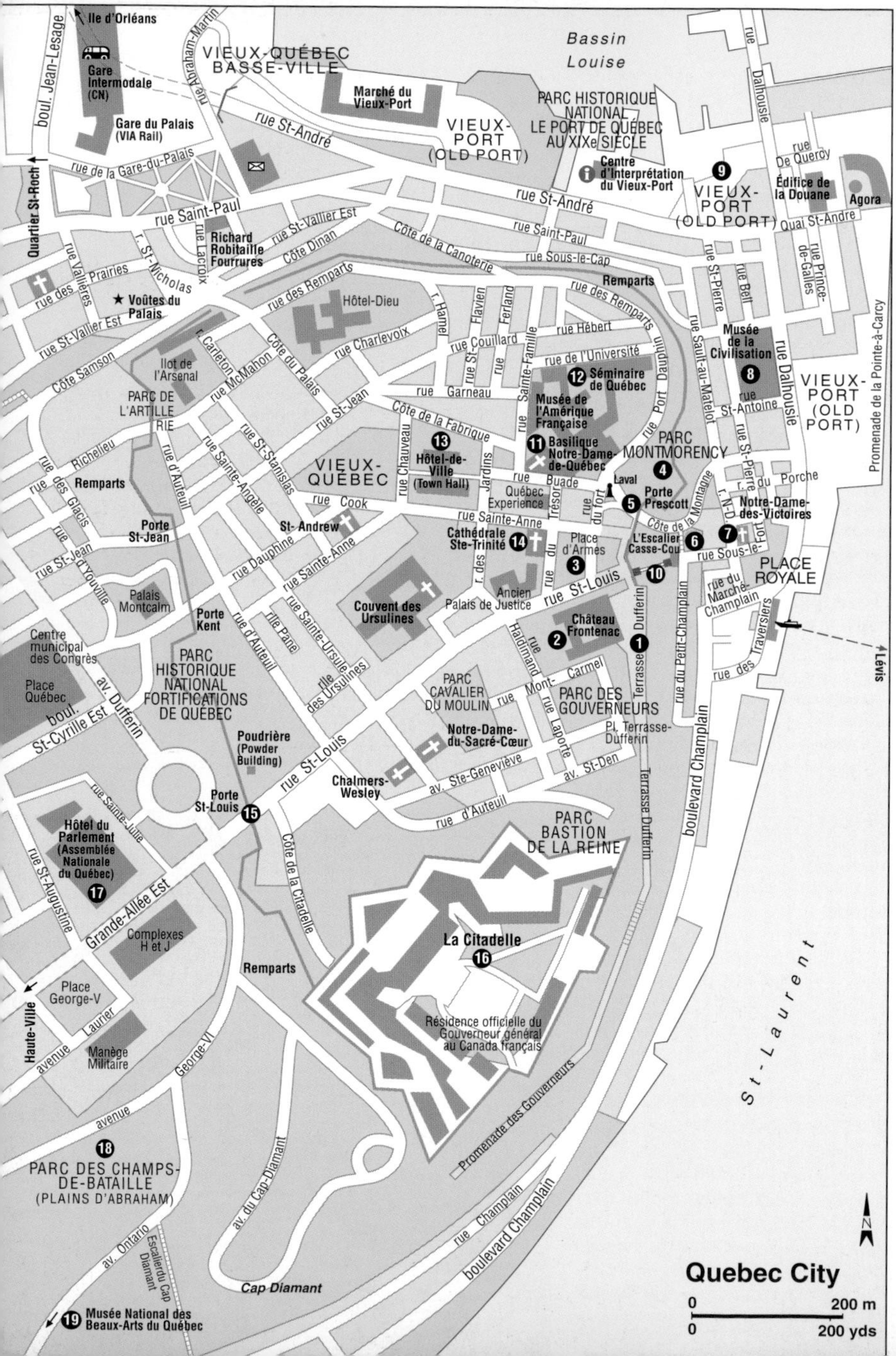
Quebec City
0
200 m
0
200 yds
N
Ile d'Orléans
Gare Intermodale (CN)
Gare du Palais (VIA Rail)
boul. Jean-Lesage
Quartier St-Roch
rue Abraham-Martin
VIEUX-QUÉBEC BASSE-VILLE
Bassin Louise
Marché du Vieux-Port
PARC HISTORIQUE NATIONAL LE PORT DE QUÉBEC AU XIXe SIÈCLE
VIEUX-PORT (OLD PORT)
Centre d'Interprétation du Vieux-Port
rue St-André
rue Dalhousie
rue De Quercy
Édifice de la Douane
Agora
Quai St-André
rue de la Gare-du-Palais
rue Saint-Paul
rue St-Vallier Est
Richard Robitaille Fourrures
Côte Dinan
Côte de la Canoterie
rue Sous-le-Cap
rue Lacroix
r. St-Nicholas
rue des Prairies
rue Vallières
Voûtes du Palais
rue des Remparts
Remparts
Hôtel-Dieu
r. Hamel
rue Flavien
rue Ferland
rue St-Pierre
rue Bell
rue Prince-de-Galles
Promenade de la Pointe-à-Carcy
rue Couillard
rue Hébert
rue de l'Université
rue Sault-au-Matelot
Musée de la Civilisation
rue Charlevoix
r. Carleton
Côte du Palais
Ilot de l'Arsenal
Côte Samson
rue McMahon
PARC DE L'ARTILLERIE
rue Garneau
rue Sainte-Famille
Séminaire de Québec
Musée de l'Amérique Française
rue Port Dauphin
rue St-Antoine
rue Dalhousie
VIEUX-PORT (OLD PORT)
rue St-Jean
Côte de la Fabrique
Basilique Notre-Dame-de-Québec
PARC MONTMORENCY
rue Richelieu
rue St-Stanislas
rue Sainte-Angèle
rue d'Auteuil
rue Chauveau
Hôtel-de-Ville (Town Hall)
VIEUX-QUÉBEC
rue Jardins
rue Buade
Laval
Porte Prescott
Côte de la Montagne
r. du Porche
r. N-D
Notre-Dame-des-Victoires
Remparts
rue des Glacis
rue Cook
Québec Experience
rue Trésor
rue du Fort
rue Sainte-Anne
Porte St-Jean
St- Andrew
Cathédrale Ste-Trinité
Place d'Armes
L'Escalier Casse-Cou
rue Sous-le-Fort
rue St-Jean
rue d'Youville
rue Dauphine
rue Sainte-Anne
r. des
rue du
PLACE ROYALE
Palais Montcalm
Couvent des Ursulines
Ancien Palais de Justice
rue St-Louis
rue du Marché-Champlain
Porte Kent
rue d'Auteuil
rue Pane
rue Sainte-Ursule
Château Frontenac
rue Haldimand
Terrasse Dufferin
rue du Petit-Champlain
rue des Traversiers
Lévis
Centre municipal des Congrès
Place Québec
av. Dufferin
boul. St-Cyrille Est
PARC HISTORIQUE NATIONAL FORTIFICATIONS DE QUÉBEC
rue des Ursulines
PARC CAVALIER DU MOULIN
rue Mont-Carmel
PARC DES GOUVERNEURS
rue Laporte
Pl. Terrasse-Dufferin
boulevard Champlain
Poudrière (Powder Building)
Notre-Dame-du-Sacré-Cœur
av. Ste-Geneviève
av. St-Den
rue St-Louis
Chalmers-Wesley
Porte St-Louis
rue Sainte-Julie
rue d'Auteuil
PARC BASTION DE LA REINE
Terrasse Dufferin
Hôtel du Parlement (Assemblée Nationale du Québec)
rue St-Augustine
Grande-Allée Est
Côte de la Citadelle
Complexes H et J
La Citadelle
Remparts
St-Laurent
Place George-V
Haute-Ville
avenue Laurier
Manège Militaire
Résidence officielle du Gouverneur général au Canada français
George-VI
avenue
Promenade des Gouverneurs
PARC DES CHAMPS-DE-BATAILLE (PLAINS D'ABRAHAM)
av. du Cap-Diamant
rue Champlain
boulevard Champlain
av. Ontario
Escalier du Cap Diamant
Cap Diamant
Musée National des Beaux-Arts du Québec

forced to make major concessions to them with the 1774 Québec Act.

The colonists in America were not pleased with the new coziness between its two main enemies, and their armies marched through Maine to Québec City in the harsh winter of 1775, just months before their Declaration of Independence. The combined efforts of British and French forces swiftly repelled them, and to ensure the incident would not be repeated, the city's distinctive walls were constructed. Today Québec City is the only fortified city in North America north of Mexico.

The British divided Canada in half in 1791, naming Québec City the capital of what was then Lower Canada. When Canada became a distinct nation, on 1July 1867, Québec City remained the administrative and political capital of its province.

The early 19th century was a time of rapid change, as waves of immigrants poured in and shipping boomed. Soon Montréal began to flourish, as Canada began boosting trade with the United States – using Montréal's extensive rail lines – and reducing trade by sea with Britain. Québec City became a second city, inhabited by government paper-pushers, reverting almost exclusively to its previous Frenchness.

Standing sentinel

Québec City retains its 18th-century ambience, with narrow, winding streets and horse-drawn carriages and fine French cooking behind charming facades. The only dramatic change in the old town is the century-old Château Frontenac, a castle-like hotel that perches on its promontory overlooking the St Lawrence River.

The province of Québec's cryptic motto, *Je me souviens* (I remember), insists upon the defence of Québécois tradition, language and culture. Here, in the provincial capital, there are reminders everywhere that this defence was once performed by armed soldiers on turrets and bastions. Today, the politicians and civil servants of Québec City have taken over the job, using the milder instruments of democracy, but are hardly less ardent in their purpose.

Map on page 200

TIP

In 2008, the city celebrate's its 400th anniversary – a milestone shared by few North American cities. The commemoration begins on 3 July, and a round of attractions and special events continue throughout the year (for information: www.quebec400.qc.ca).

BELOW: approaching the fortified city by ferry.

The Sun King immortalised in place Royale.

The walled city of Québec still stands sentinel over the St Lawrence, and the views are lovely. From the **Terrasse Dufferin** ❶ in front of the **Château Frontenac** ❷ you can look out at Ile d'Orleans and, in the distance, on a clear day, the rolling countryside of the Laurentians and Mont St-Anne. At the foot of the cliffs, a variety of boats ply the sunkissed St Lawrence River 60 metres (195 ft) below.

To the Lower Town

Diagonally opposite **Place d'Armes** ❸, the former drill and parade ground, rue du Trésor runs down to rue Buade. Rue du Trésor, named after the building where colonists used to pay their dues to the Royal Treasury, is today the artists' row, hung with reasonably priced watercolours, etchings and silkscreens.

Rue Buade winds downhill to **Parc Montmorency** ❹, usually tranquil no matter how busy the rest of the old town. Opposite the park is the grand Ancien Bureau de Poste (Old Post Office) with its rather pompous monument to Bishop François-Xavier de Laval-Montmorency, first bishop of Québec and founder of its largest university.

Côte de la Montagne drops steeply to the left, winding down into the **Lower Town**, following the ravine that Québec's first settlers used to climb from the Lower to the Upper Town.

Beyond the **Porte Prescott** ❺, a reconstruction of the original erected here in 1797, is **L'Escalier Casse-Cou** ❻, the "Breakneck Stairway". This staircase, not quite as daunting as it sounds, leads to the narrow **rue du Petit-Champlain**, lined with craft shops and clothing boutiques, which claims to be the oldest shopping street in North America. From the foot of L'Escalier Casse-Cou, place Royale, spruced up for the 400th anniversary, is just around the corner. Thus one tumbles from the Château Frontenac into the cradle of French civilization in North America.

Place Royale, where the first settlement in America stood, was the business centre of Québec City until about 1832. Its name derives from

RIGHT: cycling through the lower city.

The founders

When Jacques Cartier sailed up the river to the village in 1535, his men were weary and sick. They managed three voyages without serious incident, then sailed home to France carrying a cargo of what they thought was gold. It turned out to be "fool's gold" (pyrite), but the beaver pelts Cartier also brought home would eventually seal Québec's fate as a colonial trading outpost. It was the explorer Samuel de Champlain who established the city in 1608 as the first permanent settlement in what would become New France, then Canada. He named it for what the natives called the spot: Kebec, meaning "narrowing of the river". It was not until the fur trade began picking up steam in the early 18th century, largely fuelled by fashions in Europe, that Québec City began to grow.

However, the British also coveted the river city, for its strategic position and for its port. From here they could both explore Canada's vastness and control their restless American colonies to the south. Eventually a decisive battle in late 1759, fought on the Plains of Abraham above the Old Town ended in defeat for the French. The conflict is etched into the heart of every Québécois.

the bust of Louis XIV, the great Sun King of Versailles, that was erected here in 1686.

Today, it is the scene of constant performances of plays and concerts, usually re-creating the culture of the 17th and 18th centuries. **Eglise Notre-Dame-des-Victoires** ❼, dominating the square, was built in 1688 and reconstructed after Wolfe's devastation of the Lower Town in 1759. The church is named for two early victories against the Anglo-Americans – or rather, one victory and one lucky accident.

The victory was against a Bostonian, Sir William Phipps (knighted for discovering 32 tonnes of shipwrecked bullion), who sailed to Québec with 34 boats and 2,000 men in October 1690, and demanded its surrender. Governor Frontenac promised to reply with his cannon, and during six days of fighting his guns hammered the fleet. By land, snipers, fighting First Nations-style against Phipps's troops drawn up in formal battle-order, killed 150 men with only one loss to their own party. Phipps withdrew on the sixth day, unaware that the French had just run out of ammunition.

The lucky accident – or, to the French, Our Lady's victory – was the storm in the Gulf of St Lawrence that destroyed the enormous British fleet of Sir Hovendon Walker in 1711, saving Québec from almost certain defeat. Both these events are depicted in little scenes above the odd, turreted altar.

Modern "old port"

Crossing rue Dalhousie, the road that runs along the waterfront and then feeds into boulevard Champlain, you leave the 18th century behind and encounter the more modern world of Québec City's working harbour. (The boulevard hugs the St Lawrence River and is, incidentally, the most scenic route into the city from autoroute 20.) At the southern end of this stretch of road, is the entrance to the government-operated ferry services to Lévis across the river, while straight ahead the *Louis Jolliet*, a popular cruise boat, docks. Moored behind

Map on page 200

The breakneck Stairway leads to a street of interesting crafts shops.

BELOW: artists on rue Trésor.

Delicious crêpe at Au Petit Coin Breton, rue St-Jean.

BELOW: at the farmers market in the old port.

the ferry is the *Amundsen*, a Garde Côtière Canadienne (Canadian Coast Guard) icebreaker named after Roald Amundsen, the Norwegian explorer who was the first person to successfully navigate the Northwest Passage.

At the northern end is the award-winning modern **Musée de la Civilisation** ❽ (85 rue Dalhousie; tel: 418-643 2158; www.mcq.org), which presents thematic exhibitions on such subjects as language, thought, the body and society.

The museum is the centrepiece of the modern commercial and community complex, called the **Vieux-Port** ❾ (Old Port) despite its thoroughly contemporary design featuring overhead walkways of red and silver tubing and perspex walls that connect spacious, functional pavilions. The complex surrounds the Agora, a 6,000-seat amphitheatre set among flower-beds, waterfalls and fountains, used for cultural events, particularly evening concerts throughout the summer.

Within the complex is a visitor centre that gives an overview of the harbour's history and the **Marché du Vieux-Port** (16 quai St-André; tel: 418-692 2517), a farmers' market with regional produce such as seafood from the Gaspé, blueberry brioches, duck and maple products of every kind.

Venture further along rue St-Paul and you'll land in the middle of Québec City's hottest *quartier*, an area that is a little off the beaten tourist path, but which is popular with the locals.

Hot spot

St-Roch, which runs off boulevard Charest Est, was once the industrial heartland of Québec City, home to tanneries and textile factories. When the heavy industries died out, developers started to renovate the large, open spaces, turning them into offices for dot.com companies and studios for craftspeople and artists.

Rue St-Joseph, one of the main east–west streets, is really a revitalization work-in-progress. Second-hand shops stand cheek-by-jowl with designer boutiques, condominiums and trendy restaurants.

If you're walking back toward the Lower Town, be sure to pop into **Richard Robitaille Fourrures** (329 rue St-Paul; tel: 418-692 9699), a combined fur store and *economusée* (craft museum) that is opposite the Gare du Palais, Québec City's 1915 train station. Rue St-Paul is an up-and-coming street lined with antiques shops and stores selling chic home accessories.

The fur museum, which has a workshop at the back, has some fascinating snippets about Canada's fur trade. According to one account, in the 19th century, hatters working with beaver pelt cured the skins with a blend of chemicals that included mercury salts. Prolonged exposure to the fumes could cause brain damage – hence the expression "mad as a hatter".

The Upper Town

The easiest way to get back to the **Upper Town** is to take the little **funicular** ⑩ (daily 7am–11.50pm) at the head of rue Sous-le-Fort, which is worth the small charge to save wear and tear on the feet in this city-made-for-walking. It shinnies up the cliff from the house of Louis Jolliet (the explorer of the Mississippi River) to the Terrasse Dufferin.

At the intersection of rue de Buade and Côte de la Fabrique is the baroque cathedral, **Basilique Notre-Dame-de-Québec** ⑪ (daily 8am–4pm; sound and light show May–Oct only; tel: 418-694 4000). The city's main church since 1633, Notre-Dame-de-la-Recouvrance was built by Samuel de Champlain in gratitude for the recovery of New France from the British.

Next door are the **Séminaire de Québec** ⑫ (guided tours in summer; entrance charge) and the Université Laval. The Jesuits established a college here in 1635, a year before Harvard opened, but the seminary was officially founded only in 1663, by Bishop Laval. The seminary's museum, **Musée de l'Amérique Francaise** (June–early Sept 9.30am–5pm; tel: 418-692 2843; www.mcq.org) is probably the city's finest general museum, with splendid modern facilities for the displays of baroque and Renaissance art and some of the best 19th-century Canadian art. There is also a gruesome mummy dating from the time of Tutankhamun.

Also in this area are the grey **Hôtel-de-Ville** ⑬ (Town Hall) and the **Cathédrale Ste-Trinité** ⑭, the first Anglican cathedral built outside the British Isles. It is thoroughly English, from its design (modelled on St Martin-in-the-Fields in London's Trafalgar Square) to its pews made of oak imported from the Royal Windsor Forest.

Porte St-Louis

Lively rue St-Louis, with its snug little restaurants and pensions, slopes up from the end of rue des Jardins to the **Porte St-Louis** ⑮, rebuilt in a grand neo-Gothic style (complete with turret and crenellated gun-ports) to replace the 17th-

Map on page 200

Canadian staple – authentic maple syrup can be bought at the farmer's market.

LEFT: rue Sous-le-Fort with the funicular in the background.
BELOW: shopping in the rain.

Try to catch the changing of the guard at La Citadelle on summer mornings.

century original. In the old Poudrière (Powder Building) beside the gate, an interpretive centre has been set up, providing information on the history of the **city walls**. The walls have been restored and are a protected historic site, but visitors can walk along the top of them (no charge) in a complete 4.6-km (2¾-mile) circuit around the Old City.

A military role

Back in front of the Porte St-Louis is the lane that leads to the impressive military installation, **La Citadelle** ⑯ (tours Apr–Oct daily; Changing of the Guard mid-June–Labour Day daily 10am; Beating of the Retreat July–Aug Fri–Sat 6pm; entrance charge; tel: 418-694 2815; www.lacitadelle.qc.ca), the star-shaped fortress on the summit of Cap Diamant, 100 metres (330 ft) above the St Lawrence River.

With its Changing of the Guard ceremony and Beating of the Retreat, the Citadel appeals to childhood notions of soldierly glory and adventure, but, however colourful, the Citadel continues to play a military role. It is the headquarters of Canada's Royal 22e Régiment, known as the "Vandoos" (a corruption of *vingt-deux*), and as such, security is an issue – visitors must stay with the guided tour and not wander off on their own.

There is a museum outlining the history of the regiment, as well as a more general military museum. Built by the British in the early 1800s according to plans approved by the Duke of Wellington, with double granite walls and a magnificent position above a sheer cliff, the Citadel was considered one of the most impregnable strongholds in the British Empire.

Outside the city walls

Beyond the confines of the walls, the city becomes suddenly roomy, opening out onto the **Grande-Allée** and the lawns of the **Hôtel du Parlement** ⑰, the seat of the National Assembly, Québec's provincial government. Though not old by the city's standards (building began in 1881), the elaborate French Renaissance design by Eugène-E. Taché does seem to embody Québec City's distant roots in the court of Louis XIII. Its symbols, however, are purely Québécois.

The important figures of the city's history are all there, each trying to outdo the others' elegant poses in his alcove on the facade – Frontenac, Wolfe, Montcalm, Lévis, Talon… Below, sculptor Louis-Philippe Hébert's bronze works include dignified First Nations groups, the "noble savages" of the white man's imagination.

Outside, on the terraces of the Georgian houses that border the Grande-Allée, west from the National Assembly, visitors and civil servants alike enjoy the cuisine, wines and live entertainment in some of the city's most popular restaurants.

BELOW:
an artist at work.

Map on page 200

Love and war

A block south, there is peace. **Parc des Champs-de-Bataille ⓲**, or the Plains of Abraham, runs parallel to the Grande-Allée, with spectacular views across the St Lawrence. Its rolling lawns and broad shade trees have known more romance than fighting, more wine-and-cheese picnics than violent deaths but, however incongruously, it commemorates a vicious 15-minute battle in 1759 in which Louis-Joseph, Marquis de Montcalm, lost half of North America to the British *(see page 202)*.

It wasn't quite that simple, but the fact remains that the First Nations fighting style of the *canadiens* had won them successes against the British until the Marquis de Montcalm, a traditionalist and a defeatist, became head of the land troops.

Montcalm would not emerge to fight a pitched battle and, in a last-ditch, desperate attempt to capture the city, Wolfe, the British general, took 4,400 men up the cliff in silence by cover of night to the heights, where there was no hope of turning back. Montcalm had been expecting Wolfe at Beauport, to the north, and he rushed back to fight on the Plains. Throwing away every advantage – time, the possession of the city stronghold, and the sniping skills of his men – Montcalm fought the kind of European-style set battle for which his troops had been trained. Wolfe was killed, Montcalm mortally wounded and the French surrendered the city.

An interesting interpretive centre documenting the dramatic military history of the park can be found on the first (ground) floor of the Pavillon Baillairgé, part of the **Musée National des Beaux-Arts du Québec ⓳** (tel: 418-648 4071/5641; www.mnba.qc.ca). The imposing neoclassical beaux-arts building is also home to some of the best Québec art in the province, with works by such masters as Alfred Pellan, Marc-Aurèle Fortin and Jean-Paul Riopelle.

East of the city

After seeing the sights held inside the city you might want to relieve you sightseeing fatigue by explor-

Street lamps light the way and decorate the colonial architecture in the old city.

BELOW:
a calèche ride past the Hôtel du Parlement.

Map on page 200

ing further afield. Pack your swimsuit and head east for 10 km (6 miles) along route 138, to **Parc de la Chûte-Montmorency** (daily; chairlift charge; tel: 418-663 3330; www.sepaq.com). These falls, at 83 metres (272 ft), are considerably higher than Niagara Falls, though less dramatic because they are so much narrower. Here, however, instead of looking at the falls from the top down, you approach the base, which means that the closer you get, the wetter you get from the spray, so come prepared.

The best view of the falls at Parc de la Chute-Montmorency is from the purpose-built viewing platform.

The province has thoughtfully built a large granite platform at the base of the falls so that visitors can actually stand inside the chilly cloud of spray. In winter, the spray forms a solid block, which grows up from the bottom into a "sugarloaf" of ice and snow, providing a splendid slope for tobogganing.

South of the falls, the bridge to the **Ile d'Orléans** turns off the autoroute. In 1970, the provincial government declared the island an historic district to protect one of Québec's most picturesque and historic areas. The exceptionally fertile soil brought early prosperity to the island. In the 1600s there were as many inhabitants here as in Montréal or Québec City, and farming is still the vocation of most families, many working land that has been passed down since Québec's earliest days.

In summer few visitors can resist indulging themselves at the roadside stands offering juicy, fat strawberries swimming in lakes of thick, fresh cream topped with Canadian maple sugar.

Back on the north shore of the St Lawrence is the town of **Ste-Anne-de-Beaupré**, the site of the 1922 **Basilica of Ste-Anne-de-Beaupré** (tel: 418-827 3781; www.ssadb.qc.ca), where a large annual pilgrimage takes place in late July. The fountain of Ste-Anne, in front of the church, is said to have healing powers. The town has some tacky tourist attractions showcasing religious objects, but the imposing cathedral, with its stained glass windows and gardens scattered with holy statues, is worth a visit. ❑

BELOW: Basilica of Ste-Anne-de-Beaupré.

RESTAURANTS & BARS

Restaurants

Aux Anciens Canadiens
34 rue St-Louis. Tel: 418-692 1627. L & D daily.
$$$–$$$$
Restaurant with waitstaff in period costume, serves the rib-sticking fare that fuelled early settlers. Its *habitant* food includes pea soup and pork and beans, but it also has more refined Québec dishes, such as Lake Brome duckling flavoured with maple syrup.

Café Buade
31 rue de Buade. Tel: 418-692 3909. L & D daily.
$$–$$$
In business for almost a century, this 250-seat restaurant has long been a favourite with locals and visitors alike for its grills, pasta, pizza and smoked meat. The house speciality is prime rib au jus.

Le Café du Monde
84 Rue Dalhousie. Tel: 418-692 4455. L & D daily; Br Sun. **$$–$$$**
Popular for business lunches, and if you've never tried black pudding with apples, onions and calvados, or classic beef tartare (with fries), this is the place.

Casse-Crêpe Breton
1136 rue St-Jean. Tel: 418-692 0438. L & D daily. **$**
In a city full of crêpe places, this is the best – and right on one of Québec City's main people-watching streets. Choose your filling from over 20 on the menu; save room for a crêpe.

Chez Victor
145 rue St-Jean. Tel: 418-529 7702. L & D daily. **$**
Stone and brick walls, and hearty burgers topped with Swiss, blue or goat's cheese make this fast-food spot popular with the local arty crowd.

Le Cochon Dinge
46 boulevard Champlain. Tel: 418-692 2013. L & D daily. **$–$$**
One of three "crazy pigs" in town. Inexpensive family fare – burgers, fish, pasta and desserts.

Le Commensal
860 rue St-Jean. Tel: 418-647 3733. L & D daily. **$**
Cheap 'n' cheery vegetarian restaurant with a good buffet, juices and desserts.

L'Échaudé
73 rue du Sault-au-Matelot. Tel: 418-692 1299. Open: L & D daily. **$$**
A typical French gourmet restaurant with moderately priced but good food in a stylish art deco room. Extensive wine list.

L'Entrecôte Saint-Jean
1080 rue St-Jean. Tel: 418-694 0234. L & D daily.
$$–$$$
Locals enjoy this steak-house, which specializes in steak frites. End the meal with delicious chocolate profiteroles.

L'Initiale
54 rue St-Pierre. Tel: 418-694 1818. L & D daily.
$$$–$$$$
Regional ingredients in a swirl of elegant, colourful arrangements that look too good to eat. try warm foie gras of duck and roast suckling pig served with rhubarb and puréed beets.

Laurie Raphaël
117 rue Dalhousie. Tel: 418-692 4555. L & D Tues–Sat.
$$$–$$$$
Stylish restaurant, among the first in Québec City to showcase Canadian nouvelle cuisine.

Mistral gagnant
160 rue St-Paul. Tel: 418-692 4260. L & D daily.
$$–$$$
A neighbourhood bistro near the Vieux Port. A jolly eatery serving down-to-earth fare from the South of France. Cod fillet with black olives, mustard flavoured rabbit and sautéed veal in curry sauce.

Panache
10 rue St-Antoine. Tel: 418-692 1022. L & D daily.
$$$–$$$$
One of the best dining rooms in Canada, it lives up to its name. The restaurant is part of l'Auberge St-Antoine, a member of the prestigious Paris-based Relais et Chateaux chain. Sophisticated regional cuisine, such as sweetbreads from the Mauricie region, Mingan Island scallops, and Cap-St-Ignace guinea hen might be on the menu. Or try the seven-course "signature menu".

L'Utopie
226 1/2 rue St-Joseph Est. Tel: 418-523 7878. Open: L & D daily. **$$–$$$**
One of the trendiest eateries in lively, up-and-coming St-Roch, it has an ambitious menu with food pairings as quirky as the décor.

Bars and Cafés

Bar l'Emprise
Hotel Clarendon, 57 rue Ste-Anne. Tel: 418-692 2480.
A hang-out for jazz fans with live entertainment every night).

Bistro le Sainte-Victoire
380 boulevard Charest Est. Tel: 418-525 5656.
Live jazz (Fri–Sat) at this European-style bistro; it attracts a younger crowd.

Bar Chez son Père
24 rue St-Stanislaus. Tel: 418-692 5308.
A traditional *boite à chanson*, with guitar-playing folk singers who perform political or humorous songs.

PRICE CATEGORIES

Prices for three-course dinner per person with a half-bottle of house wine:
$ = under $25
$$ = $25–50
$$$ = $50–70
$$$$ = more than $70

TRANSPORT

GETTING THERE AND GETTING AROUND

GETTING THERE

By Air

Montréal is linked to Europe, the US and the rest of Canada via **Pierre Elliott Trudeau International Airport** (YUL), 22 km (14 miles) west of downtown. It is reached by autoroutes 20 and 40. Rush-hour traffic and construction can make the journey time up to an hour. The airport is being enlarged (due to complete in 2009), so allow plenty of time to get from one end of the terminal to the other.

Pierre Elliott Trudeau International Airport is served by most major North American airlines and/or their regional subsidiaries. International schedule and charter carriers, including Air France, British Airways, Lufthansa, Mexicana and Thomas Cook Airlines (UK) also fly into Montréal.

Québec City is served by **Jean-Lesage Airport** (YQB), which handles more than a dozen North American schedule airlines and a handful of charter companies that fly to Mexico and the Caribbean.

By Rail

VIA Rail (tel: 888-842 7245; www.viarail.ca) is Canada's trans-national train company, connecting Montréal and Québec City with the rest of the country. **AMTRAK** (tel: 800-872 7245; www.amtrak.com) links Montréal with New York City. Montréal's Central Station is at 876 rue de la Gauchetière Ouest. Visitors can catch the metro trains (underground) from here.

By Road

The majority of road signs in Québec are in French (bilingual on federally run bridges) and seat belts are mandatory. **Highway 401**, central Canada's principal east–west route, connecting Toronto, Canada's main gateway, to Montréal, becomes **Autoroute 20** at the Ontario/Québec border. The main thoroughfares through Montréal are **Autoroute 40** (which leads to Québec City), **Highway 15** (north to the Laurentians or south to New York, becoming I87 south of the US border), **Highway 10** (to the Eastern Townships and New England) and **Highway 20** (to Québec City via the south shore of the St Lawrence River).

Within Montréal's city limits, the quickest access routes (outside rush hours) are **Bonaventure** and **Metropolitan** (east–west) or **Décarie** and **boulevard Louis-Hippolyte**

AIRLINES

Air Canada/Air Canada Jazz, tel: 888-247 2262; www.aircanada.ca.

air transat, tel: 866-847 1919; www.airtransat.com. Charter company serving mainly Europe in summer and southern destinations in winter.

American Airlines/American Eagle, tel: 800-433 7300; www.aa.com.

CanJet Airlines, tel: 800-809 7777; www.canjet.com. Low-cost carrier serving New York and various destinations across the country and in Florida.

Delta Air Lines/Delta Connection, tel: 800-221 1212; www.delta.com.

First Air, tel: 800-267 1247; www.firstair.ca. Cargo and passenger carrier that flies to the Arctic.

WestJet, tel: 800-538 5696, www.westjet.com. Budget airline with routes around Canada and to southern sun destinations.

Zoom Airlines, tel: 866-359 9666; www.flyzoom.com. Regional and transatlantic destinations (UK and France).

Lafontaine (north–south).

Montréal's **Central Bus Station** (505 boulevard de Maisonneuve Est, tel: 514-843 4231) serves long-distance bus routes.

Québec City's **bus terminal** is at 320 rue Abraham-Martin (tel: 418-525 3000).

GETTING AROUND

On Arrival

Orientation

Montréal is an island in the **St Lawrence River**. The city's hilly streets and curving coastline mean the streets twist and turn, coming to a dead end in places where a building or an overpass has dissected the original thoroughfares, only to continue several blocks away. Many downtown streets operate as one-way systems.

Three east–west arteries will help you get oriented – **rue Ste-Catherine** (the main shopping area), **Maisonneuve** and **Sherbrooke**. Crossing these long streets, which stretch from one end of the downtown core to the other, in a vertical direction are **rue de la Montagne** at the western end and **boulevard St-Laurent** (the "Main" in local parlance) in the east. Cutting across the middle is **rue University**, which feeds off **autoroute Bonaventure** along the river and heads north to the main campus of McGill University.

Airport/City Transportation

Montréal: **L'Aérobus** runs a three-times-per-hour shuttle service (until 2am) from Pierre Elliott Trudeau International Airport to the Central Bus Station in Montréal. The journey takes 40 minutes (though it can be longer in rush hour) and the bus stops at three downtown hotels – Château Champlain, the Fairmont Queen Elizabeth and the Sheraton. One-way fares are $13 for adults, $9.25 for children aged 5–12 (under 4s travel free), and $11.50 for seniors. The round-trip fare for adults is $22.75. Tickets should be purchased before boarding at the airport ticket kiosk (tel: 514-842 2281).

Taxis, which leave from outside the domestic and international arrivals level, charge a flat rate of $35 to downtown. **Limousines** charge from $50 to $80, depending on which company you use.

Québec City: There is no shuttle bus service from Jean Lesage International Airport to downtown. **Taxis** take only 15 minutes, and the fare is $30. **Limousine companies** offering a service from the airport to downtown include Groupe Limousine A-1 (tel: 418-523 5059), Limousine Robert Boucher (tel: 418-654 8884) and Service de limousine Guy Samson (tel: 418-652 7316). Rates vary according to the company.

Public Transit

Metro, Buses and Commuter Trains

Montréal: Public transit in Montréal is efficient, clean and comfortable. The **Sociéte de Transport de Montréal (STM)** administers both the 168 bus routes and the metro, the city's underground trains. The **metro** is currently being upgraded. The system has four lines, confusingly numbered 1, 2, 4 and 5 (line 3 was not built due to lack of funds) – Angrignon to Honoré Beaugrand (east–west, green line 1), Henri-Bourassa to Côte-Vertu (U-shaped orange line 2, which loops north–south–north), the yellow Longueil-Berri UQAM line 4 (from the south shore of the St Lawrence to the Central Bus Station) and Snowdon to St-Michel (east–west, blue line 5, in the north of the city). Single fares are $2.50 for adults, or $11.50 for a six-ticket strip. Reasonably priced passes are a good bet if you're planning to travel around the city for a day or longer. A Tourist Card costs $9 for one day, or $17 for three days. The metro runs from 5am to just after midnight (1am on Saturday). For further information tel: 514-786 4636 (press 8 for English, then 7 for travel information) or visit www.stm.info.

As part of the public-transit upgrade, electronic fare boxes are being installed in **buses**. These accept both coins and prepaid tickets (available at metro stations). Just follow the instructions on the display screen. A beeping noise and coloured lights indicate that the machine has accepted payment.

Please note that bus drivers do not carry cash, nor can they give change. Tickets *must* be purchased in advance. Transfers can be used on either the buses or the metro.

Agence Métropolitan de Transport (AMT) operates Montréal's **commuter trains**. Five lines connect downtown with the outlying communities north and south of the St Lawrence River – Dorion-Rigaud, Deux Montagnes, Blainville, Mont-St-Hilaire and Delson-Candiac. Some stations

BELOW: on the metro in Montréal.

link with the metro network, others are connected via express bus. Fares vary according to the zone and passenger category (adult, student, senior or child). Tickets can be purchased at train stations, local drug stores or *depanneurs* (convenience stores). For information tel: 514-287 8726 (press 2 for English) or visit www.amt.qc.ca.

A novel way to get around and enjoy a history lesson at the same time, in both Old Montréal and Québec City, is on a **horse-drawn *calèche*** driven by a local guide. You can hail one in the street just like a taxi (if it isn't carrying passengers, of course), or find one at various horse and carriage "parking" spots around town. The fee is around $50 per hour.

Québec City: Réseau de Transport de la Capitale (RTC) operates the city **buses**, both downtown and to the outlying areas. Flat-rate fees vary according to the category of passenger: $2.25 for adults, $1.50 for children under 13, seniors over 65, and students. A one-day pass costs $5.80. You can buy a ticket from the driver, but you need the exact change. For information tel: 418-627 2511 or visit www.rtcquebec.ca.

A **funicular railway** connects the Lower and Upper Towns. The cost is about $1.50 (free for children under 5 years or of a certain height). The funicular runs from 7.30am–11.50pm.

A **ferry** runs back and forth from boulevard Champlain, in the Lower Town, to Levis, a 10-minute trip across the St Lawrence River. It crosses every half hour in each direction, with a more frequent service on weekend mornings and late afternoon. The first ferry leaves at 6.30am, the last at 2.20am. Tickets, which must be purchased at the ferry terminal prior to boarding, cost $2.60 one way for adults, $1.80 for children aged 5–11 and $2.35 for seniors. For information tel: 877-787 7483 or visit www.traversiers.gouv.qc.ca.

Taxis

Montréal: Taxis are often driven by newcomers to Canada, who may not always speak English or know where you want to go, so it's important to give detailed instructions to the driver. Rates are fixed at an initial $3.15, plus $1.75 per kilometre. Tipping (10–15 percent of the fare) is not expected, but is always appreciated. A ride across downtown costs about $8–15. Some drivers accept credit cards; if that is the case, there is usually a sign posted in the window of the car. Also posted is the name and licence number of the driver, with a photo, should passengers encounter any problems. Provincial legislation banning smoking in public places means that the interiors of most cabs are now clean and odour-free. Major cab companies include:

Coop de Taxi de Montréal, tel: 514-725 9885
Royal Taxi, tel: 514-274 3333
Taxi Diamond, tel: 514-273 6331
Taxi Veteran, tel: 514-273 6451

Québec City: It's unlikely you'll need a taxi in Québec City, unless you're travelling outside the downtown core. It's a small city and eminently walkable. Its narrow, winding streets are a nightmare for drivers though – local and otherwise – and parking is at a premium. Taxi drivers, not wishing to linger lest they cause a traffic jam, practically throw passengers out of the door when they get to their destination. The drivers are, however, chatty and friendly and immensely proud of their historic city. Taxi companies include:

Taxi Coop, tel: 418-525 5191
Taxi Québec, tel: 418-525 8123

Car Rental

Most of the major car rental companies have offices at the airports as well as in downtown locations. Rates vary by firm and by the size of car, but they are pretty competitive. Most companies also offer unlimited mileage, weekend rates and special deals on insurance. Petrol is expensive for North America – but still half the price it is in Europe – and has been running more than $1 per litre for some time. Sales tax of 6.5 percent provincial plus 7 percent federal is added to the final bill.

Avis, tel: 800-879 2847; www.avis.ca
Budget, tel: 514-938 1000; www.budget.com
Dollar, tel: 800-800 4000; www.dollarcanada.ca
Hertz, tel: 800-263 0600; www.hertz.ca
National, tel: 800-227 7368; www.nationalcar.ca

Private Transport

By Car

The Québecois navigate the roads with style and skill, and while they often drive a little too fast, they are in constant contact with other drivers, either by way of a hand signal, a glance in the mirror or a friendly nod, to check if it's alright to change lanes or make some other manoeuvre. Tailgating when they are impatient to pass is a bad habit that can be disconcerting, not to say downright dangerous. Jay-walkers are another hazard. When driving, especially in Montréal, it's essential to keep your wits about you.

Right turns on a red light are not allowed within Montréal (though they are in other cities in the province). A blinking green light or a lit green arrow mean that a left turn is allowed; a solid green light means that a left turn is only allowed if traffic is clear.

Take special care on both Montréal and Québec City's bridges, where construction work often leads to sudden lane closures, lane changes and lane mergers at breakneck speed.

Signage is also sometimes poor. It's a good idea to map out your route in advance, noting the exit numbers.

In case of an accident, contact the police immediately (dial 911 for emergency help in both cities). You will need to fill out an accident report and also contact your car rental agency if applicable. If you are a member of the AAA (in the US) or AA (in the UK), you may use the towing and repair services of the CAA (tel: 514-861 1313 in Montréal or 418-624 0708 in Québec City). There is also a CAA office in downtown Montréal at 1180 rue Drummond, which can supply maps and other services.

Parking is at a premium in both cities, and regulations are strictly enforced, though the enforcement usually means a ticket, rather than the vehicle being clamped or towed away. Note that all parking-related signage is in French – ask a shopkeeper for guidance if you are confused.

In Montréal, parking in residential neighbourhoods is usually restricted to residents who display stickers on their car windshield. The largest central parking facility is on Dorchester Square, beside the Infotouriste building. In Québec City, try one of the private parking lots along rue St-Jean or a hotel parking lot (some downtown hotels reimburse the cost of parking to their guests). In both cities, privately run parking lots can be pricey. Municipal parking lots, indicated by a large green "P", are less expensive, between $12 and $15 per day.

Montréal's rush hours (7–9am and 4–6pm) are worst on Friday evenings and Monday mornings.

By Bicycle

Montréal: The most enjoyable place to ride a bike is along the quiet side streets, within the city parks or along the designated trails. There's a network of cycle paths covering 225 km (140 miles), and you can buy maps from sports stores. Best routes include: the Lachine Canal *(see page 87)*, the banks of the St Lawrence Seaway, rues Christophe Colomb and Berri, rue Rachel, Parc Angrignon and Parc du Mont-Royal. Des Berges is a scenic 21-km (13-mile) cycle trail running along the river, between Verdun and the western end of the Lachine Canal. This route offers great views over Lac St-Louis and the Lachine Rapids.

Velo Québec (tel: 514-521 8356; www.qc.ca) is the umbrella organization for cycling in the province. The office at 1251 rue Rachel Est has brochures, guidebooks and tourist information. Velo Québec is also the driving force behind the **Route Verte** (www.routeverte.com), the 3,600-km (2,237-mile) network of cycle trails that stretch from one end of Québec to the other. Some city trails link to the "green route".

The following companies rent bicycles in Montréal:

Bicycletterie J.R. Cyclery, 151 rue Rachel Est, tel: 514-843 6989

Quadricycle International, boulevard St-Laurent, tel: 514-849 9953

Velo Adventure, Promenade du Vieux-Port de Montréal, tel: 514-847 0666

Québec City: There are few cycle paths in Québec City, but it's possible to get around the Upper or Lower Town efficiently by bicycle. You'll need a bike with at least 27 gears, though, and the hilly streets are daunting unless you're in very good shape. An easier, picturesque option is the recreational trail along boulevard Champlain, which skirts the St Lawrence River.

To rent a bicycle in Québec City contact:

Cyclo Services, 160 rue du Quai St-André (Marché Vieux Port), tel: 418-692 4052

On Foot

Montréal: In Montréal, the challenge is to get from one end of the city to the other, which is much easier by public transit than on foot. It is, however, enjoyable to wander around the parks or to explore individual neighbourhoods. Many of these have the air of a village, especially Old Montréal, which, though it has been gentrified, also has a sizeable resident population. The narrow streets run back from the Vieux Port, another pleasant place to stroll.

Walking around Montréal in winter isn't so pleasant, as city streets can be slippery, but you can take refuge in the **Ville Souterrain** (Underground City), a network of 32 km (20 miles) of corridors that meander beneath the city, linking major shopping malls and office complexes – and if you walk up an appetite, there are plenty of cafés and restaurants along the way.

For guided walking tours of Montréal contact **Guidatour** (tel: 514-844 4021; www.guidatour.qc.ca) or **Kaléidoscope** (tel: 514-990 1872; www.tourskaleidoscope.com).

Québec City: For a bird's-eye view, you can wander along much of the wall that encircles the city. Terrace Dufferin, which runs along the top of the promontory on which the city stands, gives more lofty views – over the St Lawrence River and, in the distance, the rolling farmland of Ile d'Orleans. There's always so much to see – stunning architecture, hidden alleyways and courtyards, squares filled with street musicians and marvellous opportunities to just stop and people-watch. Even in winter, when the narrow streets and old stone buildings turn into scenes from a Christmas card and footsteps crunch along snowy sidewalks, there's always a magical air about the old town. Several companies give guided tours themed around a particular activity associated with Québec City, including famous writers with **La Promenade des Ecrivains** (tel: 418-264 2772) or hauntings with **Les Visites Fantômes de Québec** (tel: 418-692 9770).

ACCOMMODATION

SOME THINGS TO CONSIDER BEFORE YOU BOOK THE ROOM

Before You Book

The majority of hotels are located downtown. All the major chains are represented in Montréal. Along with the modern hotels, there are a slew of boutique hotels that have been converted from offices, banks and warehouses. There are over a dozen of these attractive, unique hostelries, some are decorated in traditional style, with antique furniture and wood floors. Others have been turned into temples of haute design.

Room rates vary according to the season (most hotels offer packages) and whether or not there is a major event in town. Normally, however, rooms range from $70 per night at a budget hotel, through $140–60, up to hundreds (even thousands) of dollars per night for a posh penthouse suite. To those rates are added provincial and federal sales taxes (14.5 percent), as well as a 3 percent room tax, a fee that contributes to the cost of marketing Montréal outside the city. (Levying a room-tax fee is common practice in many North American cities.)

Booking a room online rather than going through a travel agent or reservations office, is generally the cheapest way of securing hotel accommodation, but in Montréal this is not always the case. If you're planning a trip on the spur of the moment, it might be worth calling the hotel directly to check if there are any last-minute "specials". If hotels have a lot of free rooms from Friday to Sunday, they are often willing to sell them at below official "rack" rates rather than leave them empty. Last-minute deals are also posted on the Tourism Montréal website: www.tourisme-montreal.org

Virtually all hotels (except budget establishments like the YMCA) have private bathrooms, radios and/or televisions in the rooms. Complimentary continental breakfast, exercise facilities (sometimes with a swimming pool) and internet access are common features of mid-range to luxury hotels, the majority of which, during the week, cater to business travellers. Some city hotels offer all-inclusive packages to leisure travellers at weekends which may include meals, tickets to exhibitions and art galleries or discounts at local retail stores.

For more information about the accommodation available in the city and the province, call the Montréal office of Tourisme Québec, tel: 514-873 2015 or if calling from outside Montréal, tel: 1-877 BONJOUR.

Bed and Breakfast

Bed and breakfasts, or B & Bs (sometimes called *gîtes* in French), although common in the country, were slow to catch on in the city. Rural areas are replete with centuries-old farmhouses, pioneer homes and Victorian mansions which lend themselves to being converted into bed and breakfasts. As Montréal's *quartiers* are being gentrified, B & Bs are springing up in the city too. Québec City, with its rich stock of heritage buildings, has lots of small, family-run guesthouses and hotels.
For more information, call the Québec City tourism office, tel: 418-641 6290.

Staying at a B & B isn't necessarily the cheapest option, but it does allow you to meet with the host and other guests in a homey, comfy environment and in the process learn more about the country than you would by staying in a large, impersonal hotel.

The cost of a double room (with breakfast) rarely costs less than $70 per night. Unfortunately, the simple B & Bs of a decade or so ago no longer satisfy today's North American consumers, who demand luxuries like private bathrooms and fancy furnishings. In this part of the world, B & Bs are more like inns (some hosts will even prepare dinner, if ordered in advance), albeit with fewer rooms. Three to four are typical. Five is the maximum allowed under city regulations.

For further information about Montréal B & Bs, visit www.bbcanada.com or contact one of the following associations:

Downtown B & B Network in Montréal, 3458 avenue Laval, tel: 1-800-267 5180/514-289 9749; www.bbmontreal.qc.ca

Montréal Reservation, 3711 rue Ste-Famille, tel: 1-800-917 0747; www.montrealreservation.com

Relais Montréal Hospitalité, 2977 avenue Laval, tel: 1-800-363 9635; www.martha-pearson.com

Hostels and University Residences

Youth hostels offer reasonably priced accommodation. A single room at the renovated Auberge YWCA starts at $45 per night for students, $50 for others. The Montréal International Youth Hostel charges about $30 for dormitory accommodation and $50–$70 for a single room.

Auberge YWCA Montréal, boulevard 1366 René-Lévesque Ouest, tel: 514-866 9942; www.ydesfemmesmtl.org.

Montréal International Youth Hostel, rue 1030 Mackay, tel: 1-866-843 3317/514-843 3317; www.hostelling.montreal.com

Staying at a university residence when the students have finished their school year can be a modestly priced option for summer accommodation (available mid-May to mid-August). Prices are not rock-bottom – they range from about $45–$85 per night – but because the residences are downtown (one of UQAM's residences is in the heart of the trendy Latin Quarter), they compare favourably with the cost of a hotel room in the same area. Some student accommodation also has cooking facilities.

Les Résidences Universitaire de l'UQAM, 303 boulevard René-Levesque, tel: 514-987 0344; www.residences-uqam.qc.ca

Aux Résidences de L'UQAM Ouest, rue St-Urbain, tel: 514-987 7747; www.residences-uqam.qc.ca

McGill University – New Residence Hall, 3625 avenue du Parc, tel: 514-398 3471; www.mcgill.ca/nrh

McGill University – Traditional Residences, 3935 rue University, tel: 514-398 5200; www.residences.mcgill.ca

Apartment Rentals

A handful of suite hotels and holiday apartments offer self-catering accommodation. Prices vary according to the season, the size and style of apartment. The weekly rental for a studio runs from about $400 per week in winter, to $700 during the high season, while a 2-bedroom flat ranges from about $800 per week, to over $1,000. Monthly rentals average $1,500 for a studio flat, $2,000 and up for a 2-bedroom flat or hotel suite.

Studios Montréal, 3711 rue Ste-Famille, tel: 1-800-917 0747/ 514-738 2393; www.studios.montreal.com
In the cultural centre of Montréal, near Place des Arts.

Appartements touristiques du centre-ville, 3463 rue Ste-Famille, tel: 1-877-845 0427/514-845 0431; www.touristicapartments.com
Fully furnished flats with kitchenettes in a high-rise building, near Place des Arts.

Clarion Hotels & Suites Downtown, 2100 boulevard de Maisonneuve Ouest, tel: 1-800-361 7191/514-931 8861; www.clarionmontreal.com
A chain hotel offering daily rates as well as long-term rentals.

Marriott Residence Inn, rue 2045 Peel, tel: 1-888-999 9494/514-982 6064; www.residenceinn-mtl.com
Four-star downtown hotel offering week-long and monthly rentals. Popular with business travellers.

L'Appartement Hôtel, 455 rue Sherbrooke Ouest, tel: 1-800-363 3010/514-284 3634; www.appartementhotel.com
A high-rise apartment block 15–20 minutes' walk north of Old Montréal; apartments with living rooms, work areas and fully equipped kitchens.

La Tour Belvédère, 2175 boulevard de Maisonneuve Ouest, tel: 1-888-922 9052/514-935 9052; www.tourbelvedere.com
A selection of studios and one- and two-bedroom suites rented by the week or the month. Facilities include high-speed internet access, a sun deck, an exercise room, saunas and a swimming pool.

BELOW: a luxurious room at Auberge St-Antoine, Québec City.

ACCOMMODATION LISTINGS

OLD MONTRÉAL

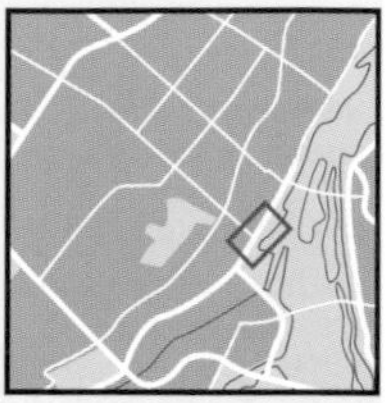

Luxury

Hotel Le St-James
355 rue St-Jacques
Tel: 1-866-841 3111/514-841 3111
www.hotellestjames.com
A 60-room hotel in a former 19th-century merchant bank. Restored in 2002 to its former glory and filled with 18th-century Russian armoires, dressers from Venice, hand-woven rugs, Ming vases and a palanquin that once belonged to a maharaja.

Expensive

Hôtel InterContinental Montréal
360 rue St-Antoine Ouest
Tel: 1-800-361 3600/ 514-987 9900
www.montreal.intercontinental.com
This mid-size, modern hotel has 357 rooms and suites. Across the street from the Palais des Congrès (convention centre), the hotel is also connected to the Montréal World Trade Centre, so during the week it caters to a mostly business clientele with leisure travellers at weekends.

Boutique Hotels

The following hotels in historic buildings in Old Montréal are characterised by exposed brick walls, beamed ceilings and high windows. All are close to: the Vieux Port, Notre-Dame Basilica, place Jacques-Cartier and the museum of archaeology.

Hotel XIXe Siècle
262 rue St-Jacques Ouest
Tel: 1-877-553 0019/ 514-985 0019
www.hotelxixsiecle.com
Spacious rooms in a converted bank building with grand Second Empire architecture.

Auberge Bonaparte
447 rue St-François-Xavier
Tel: 514-844 1448
www.bonaparte.com
There are vestiges of the past in this cosy, small hotel. There are 30 bedrooms and one suite, which has a secluded rooftop balcony with a view of Notre-Dame Basilica.

Hôtel Nelligan
106 rue St-Paul Ouest
Tel: 1-877-788 2040/ 514-788 2040
www.hotelnelligan.com
Gorgeous boutique hotel with 35 rooms and 28 suites. Meeting rooms, fitness centre and a rooftop terrace. Verses restaurant is known for its romantic ambience. Complimentary downtown shuttle service in the morning.

Le Place d'Armes
55 rue St-Jacques
Tel: 1-888-450 1887/ 514-842 1887
www.hotelplacedarmes.com
Urban chic in three 19th-century buildings. Large hotel with 83 rooms, 52 suites, meeting rooms, restaurant, rooftop terrace, fitness centre, parking and complimentary morning downtown shuttle service. Also has a spa with a Turkish-style *hammam* (steam bath).

Inexpensive

Auberge Casa de Matéo
444 rue St-François-Xavier
Tel: 514-286 9589
www.casadémateo.com
The small hotel has 22 rooms decorated with flashes of Mexican colour; with kitchenette. The restaurant has won awards for its authentic fare, but don't expect a quiet evening. *Mariachi* musicians stroll between the tables, serenading diners as they go.

DOWNTOWN

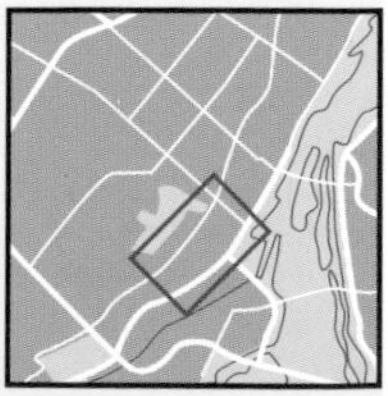

Luxury

Fairmont The Queen Elizabeth
900 boulevard René-Lévesque Ouest
Tel: 1-800-441 1414/ 514-861 3511
www.fairmont.com
A grand, 1950s railway hotel attached to the Central Station. Modernized with over 1,000 rooms and suites. The legendary Beaver Club is one of its three restaurants.

W Montréal
901 Square Victoria
Tel: 1-888-627 7081/ 514-395 3100
www.whotels.com
Converted bank building with swanky, leading-edge decor. The hotel has a spa, sunken cocktail bar and large windows overlooking the square. A 10-minute walk to the Vieux Port and the shops on rue Ste-Catherine.

Hôtel Le Germain
Rue 2050 Mansfield
Tel: 1-087 70333 2050/ 514 849 2050
www.hotelgermain.com
Part of a group of upscale Canadian hotels. This one has more than 100 bright, airy, loft-style rooms, with stylish,

minimalist decoration. Appeals to a youngish, hip clientele.

Expensive

Loews Hôtel Vogue
1425 rue de la Montagne
Tel: 514-285 555
www.loewshotels.com
On a lively street of pubs and restaurants, this 142-room hotel is attractive and intimate with comfy, lavishly decorated rooms.

Château Versailles
1659 rue Sherbrooke Ouest
Tel: 514-933 3611
www.versailleshotels.com
Close to posh galleries and boutiques, this 72-room hotel feels like an old European apartment block. Converted from two grand Edwardian residences. Across the street is sister hotel, Le Meridien Versailles.

Le Meridien Versailles
1808 rue Sherbrooke Ouest
Tel: 514-933 8111
www.versailleshotels.com
Hotel with 109 good-sized rooms and spacious suites in a modern tower block. Sister hotel to the Château Versailles.

The Ritz-Carlton
1228 rue Sherbrooke Ouest
Tel: 514-842 4212
www.ritzcarlton.com
Montréal's dowager duchess was built in 1912 and though it has been modernized over the years, its lavish décor still reflects a bygone era. Catering to an elite clientele; rooms are on the small side.

Inexpensive

Best Western Ville-Marie Hotel & Suites
3407 rue Peel
Tel: 514-288 4141
www.hotelvillemarie.com.
A cheap and cheery hotel downtown on the corner of rues Peel and Sherbrooke, a rare find in this part of town.

Hôtel du Fort
1390 rue du Fort
Tel: 514-938 833
www.hoteldufort.com
Cosy rooms, some with kitchenette. Near Concordia University and the Forum.

Hôtel Maritime Plaza
1155 rue Guy
Tel: 514-932 1411
www.hotelmaritime.com
This conventional,

ABOVE: the Grande Dame of Sherbrooke.

middle-of-the-road property has comfy traditionally decorated rooms, an indoor pool and sun deck.

Budget

Hôtel Le Saint-Malo
1455 rue du Fort
Tel: 514-931 7366
www.hotel-saint-malo.com
This European-style three-star property has snug, but brightly decorated rooms, with private bathrooms. Not far from the Canadian Centre for Architecture, and it's handy for the Ville-Marie highway which feeds into autoroutes that lead out of town.

Hôtel Le Saint-André
1285 rue Saint-André
Tel: 1-800-265 7071/
514-849 7070
One block from the bus station. Rates include continental breakfast.

Days Inn Montréal Downtown
215 boulevard René-Lévesque
Tel: 1-800 668 3872/
514-393 3388
www.daysinnmontreal.com
A modern glass tower, contrasting with the down-at-heel buildings of nearby Chinatown. Excellent value for money.

MONTRÉAL BRANCHÉ/AROUND THE QUARTIER LATIN

If you are on a limited budget, this district has good places to stay. Accommodation in this area is less expensive than downtown or in Old Montréal.

PRICE CATEGORIES

Price categories are for a double room without breakfast:
Luxury = more than $200
Expensive = $150–200
Inexpensive = $100–150
Budget = under $100

Inexpensive

Auberge Le Jardin d'Antoine
2024 rue St-Denis
Tel: 1-800 361 4506/
514-843 4506
www.hotel-jardin-antoine.qc.ca
A cute little hotel in the heart of the action. Substantial buffet breakfast included in the price of the room. The 25 rooms have Wi-Fi internet access.

Hôtel St-Denis
1254 rue St-Denis
Tel: 1-800 363 3364/
514-849 4526
www.hotel-st-denis.com
This modestly priced, three-star hotel just south of busy rue Ste-Catherine, offers the kind of in-room extras usually associated with more expensive

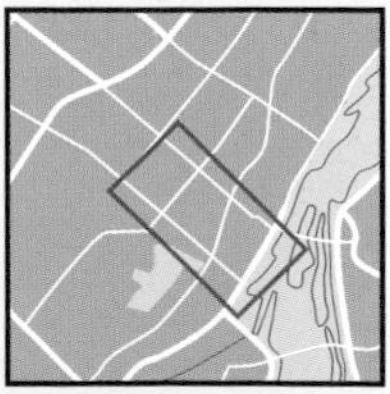

properties: coffee maker, ironing board, hairdryer and a free daily English or French newspaper.

Budget

Hôtel Manoir des Alpes
1245 rue St-André
Tel: 1-800-465 2929/
514-845 9803
www.hotelmanoirdesalpes.qc.ca
On the edge of the Quartier Latin (but it is quieter than noisy rue St-Denis), this homey little hostelry has 29 simply renovated rooms with bathroom. There is also an all-you-can-eat continental breakfast and free parking for guests.

Montréal Espace Confort
2050 rue St-Denis
Tel: 514-849 0505
www.montrealespaceconfort.com
This family-run hotel lives up to its name: "comfortable space". It is a charming place, which was once a private residence, within walking distance of the bus station, Theâtre St-Denis and Chinatown. Budget prices in winter but also inexpensive even in the height of summer.

Hotel Quartier-Latin Montréal
1763 rue St-Denis
Tel: 514-842 8444
www.hotel-quartierlatin.com
Basic, but clean and bright rooms, with air conditioning. Three minutes' walk from the Berri-UQAM metro stop.

Manoir St-Denis
2006 rue St-Denis
Tel: 1-888-567 7654/
514-843 3670
www.manoirstdenis.com
The hotel is situated within a row of stone town houses – typical architectural style of this *quartier*. The basic rooms are popular with students and artistic types. On the corner of Ontario Street, with ethnic eateries on the doorstep.

Castel St-Denis
Tel: 514-842 9719
www.castelsaintdenis.qc.ca
One step up from a hostel. Basic, clean rooms with private bathrooms, televisions, air conditioning and high-speed internet access.

THE PLATEAU

Expensive

Hôtel de l'Institut
3535 rue St-Denis
Tel: 1-800-361 5111/
514-282 5120
www.hotel.ithq.qc.ca
A 42-room hotel that is part of the government-run school for the hospitality industry. The building was renovated in 2005 when a restaurant was added. The service is excellent.

DoubleTree Plaza Hotel Downtown
505 rue Sherbrooke Est
Tel: 1-800-561 4644/
514-842 8581
www.plazamontreal.com
Large chain hotel with more than 300 functional rooms and suites with all the mod-cons – a sitting area, desk, two telephones, wireless internet access, coffee maker, hairdryer. There is also an indoor swimming pool. Located next to the Sherbrooke metro station, on the southern edge of the trendy Plateau area.

Inexpensive

Anne ma soeur Anne Hôtel-Studio
4119 rue St-Denis
Tel: 514-281 3187
www.annemasoeuranne.com
This renovated 19th-century heritage building is the perfect pied-à-terre for enjoying the buzz in the cafes, bars, bookstores and theatres on rue St-Denis. The 17 studio rooms have kitchenettes.

Auberge de La Fontaine
1301 rue St-Rachel Est
Tel: 1-800 597 0597/
514-597 0166
www.aubergedelafontaine.com
Don't be put off by the stern exterior of these Victorian greystones. The bright, modern rooms are decorated in all colours of the rainbow. Some have patios and balconies overlooking Parc la Fontaine.

Hôtel Armor Manoir Sherbrooke
157 rue Sherbrooke Est
Tel: 514-285 0140
www.armormanoir.com
Though it isn't quite a manor house, this century-old building has a turret with a pointed roof, so the rooms are an unusual shape. Rates include continental breakfast. A stone's throw from rue Prince Arthur, a pedestrian-only street with modestly priced *"Apportez votre vin"* (BYOB) eateries.

Hôtel Château de l'Argoat
524 rue Sherbrooke Est
Tel: 514-842 2046
www.hotel-chateau-argoat.qc.ca
This European-style hotel is where the Quartier Latin and the Plateau come together, the best of two neighbourhoods. Some rooms have whirlpool baths. Free parking.

Budget

Hôtel de Paris
901 rue Sherbrooke Est
Tel: 514-522 6861
www.hotel-montreal.com
Hotel in an old mansion with a turret – a common architectural feature on this section of rue Sherbrooke. Simple rooms and a licensed bistro. At the junction of the Plateau and the Quartier Latin, handy for restaurants and public transport.

Hôtel La Résidence du Voyageur
847 rue Sherbrooke Est
Tel: 514-527 9515
www.hotelresidencevoyager.com
One of the best deals in town, this budget hotel has many of the same facilities as pricier properties: private bathrooms, work space, cable TV. The front desk is open around the clock and staff speak a multitude of languages. A couple of minutes' walk from Place des Arts with its theatres and concert hall.

EXCURSIONS FROM MONTRÉAL

The hotels in the Laurentians and the Eastern Townships often include breakfast and dinner in their room rates. Some also require a minimum two-night stay. Hotel operators are, however, more flexible in the off season. The designations shown here are based on the overall price level of a property rather than just the room rate.

THE LAURENTIANS

Luxury

Hôtel l'Eau à la Bouche
3003 Boulevard, Ste-Adèle
Tel: 1-450 229 2991
www.leaualabouche.com.
The 25-room hotel, which added a spa in 2006, is in a lively ski resort and artists' colony. Better known for its restaurant and pioneering chef-owner Anne Desjardins.

Hôtel Quintessence
3004 chemin de la Chapelle
Mont-Tremblant
Tel: 819-425 3400
www.hotelquintessence.com
Boutique hotel in a stunning setting with 30-suites; an elegant blend of granite and mahogany. Lake and mountain views and luxurious marble bathrooms.

Expensive

Le Grand Lodge
2396 rue Labelle
Mont-Tremblant
Tel: 1-800-567 6763/
819-425 2734
www.legrandlodge.com
A five-minute drive from Mont-Trembant resort, this 112-unit hotel, which looks like a giant log cabin, is quieter than the mountain complex but it's no less scenic. The lodge overlooks Lac Ouimet. Family packages and a wide choice of accommodation – from studios to two-bedroom suites.

Inexpensive

Comfort Inn & Suites
860 rue Lalonde
Mont-Tremblant
Tel: 1-888-429 6000/
819-429 6000
www.comforttremblant.com
A chain hotel that is a good choice for families. Simple good-sized rooms and children under 18 stay free, if sharing their parents' room. Facilities include an indoor pool, internet access, DVD players and a children's play area.

Budget

Auberge de Jeunesse
2213 chemin du Village
Mont-Tremblant
tel: 1-866-425 6008/
819-425 6008
www.hostellingtremblant.com.
This youth hostel is in the village of Mont-Tremblant, not at the ski resort, but the slopes and hiking trails of the mountain are only minutes away. A choice of dormitories, family rooms (4–8 beds) and private rooms. The hostel has a fully equipped kitchen, a laundry, TV room, café and bar. There's a small charge for internet access: none if you have a Wi-Fi-enabled laptop. Access to Lake Moore, volleyball court and bike rentals on the premises.

Camping

Parc National du Mont-Tremblant
Lac Munroe entrance
chemin du Lac-Supérior
Tel: 819-688 2281
www.parcsquebec.com
Within the national park's 150,000 hectares (370,658 acres) lie 160 km (100 miles) of hiking trails, 400 lakes and six rivers. Visitors can camp at one of several serviced campsites or opt for more luxurious (relatively speaking) accommodation in a rustic, lake-side cabin, which has no electricity or running water.

THE EASTERN TOWNSHIPS

Luxury

Manoir Hovey
575 rue Hovey
North Hatley
Tel: 1-800-661 2431/
819-842 2421
www.manoirhovey.com
Stunning lakeside property modelled after George Washington's home in Mount Vernon. It retains the air of a private country house with 40 romantic and cosy rooms that vary in size and luxuriousness. Award-winning dining room and a terrific selection of fine wines.

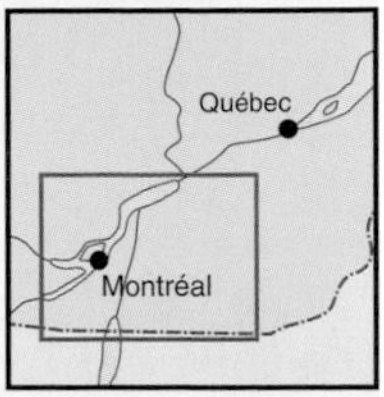

Auberge Ripplecove Inn & Spa
700 chemin Ripplecove
Ayer's Cliff
Tel: 1-800-668 4296/
819-838 4296
www.ripplecove.com
Situated at the opposite end of Lac Massawippi from North Hatley, this luxurious, five-star property is surrounded by 5 hectares (12 acres) of manicured gardens and pines. Comfortable spacious rooms. Tennis, swimming, sailing and gourmet dining.

Expensive

Auberge Georgeville
71 chemin Channel
route 247, Georgeville
Tel: 1-888 0843 8686/
819-843 8683
www.aubergegeorgeville.com
One of the oldest hotels in Canada (built in 1889), this hostelry is situated in the picture-perfect hamlet of Georgeville. The wrap-around veranda is an ideal spot to sip the glass of sherry included

PRICE CATEGORIES

Price categories are for a double room without breakfast:
Luxury = more than $200
Expensive = $150–200
Inexpensive = $100–150
Budget = under $100

ABOVE: relaxing in Tremblant Spa.

in the price of the room. Its pink and white exterior favours a giant wedding cake and indeed the inn is popular for celebrations.

Auberge L'Étoile-sur-le-lac
1200 rue Principale Ouest
Magog
Tel: 1-800-567 2727/
819-843 6521
www.etoile-sur-le-lac.com
Hotel and condominium complex within walking distance of one of the Townships' liveliest resort towns. A 10-minute drive from Mont-Orford park and ski station. The dining room, which has a patio in summer, overlooks Lac Memphrémagog. Swimming, sailing, inline skating.

Auberge Lakeview Inn
50 rue Victoria, Lac-Brome
(Knowlton)
Tel: 1-800 661 6183/
450-243 6183
www.aubergelakeviewinn.com
A romantic historic inn with comfy rooms, in a romantic historic village. Victorian decor, heated pool, bistro-pub. Near galleries and boutiques.

Inexpensive

Auberge Knowlton
286 chemin de Knowlton
Tel: 450-242 6886
www.aubergeknowlton.ca
A landmark since 1849 this former coaching inn in the centre of Knowlton (Lac-Brome) is a family-run hotel. Traditionally decorated with antiques and Québec armoires but the 12 modernized rooms have private bathrooms and internet access. The dining room specializes in dishes featuring locally-raised Lac Brome duck.

Auberge du Château
90 rue de Stanstead
Tel: 1-800-304 3433/
450-534 3433
www.chateaubromont.com
The plain-Jane budget property that belongs to the four-star Château Bromont complex. Next to Mont-Bromont, the closest Eastern Township mountain to Montréal. There is a golf course and Bromont has several restaurants, and it's an easy drive to the Granby Zoo from the village.

Budget

Motel Bon Soir
1587 rue Principale
Granby
Tel: 450-378 7947
www.motelbonsoir.com
Simple accommodation with all the basics: air conditioning, TV, pool, picnic area and barbecue facilities, kids' playground, go-kart circuit and mini-golf.

Camping

Camping au Diable Vert
169 chemin Staines
Glen Sutton
Tel: 450-538 5639
www.audiablevert.qc.ca
Thirty wooded sites amid the stunning scenery of the upper reaches of the Appalachian Mountains. There are also hiking trails at 300 metres (1,000 ft) above sea level. Reservations recommended.

QUÉBEC CITY

Québec City has a number of modern chain hotels, including Best Western, Travelodge, Holiday Inn, Marriott and Hilton, but more are situated outside the city walls, and catering primarily to business travellers and conventioneers. The branded properties are a good choice for families seeking diversions that are not centred around history, because they have facilities such as games rooms, gyms and swimming pools. For the majority of tourists who come here, however, it is Québec City's colourful past that is the main drawing card. The hotels listed here are in, or close to, the Upper and Lower Town.

Luxury

Fairmont Le Château Frontenac
1 rue des Carrières
Tel: 1-800 441 1414/
418-691 2162
www.fairmont.com
You can't miss this huge castle-like hotel with towers, turrets and copper roof. The Château Frontenac has been a Québec City landmark for over a century and it dominates the Upper Town, looming over the St Lawrence River.

Expensive

Auberge Saint-Antoine
8 rue Sainte-Antoine
Tel: 1-888-692 2211/
418-692 2211
www.saint-antoine.com
Rooms and suites are stylish and luxurious in this award-winning 94-room hotel. When the complex of 18th- and 19th-century commercial buildings was being converted thousands of artefacts from Québec City's military and mercantile past were discovered. Some 700 pieces have been incorporated into the design of the property. Shards of pottery, clay pipes and wrought- iron keys are displayed in glass wall cases.

Le Hôtel Dominion 1912
126 rue Saint-Pierre
Tel: 1-888-833 5253/
418-692 2224
www.hoteldominion.com
An elegant boutique hotel in the old town, which has been named one of the top hostelries in Canada. Luxury rooms are stylishly decorated and attract an upscale trendy clientele. One of four properties owned by Groupe Germain, with sister hotels in Montréal and Toronto.

L'Hôtel du Capitole
972 rue Saint-Jean
Tel: 418-694 4040
www.lecapitole.com
A theatre/hotel complex with 40 rooms. The "capitole" was a 1903 music hall which hosted showbiz greats like Maurice Chevalier, Edith Piaf and Yves Montand. Replete with crimson carpets, crystal chandeliers and gilded balconies, the theatre was restored in the early 1990s. Also includes Ristorante Il Teatro, with Italian-style haute cuisine.

Auberge Saint-Pierre
79 rue Saint-Pierre
Tel: 418-694 7981
www.auberge.qc.ca
The inn was built in 1921 as the head office for the Québec Fire Assurance company, whose name is carved into the stone exterior. The exterior might be old but the rooms are bright and modern. Bistro/bar and a reading room with a fireplace.

Inexpensive

Hôtel Le Priori
15 rue Sault-au-Matelot
Tel: 1-800 451 3992/
418-692 3992
www.hotellepriori.com
This 26-room boutique hotel isn't as fancy as some of the others in the old city but the rooms are stylish and it's handy for the Vieux Port and the Musée de la Civilisation. It's also easy to park in this area.

Hôtel Le Saint-Paul
229 1–2 rue Saint-Paul
Tel: 418-694 4414
www.lesaintpaul.qc.ca
A couple of blocks from the tourist bustle, this jolly yellow hostelry has elegant rooms and a silver roof with capped dormer windows. It's on a street that has become a mecca for antiques hunters.

Hôtel Belley
249 rue Saint-Paul
1-888-692 1694/
418-692 1694
www.oricom.ca/belley
Eight simple, homey rooms on a road good for antiquing. If antiques aren't your thing, wander across the road to Marché du Vieux-Port, a farmers' market selling regional produce, or stroll along rue Saint-Paul into St-Roch, an up-and-coming *quartier* with designer boutiques and trendy restaurants.

Hôtel Manoir des Remparts
3 1/2 rue des Remparts
Tel: 418-692 2056
www.manoirdesremparts.com
Across the street from the city ramparts; 34 comfy rooms, some with views over the old city. There are also eight budget-priced rooms with shared bathrooms. A good bet if you want to be in the heart of the action.

Hôtel Terrasse-Dufferin
6 place de la Terrasse-Dufferin
Tel: 418-694 9472
www.terrasse-dufferin.com
Historic exterior. Modern interior. The 22-unit 19th-century hotel and condominium complex once served as the posh town house of a master brewer. The cheapest rooms are at the back, which doesn't have much of a view, but the hotel is right on Terrasse Dufferin, which overlooks the St Lawrence River.

Hôtel Jardin Sainte-Anne
109 rue Sainte-Anne
Tel: 418-694 172
www.jardinsteanne.com
Early 19th century building with fireplaces and exposed brick walls. Breakfast is served in a charming walled garden hidden from the street. Rue Sainte-Anne is lined with restaurants, hotels and it's busy with traffic and sightseers, so it can get noisy.

Budget

Hayden's Wexford House
rue 450 Champlain
Tel: 418-524 0524
www.haydenwexfordhouse.com
A bed and breakfast in Cap Blanc on a quiet street at the foot of the Plains of Abraham. Shared bathrooms, though some also have bathrooms en-suite.

Auberge de la Paix
31 rue Couillard
Tel: 418-694 0735
www.aubergedelapaix.com
Constructed in 1850, this hostelry houses up to 60 guests – from couples to eight sharing – in 12 bright, attractive rooms. Fully equipped kitchen and communal lounge.

Auberge international de Québec
19 rue Sainte-Ursule
Tel: 418-694 0755
www.aubergeinternationalede
quebec.com
Within the city walls and fancy as far as hostels go. It's heaving with young people in the height of summer and there is a wide choice of options – dormitories with shared bathrooms and no meals, to single rooms with private bathrooms and breakfast. Private rooms have bunks with a double bed on the bottom and a single bed on top – ideal for couples travelling with a child.

PRICE CATEGORIES

Price categories are for a double room without breakfast:
Luxury = more than $200
Expensive = $150–200
Inexpensive = $100–150
Budget = under $100

ACTIVITIES

THE ARTS, NIGHTLIFE, EVENTS, CHILDREN'S ACTIVITIES, SHOPPING AND SPORTS

THE ARTS

Montréal has a vibrant arts scene born of its French/British heritage and of the newcomers who add their unique talents to the rich cultural mix. Art galleries, book shops and entertainment venues abound. Montréal is also Canada's self-proclaimed festival "capital", hosting events to celebrate every season.

Theatre

Montréal has over 50 theatres and theatre companies – from small fringe groups to major stages which mount ambitious, expensive productions with well known actors and musicians. Most performances are in French but there are two leading English-language theatres as well: **Centaur Theatre** (453 rue St-François Xavier; tel: 514-288 3161; www.centaurtheatre. com) and the **Saidye Bronfman Centre for the Arts** (5170 chemin de la Côte Ste-Catherine; tel: 514-739 2301; www.saidyebronfman.org). The latter stages productions in Yiddish as well as in English.

The main French theatres are: **Théâtre Saint-Denis** (1594 rue St-Denis, tel: 514-849 4211 or 514-790 1111; www.theatrestdenis.com); **Théâtre du Nouveau Monde** (84 rue Ste-Catherine Ouest; tel: 514-866 8668); **Théâtre du Rideau Vert**, (4664 rue St-Denis, Montréal; tel: 514-844 1793; www.rideauvert.qc.ca); **Théâtre de Quat'Sous** (100 avenue des Pins Est; tel: 514-845 7277); **Theatre Usine C**, which stages edgy, avant-garde productions (318 Ste. Catherine Ouest; tel: 514-861-5851) and **TOHU Cité des Arts du Cirque**, 2345 Jarry Est; tel: 514-376 8648. The name TOHU – derived from a French word "tohu-bohu", meaning the chaos and energy that precedes renewal and transformation – describes it well. As well as putting on shows and organizing arts lectures in a huge theatre-in-the-round modelled on a a circus big top, TOHU is home to the National Circus School and the headquarters of the famous Cirque du Soleil.

Dance

Les Grands Ballets Canadiens (tel: 514-842 2112; www.grands ballets.qc.ca), is Montréal's venerable ballet company Their repertoire includes classical and modern pieces and work by up-and-coming Canadian composers and choreographers.

Ballets Classiques de Montréal (372 Ste. Catherine Ouest; tel: 514-866 1771), as its name suggests, focuses on classical works. At the other end of the dance spectrum are the ultra-hip **Les Ballets Jazz de Montréal** (3450 St. Urbain; tel: 514-982 9145; www.bjmdanse.ca) and the zany **La La La Human Steps**, a group whose contortions on stage defy gravity (5655 avenue du Parc; tel: 514-277 9090). Montréal-based **Margie Gillis** (5143 boulevard St-Laurent; tel: 514-845 3115), a renowned dancer and choreographer who runs a foundation that coaches young dance stars is an amazing performer. She has long hair, which she whips around her body in astonishingly fluid movements. An even more provocative (and controversial) dancer is **Marie Chouinard** (3981 boulevard St-Laurent; tel: 514-843 9036; www.mariechouinard.com), who founded her dance company in 1990. Their performances are too obscure for some.

Opera

Opera buffs look jealously over at Toronto's gleaming opera house which opened in 2006. Montréal too, has hankered after a decent hall for decades, but so far several projects have been cancelled because of a lack of funding. however, there are plans to build a new concert hall by 2011.

l'Opéra de Montréal (tel: 514-985 2258) stages between four and five shows a year at the (much criticised) Place des Arts, where the opera company is based. Founded in 1980 it is considered among the 15 best opera companies in North America.

Music

Montréal has a number of internationally renowned orchestras, among them the **McGill Chamber Orchestra**, which performs at the Pollack Hall and **St-Jean-Baptiste church** (5459 Earnscliffe; tel: 514-487 5190; www.ocm-mco.org). Founded in 1939 by the Brott family, leading lights in the Canadian classical-music world, the chamber ensemble is closely allied to McGill University, famed for its Faculty of Music.

I Musici de Montréal (934 rue Ste-Catherine Est, tel: 514-982 6038; www.imusici.com), under the fiery baton of long-time musical director Yuli Turovsky, is a fine chamber group. **Orchestre Métropolitain du Grand Montréal** performs tried-and-tested classical favourites by composers such as Bruckner, Mozart, Tchaikovsky and Strauss. The orchestra plays for most of the year (except summer) at **Théâtre Maisonneuve** (486 rue Ste-Catherine Ouest; tel: 514-598 0870) in Place des Arts.

The Orchestre Symphonique de Montréal (MSO; 260 boulevard de Maisonneuve Ouest; tel: 514-842 2112; www.osm.ca) is perhaps the best known of all the city's orchestras – not least because it tours the globe and has made numerous recordings. When back at home base, the MSO, with flamboyant Japanese-American conductor, Kent Nagano, performs at Place des Arts.

Concert Venues

In addition to **Place des Arts** (175 rue Ste-Catherine Ouest; tel: 514-285 4200), a complex of five halls and studios, the main performance spaces for concerts and special events are: **Pollack Hall** (555 Sherbrooke Ouest; tel: 514-389 4547); **Redpath Hall** at McGill University (3461 McTavish; tel: 514-355 1825); **Salle Pierre Mercure** (300 de Maisonneuve Est; tel: 514-987 6919; and **Tudor Hall** (1307 Ste-Catherine Ouest; tel: 514-982 6038), a 300-seat concert venue with excellent acoustics. Built in 1928, this intimate theatre is situated on the fifth floor of Ogilvy's department store.

The Bell Centre (formerly the Molson Centre; 1260 rue de la Gauchetière Ouest; tel: 514-989 2841; www.centrebell.ca), which seats over 14,000 people is for big box-office productions featuring megastars such as Barbra Streisand and Madonna. It is also the home base of the Montréal Canadiens hockey team. The other major forum, particularly for rock concerts, is the **Spectrum** (318 rue Ste-Catherine Ouest; tel: 514-861 5851; www.spectrumdemontreal.ca).

Cinema

Québec has a well-developed star system that promotes its own actors and celebrities and many feature films are shot on the streets of Montréal, contributing millions of dollars to city coffers. When Hollywood crews come north, the city often doubles as a North American or European destination. Montréal has a mix of architecture – from narrow old lanes lined with historic buildings in Old Montréal to concrete and glass highrises. Don't be surprised to see entire streets blocked off to accommodate a film crew. Sophia Loren, Kim Basinger, Julia Roberts, Arnold Schwarzenegger, Elizabeth Hurley, Tim Robbins and Susan Sarandon have all shot movies here.

Montréal also hosts a variety of film festivals including: **Journée du Cinéma** (67 rue Ste-Catherine Ouest; tel: 514-284 3322; www.vuesdeafrique.org), a celebration of African and Creole movies, and **Festival International des Films du Monde** (World Film Festival;

Getting Tickets

Expect to pay $40 and up for tickets to large-scale theatre, dance and music productions. However, many excellent smaller theatres have seats in the $10–20 range and some musical performances – in genres from classical to hip-hop to country to jazz – charge modest fees. During the big musical festivals held throughout the year (the International Jazz Festival is an example), many performances are free.

Most theatre and concert venues are closed on Monday. Shows start at 7.30pm or later. On weekends there are sometimes two performances – a matinée and one in the evening. There are usually discounts for seniors and students.

Ordering tickets by phone and credit card sometimes involves a small administration charge. When you pick up your ticket, you will be asked to show your credit card and you will probably need to provide additional identification.

Some theatres and concert halls allow online booking through this website, while others just give a list of upcoming events and ticket prices.

Canada's largest ticket agency, the **Admission Network** (Tel: 514-790 1245; www.admission.com), which is affiliated with TicketMaster, has a comprehensive website, where you can buy tickets to Montréal's festivals, sporting events, shows, plays and concerts. The network has over 100 ticket outlets around the province (30 in Montréal) where you can purchase tickets in person.

1432 de Bleury; tel: 514-848 3883; www.ffm-montreal.org), which showcases the work of actors, producers and directors from over 70 countries.

Most foreign movies are either dubbed into French or carry subtitles. The titles of the films are also translated into French, which can be confusing. To help the viewer determine whether or not a film has English dialogue, cinemas and newspaper entertainment pages will list either VO (original version), VA (English version) or VF (French version), after the title.

Films on a second run, and a selection of art films and foreign movies can be seen at **Cinéma du Parc** (3575 avenue du Parc, tel: 514-281 1900). **Ex-Centris** (3536 boulevard St-Laurent, tel: 514-847 3536; www.ex-centris.com) also specializes in alternative and independent films. For wide-screen epics try the **IMAX Theatre** (quai King-Edward, Vieux Port, tel: 514-496 4629; www.centredessciencesdemontreal.com).

The **National Film Board** (NFB) is headquartered at 1564 rue St-Denis in the Quartier Latin; tel: 514-496 6887; www.nfb.ca. Movie buffs can spend hours trolling through its huge collection – 6,000 films at last count. The archives of the **Cinémathèque Québecoise** (335 boulevard de Maisonneuve; tel: 514-281 1900; www.cinematheque.qc.ca), also in the Quartier Latin, includes some 35,000 film titles (foreign as well as North American), in addition to 15,000 hours of video and television.

NIGHTLIFE

Montrealers are party people. They like to eat and go out late so by 9pm the streets are hopping. You'll find non-stop action and entertainment in the bars, clubs, discos and pubs on rues Crescent, St-Denis, Ontario and around the Quartier Latin. Cocktail lounges are open until 2am, bars about an hour later. Large hotels have nightclubs with discos, comedy shows and other entertainment.

Pubs

Local beers are big in Montréal. Brands to try: Boréale, La Maudite, Blanche de Chablis. **Le Cheval Blanc** (rue Ontario Est, tel: 514-522 0211) is a brewpub and student hangout. **Brutopia** (1219 rue Crescent, tel: 514-393 9277) is another tavern where beer is made on the premises. It is known for its samplers of different styles of beer, one of the most popular being the hearty Scotch Ale. The city has several Irish- and British-style pubs which are surprisingly like the genuine article. **Hurley's Irish Pub** (1225 rue Crescent, tel: 514-861 4111) is the most realistic. With just the right degree of scruffiness, it's a venue for Celtic musicians and for toe-tapping music.

Bars

Old Montréal's boutique hotels all have cooler-than-cool bars but one of the coolest is the **GoGo Lounge** (3682 rue St-Laurent; tel: 514-286 0882). The furniture is retro, the decor psychedelic. Martini cocktails are the house speciality. There are more martini cocktails at **U Lounge** (191 rue St-Paul Ouest: tel: 514-849 8881), and with live entertainment too. **Bar à Vin** is a chic wine bar that is part of **Restaurant Les Remparts** (93 rue de la Commune Est; tel: 514-392 1649), one of Montréal's hottest restaurants. **Winnie's** (1355 rue Crescent, tel: 514-288 3814) has been around since the 1960s. Unlikely though it seems, this three-in-one venue, which comprises a pub, restaurant and swanky Karina's Club Lounge, was named after Sir Winston Churchill, who enjoyed a tipple.

Grumpy's Bar (1242 rue Bishop, tel: 514-866 9010) is far from miserable. Its slogan is "live bands, cold beer, good company". There is a variety of live entertainment; weekly line-ups include poetry readings, bluegrass jams and stand-up comedy. **Whisky Café** (5800 rue St-Laurent, tel: 514-278 2646) has soft lighting, leather couches and a choice of more than 150 single malts. Jump to reggae music at **Bar St Laurent 2** (5550 rue St-Laurent, tel: 514-273 2359). There is blues and hip-hop during the week too; weekends are reserved for the tropical beat of *rai* and salsa. **Les Deux Pierrots** (104 rue St-Paul Est, tel: 514-861 1270) is more than just a *"boite à chanson"*, it's a place where new Québec talent has been nurtured by the owners for over three decades and where patrons, carried away by the music, sing along with the artists onstage: lively and fun. For booze with a bird's-eye view, head for **Altitude 737** (1 Place Ville-Marie). The chic bar and nightclub (dress smartly) is at the top of an office and shopping complex. Sip your cocktail and enjoy a great view over the city and the St Lawrence River.

GAMBLING

Gambling (or gaming) is the *raison d'etre* of the **Casino de Montréal** (1 du Casino Avenue, Île Notre-Dame, tel: 1-800 665 2274/514-392 0909, www.casino-de-montreal.com) but it's also one of the best places to dine out and to watch bilingual Las Vegas-style shows. The landmark building on the St Lawrence River served as the French and Québec pavilions during Expo '67, and it has been enlarged several times since it opened in 1993. There are 120 gaming tables, 3,000 slot machines and a 500-seat performance hall (The Cabaret). The minimum gambling age at the government-run casino, is 18 years old.

Jazz Bars

Some bars have live jazz during the International Jazz Festival: **Les Bobards** (4328 rue St-Laurent, tel: 514-987 1174); **Cubano's Club** (316 rue Ste-Catherine Ouest, tel: 514-276 7464) and **Café Sarajevo** (2080 rue Clark, tel: 514-284 5629). **House of Jazz** (2060 rue Aylmer, tel: 514-842 8656) is the former Biddle's, named after the late Charlie Biddle, a famous bass player who brought some of the biggest names in local and international jazz to play at his restaurant. Biddle died in 2003 but the same crowd still hang out here. **Upstairs Jazz Bar and Grill** (1254 rue MacKay, tel: 450-931 6808) is actually downstairs, in a bistro. There is live jazz nightly at 8.30pm. Grumpy's *(see page 224)* has a jazz night on Wednesday, when musicians are jam, from 10pm onwards.

EVENTS

January

Le Fête des Enfants de Montréal (Children's festival), tel: 514-872 0060
Fête des Neiges, tel: 514-872 6120; www.fetesdesneiges.com

February

Les Rendez-vous du Cinéma Québécois, tel: 514-526 9635; www.rvcq.com
Montréal Highlights Festival, tel: 514-288 9955; www.montrealhighlights.com
Québec City
Carnaval de Québec M. Christie, tel: 418-626 3716; www.carnaval.qc.ca
La Ville de Québec, 400th anniversary celebrations throughout 2008, tel: 418-691 7337; www.quebec400.qc.ca

March

Montréal International Children's Film Festival, tel: 514-842 7750; www.fifem.com
St Patrick's Day Parade (rues Fort and Ste-Catherine); www.montrealirishparade.com

April

Blue Metropolis International Literary Festival, tel: 514-814 2538; www.bluemetropolis.org

May

La Biennale Montréal tel: 514-288 0811; www.ciac.ca (modern art exhibits), runs till July.
Montréal Chamber Music Festival, tel: 514-489 7444; www.festivalmontreal.org

June

Canada Grand Prix (Formula 1), tel: 514-350 0000; www.grandprix.ca
Fashion & Design Festival, tel: 514-876 1499; www.sensationmode.com
Fête Nationale, Québec's provincial holiday. Parade downtown and events throughout the province.
Festival International de Jazz de Montréal, tel: 1-888-515 0505/514-871 1881; www.montrealjazzfest.com
International des Feux Loto-Québec (Montréal International Fireworks Competition), tel: 1-800 361 4595/514-790 1245; www.internationaldesfeuxloto-quebec.com
Les Francofolies de Montréal, tel: 1-888-444 9114/514-876 8989; www.francofolies.com
Montréal Bike Fest, tel: 1-800-567 8356/514-521 8687; www.velo.qc.ca
St Ambroise Montréal Fringe Festival, tel: 514-849 3378

July

Canada Day (1 July)
Just for Laughs Festival, tel: 1-888-244 3155/514-845 2322; www.hahaha.com
Divers/Cité Festival (gay), tel: 514-285 4011; www.diverscite.org
Festival International Nuits d'Afrique, tel: 514-499 9239; www.festivalnuitsdafrique.com
Québec City
Festival d'été de Québec, tel: 1-888-992 5200/418-529 5200; www.infofestival.com

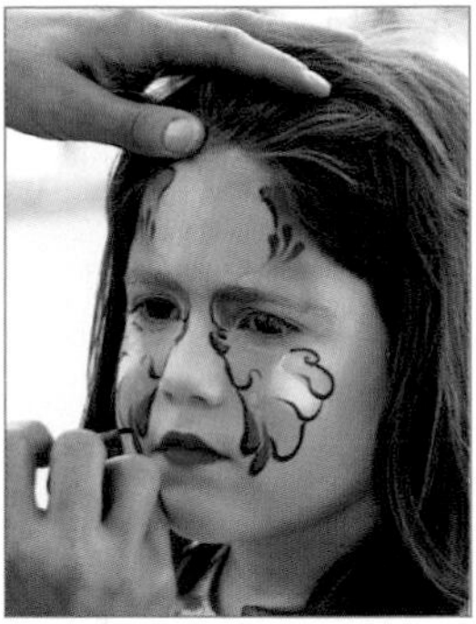

ABOVE: face painting for kids.

August

Montréal World Film Festival, tel: 514-848 3883; www.ffm-montreal.org
Rogers Cup (tennis), tel: 1-866-338 2685/514-273 1515; www.tenniscanada.com
Québec City
Fêtes de la Nouvelle-France (Medieval festival), tel: 1-866-391 3383/418-694 3311; www.nouvellefrance.qc.ca

September

Autumn festivals and country fairs in the Eastern Townships and the Laurentians.

October

Black & Blue Festival (gay), tel: 514-875 7026; www.bbcm.org
Festival du nouveau cinéma de

HOT AFRICAN NIGHTS

In July Montréal hosts North America's biggest festival of Afro-Caribbean and Latin American music, Nuits d'Afrique. For 12 nights 450 musicians and dancers perform in 40 venues across the city, including Metropolis, Tulipe and Kola Note. Featured artists at past festivals have included Youssou N'Dour, Alpha Blondy and Maria de Barros. An open-air event downtown at Place Emilie-Gamelin (Berri Square) has workshops and activities for children.

Montréal, tel: 514-282 0004; www.nouveaucinema.ca
Québec Intercultural Storytelling Festival, tel: 514-272 4494; www.festival-conte.qc.ca
Québec City
Festival de l'Oie des Neiges de Saint-Joachim (migration of the snow geese), tel: 418-827 4052; www.festivaldeloiedesneiges.com

November

Santa Claus Parade, tel: 514-398 9438; www.destinationcentreville.com

December

Christmas at the Montréal Botanical Garden, tel: 514-872 1400; www.2ville.montreal.qc.ca

Children's Activities

Montréal and its environs have a range of activities for children, from the Granby Zoo *(see Around Montréal page 179)* to theatre productions designed for small fry. Most of the major sightseeing spots, including some of the city parks, have special programmes for children. For older kids, the numerous historic sites of Québec City *(see Québec City page 199)* are of interest. Costumed animators at some of those sites help to make a visit more lively.

In Montréal, on Île Ste-Hélène, one of the most popular spots for families is **La Ronde** (22 chemin MacDonald, tel: 514-397 2000; www.laronde.com), an amusement park with Ferris wheels, boat rides and simulator rides. The park has the highest, fastest roller coaster in Canada. The ride reaches speeds of up to 110 kph (68 mph) as it plunges earthwards from 53 metres (175 ft) above ground level. Also on Île Ste-Hélène is the **Biosphère** (160 chemin Tour-de-l'Isle, tel: 514-283 5000; www.biosphere.ec.gc.ca), a geodesic dome that is an interpretation centre for the environment. Hands-on exhibits and workshops cover topics such as the effects of climate change.

The **Biodôme** (4777 avenue Pierre de Coubertin, tel: 514-868 3000; www.2ville.montreal.qc.ca/biodome) is a combination of a zoo and a botanical garden. Housed in the former Velodrome for the 1976 Olympic Games, it contains areas that mimic four ecosystems – a tropical jungle, a polar landscape, the boreal forest and the St Lawrence River, with native animal and plant life.

Musée d'Archéologie et d'Histoire de la Pointe-à-Callière (350 Place Royale, tel: 514-872 9150; www.pacmusee.qc.ca) was 10 years in the making, its contents and foundations having been formed from an underground crypt and artefacts discovered in archaeological digs. Across the street at the Vieux Port is the **Science Centre and IMAX TELUS** movie theatre (King Edward Pier, tel: 514-496 4724; www.MontréalScienceCentre.com) with high-tech games, multimedia quizzes and interactive areas for youngsters.

Shopping

Canadian art, music, literature, industrial design, jewellery and other craft items are held in high esteem around the world and they are easy to track down in Montréal, especially along rue Ste-Catherine, the main drag. The city also has plenty of shops with luxury items and electronics. Rue Notre-Dame, east of rue Atwater, has antique dealers specializing in Victorian furniture from Europe and around the province.

For fashion mavens, Montréal is the motherlode. The city is home to Canada's rag trade and you can find fur coats and designer clothing (or fakes) at reasonable prices. The city also has a slew of homegrown clothes designers who sell one-of-a-kind garments from their studios, workshops and boutiques in such areas as Old Montréal and around the Lachine Canal. For fancy couture clothes, head for the stores along rue Sherbrooke, near the Museum of Fine Arts. Then there is Montréal's underground pedestrian city – 30 km (18 miles) of walkways lined with every conceivable kind of store.

There are seasonal sales and from 26 December most shops have very low prices; sales may continue for a week or longer. Winter merchandise is generally reduced from January to April and summer goods may be reduced from June to early August, though given that the retail market in Montréal is highly competitive, you might find one-off sales at other times of year as well.

Spas

Chilling out at a day spa is the perfect antidote to shopping and sightseeing. Prices vary, but as a rough guide, a manicure runs between $15–35, a pedicure $30–50 and a massage from $80 for one hour to $115 for 90 minutes. It is customary to give a tip to the therapist of at least 10 percent of the cost of the treatment.
Spa Eastman Montréal (666 rue Sherbrooke Ouest, tel: 514-845 8455; www.spa-eastman.com). One of three branches of Canada's oldest spa. It has relaxing views over Mont-Royal.
Spa Diva (Les Cours Mont-Royal, 1455 rue Peel, tel: 514-985 9859; www.spadiva.ca).
Rainspa at Hôtel Place des Armes (55 rue St-Jacques Ouest, tel: 514-842 1887; www.hotelplacedarmes.com).
Gibson Salon Spa at Fairmont The Queen Elizabeth (900 boulevard René Levesque Ouest, tel: 514-861 3511; www.fairmont.com).
Spa St-James (2190 rue Crescent, tel: 514-844 4590; www.spastjames.com), on a street lined with trendy restaurants.

Sales Tax

Canadian price tags usually give the cost before taxes, so add 13.5 percent (6 percent federal sales tax, shown on a bill as GST, plus 7.5 percent provincial tax or TVQ) to the purchase price.

Shopping Centres

Complexe Les Ailes (677 rue Ste-Catherine Ouest, tel: 514-288 3759; www.complexelesailes.com) is a stunning building with a soaring glass atrium housing 60 stores, a high-end liquor store with a good selection of wines and Archaumbault, Québec's leading chain of book and music shops.

Montréal Eaton Centre (705 rue Ste-Catherine Ouest, tel: 514-288 3708; www.montrealeaton centre.com) has over 175 stores and restaurants, as well as indoor parking.

Le Faubourg Sainte-Catherine (1616 rue Ste-Catherine Ouest, tel: 514-939 3663; www.lefaubourg.com) is a favourite with foodies and students from nearby Concordia University. This is more marketplace than shopping mall, with more than 20 restaurants and food stalls selling ingredients from around the world.

Complexe Desjardins (150 rue Ste-Catherine Ouest, tel: 514-845 4636; www.complexedesjardins.com), one of Montréal's first modern shopping malls (opened in 1976) was renovated in 2001. It has a food court with 16 restaurants as well as dozens of boutiques. The mall's centrepiece, the Grande-Place, with its fancy fountain, is a venue for free events.

Place Montréal Trust (1500 avenue McGill College, tel: 514-843 8000; www.placemontreal.trust.com) has five levels of boutiques and services plus direct access to the metro. This is one of the downtown area's most popular indoor shopping malls. Shop here for children's clothing (La Cache, La Senza Girl, Souris Mini) and for lingerie (La Vie en Rose et Compagnie).

Place Ville Marie (corner of avenue McGill College and rue Cathcart, tel: 514-861 9393; www.placevillemarie.com) is in the heart of downtown. This cruciform office tower houses a range of boutiques on its bottom floors but be warned, because of its unusual shape, it's easy to get lost in the maze of underground corridors.

ABOVE: fashion in downtown Montréal.

Department Stores

The following establishments have their roots in Québec, though Holt Renfrew and La Baie (the Bay) have branches in other Canadian provinces.

La Maison Ogilvy (1307 rue Ste-Catherine Ouest, tel: 514-842 7711; www.ogilvycanada.com), which sells clothing by the likes of Jaeger and Aquascutum, began as James A. Ogilvy's linen shop in 1866. A lavish interior is graced by a huge chandelier which used to hang in Her Majesty's Theatre on rue Guy. Between noon and 1pm a bagpiper in full regalia strolls through the aisles, to the delight of shoppers.

Holt Renfrew (1300 rue Sherbrooke Ouest, tel: 514-842 5111; www.holtrenfrew.com) owes its origins to a hat shop in Québec City opened in 1837 by Irishman William Henderson. Today it's one of Canada's premier upscale retail stores, selling high-end designer clothing and cosmetics.

La Baie (585 rue Ste-Catherine Ouest, tel: 514-281 4422; www.hbc.com) started life as the Hudson's Bay Company, the fur trading firm. The Bay still sells its distinctive striped wool blanket, used for barter in days gone by, but mostly it stocks household items, clothing and electronic goods.

Arts and Crafts

Montréal's museum shops offer a good choice of hand-crafted items. A number of the museum shops sell exquisite reproductions of artefacts found at archaeological sites around the world. Museum shops also have a limited selection of modestly priced toys, cards, posters and Canadiana.

Old Montréal – for example St-Paul, Notre-Dame, St-Sulpice – are replete with independent galleries and boutiques selling art, ceramics and handmade furniture.

Galerie Le Chariot (446 Place Jacques Cartier, tel: 514-875 4994; www.galerielechariot.com) specializes in the genuine article. The gallery stocks the largest selection of Inuit and First Nations art in the country – from modestly-priced prints, to sculptures depicting the wildlife and lifestyles of Canada's Far North. Prices reach many thousands of dollars.

L'Art des artisans du Québec (tel: 514-288 5379), on the metro level of Complexe

CLOTHING CHART

Garment sizing varies widely and clothes may be tagged with North American or European sizes, or both. Some shops use approximations: XS (extra small), S (small), M (medium), L (large), XL (extra large) and XXL (extra-extra large). High-end shops tend to size more generously than inexpensive boutiques.

Women's Garments

NA	EU	UK
6	38/34N	8/30
8	40/36N	10/32
10	42/38N	12/34
12	44/40N	14/36
14	46/42N	16/38
16	48/44N	18/40

Men's Suits

NA	EU	UK
34	44	34
—	46	36
38	48	38
—	50	40
42	52	42
—	54	44
46	56	46

Men's Shirts (collars)

NA	EU	UK
14	36	14
14½	37	14½
15	38	15
15½	39	15½
16	40	16
16½	41	16½
17	42	17

Women's Shoes

NA	EU	UK
4½	36	3
5½	37	4
6½	38	5
7½	39	6
8½	40	7
9½	41	8
10½	42	9

Men's Shoes

NA	EU	UK
6½	—	6
7½	40	7
8½	41	8
9½	42	9
10½	43	10
11½	44	11
12½	45	12

Desjardins is a small shop selling beautiful *objets d'arts* made of wood, pewter and glass, as well as toys and clothing, created by local artisans.

Marché Bonsecours (350 rue St-Paul Est, tel: 514-872 7730; www.marchebonsecours.qc.ca), a one-time market, now houses 15 boutiques and studios showcasing Québec and First Nations artists, designers and artisans. The following is a sample:

Boutique des Métiers d'Art du Québec (tel: 514-878 2787) stocks the work of over 100 of the province's leading artisans, with decorative, functional and collectors' pieces.

Boutique GoGoGlass is the studio and sales outlet for glassblowers Annie Michaud (tel: 514-397 8882) and Karine Bouchard (tel: 514-878 9698). Watch them in action as they shape molten glass into gorgeous vases, paperweights and candlesticks.

Bastien Brasseur Jewellers (tel: 514-872 1811). Owners Jean Bastien and Camille Brasseur have a keen eye for modern design but their dazzling collection of gold, silver and diamond jewellery is assembled the old-fashioned way, by hand.

Bakeries, Patisseries and Chocolate Shops

You can't visit a francophone city and ignore the sweet goodies that it is known for. You'll find the same things here as in France or Belgium – crunchy baguettes, melt-in-the-mouth croissants, brioches and tangy fruit tarts – and some local favourites too, namely sugar pie made with maple syrup and bagels, whose crunchy crusts sprinkled with poppy seeds are much lighter than their New York counterparts.

Première Moisson has several branches around the city. Its name means "first harvest", which aptly describes the fresh-from-the-oven produce. The two branches closest to downtown are at Les Halles de la Gare in the Central Railway station (tel: 514-393 1247) and at 1490 rue Sherbrooke Ouest (tel: 514-931 6540).

Au Pain Doré (1415 rue Peel, tel: 514-842 3151) is a chain of Montréal *boulangeries* run by third generation bakers who pride themselves in their wide choice of speciality breads – over 40 varieties laced with everything from olives to cheese.

Fairmount Bagel (74 rue Fairmont Ouest, tel: 514-272 0667; www.fairmontbagel.com) has been churning out hand-rolled bagels made from organic whole-wheat flour since 1919. Be prepared to line up at breakfast time; this bakery has a steady stream of morning customers.

The same applies to the **St Viateur Bagel shop** (263 rue St Viateur Ouest, tel: 514-276 8044), whose bagels are every bit as good as Fairmount's.

Laura Secord (www.laurasecord. ca) is a Canada-wide chain of chocolate shops, named after a heroine of the War of 1812–14. The chocolate manufacturer, which makes over 400 products, has been around for almost a century. You'll find branches in Eaton Centre, Place Ville-Marie and Complexe Desjardins. The truffles are to die for and the ice cream is pretty good too.

Divine Chocolatier (2158 rue Crescent, tel: 514-282 0829; www.divinechocolatier.com). The name says it all. Absolutely divine chocolates, sold in attractive wooden presentation boxes adorned with satin ribbons. A branch of **Léonidas**, the renowned Belgian chocolatier with hundreds of outlets around the world, can be found at 605 de Maisonneuve Ouest, tel: 514-849 2620; www.leonidas.com.

Book and Magazines

The majority of bookstores in Montréal and Québec City sell French-language books and magazines. **Archambault**, with several branches in both cities, is the principal chain. **Librairie Paragraphe Bookstore** at 2220 avenue McGill College, tel: 514-845 5811; www.paragraphebooks.com is Archambault's English-language affiliate.

Other major English-language bookstores are **Chapters** and **Indigo**, (www.chapters.indigo.ca) national chains, with branches at 1172 Ste-Catherine Ouest, tel: 514-849 8825 (for Chapters) and 1500 avenue McGill College, tel: 514-281 5549 (Indigo). Both stores have seating areas and cafés that serve pastries and speciality brews.

Nicholas Hoare (1355 avenue Greene, tel: 514-933 4201), whose voice still rings with the distinctive cadences of his native Britain, runs elegant, distinctive bookstores in Ottawa, Montréal and Toronto. An ardent booklover, Hoare organizes readings, book signings and special events at his store in toney Westmount. He specializes in difficult-to-find titles, especially from the UK.

For international magazines and daily newspapers from Europe and further afield, head to **Maison De La Presse International** at 550 rue Ste-Catherine Est, tel: 514-842 3857 or 1166 Ste-Catherine Ouest, tel: 514-861 6767.

SPORTS

Spectator Sports

Hockey. Montréalers are mad about ice hockey *(see page 63)* and the city's premier National Hockey League team, the Montréal Canadiens, play at the Bell Centre from October to April. The team, commonly called "the habs", (from *habitants*) has won 24 Stanley Cups. For tickets call 514-790 1245; www.canadiens.com

Canadian football is similar to American football. The Montréal Alouettes of the Canadian Football League play regular outdoor games during the summer at McGill University's Molson Stadium, 475 avenue des Pins, tel: 514-871 2255.

Baseball. Montréal no longer has a baseball team, but you can watch games in Québec City. The Minor League baseball team, Les Capitales, plays at the municipal stadium, 100 rue du Cardinal Maurice-Roy, tel: 418-521 2255; www.capitalesdequebec.com.

Soccer, as football is called here, is hugely popular, thanks to programmes in Québec's schools which encourage youngsters to get involved in the game at an early age. The Montréal Impact play through the summer until late September (8770 boulevard Langelier, tel: 514-328 3668 www.impactmontreal.com).

Tennis. The Rogers Cup, an international championship that attracts some of the most famous players, is held at Jarry Park, tel: 514-790 1245. Alternating with Toronto, the women's competitions take place in even-number years and the men's in odd-number years.

Auto racing. The most exciting sporting event of the summer season is the Formula 1 Grand Prix du Canada, held in June at the Gilles Villeneuve Track on Île-Notre-Dame, tel: 514-350 0000; www.grandprix.ca.

Golf. There are more than 100 golf courses in the Greater Montréal area, including some of the best in Canada. The private Royal Montréal on Île Bizard, founded in 1873 on Mont-Royal, was the first golf club in North America. Municipal courses are open to the public, but they do require reservations; tee times are sometimes booked several days in advance.

Dorval Municipal Golf Club is only minutes away from Pierre Elliott Trudeau International Airport (formerly Dorval), 1455 avenue Cardinal, tel: 514-457 6020; www.golfmunidorval.com.

Also in this area is Golf Dorval, an 18-hole course at 2000 avenue Reverchon, tel: 514-631 4653; www.golfdorval.com.

Montréal Municipal Golf, Village Olympique, 4235 rue Viau, tel: 514-872 4653. A 9-hole, par-27 course.

Club de Golf de L'Île de Montréal, 3700 rue Damien Gauthier, tel: 514-448 6000; www.cgimgolf.com.

Golf des Îles on the islands of Boucherville (exit 1 off autoroute 20) is an 18-hole, par 70, 6,100-yard course with practice greens and a snack bar, tel: 514-670 4653; www.golfdesiles.com.

BELOW: Montréal has some of the best golf courses in Canada.

A–Z

AN ALPHABETICAL SUMMARY OF PRACTICAL INFORMATION

Admission

See Getting Tickets, page 223.

Budgeting for your Trip

An average tourist should be able to spend one day in Montréal very comfortably for about $200 (hotel, meals and public transport); a thrifty traveller $80–115 and for extravagant luxury, expect to spend at least $500–700.

Business Hours

Most offices open 8 or 9am, and close at 4.30 or 5pm Monday to Friday. Most banks open 10am–3pm Monday to Friday, with some keeping later hours on Thursday and Friday. Most downtown shops open 10am–9pm Monday to Saturday, and noon–5pm Sunday. Suburban stores have shorter opening hours, typically closing at 6pm. Most are closed on Sunday.

Climate

When to Visit

Weather ranges from extreme heat and humidity in summer to icy winters. The most best months for sightseeing are May and June and September and October. From early November to April, snow and extreme cold are possible (a certainty December to March). The Underground City provides shelter from the elements. Québec City, 250 km (150 miles), northeast of Montréal, is colder and drier.

What to Wear

In business, men wear a suit and tie; women a suit or conservative dress. Jeans and T-shirts are okay elsewhere. Dress up for theatre, concerts and formal restaurants.

In summer (June–Aug) you'll only need light clothing, with a jacket or sweater for cooler evenings (and air-conditioned buildings) and waterproofs in case of a shower. Add a layer or two for the colder seasons. In winter (November–April) you need a wind- and waterproof coat (over a warm fleece in severe weather), plus a scarf, hat and gloves. Carry these even on short car trips.

Crime and Safety

Montréal is a safe city at any time of day or night, but exercise

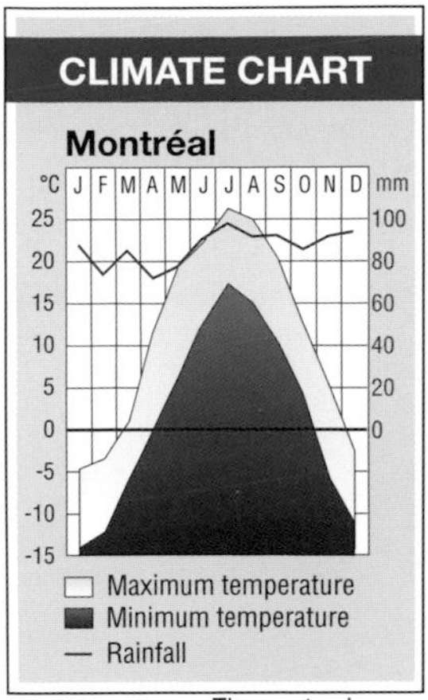

common sense. The metro is patrolled by security officers and police are in evidence on streets. Car theft is, however, a problem in deserted areas. Always lock your car if parked outside and never leave valuables inside.

Customs Regulations

Visitors are not permitted to bring in living vegetation and firearms. Full details are available from Revenue Canada, Customs and Excise (tel: 204-983 3500 or 506-636 5064; www.ccraadrc.gc.ca).

Disabled Travellers

Kéroul, (4545 avenue du Pierre de Coubertin, tel: 514-252 3104; www.keroul.qc.ca) is Québec's leading organization for disabled travellers. It also provides information about cultural events and accessibility of restaurants, museums and attractions, creating a signage system in conjunction with Québec's Ministry of Tourism. Most modern public buildings have ramps and accessible washrooms. In older buildings signage usually indicates if a disabled person needs assistance to enter. Some car parks have spaces for people with disabilities. Shopping centres and large stores have slow-moving automatic doors.

A Québec government programme (VATL) allows companions of disabled persons free entry to tourist and leisure sites. Look for the Tourist and Leisure Companion sticker. **Paratransit** (tel: 514-280 8211), a division of STM, Montréal's public transit system, can provide information on "low-floor" buses and accessibility at stations.

Important Numbers

Bell Relay Service: assistance in using TTY (teletypewriters), VCO (Voice Carry Over) and HCO (Hearing Carry Over) calls: 1-800-855 0511 (TTY only: 711)

Operator assistance for TTY users: 1-800-855 1155

Embassies & Consulates

Foreign Consulates

Australian High Commission: 50 O'Connor Street, Suite 710, Ottawa, tel: 613-236 0841

British Consulate-General: 1000 rue de la Gauchetière O, Suite 4200, tel: 514-866 6863

South African High Commission: 15 Sussex Drive, Ottawa, tel: 613-744 0330

US Consulate: 1155 rue St-Alexandre, tel: 514-398 9695

Canadian Embassies & Consulates Abroad

Australia: Commonwealth Avenue, Canberra ACT 2600, tel: 02-6270 4000 or 01-613 944 9136 (TTY)

New Zealand: Canadian High Commission, P.O. Box 8047, Level 11, 125 The Terrace, Wellington, tel: 64-4 473 9577

UK: Canadian High Commission, MacDonald House, 1 Grosvenor Square, London, tel: 020-7258 6600

US: Consulate General of Canada, 1251 Ave of the Americas, New York, tel: 212-596 1628.

Emergency Numbers

Police, fire, ambulance (emergencies only): 911

Police (non-emergency): 514-310 4141

Poison information: 1-800-463 5060

Info-Crime Québec: 1-800-711 1800

Entry Requirements

Visitors require a passport to enter Canada. Everyone travelling between Canada and the US, by air or rail, requires a passport; a birth certificate plus photo ID is not acceptable. Residents of other countries must carry a passport and in some cases a visa is also required. For more information, call 1-800-992 7037 (outside Canada); 1-888-242 2100 (within Canada), or visit www.cic.gc.ca.

Gay & Lesbian Travellers

Montréal has a large active gay, lesbian, bisexual, transgendered and transsexual community. The Village, just east of the Quartier Latin, is the main community hub, but gay and lesbian

BELOW: getting around town.

ETIQUETTE

Good manners are valued: hold doors open for people following you; don't jump the queue; let people get off public transport before you get on; offer your seat to older passengers or pregnant women; on escalators, stand on the right, walk past on the left; say "pardon" if you accidentally nudge someone or need to walk in front of them. If you are a smoker, ask the people around you if it's OK to light up. Smoking is banned in most public places.

travellers should feel at home in most places. The gay helpline is, tel: 514-866 0103.

The free monthly magazine *fugues* (www.fugues.com), for news, listings and articles about the gay community can be found at newsstands around downtown.

Health and Medical Care

Non-Canadians must pay for most medical services at the time of treatment, then claim through their medical insurance.

24-hour Hospital Emergency Rooms

Jewish General Hospital-Sir Mortimer B Davis: 3755 chemin de la Côte-Ste-Catherine.
Montréal General Hospital: 1650 avenue du Cédar (north on Guy).
Montréal Children's Hospital: 2300 Tupper (René Levesque and Atwater).
Royal Victoria Hospital: 687 avenue des Pins Ouest (south side of Mont-Royal).

Dental Emergencies

Dr Gerald Rudick & Associates: 3546 Côte des Neiges, tel: 514-342 4444.
Dr Philip Brownstein: 5845 Côte des Neiges, tel: 514-738 1842.
Centre Dentaire Danielle St-Hilaire: 1834 rue Ste-Catherine Ouest, tel: 514-933 3337.

24-hour Pharmacies

Pharmaprix has over 30 branches open 24 hours: tel: 514-933 9331, www.pharmaprix.ca
Jean Coutu has dozens of branches, some are open 24 hours, tel: 450-646 9760, www.jeancoutu.com

Internet

Most hotels offer internet access to guests. Public libraries and many cafés and bookshops offer inexpensive access to the web.

Language

Some 68 percent of Montréalers speak French at home; only 12.5 percent speak English at home, although English is widely spoken in business circles.

Left/Lost Luggage

Pierre Trudeau International has a left luggage/lost-and-found facility (tel: 514-636 0499). Luggage can be left at the cloakroom on the arrivals level. Individual airlines deal with lost luggage. The VIA Rail baggage office is behind the ticket counter in the Central Railway Station (tel: 514-871 7762). Montréal's Central Bus Station has coin-operated left-luggage lockers, as does Québec City's bus terminal. Montréal metro: for lost items, tel: 514-786 4636, press 8, then 4, then 2.

Maps

Most bookshops and hotels sell good local maps. *Plan du Métro* maps are free from the UQAM subway station. Other useful free maps are available from civic centres and tourist offices.

Media

Print

Canada's national newspapers are the *Globe and Mail* and the *National Post*. The city's principal English daily is the *Montréal Gazette* (harder to find in Québec City). Extensive nightlife listings are printed in the *Mirror* and *Hour* (English) and *Voir* (French and also available in Québec City).

Television

There are over 500 television stations in Montréal and Québec City. Montréal has 35 radio stations, 17 of which are broadcast in English. The government-supported Canadian Broadcasting Corporation (CBC) in English and Radio-Canada (French), broadcast nationwide on radio, television and the web.

Money

The currency is the Canadian dollar. Coins are the penny (1 cent), nickel (5 cents), dime (10 cents), quarter (25 cents), loonie (1 dollar) and toonie (2 dollars). Notes (bills) come in 5, 10, 20, 50 and 100-dollar denominations. Some shops will refuse to take a $50 or $100 bill.

There are banks and bureaux de change downtown. US dollars are accepted, but change will be given in Canadian dollars and the rate will not be as good as that given by a bank. Cash can be withdrawn in Canadian funds from cashpoints (ATMs) with shared banking systems. Traveller's cheques and major credit cards are widely accepted. **Note** that only Canadian debit cards are accepted.

Postal Services

Postes Canada/Canada Post locations are listed in the telephone directory; drugstores and malls have postal kiosks. Some *depanneurs* and paper shops sell stamps. Red mail boxes are located on street corners. The general information line is 1-800-607 6301.

Public Holidays

1 January: New Year's Day
24 June: Fête Nationale

1 July: Canada Day
11 November: Remembrance Day
24 December: (some places close at midday. Christmas Eve is a major holiday in Québec)
25 December: Christmas Day
26 December: Boxing Day

Movable Dates
Easter: Easter Sunday *(dimanche de Pâques)* may fall anywhere from 22 March to 25 April. The preceding Friday *(vendredi saint)* and following Monday *(lundi de Pâques)* are also holidays.
Victoria Day *(Fête de Dollard)*, Monday closest to 24 May
Civic holiday (Monday closest to 1 August)
Labour Day (First Monday in September)
Thanksgiving Day *(Action de grâces)*, second Monday in October.

Public Toilets

Montréal does not have a public washroom system. Try shopping malls, petrol stations, department stores and bus and rail stations.

Religious Services

Roman Catholicism, Judaism and Islam are the most commonly practised religions in Montréal.

Student Travellers

Students with a valid international student card are eligible for discounts on transit passes, theatre tickets and museum admission.

Taxes

Canada's 6-percent Goods and Services Tax (GST) and Québec's 7.5-percent Provincial Sales Tax (PST) apply to most purchases except groceries. However, visitors can apply for a rebate on GST paid on goods to be taken home and on up to 30 nights' accommodation. Keep receipts and get a form at a tourist office, shop or hotel. Call 1-800-668-4748 (in Canada) or 902-432 5608; www.pcra.gc.ca/visitors.

Telephones

Local calls from private phones are free. The area codes 514 or 450 must be dialled within Montréal. The 819 code applies to surrounding areas. The area code for Québec City is 418. Numbers starting 1-800, 1-866, 1-877 and 1-888 are toll-free. To call long distance within North America dial 1; for international calls dial 011 then the country code.
Directory assistance: 411
Operator assistance: 0

Coin-operated public phones are found in subway stations, restaurants and shopping malls. The charge for a local call is $0.25, and calling cards are widely available.

Visitors can use their own cell-phones in Canada but only those operating on a GSM frequency are compatible. Others can purchase a SIM card (about $25), and make an arrangement with a local carrier for billing. Contact Rogers Wireless at any Rogers Video store (Tel: 1-800-575 9090, www.rogers.com).

Tourist Information

Tourist Welcome Office, 174 Notre-Dame Est. For maps, metro cards, cycle-path information.
Infotouriste Centre, 1255 rue Peel. For provincial information. For both tourist offices: tel: 1-877-266 5687 or 514-873 2015.
Office du Tourisme et des Congrès de Québec, 835 avenue Wilfred-Laurier, tel: 418-641 6290. The main tourist office in Québec City.

Weights and Measures

Canada uses the metric system.
1 centimetre (cm) = 0.394 in
1 kilometre (km) = 0.621 miles
1 litre = 0.22 UK gallon
1 litre = 0.26 US gallon
1 gram (g) = 0.035 oz
1 kilogram = 2.2 lbs

Time Zone

Montréal is in the **Eastern Standard Time Zone**, the same as New York, five hours behind London in the UK, and three hours ahead of Vancouver and San Francisco. Daylight Saving Time starts on the second Sunday in March when clocks are set forward one hour. Clocks are set back one hour on the first Sunday in November.

BELOW: maps are available at tourist offices.

LANGUAGE

UNDERSTANDING CANADIAN FRENCH

General

Even if you speak no French at all it is worth trying to master a few phrases. The fact that you have made an effort is likely to get you a better response. Beginning a conversation with *"Bonjour"* is a good start. Indeed, some shopkeepers in Montréal hedge, with an all-purpose: *"Bonjour-Hi"*.

Pronunciation is key; locals really will not understand if you get it very wrong. Remember to emphasise each syllable, not to pronounce the last consonant of a word as a rule (this includes the plural "s") and always to drop your "h"s. Whether to use *"vous"* or *"tu"* is a vexed question; increasingly the familiar form of *"tu"* is used. However, it is better to be too formal, and use *"vous"* if in doubt. It is very important to be polite; always address people as *Madame* or *Monsieur*, and address them by their surnames until you are confident first names are acceptable.

Learning the pronunciation of the French alphabet is a good idea and, in particular, learn how to spell out your name.

Some 52 percent of the city's residents and 68 percent of those in the metropolitan area are French speakers, with 17 percent and 12 percent English speakers, respectively. In Québec City fewer people speak English.

Unique to Québec province is *joual*, a patois the name of which is derived from the French for horse: *cheval*. The earthy dialect flourishes among the city's working class.

Accents distinguish French in Québec from French in Paris or Marseilles. Québec's francophones form sounds deep in the throat, lisp slightly, voice toward diphthongs, and bend single vowels into exotic shapes. It has also incorporated some English words, such as chum, as in *mon chum*, or *ma chumme*, and *blonde*, for girlfriend, while *le fun* is a good time.

Words and Phrases

What is your name? *Comment vous appelez-vous?*
My name is... *Je m'appelle...*
Do you speak English? *Parlez-vous anglais?*
I am English/American *Je suis anglais(e)/américain(e)*
I don't understand *Je ne comprends pas*
Please speak more slowly *Parlez plus lentement, s'il vous plaît*
Can you help me? *Pouvez-vous m'aider?*
I'm looking for... *Je cherche*
Where is...? *Où est...?*
I'm sorry *Excusez-moi/Pardon*
I don't know *Je ne sais pas*
No problem *Pas de problème*
Have a good day! *Bonne journée!*
Show me the word in the book *Montrez-moi le mot dans le livre*
At what time? *A quelle heure?*
When? *Quand?*
What time is it? *Quelle heure est-il?*
Note. The Québécois sometimes use the 24-hour clock.
yes *oui*
no *non*
please *s'il vous plaît*

ON THE TELEPHONE

How do I make an outside call? *Comment est-ce que je peux téléphoner à l'exterieur?*
I want to make an international call *Je veux faire un appel à l'étranger*
local call *une communication locale*
dialling code *l'indicatif*
I'd like an alarm call for 8 tomorrow morning *J'aimerais un réveil à 8 heures demain matin*
Who's calling? *C'est qui à l'appareil?*
Hold on, please *Ne quittez pas s'il vous plaît*
The line is busy *La ligne est occupée*

thank you *merci*
(very much) *(beaucoup)*
you're welcome *de rien*
excuse me *excusez-moi*
OK *d'accord*
goodbye *au revoir*
good evening *bonsoir*
here *ici*
there *là*
today *aujourd'hui*
yesterday *hier*
tomorrow *demain*
now *maintenant*
later *plus tard*
right away *tout de suite*
this morning *ce matin*
this afternoon *cet après-midi*
this evening *ce soir*

On Arrival

I want to get off at... *Je voudrais descendre à...*
Is there a bus to...? *Est-ce qui'il ya un bus pour...?*
What street is this? *Quel est le nom de la rue?*
Which line do I take for...? *Quelle ligne dois-je prendre pour...?*
How far is...? *A quelle distance se trouve...?*
airport *l'aéroport*
train station *la gare de train*
bus station *la gare routière*
metro stop *la station de métro*
bus *l'autobus*
bus stop *l'arrêt d'autobus*
platform *le quai*
ticket *le billet*
return ticket *aller-retour*
transfer *correspondance*
hitchhiking *faire du pouce*
toilets *les toilettes*
This is the hotel address *C'est l'adresse de l'hôtel*
I'd like a (single/double) room... *Je voudrais une chambre (pour une/deux personnes)...*
...with shower *avec douche*
...with bath *avec salle de bain*
...with a view *avec vue*
Does the price include breakfast? *Le prix comprend-il le petit déjeuner?*
May I see the room? *Je peux voir la chambre?*
washbasin *le lavabo*
bed *le lit*
key *la clé*
elevator *l'ascenseur*
air conditioned *air climatisé*

On the Road

Where is the nearest garage? *Où est le garage le plus proche?*
Our car has broken down *Notre voiture est en panne*
I want to have my car repaired *Je veux faire réparer ma voiture*
the road to... *la route pour...*
left *gauche*
right *droite*
straight on *tout droit*
far *loin*
near *près d'ici*
opposite *en face*
beside *à côté de*
car park *le parking/le stationment*
at the end *au bout*
give way *céder le passage*
dead end *impasse*
no parking *stationnement interdit*
motorway *l'autoroute*
toll *le péage*
speed limit *la vitesse limite*
petrol *l'essence/gaz*
unleaded *sans plomb*
diesel *le diesel*
water/oil *l'eau/l'huile*
puncture *une crevaison*
bulb *l'ampoule*
wipers *les essuies-glace*

Dining Out

Note: *Garçon* is the word for waiter but never used directly; say *Monsieur* or *Madame* to attract attention. Adding *s'il vous plaît* doesn't hurt either.
Table d'hôte is a set menu served at a set price. *Prix fixé* is a fixed-price menu. *A la carte* means dishes from the menu are charged separately.
breakfast *le petit déjeuner*
lunch *le déjeuner*
dinner *le dîner*
meal *le repas*
first course *l'entrée/les hors d'oeuvre*
main course *le plat principal*
made to order *sur commande*
drink included *boisson compris*
wine list *la carte des vins*
the bill *l'addition*
I am a vegetarian *Je suis végétarien(ne)*
What do you recommend? *Que'est-ce que vous recommandez?*
Do you have local specialities? *Avez-vous des spécialités locales?*
I'd like to order *Je voudrais commander*
Is service included? *Est-ce que le service est compris?*

Breakfast and Snacks

baguette **long thin loaf**
pain **bread**
petits pains **rolls**
beurre **butter**
poivre **pepper**
sel **salt**
sucre **sugar**
confiture **jam**
miel **honey**
oeufs **eggs**
...à la coque **boiled eggs**
...au bacon **bacon and eggs**
...au jambon **ham and eggs**
...frits **fried**
...miroir **sunnyside up**
...tournés **over lightly**
...brouillés **scrambled eggs**
yaourt **yoghurt**
crêpe **pancake**
croque-monsieur **ham and cheese toasted sandwich**
croque-madame **...with a fried egg on top**
galette **type of pancake**

First Course

An *amuse-bouche, amuse-gueule* or *appetizer* is served before the first course.
anchoiade **olive oil, anchovy and garlic served with raw vegetables**
assiette anglaise **cold meats**
potage **soup**
rillettes **rich fatty paste of shredded duck, rabbit or pork**
tapenade **spread of olives and anchovies**
pissaladière **pizza/pie with onions, olives and anchovies**

Main Course

La Viande – Meat
saignant **rare**
à point **medium**
bien cuit **well done**

grillé **grilled**
agneau **lamb**
andouille/andouillette **tripe sausage**
bifteck **steak**
boudin **sausage**
boudin noir **black pudding**
boudin blanc **white pudding (chicken or veal)**
blanquette **stew of veal, lamb or chicken with creamy egg sauce**
boeuf à la môde **beef in red wine, carrots, onions and mushrooms**
à la bordelaise **beef with red wine and shallots**
à la bourguignonne **cooked in red wine, onions and mushrooms**
brochette **kebab**
caille **quail**
canard **duck**
carbonnade **casserole of beef, beer and onions**
carré d'agneau **rack of lamb**
cassoulet **stew of beans, sausages, pork and duck**
cervelle **brains (food)**
châteaubriand **thick steak**
choucroute **sauerkraut, bacon and sausages**
confit **duck or goose preserved in its own fat**
contre-filet **cut of sirloin steak**
coq au vin **chicken in red wine**
côte d'agneau **lamb chop**
daube **beef stew with red wine, onions and tomatoes**
dinde **turkey**
entrecôte **beef rib steak**
escargot **snail**
faisan **pheasant**
farci **stuffed**
faux-filet **sirloin**
feuilleté **puff pastry**
foie **liver**
foie de veau **calf's liver**
foie gras **goose or duck liver pâté**
cuisses de grenouille **frog's legs**
grillade **grilled meat**
hachis **minced meat**
jambon **ham**
langue **tongue**
lapin **rabbit**
lardon **small pieces of bacon**
magret de canard **breast of duck**
médaillon **round piece of meat**
moelle **beef bone marrow**
navarin d'agneau **stew of lamb with onions, carrots and turnips**
oie **goose**
pattes de cochon **pig's trotters**
pintade **guinea fowl**
porc **pork**
pot-au-feu **casserole of beef and vegetables**
poulet **chicken**
poussin **young chicken**
rognons **kidneys**
rôti **roast**
sanglier **wild boar**
saucisse **fresh sausage**
saucisson **salami**
veau **veal**

***Poissons* – Fish**

anchois **anchovies**
anguille **eel**
bar (or loup) **sea bass**
barbue **brill**
bigorneau **sea snail**
bercy **sauce of fish stock, butter, white wine and shallots**
bouillabaisse **fish soup served with grated cheese, garlic croutons and rouille, a spicy sauce**
brandade **salt-cod purée**
morue **cod**
calmars **squid**
colin **hake**
coquillage **shellfish**
pétoncles **scallops**
crevette **shrimp**
daurade **sea bream**
flétan **halibut**
fruits de mer **seafood**
hareng **herring**
homard **lobster**
huître **oyster**
langoustine **large prawn**
limande **lemon sole**
lotte **monkfish**
moule **mussel**
moules marinières **mussels in white wine and onions**
oursin **sea urchin**
raie **skate**
saumon **salmon**
thon **tuna**
truite **trout**

***Légumes* – Vegetables**

ail **garlic**
artichaut **artichoke**
asperge **asparagus**
aubergine **eggplant/aubergine**
avocat **avocado**
bolets **boletus mushrooms**
champignon **mushroom**
cornichon **gherkin**
courgette **zucchini/courgette**
chips **potato crisps**
chou **cabbage**
chou-fleur **cauliflower**
concombre **cucumber**
cru **raw**
crudités **raw vegetables**
épinard **spinach**
frites **chips/French fries**
gratin dauphinois **sliced potatoes baked with cream**
haricots verts **green beans**
maïs **corn**
mesclun **mixed-leaf salad**
navet **turnip**
noix **nut, walnut**
noisette **hazelnut**
oignon **onion**
panais **parsnip**
patate **potato**
persil **parsley**
pignon **pine nut**
poireau **leek**
pois **pea**
poivron **bell pepper**
primeurs **early fruit and vegetables**
radis **radish**
roquette **arugula, rocket**
ratatouille **stew of aubergine, courgette, tomato and pepper**
riz **rice**
salade niçoise **egg, tuna, olives, onions and tomato salad**
salade verte **green salad**
truffe **truffle**

***Fruit* – Fruit**

ananas **pineapple**
cerise **cherry**
citron **lemon**
lime **lime**
figue **fig**
fraise **strawberry**
framboise **raspberry**
groseille **redcurrant**
mangue **mango**
mirabelle **yellow plum**
pamplemousse **grapefruit**
pêche **peach**
poire **pear**
pomme **apple**
raisin **grape**
prune **plum**

***Sauces* – Sauces**

aioli **garlic mayonnaise**
bearnaise **egg, butter, wine and herbs**

forestière **mushrooms and bacon**
hollandaise **egg, butter and lemon**
lyonnaise **onions**
meunière **butter, lemon and parsley**
mornay **cream, egg and cheese**
parmentier **served with potatoes**
paysan **rustic style; ingredients depend on the region**
pistou **basil, garlic and olive oil; vegetable soup with the sauce**
provençale **tomatoes, garlic and olive oil**

***Pouding* – Dessert**
clafoutis **baked pudding of batter and cherries**
coulis **purée of fruit**
crème anglaise **custard**
crème caramel **caramelised egg custard**
crème Chantilly **whipped cream**
fromage **cheese**
gâteau **cake**
Ile flottante **whisked egg whites in custard sauce**
pêche melba **peaches with ice cream and raspberry sauce**
Poire belle Hélène **fruit with ice cream and chocolate sauce**
tarte tatin **upside-down tart of caramelised apples**

***Les Boissons* – Drinks**
café **coffee**
...au lait/crème **with milk/cream**
...déca/décaféiné **decaffeinated**
...express/noir **black espresso**
...filtre **American filtered coffee**
thé **tea**
...tisane **herbal tea/infusion**
...verveine **verbena**
chocolat chaud **hot chocolate**
lait **milk**
eau minérale **mineral water**
pétillant **fizzy**
platte **still**
limonade **fizzy lemonade**
citron pressé **fresh lemon juice served with sugar**
orange pressée **fresh orange juice**
entier **full or whole cream milk**
frais, fraîche **fresh or cold**
bière **beer**
pastis **aniseed-flavoured apéritif**
kir **white wine with cassis**
kir royal **kir with champagne**
avec glace **with ice**
sec **neat/dry**
rouge **red**
blanc **white**
rosé **rosé**
doux **sweet**
vin pétillent **sparkling wine**
panaché **mixed**
digestif **after-dinner drink**
santé! **cheers!**
Encore du vin, s'il vous plaît
More wine, please
gueule de bois **hangover**
cidre de glace **ice cider**
vin de glace **ice wine**

Emergencies

Help! *Au secours!*
Stop! *Arrêtez!*
Call a doctor *Appelez un médecin*
Call an ambulance *Appelez une ambulance*
Call the police *Appelez la police*
Call the fire brigade *Appelez les pompiers*
Where is the nearest telephone? *Où est le téléphone le plus proche?*
Where is the nearest hospital? *Où est l'hôpital le plus proche?*
I am sick *Je suis malade*
I have lost my passport/purse *J'ai perdu mon passeport/porte-monnaie*

Days and Months

Monday *lundi*
Tuesday *mardi*
Wednesday *mercredi*
Thursday *jeudi*
Friday *vendredi*
Saturday *samedi*
Sunday *dimanche*
January *janvier*
February *fevrier*
March *mars*
April *avril*
May *mai*
June *juin*
July *juillet*
August *août*
September *septembre*
October *octobre*
November *novembre*
December *decembre*

Shopping

Where is the nearest bank/post office? *Où est la banque/Poste la plus proche?*
I'd like to buy *Je voudrais acheter*
How much is it? *C'est combien?*
Do you take credit cards? *Est-ce que vous acceptez les cartes de crédit?*
I'm just looking *Je regarde seulement*
Have you got? *Avez-vous...?*
I'll take it *Je le prends*
I'll take this one/that one *Je prends celui-ci/celui-là*
What size is it? *Quelle est la taille?*
size (clothes) *la taille*
size (shoes) *la pointure*
cheap *bon marché*
expensive *cher*
enough *assez*
too much *trop*
a piece *un morceau de*
each *la pièce* (eg. $5 la pièce)
bill *la note*
chemist *la pharmacie*
bakery *la boulangerie*
bookshop *la librairie*
library *la bibliothèque*
department store *le magasin à rayons*
delicatessen *la charcuterie/le traiteur*
fishmonger's *la poissonnerie*
grocery *l'alimentation/l'épicerie*
convenience store *dépanneur*
market *le marché*
supermarket *le supermarché*

Sightseeing

old town *la vieille ville*
church *l'église*
mansion *l'hôtel*
town hall *l'hôtel de ville/la mairie*
tower *la tour*
walk *le tour*
museum *le musée*
art gallery *la galerie*
swimming pool *la piscine*
to book *réserver*
free *gratuit*
open *ouvert*
closed *fermé*
every day *tous les jours*
all year *toute l'année*
all day *toute la journée*

FURTHER READING

History

A Short History of Québec by John Alexander Dickinson and Brian Young. A little dry in parts. (McGill-Queen's University Press, 3rd edition 2003.)
An Historical Guide to Québec by Yves Tessier. An easy-to-follow read with maps and illustrations, covering the historical events and heritage sites of Québec City. (La Société historique de Québec, 4th edition 1996.)

General

Barney's Version by Mordecai Richler. An obsessive (but funny) rant about hockey, Québec separatists, vegetarians and old-guard anglos. (Washington Square Press, reprint 2003.)
Beautiful Losers by Leonard Cohen. Examines the three cultural forces (French, anglo and native) that have shaped the city. (Vintage, 1993.)
Black Robe: A Novel by Brian Moore. The harrowing tale of a proselytizing 17th-century Jesuit missionary struggling with the brutality of life among the native peoples of northern Québec. (Penguin, 2006.)
Elle by Douglas Glover. Lusty, eccentric story about a young French woman abandoned on an island in the Gulf of St Lawrence during an expedition. (Goose Lane Editions, 2003.)
French Fun: The Real Spoken Language of Québec by Steve Timmins. A humorous look at the colourful idioms in common use. (John Wiley & Sons, 1995.)
Montréal Stories by Mavis Gallant. Short stories selected by Russell Banks. (McClelland & Stewart, 2004.)
Montréal Stories: Selected Stories, Volume Three by Clark Blaise. (Porcupine's Quill, 2003.)
Montréal Up Close: a Pedestrian's Guide to the City by Kirk Johnson and David Widgington. (Cumulus Press, 1998.)

FEEDBACK

We do our best to ensure the information in our books is as accurate and up-to-date as possible. The books are updated on a regular basis, using local contacts, who painstakingly add, amend and correct as required. However, some mistakes and omissions are inevitable and we are ultimately reliant on our readers to put us in the picture.

We would welcome your feedback on any details related to your experiences using the book "on the road". Maybe we recommended a hotel that you liked (or another that you didn't), as well as interesting new attractions, or facts and figures you have found out about the country itself. The more details you can give us (particularly with regard to addresses, e-mails and telephone numbers), the better.

We will acknowledge all contributions, and we'll offer an Insight Guide to the best letters received.

Please write to us at:
Insight Guides
PO Box 7910
London SE1 1WE
United Kingdom
Or send e-mail to:
insight@apaguide.co.uk

Putting Down Roots, by Elaine Kalman Naves. Explores the work of authors whose native languages include Arabic, Italian, Yiddish and Haitian French. (Véhicule Press, 1999.)
Sacre Blues: An Unsentimental Journey Through Québec by Taras Grescoe. An entertaining examination of Québec and its ethnic, linguistic and political identities. (Macfarlane Walter & Ross, 2001.)
Stranger Music: Selected Poems and Songs by Leonard Cohen. Poetry and lyrics. (Vintage, 1994.)
The Apprenticeship of Duddy Kravitz by Mordecai Richler. An opportunistic, amoral young Jew's determination to fight his way out of the working-class neighbourhood of his youth. (Washington Square Press, reprint edition 2003.)
The Jesuits in North America by Francis Parkman. Includes some background on the New France missionaries. (Peter Smith Pub, 2000.)
The Rent Collector by Glen Rotchin. Montréal's Orthodox Jewish community and the garment district. (Vehicule Press, 2006.)
The Two Solitudes by Hugh MacLennan. The linguistic and cultural conflicts between Canada's two founding nations. (McGill-Queen's University Press, reprinted 2006.)
The Writers of Montréal by Elaine Kalman Naves. Tracks the literary heritage of Montréal. (Véhicule Press, 1993.)
Volkswagen Blues by Jacques Poulin, translated by Sheila Fischman. About a road trip from the Gaspé along the St Lawrence River to California. (Cormorant Books, 2004.)

Montreal Street Atlas

The key map shows the area of Montréal covered by the atlas section. An index of street names and places of interest shown on the maps can be found on the following pages. For each entry there is a page number and grid reference.

Map Legend

Expressway with Junction	Airport	Expressway	Metro Station
Expressway (under construction)	Church (ruins)	Highway	Bus Station
Divided Highway	Monastery	Main Roads	Tourist Information
Main Road	Castle (ruins)		Post Office
Secondary Road	Archaeological Site	Minor Roads	Cathedral/Church
Minor Road	Cave		Mosque
Track	Place of Interest	Footpath	Synagogue
International Boundary	Mansion/Stately Home	Railway	Statue/Monument
Province/State Boundary	Viewpoint	Pedestrian Area	Tower
National Park/Reserve		Important Building	

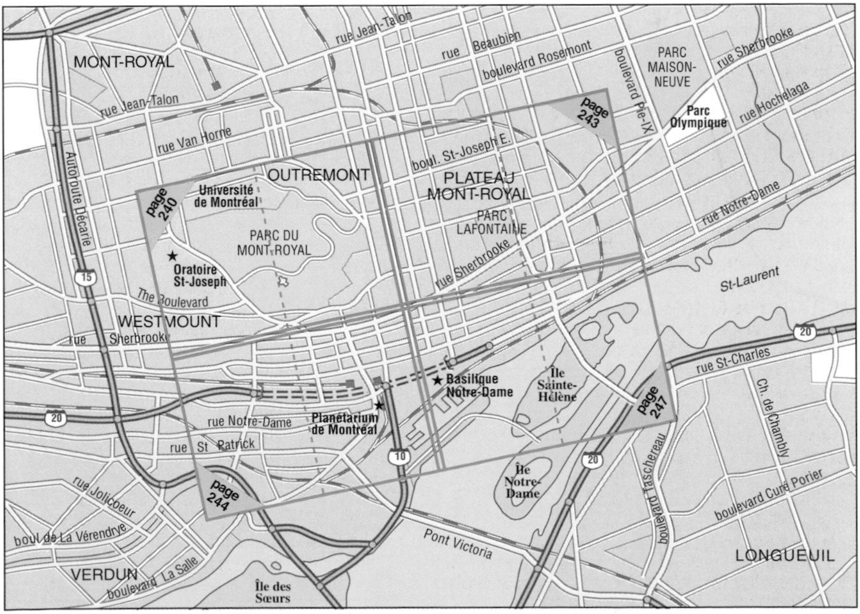

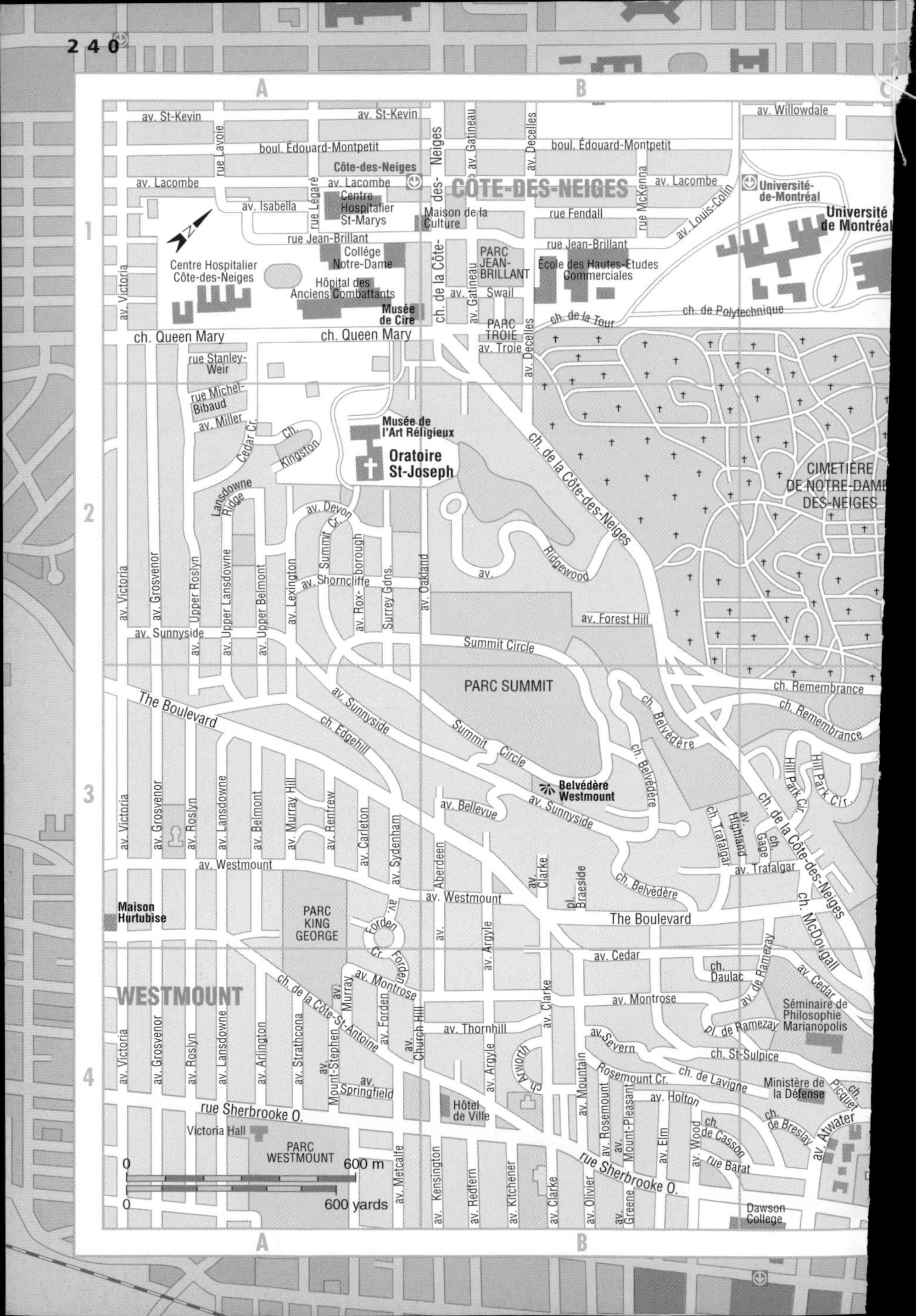
A
B
C
1
2
3
4
av. St-Kevin
av. St-Kevin
av. Willowdale
rue Lavoie
boul. Édouard-Montpetit
boul. Édouard-Montpetit
Côte-des-Neiges
av. Gatineau
av. Decelles
av. Lacombe
av. Lacombe
av. Lacombe
CÔTE-DES-NEIGES
Université-de-Montréal
Université de Montréal
rue Légaré
Centre Hospitalier St-Marys
av. Isabella
Maison de la Culture
rue Fendall
rue McKenna
av. Louis-Colin
rue Jean-Brillant
rue Jean-Brillant
Collège Notre-Dame
PARC JEAN-BRILLANT
École des Hautes-Études Commerciales
Centre Hospitalier Côte-des-Neiges
Hôpital des Anciens Combattants
ch. de la Côte-des-Neiges
av. Gatineau
Swail
av. Victoria
Musée de Cire
PARC TROIE
ch. de la Tour
ch. de Polytechnique
ch. Queen Mary
ch. Queen Mary
av. Troie
av. Decelles
rue Stanley-Weir
rue Michel-Bibaud
av. Miller
Cedar Cr.
ch. Kingston
Musée de l'Art Réligieux
Oratoire St-Joseph
ch. de la Côte-des-Neiges
CIMETIÈRE DE NOTRE-DAME DES-NEIGES
Lansdowne Ridge
av. Devon
Summit Cr.
av. Ridgewood
av. Victoria
av. Grosvenor
Upper Roslyn
Upper Lansdowne
Upper Belmont
av. Lexington
av. Shorncliffe
av. Rox-borough
Surrey Gdns.
av. Oakland
av. Forest Hill
av. Sunnyside
av. Upper Lansdowne
av. Upper Belmont
Summit Circle
PARC SUMMIT
ch. Remembrance
ch. Remembrance
The Boulevard
av. Sunnyside
ch. Edgehill
Summit Circle
ch. Belvédère
ch. Belvédère
Hill Park Cir.
Hill Park Cir.
Belvédère Westmount
av. Sunnyside
ch. de la Côte-des-Neiges
av. Victoria
av. Grosvenor
av. Roslyn
av. Lansdowne
av. Belmont
av. Murray Hill
av. Renfrew
av. Carleton
av. Sydenham
av. Bellevue
ch. Trafalgar
av. Highland
ch. Gage
av. Trafalgar
av. Westmount
av. Aberdeen
av. Westmount
av. Clarke
pl. Braeside
ch. Belvédère
ch. McDougall
Maison Hurtubise
PARC KING GEORGE
av. Forden
Forden Cr.
The Boulevard
av. Argyle
av. Cedar
ch. Daulac
av. de Ramezay
av. Cedar
av. Montrose
av. Murray
ch. de la Côte-St-Antoine
WESTMOUNT
av. Forden
av. Clarke
av. Montrose
Séminaire de Philosophie Marianopolis
pl. de Ramezay
av. Thornhill
av. Church Hill
av. Severn
ch. St-Sulpice
av. Victoria
av. Grosvenor
av. Roslyn
av. Lansdowne
av. Arlington
av. Strathcona
av. Mount-Stephen
av. Springfield
av. Argyle
ch. Atworth
av. Mountain
Rosemount Cr.
ch. de Lavigne
Ministère de la Défense
ch. Picquet
av. Holton
ch. de Breslay
av. Atwater
rue Sherbrooke O.
Hôtel de Ville
Victoria Hall
PARC WESTMOUNT
av. Rosemount
av. Mount-Pleasant
av. Elm
av. Wood
ch. de Casson
rue Barat
rue Sherbrooke O.
0
600 m
0
600 yards
av. Metcalfe
av. Kensington
av. Redfern
av. Kitchener
av. Clarke
av. Olivier
av. Greene
Dawson College

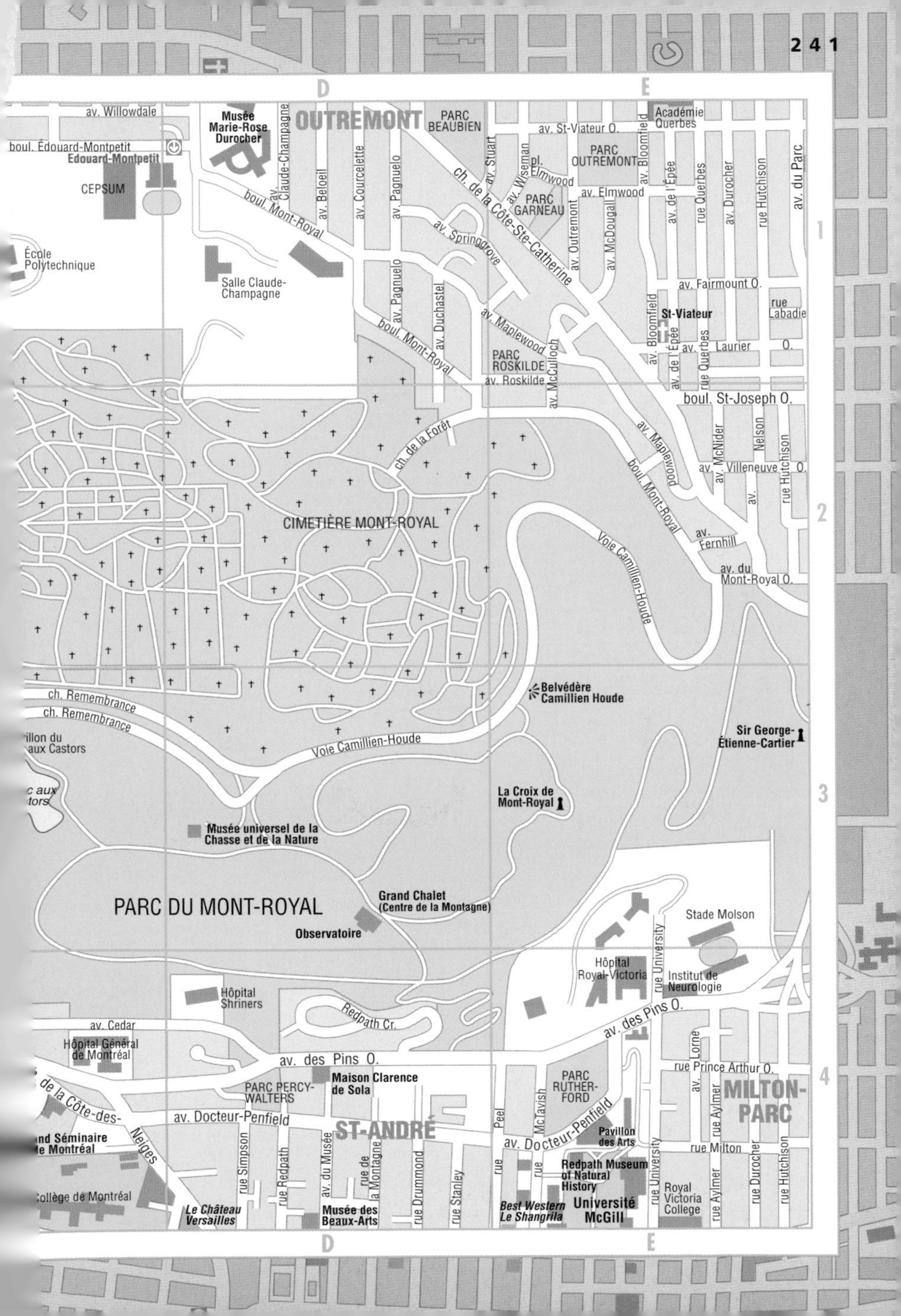
D
E
av. Willowdale
boul. Édouard-Montpetit
Edouard-Montpetit
CEPSUM
Musée Marie-Rose Durocher
av. Claude-Champagne
OUTREMONT
PARC BEAUBIEN
Académie Querbes
av. St-Viateur O.
PARC OUTREMONT
av. Bloomfield
av. du Parc
av. Beloeil
av. Courcelette
av. Pagnuelo
av. Stuart
av. Wiseman
pl. Elmwood
av. Elmwood
PARC GARNEAU
av. de l'Épée
rue Querbes
av. Durocher
rue Hutchison
boul. Mont-Royal
ch. de la Côte-Ste-Catherine
av. Springgrove
av. Outremont
av. McDougall
1
École Polytechnique
Salle Claude-Champagne
av. Fairmount O.
rue Labadie
St-Viateur
av. Duchastel
av. Maplewood
Bloomfield
av. Laurier O.
PARC ROSKILDE
av. Roskilde
av. McCulloch
boul. St-Joseph O.
ch. de la Forêt
av. Maplewood
av. McNider
Nelson
av. Villeneuve O.
rue Hutchison
CIMETIÈRE MONT-ROYAL
Voie Camillien-Houde
av. Fernhill
av. du Mont-Royal O.
2
ch. Remembrance
ch. Remembrance
Belvédère Camillien Houde
Sir George-Étienne-Cartier
Voie Camillien-Houde
La Croix de Mont-Royal
3
Musée universel de la Chasse et de la Nature
PARC DU MONT-ROYAL
Grand Chalet (Centre de la Montagne)
Observatoire
Stade Molson
Hôpital Royal-Victoria
rue University
Institut de Neurologie
Hôpital Shriners
Redpath Cr.
av. des Pins O.
av. Cedar
Hôpital Général de Montréal
av. des Pins O.
Lorne
rue Prince Arthur O.
Maison Clarence de Sola
PARC PERCY-WALTERS
PARC RUTHERFORD
MILTON-PARC
4
de la Côte-des-Neiges
av. Docteur-Penfield
ST-ANDRÉ
rue Peel
McTavish
av. Docteur-Penfield
Pavillon des Arts
av. Aylmer
rue Milton
rue Simpson
rue Redpath
av. du Musée
rue de la Montagne
rue Drummond
rue Stanley
rue McTavish
Redpath Museum of Natural History
Université McGill
rue University
Royal Victoria College
rue Aylmer
rue Durocher
rue Hutchison
Le Château Versailles
Musée des Beaux-Arts
Best Western Le Shangrila

A
B
C
1
2
3
4
MILE-END
LAURIER
ST- DENIS
PLATEAU MONT-ROYAL
ST-JEAN-BAPTISTE
LAFONTAINE
ST-LOUIS
ST-JACQUES
av. St- Viateur O.
av. St-Viateur E.
Library
av. du Parc
rue Jeanne-Mance
av. de l'Esplanade
r. Groll
r. Waverly
rue St-Urbain
rue Clark
boul. St-Laurent
rue St-Dominique
av. Casgrain
av. de Gaspé
rue Maguire
av. Henri-Julien
av. du Carmel
rue Drolet
rue St-Denis
rue St-Grégoire
rue Rivard
rue Boucher
rue Berri
rue Resther
rue St-Hubert
rue St-André
rue de Mentana
PARC SIR-WILFRED-LAURIER
rue de Brébeuf
rue Chambord
rue de Lanaudière
rue Garnier
rue Fabre
av. Fairmount O.
av. Fairmount E.
PARC DE ST-MICHEL
av. Laurier O.
av. Laurier E.
PARC LAHAIE
École Nationale de Théâtre
Laurier
av. Christophe Colomb
rue Boyer
rue de La Roche
boul. St-Joseph O.
boul. St-Joseph E.
rue Gilford
av. l'Hôtel-de-Ville
rue de Grand-Pré
av. Villeneuve O.
av. Villeneuve E.
Bullion
r. Gilford
rue Pontiac
rue de Bienville
rue Poitevin
r. de Varennes
rue Généreux
av. du Mont-Royal O.
av. du Mont-Royal E.
Mont-Royal
av. Laval
rue de Bullion
av. Coloniale
r. Marie-Anne O.
rue Marie-Anne E.
av. de Châteaubriand
rue St-Christophe
r. de Courville
PARC JEANNE-MANCE
St-Jean-Baptiste
Palais des Nains
Sir George-Étienne-Cartier
r. Rachel O.
rue Rachel E.
av. Bureau
rue Duluth O.
rue Duluth E.
rlle. de Mentana
Théâtre de Verdure
PARC LAFONTAINE
av. Parc La Fontaine
av. Calixa-Lavallée
r. Napoléon
Hôtel-Dieu de Montréal
rue Sewell
rue Roy E.
Université du Québec à Montréal (UQAM)
av. des Pins E.
r. Guilbault
Cinéma Parallèle
r. Bousquet
rue Cherrier
rue Sherbrooke E.
Sherbrooke
Sq. St-Louis
Hôtel du Parc
rue Prince Arthur O.
rue Prince Arthur E.
Institut de tourisme et d'hôtellerie du Québec
Library
rue Plessis
rue Panet
rue de la Visitation
rue Beaudry
rue de Montcalm
rue Wolfe
rue Amherst
rue Ste-Famille
rue Milton
Ecomusée du Fier Monde
Marché St-Jacques
rue Ontario E.
rue Labrecque
rue St-Timothée
CÉGEP du Vieux-Montréal
rue La Fonta
0
600 m
0
600 yards

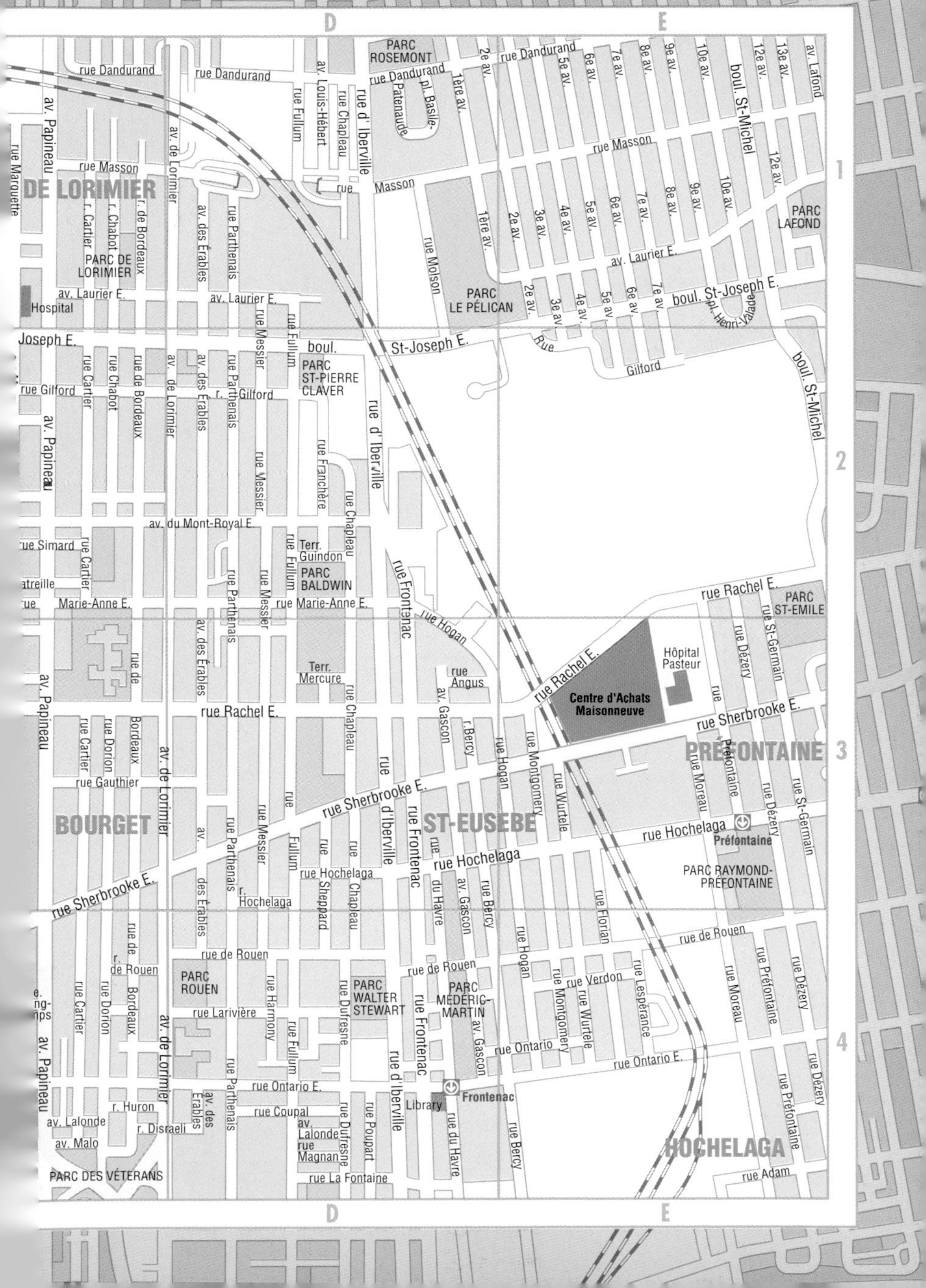
D
E
1
2
3
4
PARC ROSEMONT
rue Dandurand
2e av.
5e av.
6e av.
7e av.
8e av.
9e av.
10e av.
12e av.
13e av.
av. Lafond
boul. St-Michel
pl. Basile-Patenaude
1ère av.
rue d' Iberville
av. Louis-Hébert
rue Chapleau
rue Fullum
av. Papineau
rue Marquette
av. de Lorimier
rue Masson
DE LORIMIER
r. Cartier
r. Chabot
r. de Bordeaux
av. des Érables
rue Parthenais
PARC DE LORIMIER
av. Laurier E.
Hospital
rue Molson
3e av.
4e av.
PARC LAFOND
PARC LE PÉLICAN
boul. St-Joseph E.
pl. Henri-Valade
Rue Gilford
Joseph E.
boul. St-Joseph E.
PARC ST-PIERRE CLAVER
rue Messier
rue Gilford
r. Gilford
rue Cartier
rue Chabot
rue de Bordeaux
rue Franchère
av. du Mont-Royal E.
rue Simard
Terr. Guindon
PARC BALDWIN
rue Frontenac
rue Marie-Anne E.
rue Hogan
rue Rachel E.
PARC ST-EMILE
rue St-Germain
rue Dézery
Hôpital Pasteur
Centre d'Achats Maisonneuve
Terr. Mercure
rue Angus
av. Gascon
r. Bercy
rue Montgomery
rue Sherbrooke E.
PRÉFONTAINE
rue Préfontaine
rue Moreau
rue Dorion
rue Gauthier
BOURGET
ST-EUSEBE
rue Wurtele
rue Hochelaga
Préfontaine
PARC RAYMOND-PRÉFONTAINE
rue Sheppard
r. Hochelaga
rue du Havre
rue Florian
rue de Rouen
r. de Rouen
PARC ROUEN
PARC WALTER STEWART
PARC MÉDÉRIC-MARTIN
rue Verdon
rue Lespérance
rue Larivière
rue Harmony
rue Dufresne
rue Ontario
rue Ontario E.
Frontenac
Library
r. Huron
r. Disraeli
av. Lalonde
av. Malo
rue Coupal
rue Poupart
rue Magnan
PARC DES VÉTERANS
rue La Fontaine
HOCHELAGA
rue Adam

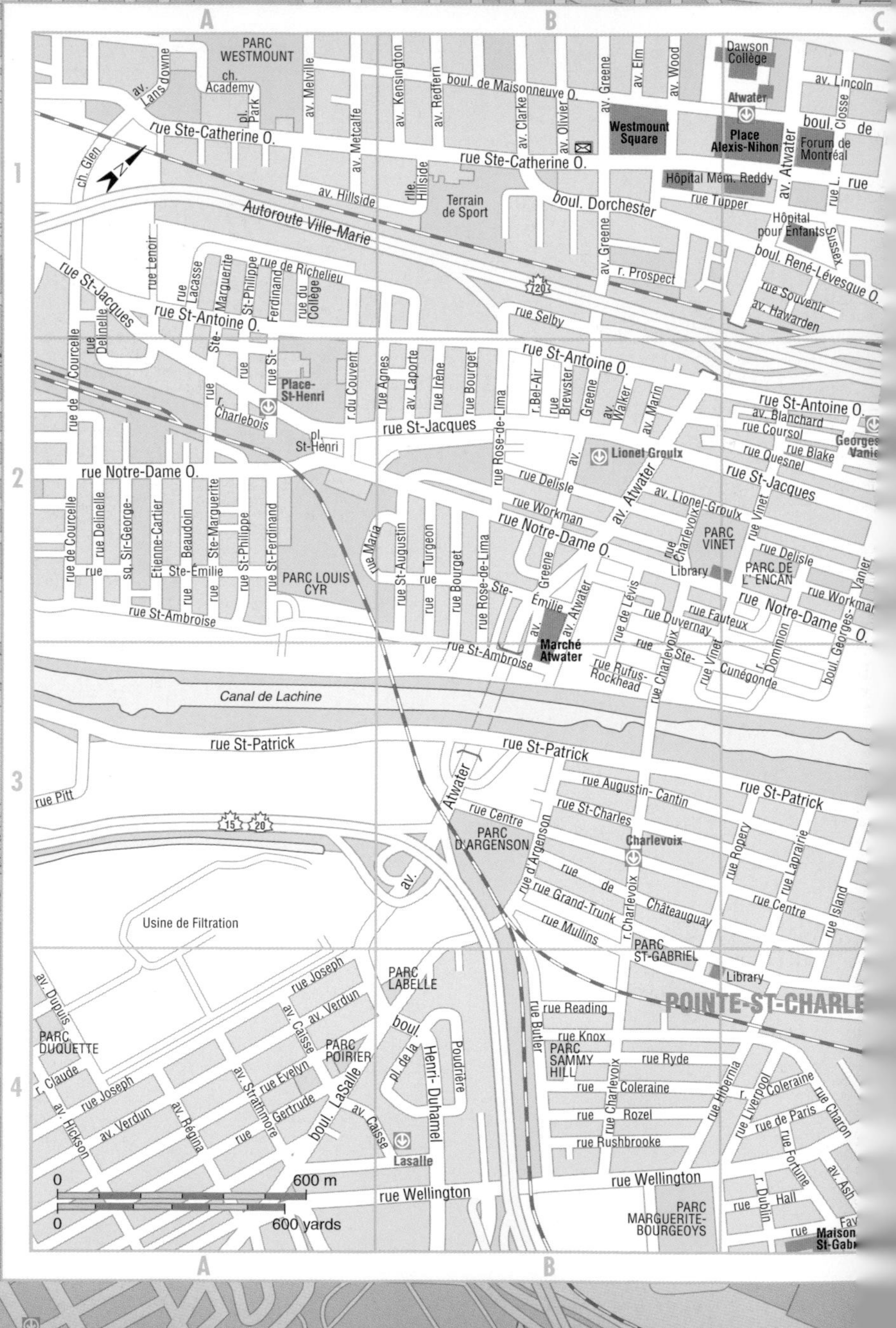
A
B
C
1
2
3
4
PARC WESTMOUNT
ch. Academy
av. Lansdowne
pl. Park
av. Melville
av. Kensington
av. Redfern
boul. de Maisonneuve O.
av. Greene
av. Elm
av. Wood
Dawson Collège
av. Lincoln
Atwater
av. Metcalfe
av. Clarke
av. Olivier
Westmount Square
Place Alexis-Nihon
boul. de
Forum de Montréal
av. Atwater
rue Ste-Catherine O.
ch. Glen
rue Ste-Catherine O.
Hôpital Mém. Reddy
rue
av. Hillside
rlle. Hillside
Terrain de Sport
boul. Dorchester
rue Tupper
Hôpital pour Enfants
Sussex
Autoroute Ville-Marie
boul. René-Lévesque O.
rue Lenoir
rue Lacasse
Marguerite
St-Philippe
rue de Richelieu
Ferdinand
rue du Collège
av. Greene
r. Prospect
rue Souvenir
av. Hawarden
rue St-Jacques
rue St-Antoine O.
rue Selby
20
rue Delinelle
rue de Courcelle
Ste-
rue
rue St-
Place-St-Henri
r.du Couvent
av. Agnes
av. Laporte
rue Irène
rue Bourget
rue St-Antoine O.
rue Bel-Air
rue Brewster
Greene
av. Walker
av. Marin
rue St-Antoine O.
av. Blanchard
rue Coursol
Georges Vanier
r. Charlebois
rue St-Jacques
pl. St-Henri
rue Rose-de-Lima
av.
Lionel-Groulx
rue Blake
rue Quesnel
rue St-Jacques
rue Notre-Dame O.
rue Delisle
av. Atwater
av. Lionel-Groulx
rue Workman
rue Notre-Dame O.
rue Charlevoix
PARC VINET
rue Vinet
rue Delisle
rue de Courcelle
rue Delinelle
sq. Sir-George-Etienne-Cartier
Beaudoin
Ste-Marguerite
rue St-Philippe
rue St-Ferdinand
rue Maria
rue St-Augustin
Turgeon
rue Bourget
rue Rose-de-Lima
Greene
Library
PARC DE L'ENCAN
Vanier
rue Workman
rue Ste-Émilie
PARC LOUIS CYR
Ste-Émilie
av. Atwater
rue de Lévis
rue Fauteux
rue Duvernay
rue Notre-Dame O.
rue Dominion
boul. Georges-
rue St-Ambroise
Marché Atwater
rue St-Ambroise
rue Rufus-Rockhead
rue Charlevoix
rue Ste-Cunégonde
rue Vinet
Canal de Lachine
rue St-Patrick
rue St-Patrick
rue Pitt
Atwater
rue Augustin-Cantin
rue St-Patrick
rue Centre
rue St-Charles
15
20
PARC D'ARGENSON
rue d'Argenson
Charlevoix
rue Ropery
rue Laprairie
av.
rue de Châteauguay
rue Grand-Trunk
rue Centre
rue Island
Usine de Filtration
rue Mullins
r.Charlevoix
PARC ST-GABRIEL
rue Joseph
PARC LABELLE
Library
av. Dupuis
av. Verdun
rue Reading
POINTE-ST-CHARLES
PARC DUQUETTE
av. Caisse
PARC POIRIER
boul. Henri-Duhamel
pl. de la
Poudrière
rue Butler
rue Knox
PARC SAMMY HILL
rue Ryde
r. Claude
rue Joseph
av. Strathmore
rue Evelyn
rue Coleraine
rue Hibernia
r. Coleraine
av. Hickson
av. Verdun
av. Régina
rue Gertrude
boul. LaSalle
av. Caisse
rue Rozel
rue Charlevoix
rue Liverpool
rue de Paris
rue Charon
rue Rushbrooke
rue Fortune
Lasalle
0
600 m
rue Wellington
rue Wellington
av. Ash
0
600 yards
PARC MARGUERITE-BOURGEOYS
r. Dublin
rue Hall
rue
rue
Maison St-Gab
A
B

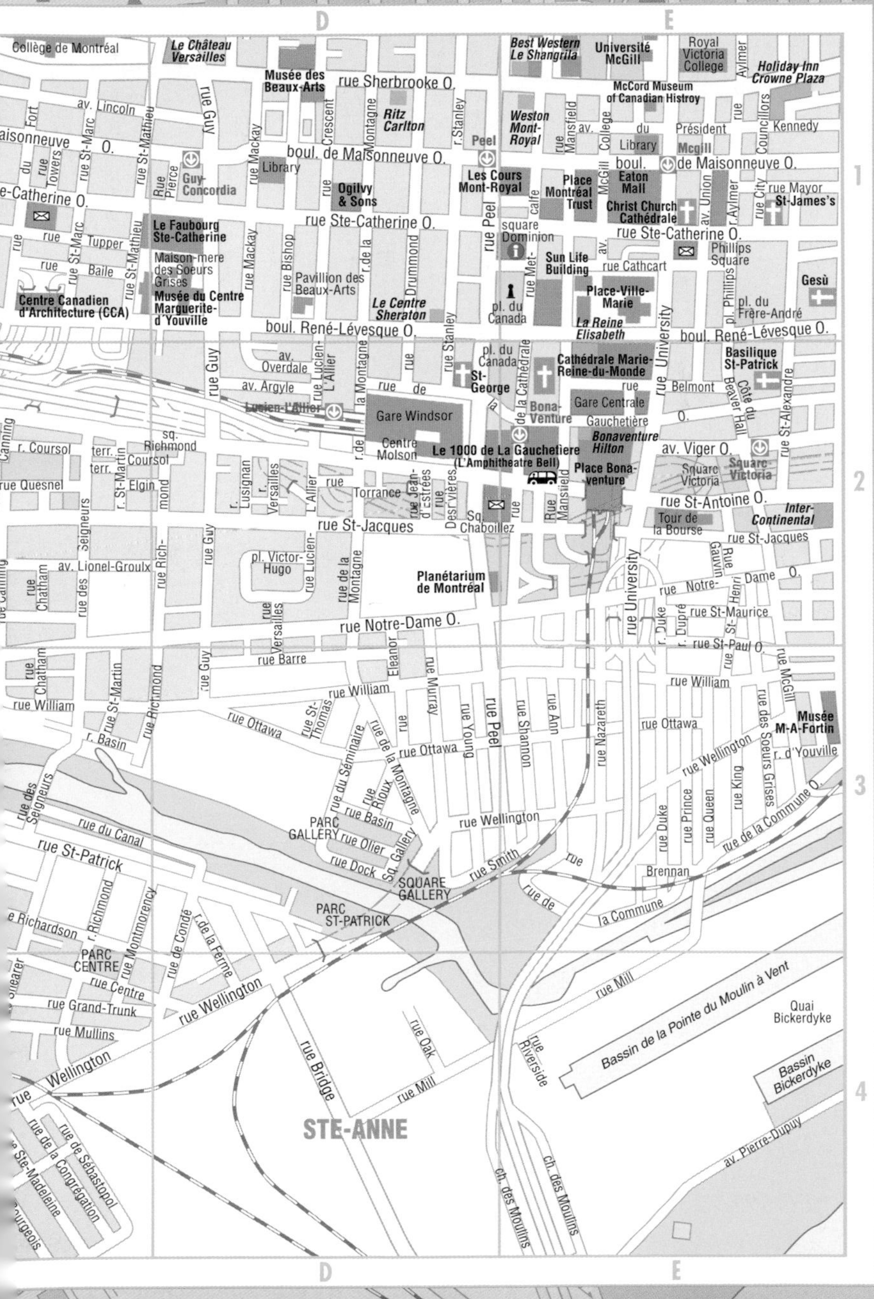
D
E
Collège de Montréal
Le Château Versailles
Musée des Beaux-Arts
rue Sherbrooke O.
Best Western Le Shangrila
Université McGill
Royal Victoria College
Aylmer
Holiday Inn Crowne Plaza
McCord Museum of Canadian Histroy
av. Lincoln
rue Guy
Crescent
Montagne
Ritz Carlton
r. Stanley
Weston Mont-Royal
Mansfield
College
av. du Président Kennedy
Councillors
Fort
Maisonneuve O.
du Towers
rue St-Marc
rue St-Mathieu
rue Mackay
Peel
Library
Mcgill
boul. de Maisonneuve O.
boul. de Maisonneuve O.
Rue Pierce
Guy-Concordia
Ogilvy & Sons
Les Cours Mont-Royal
Place Montréal Trust
Eaton Mall
rue Union
rue Mayor
St-James's
Ste-Catherine O.
Christ Church Cathédrale
rue Aylmer
rue City
Le Faubourg Ste-Catherine
rue Tupper
rue Ste-Catherine O.
square Dominion
rue Ste-Catherine O.
Phillips Square
Maison-mere des Soeurs Grises
rue Baile
rue Bishop
r. de la
Drummond
rue Peel
rue Met-calfe
Sun Life Building
rue Cathcart
Pavillion des Beaux-Arts
Place-Ville-Marie
rue Phillips
Gesù
Centre Canadien d'Architecture (CCA)
Musée du Centre Marguerite-d'Youville
Le Centre Sheraton
pl. du Canada
La Reine Elisabeth
rue University
pl. du Frère-André
boul. René-Lévesque O.
boul. René-Lévesque O.
av. Overdale
rue Lucien-L'Allier
rue Stanley
pl. du Canada
rue de la Cathédrale
Cathédrale Marie-Reine-du-Monde
Basilique St-Patrick
av. Argyle
rue de la Montagne
rue de
St-George
Bona-Venture
rue Belmont
Côte du Beaver Hall
rue St-Alexandre
Lucien-L'Allier
Gare Windsor
Gare Centrale
Gauchetière
Canning
r. Coursol
sq. Richmond
Centre Molson
Le 1000 de La Gauchetière (L'Amphitheatre Bell)
Bonaventure Hilton
av. Viger O.
terr. Coursol
terr. St-Martin
Elgin
Place Bona-venture
Square Victoria
Square Victoria
rue Quesnel
Richmond
Lusignan
r. Versailles
L'Allier
rue Torrance
rue Jean-d'Estrées
Desrivières
Rue Mansfield
rue St-Antoine O.
Seigneurs
rue St-Jacques
Sq. Chaboillez
Tour de la Bourse
Inter-Continental
rue St-Jacques
rue Guy
pl. Victor-Hugo
rue de la Montagne
Planétarium de Montréal
Rue Gauvin
av. Lionel-Groulx
rue Rich-mond
rue Chatham
rue des
rue Versailles
rue Lucien-
rue Notre-Dame O.
rue Henri
rue University
rue St-Maurice
r. Duke
r. Dupré
rue Notre-Dame O.
rue St-Paul O.
rue Chatham
rue Barre
Eleanor
rue Murray
rue McGill
rue William
rue William
rue St-Martin
rue Richmond
rue Ottawa
rue St-Thomas
rue Young
rue Peel
rue Shannon
rue Ann
rue Nazareth
rue Ottawa
rue des Soeurs Grises
Musée M-A-Fortin
r. Basin
rue du Séminaire
rue de la Montagne
rue Ottawa
rue Wellington
r. d'Youville
rue des Seigneurs
rue Rioux
rue Basin
rue Wellington
rue Duke
rue Prince
rue Queen
rue King
rue de la Commune O.
rue du Canal
PARC GALLERY
rue Olier
rue St-Patrick
rue Dock
Sq. Gallery
SQUARE GALLERY
rue Smith
rue de
Brennan
la Commune
rue Richardson
r. Richmond
rue Montmorency
rue de Condé
r. de la Ferme
PARC ST-PATRICK
PARC CENTRE
Shearer
rue Centre
rue Grand-Trunk
rue Wellington
rue Mill
Quai Bickerdyke
Bassin de la Pointe du Moulin à Vent
rue Mullins
rue Oak
rue Riverside
rue Bridge
rue Wellington
rue Mill
Bassin Bickerdyke
STE-ANNE
rue de Sébastopol
rue de la Congrégation
rue Ste-Madeleine
Bourgeois
av. Pierre-Dupuy
ch. des Moulins
ch. des Moulins
1
2
3
4
D
E

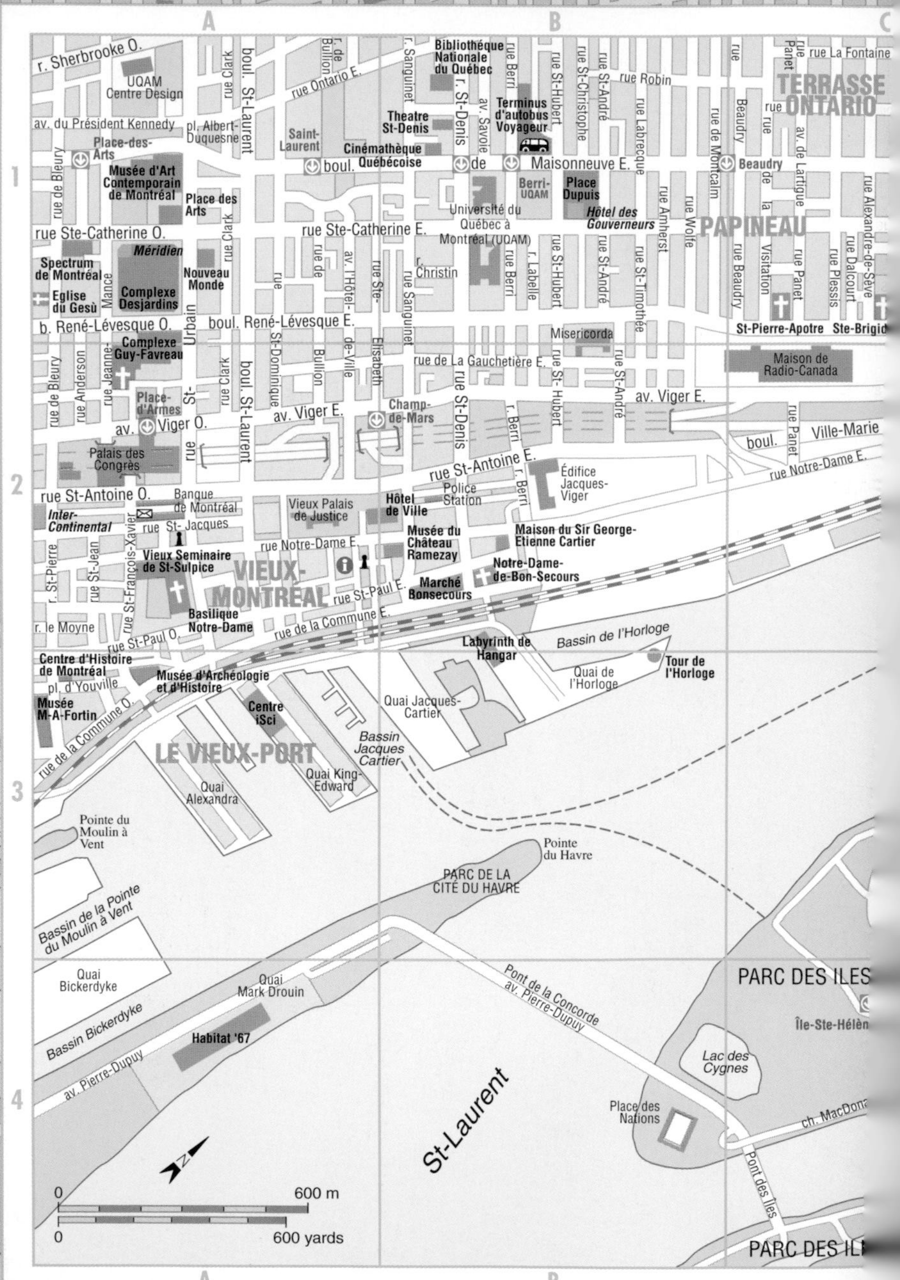
A
B
C
1
2
3
4
r. Sherbrooke O.
UQAM Centre Design
rue Clark
boul. St-Laurent
r. de Bullion
rue Ontario E.
r. Sanguinet
Bibliothèque Nationale du Québec
rue Berri
rue St-Hubert
rue St-Christophe
rue St-André
rue Robin
rue Panet
rue La Fontaine
TERRASSE ONTARIO
av. du Président Kennedy
pl. Albert-Duquesne
Saint-Laurent
Theatre St-Denis
r. St-Denis
av. Savoie
Terminus d'autobus Voyageur
rue Labrecque
rue de Montcalm
rue Beaudry
av. de Lartigue
Place-des-Arts
Musée d'Art Contemporain de Montréal
Cinémathèque Québécoise
boul. de Maisonneuve E.
Beaudry
rue de Bleury
Place des Arts
Berri-UQAM
Place Dupuis
Université du Québec à Montréal (UQAM)
Hôtel des Gouverneurs
rue Amherst
rue Wolfe
PAPINEAU
rue de la Visitation
rue Alexandre-de-Sève
rue Ste-Catherine O.
rue Ste-Catherine E.
Méridien
Spectrum de Montréal
Complexe Desjardins
Nouveau Monde
r. Christin
rue Labelle
rue St-Timothée
rue Dalcourt
rue Plessis
Eglise du Gesù
Mance
b. René-Lévesque O.
boul. René-Lévesque E.
Misericorda
St-Pierre-Apotre
Ste-Brigid
Complexe Guy-Favreau
rue de La Gauchetière E.
Maison de Radio-Canada
rue Anderson
rue Jeanne-Mance
rue St-Urbain
rue St-Dominique
rue Bullion
rue de l'Hôtel-de-Ville
rue Ste-Elisabeth
rue Sanguinet
Place-d'Armes
av. Viger O.
av. Viger E.
Champ-de-Mars
boul. Ville-Marie
Palais des Congrès
rue St-Antoine O.
rue St-Antoine E.
rue Notre-Dame E.
Banque de Montréal
Inter-Continental
Vieux Palais de Justice
Hôtel de Ville
Police Station
Édifice Jacques-Viger
rue St-Jacques
Musée du Château Ramezay
Maison du Sir George-Etienne Cartier
r. St-Pierre
rue St-Jean
rue St-François-Xavier
Vieux Seminaire de St-Sulpice
VIEUX-MONTRÉAL
rue Notre-Dame E.
Notre-Dame-de-Bon-Secours
rue St-Paul E.
Marché Bonsecours
Basilique Notre-Dame
r. le Moyne
rue de la Commune E.
rue St-Paul O.
Labyrinth de Hangar
Bassin de l'Horloge
Centre d'Histoire de Montréal
pl. d'Youville
Musée d'Archéologie et d'Histoire
Quai de l'Horloge
Tour de l'Horloge
Musée M-A-Fortin
Centre iSci
Quai Jacques-Cartier
rue de la Commune O.
LE VIEUX-PORT
Bassin Jacques Cartier
Quai King-Edward
Quai Alexandra
Pointe du Moulin à Vent
Pointe du Havre
PARC DE LA CITÉ DU HAVRE
Bassin de la Pointe du Moulin à Vent
Quai Bickerdyke
Quai Mark Drouin
Pont de la Concorde
av. Pierre-Dupuy
PARC DES ILES
Île-Ste-Hélène
Bassin Bickerdyke
Habitat '67
Lac des Cygnes
St-Laurent
Place des Nations
ch. MacDonald
Pont des Iles
N
0
600 m
600 yards

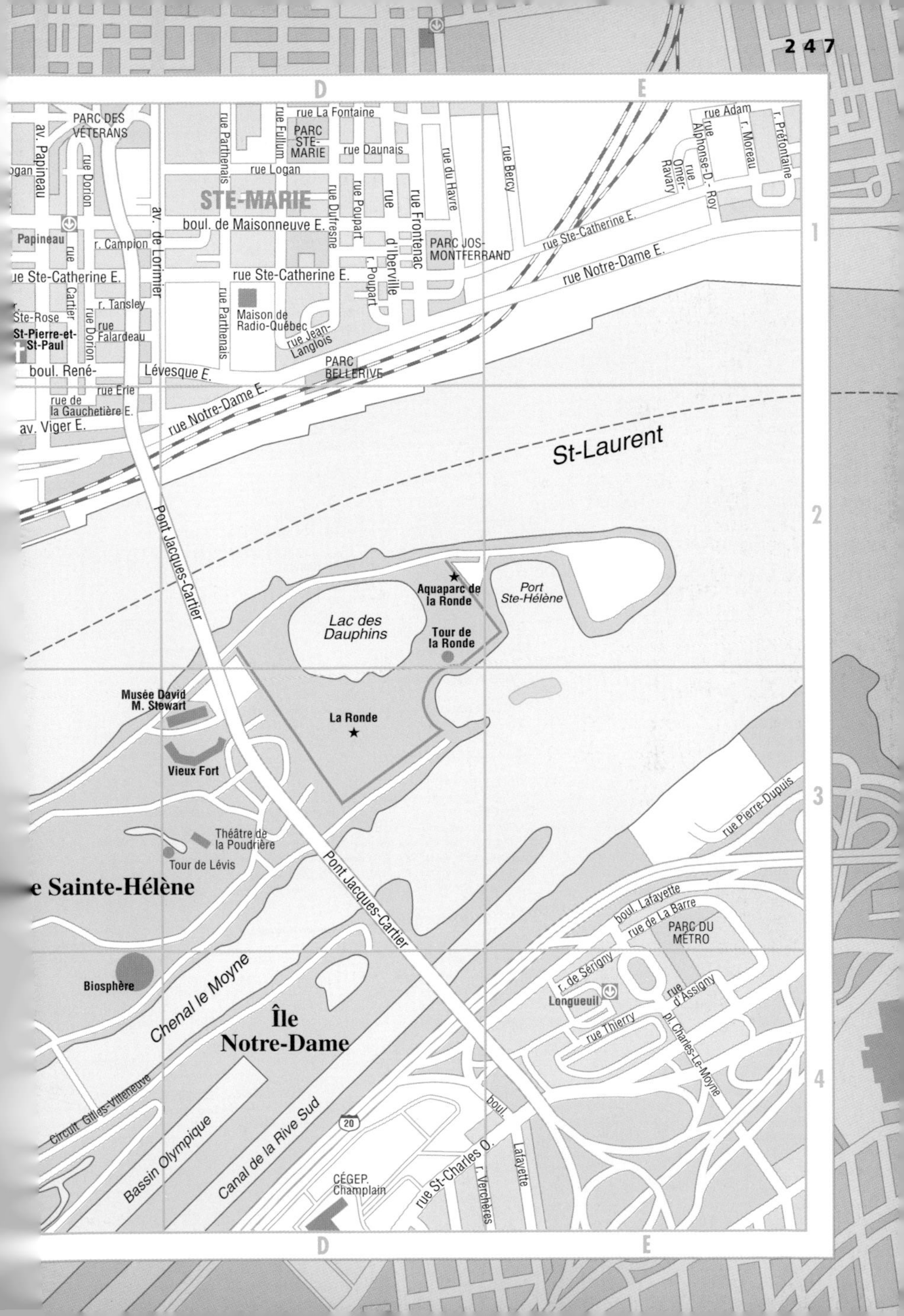
D
E
1
2
3
4
PARC DES VÉTERANS
av. Papineau
rue Dorion
Papineau
r. Campion
rue Cartier
ue Ste-Catherine E.
r. Tansley
Ste-Rose
rue Dorion
rue Falardeau
St-Pierre-et-St-Paul
boul. René-Lévesque E.
rue Erie
rue de la Gauchetière E.
av. Viger E.
av. de Lorimier
rue Parthenais
rue Fullum
rue La Fontaine
PARC STE-MARIE
rue Daunais
rue Logan
STE-MARIE
boul. de Maisonneuve E.
rue Dufresne
rue Poupart
rue Frontenac
rue d'Iberville
r. Poupart
rue Ste-Catherine E.
Maison de Radio-Québec
rue Jean-Langlois
PARC BELLERIVE
rue Notre-Dame E.
rue du Havre
rue Bercy
PARC JOS-MONTFERRAND
rue Ste-Catherine E.
rue Notre-Dame E.
rue Adam
rue Alphonse-D.-Roy
rue Omer-Ravary
r. Moreau
r. Préfontaine
St-Laurent
Pont Jacques-Cartier
Aquaparc de la Ronde
Port Ste-Hélène
Lac des Dauphins
Tour de la Ronde
La Ronde
Musée David M. Stewart
Vieux Fort
Théâtre de la Poudrière
Tour de Lévis
Île Sainte-Hélène
rue Pierre-Dupuis
boul. Lafayette
rue de La Barre
PARC DU MÉTRO
r. de Sérigny
Longueuil
rue d'Assigny
rue Thierry
pl. Charles-Le-Moyne
Biosphère
Chenal le Moyne
Île Notre-Dame
Circuit Gilles-Villeneuve
Bassin Olympique
Canal de la Rive Sud
20
CÉGEP Champlain
rue St-Charles O.
r. Verchères
boul. Lafayette

STREET INDEX

INSIGHT CITY GUIDES
The Guides That Are Streets Ahead
Insight Guides to every major country are also available
FREE Restaurant Guide
AMSTERDAM
LAS VEGAS
LONDON
MADRID
WALT DISNEY WORLD RESORT & ORLANDO
PARIS
ROME
SINGAPORE
SYDNEY
www.insightguides.com

Art & Photo Credits

Rubens Abboud/Alamy 38
Archive Photos 31, 36, 65R
Archives Canada 20, 22, 28, 29
Bettmann/Corbis 18, 35, 37, 39, 41, 46, 65L
The Bridgeman Art Library 40
Dirk Buwalde back cover CL, 62
Mary Evans Picture Library 17, 23, 27
Winston Fraser inside back flap, 6T, 53, 64, 66R, 80T, 127T, 133T, 134T, 140, 143, 148, 169, 185, 186, 187, 190, 194, 196, 201, 202T, 206, 207
Winston Fraser/Keystone Press 50R
Robert Fried 153
Jackie Garrow/APA 3BR, 44, 47, 52, 57, 79, 79T, 82T, 84T, 99, 108, 116T, 118T, 119T, 128T, 129T, 132, 133, 134, 146T, 147, 157, 158, 162, 162T, 171T, 174T, 175, 179, 181T, 183, 187T, 188T, 193, 193T, 194T, 195, 197, 217
Eduardo Gil 112
Hulton/Getty Images 16
Hulton-Deutsch Collection/Corbis 30
Illustrated London News Photo Library 21, 24, 25, 26
Earl Kowall 34, 42, 45, 80BL
Sébastien Larose/Globe Press 2/3, 198
LL/Roger Viollet/Getty Images 32
Gered Mankowitz/Redferns 50L
Steve Marcus/Reuters/Corbis 87T
Perry Mastrovito/Reflexion 189
Christinne Muschi/Reuters/Corbis 63, 67
Peter Newark's American Pictures 19
Nowitz Photography/APA back cover C, 1, 4T, 4CL, 5T, 5B, 6BL, 6BR, 7TR, 7CL, 7BR, 8TL, 8BL, 8BR, 9TL, 9CR, 9BR, 10/11, 12/13, 14, 48, 49, 51L, 51R, 56, 58, 59, 68/69, 70/71, 72, 76, 77, 81, 81T, 82, 83, 83T, 84, 85T, 86, 86T, 87L, 87R, 88, 89, 89T, 90, 90T, 91L, 91R, 91T, 92, 93, 94, 94T, 95, 95T, 96, 96T, 97, 102, 103, 105, 106, 106T, 107, 107T, 109, 109T, 110, 110T, 111L, 111R, 111T, 113T, 114L, 114R, 114T, 115, 115T, 116, 117, 117T, 118, 119, 120, 120T, 121, 124, 125, 127, 128, 129, 130, 130L, 130R, 130T, 132T, 135, 135T, 141, 143T, 144, 145, 145T, 149, 150, 151, 152T, 153T, 154, 159, 160, 161L, 161R, 161T, 166, 167, 168T, 170BL, 170T, 171, 172, 172T, 173, 174, 178, 181, 182T, 183T, 184, 184T, 185T, 186T, 191, 191T, 192T, 195T, 199, 202, 203T, 204, 204T, 205L, 205R, 205T, 207T, 208, 208T, 211, 215, 220, 225, 227, 229, 231, 233
Ontario Archives 33
Andrea Pistolesi 168, 203, 206T
Ann Purcell 155T
Reflexion 85, 113, 142T, 188
David Simson 43, 192
Tourisme Montréal 146, 152, 157
Richard Wolowicz/Corbis 66L

Picture Spreads

54/55: Winston Fraser 54BR, 55TR; **Earl Kowall** 54BL, 55BL, 55BR; **Nazima Kowall** 54CR, 55BC; **Shelia Naiman/Reflexion** 54/55, 55CL

60/61: Courtesy of Les Ballets Jazz de Montréal 60BR; **Centaur Theatre/Yanick Macdonald** 60BL; **Mick Hutson/Redferns** 61BL; **Kari Marttila/Alamy** 60TL; **Christinne Muschi/Reuters/Corbis** 61TR; **Christopher Smith/Corbis** 61BR; **Courtesy of Théâtre du Nouveau Monde** 60/61

100/101: Alain Evrard 101CL; **Winston Fraser** 100TL, 100BL, 100BR, 101TR, 101BR; **Robert Fried** 100CR; **Richard Nowitz/APA** 101BL; **Andrea Pistolesi** 100/101

138/139: Fotoman/Alamy 141CL; **Winston Fraser** 140CR, 140BL, 141TR; **Nowitz Photography/APA** 140/141, 140TL, 140BR, 141BR; **Pierre Roussel/Getty Images** 141BL

164/165: Gero Breloer/dpa/Corbis 164C; **Courtesy of Cirque du Soleil** 164BR, 165CL; **Rune Hellestad/Corbis** 164BL; **Steve Marcus/Reuters/Corbis** 165BC; **John Munson/The Star-Ledger/Corbis** 164/165, 165TR

176/177: Rubens Abboud/Alamy 178/179; **Eric Dufresne/Alamy** 178CR; **Winston Fraser** 179CL, 179BL, 179BR; **Jackie Garrow/APA** 178BL; **Earl Kowall** 178BR; **Andrea Pistolesi** 179TR; **Topham Picturepoint** 178TL

Map Production: Mike Adams, James Macdonald and **Stephen Ramsay**

©2007 Apa Publications GmbH & Co. Verlag KG, Singapore Branch

Production: Linton Donaldson

General Index

A page reference in **bold** indicates the main entry in the book. A page reference in *italics* indicates a photograph.

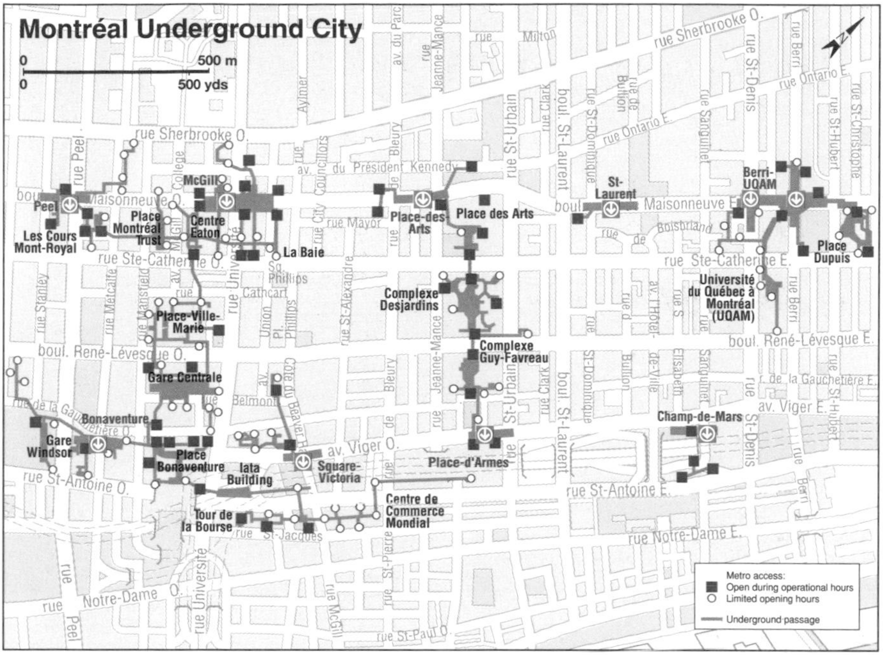
Montréal Underground City
0
500 m
0
500 yds
N
rue Sherbrooke O.
rue Ontario E.
rue Milton
av. du Parc
rue Jeanne-Mance
Aymer
boul. St-Laurent
rue Clark
rue St-Dominique
rue de Bullion
rue Sanguinet
rue St-Denis
rue Berri
rue St-Hubert
rue St-Christophe
rue Peel
College
rue Sherbrooke O.
av. du Président Kennedy
Bleury
rue City Councillors
rue Maisonneuve O.
Peel
McGill
Place Montréal Trust
Centre Eaton
Les Cours Mont-Royal
La Baie
Place-des-Arts
Place des Arts
St-Laurent
boul. Maisonneuve E.
Berri-UQAM
rue Mayor
rue de Boisbriand
Place Dupuis
rue Ste-Catherine O.
rue Ste-Catherine E.
Sq. Phillips
Cathcart
Université du Québec à Montréal (UQAM)
rue Stanley
rue Metcalfe
rue Mansfield
rue University
Union
Pl. Phillips
rue St-Alexandre
Complexe Desjardins
Place-Ville-Marie
boul. René-Lévesque O.
boul. René-Lévesque E.
Complexe Guy-Favreau
rue St-Urbain
av. de l'Hôtel-de-Ville
rue St-Élisabeth
Gare Centrale
Côte du Beaver Hall
Belmont
r. de la Gauchetière E.
rue de la Gauchetière O.
av. Viger E.
Bonaventure
Champ-de-Mars
Gare Windsor
Place Bonaventure
av. Viger O.
Iata Building
Square-Victoria
Place-d'Armes
rue St-Antoine O.
rue St-Antoine E.
Centre de Commerce Mondial
Tour de la Bourse
rue St-Jacques
rue Notre-Dame E.
rue Notre-Dame O.
rue St-Pierre
rue McGill
rue St-Paul O.
Metro access:
Open during operational hours
Limited opening hours
Underground passage

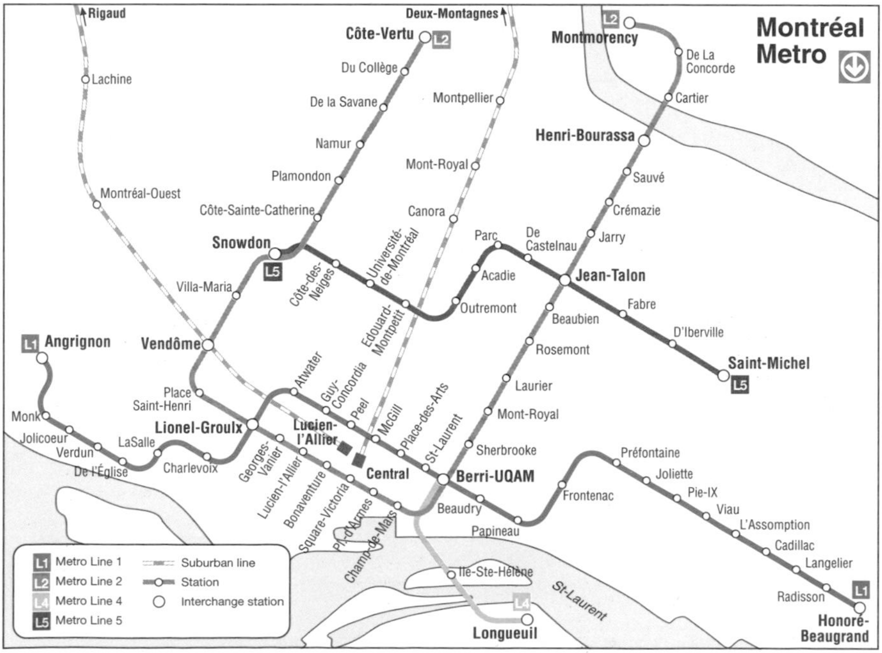
Montréal Metro
Rigaud
Lachine
Montréal-Ouest
Deux-Montagnes
Côte-Vertu
L2
Du Collège
De la Savane
Namur
Plamondon
Côte-Sainte-Catherine
Snowdon
L5
Villa-Maria
Vendôme
Place Saint-Henri
Lionel-Groulx
Montpellier
Mont-Royal
Canora
Université-de-Montréal
Côte-des-Neiges
Edouard-Montpetit
Parc
Acadie
Outremont
De Castelnau
Jean-Talon
Fabre
D'Iberville
Saint-Michel
Montmorency
De La Concorde
Cartier
Henri-Bourassa
Sauvé
Crémazie
Jarry
Beaubien
Rosemont
Laurier
Mont-Royal
Sherbrooke
Berri-UQAM
L1
Angrignon
Monk
Jolicoeur
Verdun
De l'Église
LaSalle
Charlevoix
Atwater
Guy-Concordia
Peel
McGill
Place-des-Arts
St-Laurent
Lucien-l'Allier
Central
Georges-Vanier
Lucien-l'Allier
Bonaventure
Square-Victoria
Pl.-d'Armes
Champ-de-Mars
Beaudry
Papineau
Frontenac
Préfontaine
Joliette
Pie-IX
Viau
L'Assomption
Cadillac
Langelier
Radisson
Honoré-Beaugrand
Ile-Ste-Hélène
L4
Longueuil
St-Laurent
Metro Line 1
Metro Line 2
Metro Line 4
Metro Line 5
Suburban line
Station
Interchange station

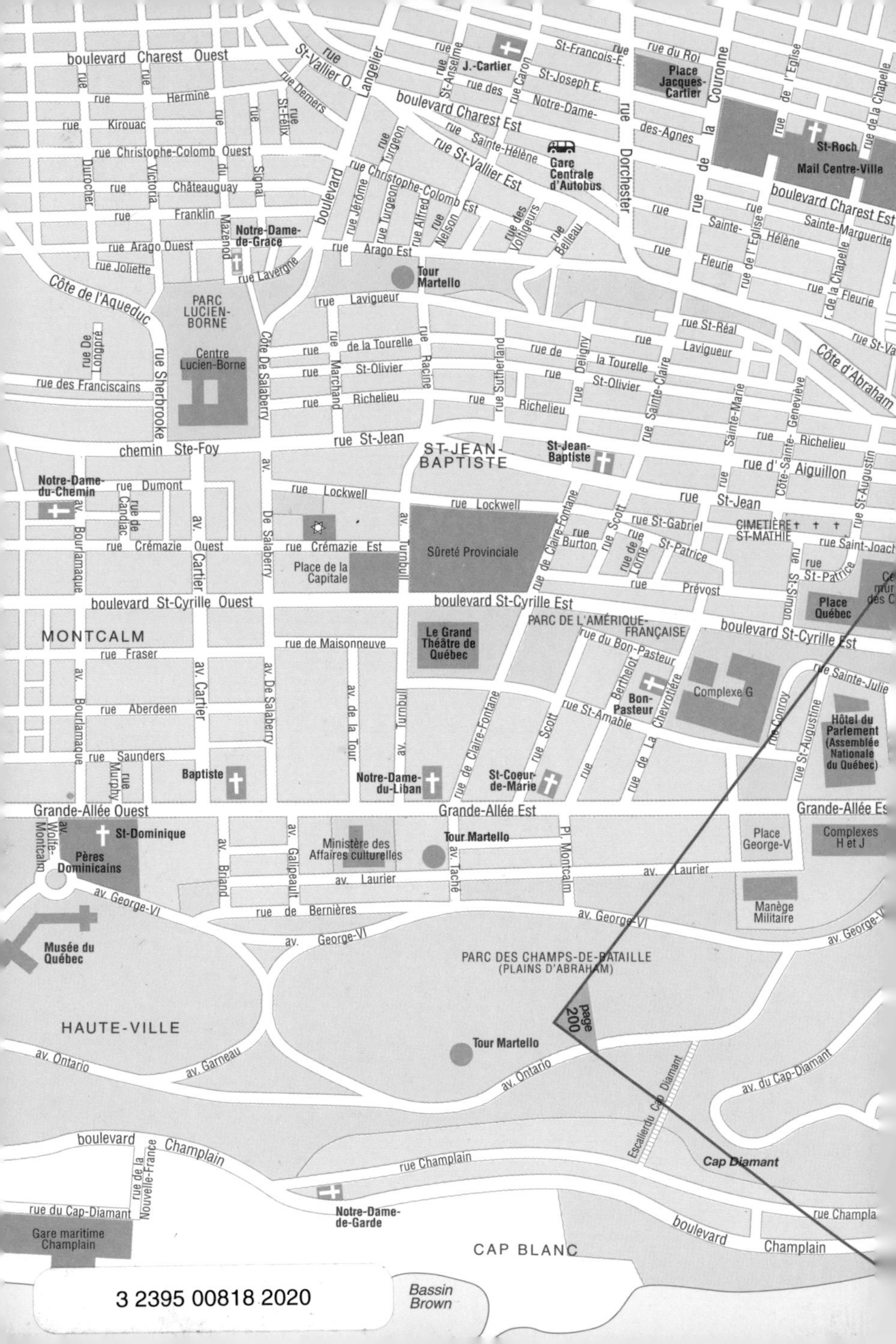

3 2395 00818 2020